A FADED LEGACY

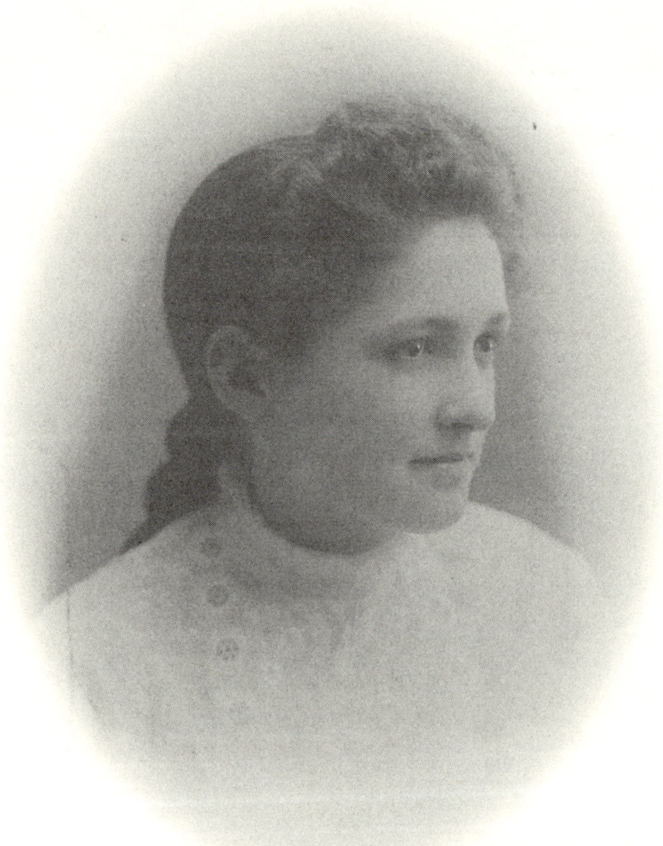

A FADED LEGACY

AMY BROWN LYMAN AND MORMON WOMEN'S ACTIVISM, 1872–1959

Dave Hall

The University of Utah Press Salt Lake City

A Faded Legacy: Amy Brown Lyman and Mormon Women's Activism, 1872–1959
is a project of the Charles Redd Center for Western Studies.
The publisher gratefully acknowledges their support.

The Defiance House Man colophon is a registered trademark
of the University of Utah Press. It is based on a four-foot-tall Ancient
Puebloan pictograph (late PIII) near Glen Canyon, Utah.

19 18 17 16 15 1 2 3 4 5

Library of Congress Cataloging-In-Publication Data

Hall, Dave, 1957–
A faded legacy : Amy Brown Lyman and Mormon women's activism, 1872–1959/Dave Hall.
pages cm
Includes bibliographical references and index.
ISBN 978-1-60781-453-5 (cloth : alk. paper)—ISBN 978-1-60781-454-2 (ebook)
1. Lyman, Amy Brown.
2. Relief Society (Church of Jesus Christ of Latter-day Saints)—Biography. 3. Mormon women—United States—Biography. 4. Social reformers—United States—Biography. 5. Relief Society (Church of Jesus Christ of Latter-day Saints)—History. 6. Mormon women—United States—History. 7. Church of Jesus Christ of Latter-day Saints—Charities—History. 8. Mormon Church—Charities—History. I. Title.
BX8695.L925H35 2015
267'.4493092—dc23 2015022958

Portions of chapter 4 of this book were previously published in Dave Hall, "From Home Service to Social Service: Amy Brown Lyman and the Development of Social Work in the LDS Church," *Mormon Historical Studies* 9 (Fall 2008): 67–88.

Portions of chapters 6 and 8 of this book were previously published in Dave Hall, "A Crossroads for Mormon Women: Amy Brown Lyman, J. Reuben Clark, and the Decline of Organized Women's Activism in the Relief Society," *Journal of Mormon History* 36 (Spring 2010), 205–49.

Printed and bound by Sheridan Books, Inc., Ann Arbor, Michigan.

FIRST

for *Teri,* who endured in patience and love

THEN

for *Tom* and *Jessie,* pioneering scholars, patient mentors, and fast friends who believed in me and the project

AND FINALLY,

for *Amy Kathryn*, *Vera*, and *Leona*, who kept the flame alive

CONTENTS

FIGURES

Following page 103

PREFACE

If the opportunity had come to you, as it did to me, to ask Mormon women who had lived through the 1930s and 1940s about Amy Brown Lyman, you would have seen their eyes brighten with recognition and pride. "Oh, Sister Lyman," was a common response, "she was wonderful!" If one could step back in time to ask prominent figures in national women's or social work organizations active in the 1920s or 1930s about her, they would have known her and been familiar with her work. Without question, Amy Brown Lyman's accomplishments rank her among the most influential women in Mormon history. Yet today, Lyman is all but forgotten among her own people and rates not even a footnote outside the Latter-day Saint community.

History is rife with such figures, prominent in their day, but for a number of reasons, forgotten by subsequent generations. Yet Lyman's case, both in her accomplishments and in the reasons why they are forgotten, seems particularly striking. A significant bridge builder to the larger community, she played a key role in the transformation of social work practices in Utah and the Intermountain West. A leader in the Relief Society, the premier women's organization of her church, she rose to the pinnacle of its leadership, inspiring generations of Mormon women, only to see her legacy all but vanish due to a scandal that rocked her family and shocked the members of her church.

My own first encounter with Lyman came many years ago when I purchased a copy of Thomas G. Alexander's *Mormonism in Transition*. This pioneering volume examines the path of accommodation and adjustment followed by Latter-day Saint leaders during the period from 1890 to 1930 as they shifted church programs from their earlier emphasis on establishing a separatist commonwealth in the West and moved toward assimilation into national economic, social, and political norms. Raised, as I was, in Southern California in a family with a non-Mormon father and a lukewarm Mormon mother at a time when the church seemed especially insular in its thinking, I found Alexander's rich and detailed volume fascinating as well as exciting in its implications. Of the many remarkable individuals I encountered in its pages, to me the most compelling by far was Amy Brown Lyman. I found her so compelling, in fact, that I entered the master's program in history at Brigham Young University in order to work under Tom Alexander and learn more about Lyman and her world. Eventually, I wrote a master's thesis on Lyman that was then transformed into a doctoral dissertation at the University of California, Santa Barbara, and finally reshaped into this volume.

As I began work on Lyman's life more than two decades ago now, I encountered a number of obstacles: first was the matter of context. In the larger study of women and social welfare work a number of seminal treatments were only then beginning to appear. As far as Mormon women, particularly in the twentieth century, there was very little in the historical literature when I began this work, and to a degree, with some notable exceptions, that is still the case. However, some were already breaking ground in this area. In particular Jill Mulvay Derr and Maureen Ursenbach Beecher, joined by Janath Russell Cannon, made a major contribution to our understanding of the Relief

Society women during this period when they published *Women of Covenant: The Story of Relief Society*. Similarly, Carol Cornwall Madsen had taken steps into the early twentieth century with her important dissertation on Emmeline B. Wells. Nevertheless, despite such key milestones and a handful of others by these and similar authors, as I began to explore many aspects of Lyman's life and experiences I frequently found myself alone in broad regions of unexplored territory. Consequently this has been an exciting, but often solitary endeavor. Recently, however, a number of scholars have begun to explore this rich area of Mormon women's history, and I hope this study might inspire others to join them.

In addition to challenges due to the sometimes fragmentary state of secondary literature regarding Lyman and her generation of women, I was also confronted by a dearth of documentary information about her activities as a Relief Society leader. While important collections of official records of the activities of Latter-day Saint leaders were stored in the archives of the Church History Library of the Church of Jesus Christ of Latter-day Saints in Salt Lake City, at the time I began my work, many of the most useful records were—and to a degree, still remain—restricted and thus unavailable to scholars. These include the official minutes of the general leadership organizations of the LDS Church, including the Relief Society. I was able to work around this limitation in part due to the generosity of a number of scholars who shared with me their insights and even their notes taken during an earlier period when the minutes of the Relief Society and other organizations had been more widely accessible. In addition, the able and extremely helpful staff at the Church History Library was able to steer me toward alternative resources and collections that remained available to scholars. In this respect, these restrictions have provided some benefit in my research as I was forced to exploit resources that provided insights I might not have discovered otherwise.

I encountered other limitations, as well, that hindered my efforts to gain insight into Lyman's thoughts and motivations. When I began my research I soon learned that comparatively few of Lyman's personal papers had survived. It should be said, however, that there are some very important documents that remain: drafts of published articles, personal addresses, and some fragmentary official and personal correspondence are located in a collection of Lyman's papers at the L. Tom Perry Special Collections at the Harold B. Lee Library at Brigham Young University. More recently, additional papers have been donated by her family to the Church History Library. Nevertheless, much of her correspondence, including what was once in the files of the Relief Society, as well as other materials related to her life and activities has simply disappeared. Lyman had kept appointment books with some pertinent personal information, for example, as well as other family records that might have provided valuable insight into her thinking, but these apparently were discarded long ago. Her surviving correspondence, both personal and official, while helpful to a biographer—sometimes extremely so—represents but a small fragment of what once existed. This is especially the case for her most productive years when she served in the leadership of the Relief Society. Her husband kept a journal, also housed at Brigham Young University, but with some important exceptions his entries were not especially introspective nor particularly informative about Lyman or her thoughts and motivations. She also left behind a brief but very helpful autobiography, however, it too was largely unreflective and devoid of intimate details.

To compensate, to a degree, for these limits on the availability of documentary information about Lyman, I have made extensive use of oral history interviews. My most important contacts in this regard were several surviving family members and coworkers who were extremely generous with their time and memories. In addition to the interviews I conducted myself, I was fortunate to be able to draw upon materials collected by others previously involved in researching the Relief Society and its activities. Particularly helpful were the oral history interviews conducted by Loretta L. Hefner, who began work on a history of the Relief Society Social Services and had herself planned a biography of Lyman some ten years before I began my own work. Although she eventually turned her energies in different directions, her interviews, which are housed in the Church History Library, proved extremely helpful as I began my research. The same is true regarding interviews conducted by others, especially Jessie L. Embry and Jill Mulvay Derr.

While oral history interviews provide a degree of immediacy and detail unavailable through other sources, they also present the researcher with special problems. Therefore, in recognition of the limitations and fluid nature of human memory, wherever possible I have sought to substantiate important observations, questioning multiple informants about specific incidents, and have sought documentary evidence, when obtainable, to reinforce the recollections of Lyman's associates.

Due to a series of especially demanding circumstances in my own life, this project has taken an excessive amount of time to complete. There were advantages that came with these delays, however. On the one hand, over the years I worked on this biography additional secondary material appeared upon which I was able to draw. On the other, it gave me far greater appreciation for the remarkable accomplishments that Lyman achieved under circumstances far more demanding than any I encountered. But this project, so long in reaching fruition, has also left me with an extensive list of individuals to whom I am indebted. At the risk of leaving out many who deserve to be recognized, I wish to mention a few of them by name.

First, I want to extend my gratitude to Marvin S. Hill, retired professor of history at BYU, who as my master's chair encouraged me to take on this topic. His deep knowledge of Mormon history helped lay a foundation for my understanding of Lyman and her contributions, while his dry, good humor helped ease my transition back, after several years away, into the life of a student. I am deeply indebted as well to the Charles Redd Center for Western Studies at BYU and to its staff and board of directors for their generous support for my research through fellowships and grants, without which this project would not have been possible.

At the University of California, Santa Barbara, I want to especially thank Jane S. De Hart, now professor emeritus, who chaired my doctoral committee and in that capacity encouraged me to continue my work on Lyman. Jane required the best of me, despite the difficult circumstances under which I was working, and I wish to thank her for helping me hone my skills as a historian and a writer—and for her enormous patience and encouragement in so doing. Also at UCSB, I am grateful to John Sutton for his insight into the history of social work, and to Patricia Cline Cohen, just this year retired, for her many valuable suggestions and kind assistance rendered despite her own extremely hectic schedule.

I am indebted as well to the personnel at several libraries for the many favors and the constant aid they rendered. David J. Whitaker, now retired from the L. Tom Perry Special Collections at BYU, was very helpful in guiding me to relevant collections and extremely generous with his time and assistance over the years. The current and former staff of the LDS Church History Library have also gone far above and beyond the call of duty in providing aid for this project. In particular Ron Barney, Jay Burrup, Randy Dixon, Michael Landon, Pauline Musig, Bill Slaughter, and Ron Watt have rendered assistance and shared their unmatched knowledge of the collections and valuable insights into many facets of Mormon history. Pauline Musig, in particular, has rendered innumerable aids to my research that have, in a very real sense, made much of this volume possible. I must express my special gratitude as well to Church Historians Elder Marlin K. Jensen and Elder Steven E. Snow for maintaining and extending an atmosphere conducive for scholarship and especially to Assistant Church Historian Richard E. Turley for his encouragement and assistance. I want to thank as well the staffs of the Marriott Library at the University of Utah, the Utah State Historical Society, and that of the National Archives at College Park, Maryland.

A number of people have read all or part of this manuscript in its various manifestations and I wish to extend to them my heartfelt thanks for taking on that onerous task and especially for providing me with their many helpful and insightful suggestions. These include Thomas G. Alexander, John Alley, Lavina Fielding Anderson, Maureen Ursenbach Beecher, Patricia Cline Cohen, Jane S. De Hart, Randolph Dixon, Liz Dulaney, Jessie L. Embry, Amy Lyman Engar, Marvin S. Hill, Jeffrey Johnson, Carol Cornwall Madsen, Susanna Morrill, Pauline Musig, Vera White Pohlman, John Sillito, John Sutton, Leona Fetzer Wintch, and anonymous reviewers at the University of Illinois and Utah State University press. I must make note of the exceptional generosity of Lavina Fielding Anderson in this regard. In addition, special thanks are due to Carol Cornwall Madsen, who took time recently to review several early chapters and provided suggestions that helped clarify and correct portions of my manuscript. Of course, I must extend my very great appreciation to John Alley, editor in chief of the University of Utah Press, for his encouragement for this project over an extended period of many years and for his infinite patience as the day-to-day demands of my life meant that progress proceeded at a glacial pace. Thanks go as well to the employees and staff at the press for all their efforts, including addressing a number of copyediting issues, among which are my idiosyncratic and stubbornly adhered to grammatical practices, and who gently prodded me in order to move this volume forward to completion. I, of course, remain solely responsible for any and all errors and limitations in this manuscript.

I owe a special debt of gratitude, as well, to the family, friends, and coworkers of Amy Brown Lyman who graciously shared their experiences with me and took the time to patiently correct my errors when I got things wrong. Those who worked with Lyman in the Relief Society, though universally self-effacing, recognized that they had been part of something remarkable and all were anxious that Lyman and her contributions not be forgotten. In their generous sharing of their time, memories, and often memorabilia as well, they brought to life not only the subject of this biography, but also the generations of Mormon women whose lives she touched. These informants included Mark Knight Allen, Keith Hayes, Evelyn Lewis Hodges, Mary Lyman Henrie, Melvin Lyman, Mary Schindler Nielsen, David and Sabey Pingree, Emily Pollei, Richard Schreiner, Perry

Sorensen, A. Z. Richards, Emmeline Wirthlin, and Evelyn Ballif Woodruff. Their names, together with others who assisted in a similar manner, are listed in the bibliography.

Of all my informants, however, there were three to whom I owe a special debt of gratitude. Vera White Pohlman first worked with Lyman in 1920 as her personal secretary, served with her again as general secretary-treasurer of the Relief Society from 1940–45 when Lyman was general president, and remained close to Lyman throughout the remainder of her life. Already in her nineties when I met her, she possessed a ready wit that enlivened her keen memory as she recalled intimate details and significant events covering a broad swath of Lyman's life. Vera was a master organizer, an insightful observer, and a generous informant, tireless in sharing her memories of "Mrs. Lyman." Leona Fetzer Wintch began employment in the Relief Society offices in 1932 as one of Lyman's social work trainees and later became a member of her general board. Lyman took Wintch under her wing, recognized her potential, and became the younger woman's mentor and life-long friend. "Lonnie" Wintch was a devoted disciple of Lyman and a woman of rare intellect and ability. She was also a kind and generous contributor to my work. The first, and in many ways most important of my contacts with Lyman's family and coworkers, was Amy Kathryn Lyman Engar—granddaughter of Amy Brown Lyman who was raised by her grandparents when first her mother and then her father met untimely deaths. An enthusiastic booster of her grandparents, she was also a careful and thoughtful source of an almost limitless supply of information related to Lyman and her life. Through her I was led into an expanding web of contacts among family members and coworkers that greatly enriched my understanding of Lyman and her times. Each of these three women shared countless hours of memories with me, on the record and off, and answered patiently and good naturedly the endless stream of questions I posed, whether in person or on the telephone. My association with them became one of the most valued experiences of my life. Without them, much of Lyman's life and contributions would have been forever lost. I am honored to have counted them among my friends. In a very real sense, this work was written for them and it is thus very appropriate that it is in part dedicated to Amy Kathryn Lyman Engar, Vera White Pohlman, and Leona Fetzer Wintch.

I owe a special debt of gratitude, as well, to Tom Alexander and Jessie Embry. My contact with Tom, now Lemuel Hardison Redd Professor Emeritus of Western History at BYU, began when he served as a member of my master's committee and as my supervisor when I worked as a graduate research assistant at the Redd Center. In the long years since he has been an interested advisor, a generous mentor, and a kind and faithful friend. Similarly, Jessie Embry, recently retired associate director of the Redd Center, has been more than generous with her time and means. She has listened patiently as I struggled to make sense of Lyman's experiences and has demonstrated (or at least successfully feigned) interest when I simply needed to talk to someone who knew of Lyman's importance and honestly cared about what I was learning of Lyman's life and times. I am pleased and honored to count this accomplished scholar and kind soul my friend. In recognition of all their assistance and years of friendship, this volume is also dedicated to Tom and Jessie.

Finally, I must thank my family. For years they lived with Amy Brown Lyman and, indeed, the whole Lyman clan, hearing of all the disappointments and new discoveries in my research. In particular I must acknowledge the tremendous patience of my wife,

Teri. The long, exhausting, and extremely stressful quest to complete this project was not what she signed up for, especially considering the more pressing task incumbent upon us at the time of raising three (wonderful) children. Yet she stuck with me through the whole difficult process and for that I am truly grateful. In recognition of her enduring love and support, it is certainly fitting then that this volume is first of all dedicated to her.

Introduction

MORMON WOMEN IN AN AMERICAN CONTEXT

> Women everywhere are leaders in helping to inaugurate movements and to establish institutions and agencies for the benefit of humanity.
>
> —AMY BROWN LYMAN[1]

The above words could have been written by any American woman active in social reform during the early twentieth century. That they came from Amy Brown Lyman, a lifelong Mormon (more properly, a member of the Church of Jesus Christ of Latter-day Saints), might seem surprising inasmuch as the historical experience of women of her faith is often assumed to be conservative, in keeping with a pattern of polygamous patriarchy believed established in Mormonism's frontier period. Such stereotypes, if uncritically accepted, not only ignore and distort important aspects of the past, but also misrepresent gender relations in the faith.

For no one would such preconceptions be less accurate than Lyman. A well-known social worker and reformer, she not only enjoyed close ties to national and international bodies of women but was outspoken in her advocacy of women's rights, expressing views that were representative of many in feminism's first wave.[2] All this she pursued from her position in the leadership of the Relief Society, the flagship women's organization of her faith. Though she is nearly forgotten today—and if remembered, often only because of a devastating family tragedy that ended her career—Lyman was the best-known and most highly accomplished Mormon woman of her generation.[3] While her prominence was admittedly extraordinary, her experiences and activities were no anomaly; rather, in many ways, they were representative of an entire generation of Latter-day Saint women.

This "second generation," born after the Mormon move west in 1847 and before the end of the 1870s, came of age during the last three decades of the nineteenth century in an environment heavily influenced both by attempts to build a religious community in the Great Basin and by simultaneous developments in the larger society. Their experiences illustrate the rich and complex history of Mormon women, one that involves far more than the oft-celebrated experiences of the founding generation. During the youth of these children of the pioneers, at a time when to outsiders the lives of women of the faith seemed most at variance with progressive views concerning gender equality, mothers and daughters embraced an agenda of women's suffrage and community activism that brought them significant advantages within their own community and led them into close association with their non-Mormon sisters. Building on these ties, second generation women created a network of social services critical to the process of state formation in the Intermountain West. Because Lyman was at the center of many of these endeavors, her life provides a valuable case study that demonstrates how these sacred and secular influences interacted to produce a generation of women who, in their maturity, were confident in the public sphere and focused on resolving societal problems. Collectively, their achievements were impressive.

During the years of Lyman's youth, America witnessed the rise of what came to be known as the Progressive Generation, whose members were noted for their role in initiating a broad range of social and political reforms. Historians have argued that progressives were often the children of local elites who themselves had been active in the great causes of mid-century, such as abolitionism and defending the Union. Leaders of Mormonism's progressive generation came from similarly prominent circumstances, though their families' status was linked to positions in the church's lay-hierarchy and their great cause pursued at mid-century was building the Mormon kingdom. Like their national counterparts, and especially followers of the Social Gospel (who drew upon Christian concepts to address societal problems), Mormon progressives adapted their parent's activism to address new challenges emerging in the economic and social climate of the turn of the century while attempting to preserve the communitarian ideals of their youth. Over time these parallel generations came to closely resemble one another in the strategies and goals they pursued, including their advocacy of a stronger role for government. Illuminating the similarities and distinctions between these two groups is one purpose of this study.

To understand the political activism that arose among Mormon women one must grasp the circumstances that led them to develop a sense of common interest and purpose. Next, the question must be addressed of how these qualities were transferred between generations confronting very different environments. This study builds upon existing treatments of sisterhood and activism among Latter-day Saint women chronologically and contextually and examines the largely unexplored role of an institutionalized framework for mentoring and role modeling within the church to address the latter of these issues.[4] Using Lyman as a focal figure, LDS women's organizations—the Relief Society, Young Ladies Mutual Improvement Association, and Primary Association—are revealed as venues where Mormon girls and women of the second generation experienced opportunities to build skills and were self-consciously mentored for public roles in community affairs.

To address the former issue—tracing the origins of common interest and identity among women of the faith—a central, if unlikely, force is found in polygamy. A number of scholars have considered how this radical departure in marriage practices affected Mormon women and influenced their relationship with other Americans of the period.[5] Lyman, as a daughter of the third wife of a locally prominent church leader, was embedded in a family form and experience that can extend our understanding of polygamy's effect on women by examining the generation born and raised in the system. Her personal history also highlights the interplay between the commitment of Latter-day Saint women to the larger goals and distinctive practices of their community and their dedication to such causes as suffrage and equal rights.

Her life-story also provides a vehicle to explore late-nineteenth and twentieth-century gender relations in this seemingly atypical example, demonstrating in particular how the precepts of Mormonism—including polygamy and the woman's culture that grew around it—shaped the gender expectations of girls and young women raised in the faith. The results are counterintuitive. A combination of factors produced a forward-looking and self-confident generation who pushed the boundaries of traditional gender norms. Certainly one must closely qualify any claim that polygamy was liberating to women. Yet, at a time when the concept of separate spheres was common in both the Mormon world as well as in the larger society, Latter-day Saint women proved especially adept at expanding their own sphere of influence and, within it, came to enjoy considerable autonomy. Lyman's story allows us to explore this sphere, one that waxed and waned in size and prerogatives over time, and examine what Mormon women were able to accomplish within its often very broad parameters. While women's groups in the larger society did not commonly recognize or accept the real advantages Mormon women were able to carve out for themselves, importantly, two generations of Mormon women did, and they frequently saw themselves as uniquely empowered over their non-Mormon sisters.

Historical accounts of Mormon families have understandably focused on the earlier polygamous era and there has been very little investigation into adaptations to the mores of Victorian America that took place in the immediate post-polygamy period. Many women among this transitional generation were advantaged not only over their polygamous mothers but over their own daughters and granddaughters, who, because of increasing assimilation, grew to maturity in a society more closely aligned with national gender and family norms at a time when those norms were becoming conservative. How Lyman and her contemporaries were able to build upon the legacy of greater women's autonomy and a broader gendered sphere, facilitated in part by polygamy and necessitated by Mormon separatism, is but one achievement. That freed of polygamy's constraints, some managed to establish companionate marriages and share family responsibilities with their spouses while embracing a rigorous regimen that many of their non-Mormon counterparts could pursue only by rejecting the family claim, is a second.

Yet, precisely because they were married and had children, Lyman and the women of her generation while balancing heavy commitments to family, church, and community—and sometimes professional careers—anticipated the struggles of later generations of American women. In Lyman's case, the consequences of marriage proved mixed. On the one hand, her relationship with her husband was remarkably empowering, in part accounting for her entry into the leadership of the Relief Society and her introduction to national networks of reform. On the other hand, it produced the devastating tragedy that destroyed her career and undermined her legacy.

Ironically, at the very time the second generation came to maturity and began families of their own, the circumstances that gave rise to their activism were changing as coercive federal measures forced the church to bring its actions into line with the cultural practices of the larger American society. But women of Lyman's generation were unwilling to give up their public role. To preserve it, they turned to the burgeoning club movement then sweeping the nation. Clubs, with their ideology of municipal housekeeping and maternalist agenda of reform, provided a new justification for women's continued presence in the public sphere.[6] Lyman's entry into club work in the latter 1890s provides an occasion to examine the club experience in the context of the Mormon community, revealing how second generation women used clubs to form a bridge from the church-centered world of their youth to the more secular society in which they lived in adulthood.[7] In an illustration of the political acumen and resourcefulness that characterized this generation, Lyman and her cohort then grafted this new club agenda onto that of the Relief Society and drew upon the strength of that organization's broad membership base to further their quest for community betterment and social reform. By the 1910s, Lyman and her associates, who then predominated in the leadership of the Relief Society, were actively working to build social services in Utah and several adjacent western states.

Much has been written regarding the importance of a "female dominion" in the development of social reform and state formation in studies based largely on the experience of Eastern elites.[8] Whether the Eastern experience reflects Western realities is as problematic as are the prevailing stereotypes of Mormon women. The story of Amy Brown Lyman reveals a significant amount of influence exercised by these Eastern women upon those of the Relief Society as they interacted in cooperative activities with government agencies and in such organizations as the National Conference of Social Work and the National Council of Women. But it also suggests that there was a richer and more complex level of interaction occurring in these relationships upon which historians as well as contemporary Mormons might draw. In particular, an examination of Lyman's activities both enhances our understanding of the distinct Mormon experience as part of this female dominion and sheds light on the larger question of its role in the development of the welfare state in the West.

Issues of particular interest to Western women of the time included the health of mothers and children. General studies of health care and American women portray the grim reality facing them during the latter nineteenth and early twentieth centuries when lack of medical knowledge and inadequate care at childbirth led to high maternal mortality rates and frequently to lifetime disabilities.[9] The story of Lyman's family indicates that women in the West shared most of the disadvantages and few of the advantages afforded their Eastern sisters. Such health-related experiences forged women of her generation into an effective force pushing for improvements in infant and maternal health during the first decades of the twentieth century. Perhaps surprisingly, in light of the current pattern of political conservatism among the faithful, Mormon progressives recognized that such improvements could only be achieved through greater intervention by all levels of government, and worked assiduously to expand its role in the field of public health.

Recent studies have emphasized the importance of federal measures in addressing such issues. Lyman's experiences suggest that, as women joined the call for national action and then worked to support the resulting initiatives, the federal government played an equally important role in stimulating further social activism among women.[10] Two under-examined measures proved critical to this process. The first, the Smith-Lever

Agricultural Extension Act of 1915, provided funding to land-grant colleges for extension work in the latest farming techniques. As a result of lobbying by the National Home Economics Association, the legislation also included monies for instruction in domestic science. In Utah, administrators at the state agricultural college turned to private organizations for help in carrying out the measure which, with the encouragement of Lyman and like-minded women in its leadership, led to the involvement of the Relief Society. Consequently, women in its local branches organized lectures on nutrition and health as well as clinics where mothers and children were examined by physicians. This resulted in significant improvements in public health even as these same activities initiated Relief Society women into a larger role in community affairs. Under Smith-Lever, women of the organization engaged in, albeit at a limited level, all the activities that characterized later and more thoroughly studied federal measures.

A second under-explored area with far reaching effects for women was the home service work organized during the First World War, an effort that hastened the adoption of modern social work methods in many areas of the country.[11] At the request of the federal government, the American Red Cross assumed the task of providing for the welfare of servicemen and their families. The Red Cross, in turn, sought the assistance of private community organizations. With Lyman coordinating its efforts, the Relief Society assumed responsibility for looking after the families of Latter-day Saint servicemen. In performing this work, the Red Cross required cooperating organizations to utilize the latest social work techniques. Lyman immediately recognized the benefits to be obtained by adopting these modern methods and, with the support of church leaders, moved quickly to establish a central office in Salt Lake City staffed by a handful of professionally trained workers. She then organized social service institutes where hundreds of Relief Society women received instruction in modern social work techniques and, carrying her efforts still further, arranged for lessons on sociology and social work to be incorporated into the Society's official curriculum. Accordingly, each month as many as fifty thousand Relief Society women studied social problems and their solutions. Presiding over this veritable army of social workers, para-professionals, informed volunteers, and interested observers committed to improving conditions in their communities, Lyman was able, not only to transform Mormon charitable practices, but to organize Relief Society women into disciplined lobbyists for improved public services at the local, state, and national levels. The result was a revolution in social welfare provision, especially in Utah, where, as elsewhere in the West, public social services had been virtually non-existent.

Recently, historians have noted the important role played by private charities in administering services in the decades before the New Deal when the need was high but when under-funded public agencies were unable to provide them.[12] An examination of Lyman's actions in revolutionizing Mormon charity work sheds light on this process, showing how Relief Society social workers struggled to provide assistance to their communities even as they lobbied for permanent public agencies in Utah and several adjacent western states. In the context of recent discussions concerning the efficiency of private versus public charity efforts, the Relief Society's activities give valuable insight into the chronic inability of even such well-organized efforts to meet growing demands for services in relatively flush times, much less in times of crisis. Indeed, during the Great Depression, while the charity work of Relief Society women continued, one of the greatest benefits derived as a result of their years of experience came in an unexpected manner. When the New Deal ushered in an era of public social services and state building, the church was ready to contribute women prepared to become core public sector social workers.

Among the many factors stimulating the rise of women's activism in social welfare matters, the role played by the Federal Children's Bureau has been carefully examined in literature of women and the welfare state.[13] This account of Lyman's leadership of the Relief Society's cooperative efforts in support of such measures as the Children's Year and the Federal Maternity and Infancy Act of 1921, better known as the Sheppard-Towner Act, does not challenge existing interpretations. But, what these other accounts do not convey are the extraordinary benefits of these initiatives for the West. Neither do they focus on the consequences of these measures at the local level, or adequately acknowledge the immensely effective voluntary support offered by women such as those in the Relief Society, required, for example, because of Sheppard-Towner's meager funding provisions. As in the case of developing social work practices, the account of Lyman's activities thus reveals the dramatic contribution the Relief Society made to the improvement of infant and maternal health in the Intermountain West. There, on a much larger scale then they had achieved under Smith-Lever, Relief Society members joined state and local officials and federal administrators to organize clinics, provide motherhood education classes, and arrange for medical care and other services for tens of thousands of children and expectant mothers. This study seeks to expand previous studies of these developments to better illuminate the resulting dramatic reductions of infant and maternal mortality.[14] It was no coincidence that under Sheppard-Towner, Utah, where organized cadres involving thousands of Mormon women made such an immense contribution, experienced the greatest reduction of mortality rates of any state in the nation. The activities of Lyman and the Relief Society also provide an important example of the impact of federal leadership in local social welfare matters, even when largely unaccompanied by federal funds.

As impressive as these accomplishments were and as satisfying as they must have been for Latter-day Saint social workers, the process of cooperation with federal initiatives had its negative consequences as well. As social welfare work became increasingly important during the Great Depression, historians and political scientists have shown that male politicians and bureaucrats scrambled to take control of public charitable agencies and the distribution of relief. Because Mormon women shared the goals and strategies of their non-Mormon sisters, their activism became increasingly vulnerable to these same influences that eventually forced American women into a diminished role in welfare matters.[15] An examination of Lyman's efforts during these years enhances our understanding of the dynamics of this process both at the national and local levels while demonstrating the unique vulnerability faced by Latter-day Saint women. Precisely because of the unusually large role played by the federal government in the West and the close link between the Relief Society's agenda and federal initiatives, their welfare activism was especially hard-hit when the New Deal terminated cooperative activities and public agencies took over the lion's share of welfare services. While the loss of women's dominance in welfare matters occurred throughout the nation, Mormon women were dealt a double blow inasmuch as the male church hierarchy simultaneously assumed control over LDS charity matters, further constricting the Relief Society's sphere of influence.[16] The examination of this process and its consequences for Mormon women's activism is another goal of this study.

This study also seeks to illuminate the role personalities play in organizations, in particular in policy making and program development in the LDS Church. While sharing common goals, Mormon leaders often find themselves following very different paths toward achieving them. In particular, based on her experience and knowledge, Lyman at times found herself in disagreement with some church leaders concerning the proper course to pursue in regard to social welfare work as well as the proper role for Mormon women. The environment of the Great Depression and the Second World War brought this divergence to the forefront and resulted in shrinking boundaries for the sphere occupied by Mormon women, and diminished autonomy within that sphere. The period provides an opportunity to examine, as well, the strategies women have utilized to influence the decision-making process in male-dominated organizations.

Continuing our examination of Lyman as she became Relief Society president in 1940, allows us to see how despite the challenges confronting her, she struggled to broaden Relief Society responsibilities in order to provide new outlets for later generations of women in community affairs; and, in addition, how restrictions on travel and activities during the Second World War and changes in the church hierarchy limited her options, even as personal tragedy undermined her effectiveness as a leader and resulted in her resignation in 1945. After the loss of her dynamic leadership, the legacy of activism developed by the second generation was lost and the agenda of the Relief Society became less ambitious. As a result, Mormon women were left with few legitimate alternatives to the idealized and much touted domesticity of the post-war period. In sum, Lyman's story provides an opportunity to examine the roots and trajectory of Mormon women's activism, following both its rise during a period of separation from mainstream society and its decline as women of the faith assimilated to national norms. And, because of Lyman's long association with leaders of national and international women's organizations, it also shows how the fate of Mormon women was linked to that of other first wave feminists.

The final period of Lyman's life illuminates the process through which Mormon women, despite their activist heritage, came to resemble the conservative stereotype often thought to typify women of the faith today. Because little has been written about LDS women during this period we have a limited understanding of the process through which their tradition of activism was lost. Historians of American women, while documenting the heightened domesticity of the later 1940s and 1950s, have made clear that this was not the only option available.[17] This examination seeks to reveal other alternatives open to Mormon women that might have allowed their earlier dynamic to continue.

The chapters in this study are divided roughly into three sections. Part I, comprising chapters one and two, explores the religious and political environment that gave birth to the intense activism characteristic of the second generation of Latter-day Saint women. Chapter one introduces the Mormon world of Lyman's youth showing both its unique aspects and its similarities to the larger society. It challenges the assumption that nineteenth-century Mormon women were merely oppressed victims of a patriarchal society by demonstrating how, during Lyman's girlhood and youth, her mother's generation used community goals aimed at establishing a semi-autonomous commonwealth and defending their faith to create, legitimize, and extend their activism within the public sphere. Chapter two examines Lyman's entry into the larger world during the period surrounding the 1890 Manifesto that ended the public practice of polygamy and signaled the acceleration of Mormon assimilation into the national mainstream. It considers her own expectations and those of her generation as she prepared for a career, married, and joined the world of club women, seeking meaningful outlets in a rapidly changing society. It follows her further through life-changing experiences at the University of Chicago and Cornell where she gained a firsthand look at new approaches to social activism.

Part II (chapters three through five) depicts Lyman and her generation of Relief Society women at the apex of their influence as they adapted their heritage of activism to new realities faced by women of the period. Chapter three traces Lyman's entry into the leadership of the Relief Society and exposes efforts to modernize the organization and make it a relevant player in the lives of second generation Mormon women. This occurred when the agenda and techniques of club work were grafted onto Mormon women's tradition of public activism. Chapter four describes how the organization became a pivotal player in the development of the welfare state in the West as the Relief Society began to work closely with local, state, and federal officials in Smith-Lever, Children's Bureau, and Red Cross activities. In addition, it details Lyman's efforts to modernize church charity practices and transform Relief Society women into a progressive lobbying force. Chapter five, spanning the high point of Mormon women's activism from 1921–1928, focuses closely on the Relief Society's maternity and infancy work under the Sheppard-Towner Act.

Chapters six through nine, which make up the third and final segment, follow Lyman and the Relief Society through a period of continued relevance but declining activism. Beginning with the advent of the Great Depression and the New Deal, chapter six explores the federalization of relief and the displacement of women from positions of prominence in welfare matters. While acknowledging that this process represented the beginning of a significant decline in activism among LDS women, this chapter argues that such an outcome was not inevitable. Chapter seven represents a departure, literally and figuratively for Lyman, when she accompanied her husband for two years to preside over the European Mission of the church. This was a period when she was able to judge the applicability of church programs she had helped devise back in the Intermountain American West to the realities facing women in a far different environment. While dwelling on the insights this period provided her, it also shows Lyman as a pioneering figure in Mormonism's transition away from being a strictly American faith. Chapter eight covers the years 1940–45, when Lyman was president of the Relief Society. Despite the losses of the 1930s, Lyman hoped to rebuild the relevance of the organization by broadening its remaining responsibilities. Her efforts to recapture a prominent role in community affairs proved unsuccessful due to circumstances beyond her control and ended with her departure from the Relief Society leadership in April 1945. Chapter nine spans the years from Lyman's resignation to her death in 1959, a period in which the ideals and goals of Mormon women embraced the exaggerated domesticity that seemed to typify the period. It concludes by examining Lyman's remarkable legacy, and how it faded from the collective memory of those of her faith.

Among her contemporaries Lyman was remembered for her dynamic personality, her inspiring public addresses, and especially for her remarkable vision of what Mormon women and the Relief Society could accomplish. She was the most admired woman of her generation, not because she was out of the mainstream, but because she was a leader who embodied the values held dear by LDS women of the time. This study seeks to place Lyman and her peers in the context of that time, both locally and nationally, showing them as both similar to and, in some ways, significantly different from their American sisters. Pursuing a path that at times intersected, sometimes diverged, and, at other times, paralleled that followed by other American women, these children of polygamy left behind an impressive record of accomplishments that resulted in remarkable benefits for themselves and subsequent generations. It is the intent of this volume to help restore these accomplishments, as well as the stories of Lyman and the women who joined her in achieving them, to the shared memory of later generations.

At this point a word regarding Latter-day Saint terminology may be helpful for some readers. Like most organizations or social groups, Mormons use language in a way that has meaning specific to themselves, some of which is unavoidably used in this study. The word Mormon, for example, is a nick-name originally bestowed upon members of the faith because of their belief in the *Book of Mormon*. However, the church is more properly known as the Church of Jesus Christ of Latter-day Saints. Its members, while most often known as Mormons are also referred to as Latter-day Saints, or simply as Saints, while things relating to the church and its members are also known as LDS. All four terms are used here interchangeably. Mormon congregations, roughly equivalent to a Catholic parish, are known as wards, while several wards are combined in an ecclesiastical unit known as a stake, the rough equivalent to a diocese. In areas with smaller numbers of members, where a full ward organization is not possible, congregations are organized into branches. Mormonism is governed through an all-male lay priesthood divided into different offices that eventually came to include all male members over twelve years of age judged worthy to hold it. Members of this lay ministry designated as bishops, along with two counselors, preside over a ward. Stakes are presided over by a stake president and his two counselors, as well as a twelve man high council. General authorities preside over the church at large with the president of the church, also known as the prophet, at the top of this organizational structure. Together with his two counselors this is known as the First Presidency. Serving under their direction is the Council of Twelve Apostles. For the purpose of this study it will also be helpful to know that a presiding bishopric also serves at the general level. The Presiding Bishop and his two counselors are responsible, at the general church level, for the temporal welfare of church members.

The women of the church have their own organizations that parallel in many ways the priesthood organization, although women also serve under the direction of priesthood leaders. Their relation to the priesthood, as well as the autonomy and empowerment they enjoy in church affairs varies over time, as I hope to make clear in the pages that follow. The first and flagship women's organization of the church is the Relief Society. In the wards it is presided over by a president and her two counselors as well as various other officers called to assist them. A stake Relief Society presidency and board presided over the affairs of the organization at the stake level during the period covered in this study. A general Relief Society presidency consisting of a president, her two counselors, and a general secretary (as well as sometimes a separate treasurer) presided over the organization at large. They were assisted by women called to join with the Relief

Society General Presidency, in forming what is known as the Relief Society General Board. Numbers of women serving on the board varied over time, but during Lyman's years of Relief Society service, in addition to the Relief Society General Presidency, an additional twenty women served on average as members of the board.

It is also helpful to understand that Mormonism teaches that church leaders are entitled to inspiration and revelation in regard to their varied church responsibilities. In this context, the term "call" has a different meaning for members of the faith than is common among many Christians. A call in the Mormon sense is an invitation by church leaders for a member to serve in a specific capacity. Finally, other than general authorities who receive a modest living allowance, the practice has been for church members to donate their service to the church without financial compensation.

1

A MORMON GIRLHOOD

> That greater liberty has been given to women in our Church than elsewhere is indeed true; that more equality of sex prevails is undeniable.
>
> —EMMELINE B. WELLS[1]

> With the advent of the gospel came liberty and freedom for L.D.S. women.
>
> —AMY BROWN LYMAN[2]

Counted among Amy Brown Lyman's earliest memories were those linked to the unusual status of her sex in Mormon society. Eliza R. Snow and Zina D. H. Young, perhaps the best known women of Mormonism's founding generation, visited her hometown of Pleasant Grove, Utah, several times during her youth. These women, together with others of the so-called leading sisters, helped create a vibrant culture among women of the faith, one that served community needs even as it functioned as a bridge to movements in the larger society aimed at establishing equality between the sexes.[3] Amy vividly recalled one occasion when the two women made their way to the Brown home to "bless and comfort" her invalid mother, Margaret Zimmerman Brown. As the children of the family knelt in prayer by their mother's bedside, Snow and Young placed their hands on Margaret's head and promised that through the united faith of all present she would be "spared to the family." "This was an impressive spiritual experience for us," Lyman later recalled, "and the fulfillment of this promise was a testimony."[4]

Such shared events were not uncommon for Mormon women during this era of spiritual and social empowerment for their sex.[5] In the larger American community, the nineteenth century had witnessed the rise of organized womanhood first in benevolent associations and missionary societies and eventually in reform associations and the club movement. Such combinations gave women a voice in important issues of the day ranging from moral purity early in the century to the abolitionist cause of the middle decades, as well as to the task of ameliorating the consequences of urban growth and industrialization during the Gilded Age. In the pursuit of such agendas, many developed a growing commitment to achieving suffrage and equal rights.[6] Mormon women were moved by these national trends and, surprising as it may seem, saw themselves as especially advantaged by their faith over their non-Mormon sisters. For them, the hand of God was manifest in events that were leading to greater equality between the sexes, with Latter-day Saints singled out to play a leading role in the drama.[7] Women of Lyman's generation were thus taught from their youth that they were uniquely empowered in the spiritual realm even as they were urged toward the forefront of a larger national movement aimed at women's social and political equality. Tiny Pleasant Grove was not isolated from such heady concepts that stirred the souls of its young women and broadened their expectations.

Amy Brown Lyman's early life illustrates how the interplay of sacred and secular sometimes worked to the advantage of Mormon women. Not surprisingly, the most important influences upon her emerged from her parents' devotion to their faith. Among the vanguard of the pioneers and entrenched in the second tier of the religion's lay leadership, their credentials were unassailable. In 1820, the year Joseph Smith experienced the first of his visions that would lead to the establishment of the Mormon Church, Lyman's father, John Brown, was born in Tennessee, the twelfth of fourteen children. His family moved to Illinois when he was a boy. A short time later his father died and perhaps because of this loss John became a religious seeker. By the time he reached his young adulthood and began a career as a school teacher, he had aligned himself with the Baptists—at least until two Mormon missionaries found him. In 1841 John Brown cast his lot with the Latter-day Saints, then gathering in Nauvoo, Illinois.[8] As was common in the early days of Mormondom, Brown soon made the transition from convert to missionary, in which capacity he proselytized in the South. There, in 1843, he met and married Elizabeth Crosby, the daughter of a prosperous Mississippi slave-owning family, who was drawn both to the Mormon message and its messenger.[9] When Joseph Smith was murdered the following year by a mob fearful of the church's growing power, John and Elizabeth moved to Nauvoo and joined those loyal to Brigham Young. In 1846 when Mormons began to evacuate Nauvoo, Brown returned to Mississippi to lead a party of converts to an anticipated rendezvous with the Saints whom he believed were then enroute to the Rocky Mountains. When the main body delayed their journey a year, Brown left his charges to winter in Pueblo, Colorado, and, accompanied by a small party of leaders, traveled to the Mormon encampment near present-day Omaha, Nebraska. There Young asked him to accompany the pioneer company then preparing to begin its journey. It was a matter of family pride that Brown was consequently among the first of the Mormon pioneers to enter the Salt Lake Valley in July of 1847.[10]

For the next fifty years, while Mormons built a string of communities in the valleys of the Intermountain West, John Brown devoted his energies to the cause even as he carried out additional missionary assignments in the East and England. In all, Brown crossed the plains thirteen times before the coming of the railroad.[11] In the 1850s, he took up residence south of Salt Lake City in the Utah Valley town of Lehi, and in 1862 moved again to nearby Pleasant Grove where he was called to preside over the community as bishop. Family lore has it that Brown owed this position to his reputation as a conciliator, a trait he used to bring peace to a badly divided community.[12]

Lyman's maternal grandparents, George and Juliana Zimmerman, were immigrants from Germany who had also been drawn to the Mormon message. In 1842 they left their home in Pennsylvania and moved to the area around Nauvoo. After the trek west, the family settled in Lehi, where Amy's mother Margaret came to know and admire John Brown. In 1857, just three weeks before her twenty-first birthday, she joined Brown's family as his third wife—his second plural wife after Amy Snyder, whom he had married four years previously.[13] It is here, in the distinctive practices of Mormonism, that Lyman's story most strongly diverges from that of other prominent American women of her generation. It is in polygamy, as well, that one finds reasons why women of her faith developed roles that challenged traditional gender norms and why those of Lyman's generation learned to take an active part in social reform and public activism.

Joseph Smith introduced polygamy—or plural marriage, as it came to be known—to a select group during the Nauvoo period. But only in 1852, five years after their arrival in the Salt Lake Valley, did church leaders openly declare it a tenet of the faith.[14] While apparently limited to a minority of church members, over time, especially during a period of intense religious recommitment in the mid-1850s known as the Reformation, almost all of the church's general and local leaders took plural wives, making polygamy a sign of faithfulness and status within the community.[15]

John Brown first entered the practice in 1853 at age thirty-three when he married twenty-one-year-old Amy Snyder. He was thirty-six when he married Margaret Zimmerman.[16] According to family lore, Elizabeth Brown supported her husband's entry into polygamy, though it appears neither she nor John had any illusions about Mormonism's "peculiar institution." Instead, they viewed it as part of their religious obligation to build God's kingdom. According to one daughter, Amy Snyder and Margaret Zimmerman shared this commitment and even gave up relationships with "promising young men" to join Brown's family as plural wives.[17]

Polygamy was laden with difficulties for its practitioners. Some wives were anxious about their place in their husband's affections and struggled to ensure that they and their children received a fair share of family resources.[18] For their part, polygamous husbands, at least the conscientious ones, walked a tightrope as they tried to maintain harmony among wives and children. Annie Clark Tanner, herself a child of polygamy as well as a polygamous wife, gave a perceptive analysis of how the practice affected family relationships. A man "would need to be almost a super-human," she observed, "to help each wife *equally* with the problems of rearing a family and to resist the biased influence of other family members." As a result, she asserted, "the wife in polygamy does not feel the security that I imagine monogamous women feel."[19]

All this came at a time when romantic ideals regarding the marital relationship, fed by popular novels of the period, were becoming commonplace in the larger society. Many Mormon women shared similar hopes for their own unions, though church leaders, recognizing the special strains of polygamy, tried to disabuse them. In regard to the challenge of trying to achieve a companionate relationship among spouses, Tanner herself observed that a polygamous husband "could scarcely assume the same responsibility of a plural wife's happiness or welfare as a monogamous marriage makes possible."[20] Indeed, polygamous marriages seem not only to have been less romantic in tone but also less stable than monogamous ones. In recognition of this, Brigham Young offered Utah women access to liberal divorce laws and recent research indicates that as many as one in four polygamous unions ended in dissolution.[21]

John Brown's family seems to have been more successful than most in preserving harmony, perhaps due to early commitments by John, Elizabeth Crosby, Amy Snyder, and Margaret Zimmerman to strict self-discipline. They knew that petty jealousies had to be avoided, and agreed there would be no discussion of personality flaws, no bickering, and perhaps, most difficult of all, no public displays of affection.[22] This austere behavior and reserved demeanor was not easily maintained and its consequences for family dynamics are unknown, though it may in part account for aspects of Lyman's personality that some later interpreted as evidence of coldness. Yet, this strategy that seems to have been successful in maintaining marital harmony, did not negate the role of personalities in the Brown's family life. John was remembered as firm in resolve but genial and even-tempered. Elizabeth and Margaret were seen as very similar: intelligent and strong-willed, who, according to one of Margaret's daughters, "had to be obeyed." Amy Snyder, gentle and soft-spoken, was a conciliator. Until her death in childbirth in 1871, it was she who indulged the whims of the Brown girls and helped them through the trials of adolescence. Perhaps due to their shared status as plural wives, she and Margaret seem to have grown especially close. All three women comforted and helped one another in times of sickness and tragedy and appear to have been sister wives, not just in the common Mormon usage, but more fully than was sometimes the case.[23] These three wives bore Brown a total of twenty-five children: Elizabeth gave birth to ten, although four died in infancy, as did two of Amy Snyder's five. Likewise, of Margaret's ten, four died in infancy or childhood.

It is unclear what the Brown offspring thought about polygamy. Although Elizabeth, Amy, and Margaret sought to make them feel a part of one large family, there were at least occasional jealousies. Margaret's children, and those of Amy, for instance, felt that Elizabeth's children sometimes got special privileges. This was not unusual in polygamy, where the first wife and her children sometimes enjoyed a special status.[24] But such feelings were not allowed to fester in the Brown home. Instead, all were admonished to make willing sacrifices for the common good, a philosophical thread common in American society at the time but especially characteristic of the Mormon community building experience. While family stresses may have been minimized, the marital choices made by the Brown children reveal a certain dissatisfaction with the system nonetheless, as most of them remained in monogamous relationships. A number of reasons could account for this, including discontent, spoken or implied among the wives—some in the family felt that Margaret, at least, did not raise her daughters to become polygamists—as well as government attempts to suppress the practice that added enormous tension to an already difficult situation. [25]

As for Lyman, she left no surviving record of her thoughts regarding the pros and cons of polygamy and as an adult avoided the topic as too private and controversial to be discussed, even among Mormons.[26] Of her father's plural wives, she never knew Amy Snyder, who died before she was born, while she probably found Elizabeth a little distant and, like her own mother, a little severe. Loyalty would have prevented her from looking too critically at the circumstances of her family life, yet she must have been aware of the stresses inherent in the system.

Like others involved in the practice, the Browns encountered a host of additional strains linked to their unusual family circumstances. Surprisingly, some may have been rooted in prejudices within the Mormon community itself. While plural marriage signified membership among the elite, it was a double-edged sword, sometimes giving focus to jealousies toward those in power that especially affected polygamous wives and children. Further, a plural wife might garner sympathy and emotional support if neglected by her husband, but might also be the focus of resentment if her marriage encouraged him to neglect another. Added to this, most Mormons seemed to have accepted polygamy in principle but many were never fully comfortable with this practice, which was so different from long-standing Christian tradition.

Such strains, however, paled when compared with those that emerged from outside the community. After the Civil War and especially with the close of Reconstruction, Congress turned its attention to Utah and Mormonism's distinctive religious practices. In the years after Brigham Young's death in 1877, a shift in policy by federal officials signaled a new drive to crush plural marriage through the arrest of prominent polygamists. This reached a high point in the latter 1880s, a period known as the Raid. In response to this, Young's successor, John Taylor, set an example of resistance by going into hiding in the spring of 1885 rather than face incarceration. Hundreds of polygamous men followed him, something Mormons termed "going on the underground." Others were arrested, tried, and sentenced to stiff jail terms. As for plural wives, many were left alone to fend for their families or spent extended periods hiding to avoid testifying against their spouses. Some faced jail time of their own.[27] While most polygamists were never prosecuted, the aggressive federal policies sent many experienced leaders into flight, which thus sapped the community's ability to function efficiently, even as these same forces adversely affected family life.[28]

Beginning in February 1886, when Amy was fourteen, John Brown joined those on the underground. He spent a year and a half hiding from authorities, sometimes secreted in the foothills overlooking Pleasant Grove, at others traveling far afield under an assumed name. His infrequent visits home required constant alertness and ready access to a secure hiding place to avoid capture. The anxiety his children felt due to his absence and their unending fear of his possible incarceration was intense.[29] Family members, convinced that they were following a higher law, felt justified in their disobedience to what they saw as unrighteous federal statutes. To prevent their betrayal of his location and to avoid aiding those gathering evidence for a possible trial, whenever asked, the children were taught to say that their father was out of town. To strangers who might be informants or federal marshals, they gave false names. At one point, several of the family were summoned before a grand jury in Salt Lake City, but with John in hiding, the case was dismissed.[30] Perhaps in some regard the events of the anti-polygamy crusade had a positive consequence for Lyman as they prepared her for her later life as a social worker, when it would be vitally important to closely guard the sensitive information of her client families. At the very least these experiences reinforced her familial tendency toward reticence in personal matters.[31]

Less dramatic events during Lyman's youth may have been similarly useful in her later life by providing her with firsthand insight into the challenges of maintaining a family during hard economic times. The Brown family's financial status reportedly fell well short of their social rank in the community. Margaret's daughter Rose recalled that they were "always poor," and while there was generally enough for necessities, little was left for anything else. In the interest of frugality, the family took great pains to waste nothing.

Flour sacks, for example, were bleached in the sun and refashioned into underwear and petticoats while such non-essentials as candy or store-bought clothing were rare treats. The only luxuries the family indulged in were related to education, such as the purchase of the occasional book, particularly works of history or classics of literature. John had aspired to be a schoolteacher before his conversion and never lost his love of learning. Reportedly he devoted every spare penny toward building a modest library. Newspapers were another indulgence—Amy's mother, Margaret, tried to stay well-informed through a family subscription to the church-owned *Deseret News* as well as the semi-official voice of Mormon women, the *Woman's Exponent*, which she read together with her children.[32]

Of course, concerns about making ends meet were common for large rural families of the period and seem to have been the norm for polygamists like the Browns. Even in the insular society of the Mormon settlements, the full energy of all family members was required to ensure bare minimums of fiscal solvency.[33] In early Utah, conditions proved particularly burdensome to women. It has been said that as nineteenth-century American women went west, they traveled back in time, giving up modern conveniences and taking on tasks of home production more typical of their grandmothers' generation than their own.[34] While conditions had improved somewhat by the time Amy was born, this had been applicable to the Browns' experience. Elizabeth had come from a prosperous southern family and when she first married was so unaccustomed to household work that John had to return to Mississippi to "fetch a servant" to help her.[35] Yet over time she came to excel in all forms of home production, even the difficult task of stripping cane used to weave hats or chair bottoms.[36] In contrast, from an early age Amy Snyder and Margaret Zimmerman were accustomed to hard work, having spent much of their youth in modest households on the frontier. John was fortunate that in his large family he was assisted by three wives who made significant contributions to the family economy. Elizabeth not only helped with home production but often worked behind the counter of a family store in Pleasant Grove; Amy Snyder took in washing; and Margaret was an accomplished weaver of cloth. Each was aided by children schooled in similar skills.[37]

Some scholars have argued that the difficult conditions encountered in the West were a liberating force for women who, by necessity, were forced to take upon themselves traditionally male functions such as managing farms and ranches in place of absent, disabled, or deceased husbands. Several historians have also seen the distinct factors of Mormon society, especially polygamy, as furthering this trend.[38] At first glance these views gain credence through the example of the Brown women, who had to fend for themselves when John was away on church business or on the underground. Indeed, even when free to look after his own affairs, John divided his time among three households. Under the circumstances, his wives exercised an unusual degree of independence compared to most monogamous women, with each forced to function in areas that extended beyond the era's prescribed gender roles. Elizabeth, Amy, and Margaret cared for stock and tended crops in the absence of their husband and all joined in the work of the harvest, even when he was present.[39]

This broadening of gender roles extended to the next generation as well. Of the seventeen Brown children who survived to maturity, fourteen were girls. From an early age they worked the fields, looked after the animals, took a turn behind the counter of the family store, and otherwise assumed what were then considered male responsibilities, even as they became expert in the traditional female skills of weaving, sewing, and managing a home.[40] At a time when the contributions of many middle-class American women to the household economy were growing invisible and devalued, women of the Brown family, like many other Latter-day Saint women, were taking on an increasing share of visible and valued tasks. As they carried out these responsibilities, they grew secure in their judgment and seem to have won respect and status in their communities. Annie Clark Tanner articulated such an argument, seeing among polygamy's advantages the greater confidence it generated among women in their own abilities as they became efficient managers of family affairs and, not least, their children's labor.[41]

Yet there is little evidence that the Brown women, or most others in similar circumstances, saw these experiences as anything more than a temporary expedient requiring extra work in addition to their already overwhelming household burdens.[42] Indeed, Tanner herself maintained that Mormon women had few, if any, real advantages over their non-Mormon sisters. Although polygamous husbands were happy to surrender some control over household affairs when it was to their advantage, like other Victorian men, she asserted, they retained for themselves the final say in matters they cared about.[43]

The advantages born of rural life and polygamy thus remain matters of debate. Easier to discern are the effects of realigned gender roles on second generation women like Lyman. Their youth in an environment of blurred gender distinctions is perhaps the most important reason why, as mature adults, many of these younger women felt no qualms about taking on traditionally male roles in politics and community affairs, even as they continued to fulfill responsibilities in the home and family.

Typical of the ever changing dynamics of family life, to which polygamous families were no exception, by the late 1860s, Elizabeth's children were beginning to mature, marry, and start families of their own, even as the other Brown wives continued to bear sons and daughters. Amy Cassandra, born on February 7, 1872, was one of these. Named for Amy Snyder, who had died the previous year, she was the youngest daughter of John Brown's three families, though Margaret soon provided her with two younger brothers.[44] Despite his frequent absences, it was John who most influenced the circumstances of Amy's youth. As the ecclesiastical leader of Pleasant Grove, he was at the center of all the town's activities and it was his status that determined the social standing of the family. In adulthood, Amy took great pride in what he achieved and modeled many of her own actions on his example. As bishop, he settled disputes, gave counsel on matters ranging from business to marriage and assumed general responsibility for managing church and town affairs. The importance of his position is indicated by his simultaneous service as local mayor and representative to the territorial legislature.

Brown's preeminence in spiritual and secular affairs made it imperative that he and his family set the pace in all church sponsored community endeavors. This represented both boon and burden to his children.[45] Some of his responsibilities were especially challenging, few more so than the United Order experiment of the 1870s intended to stimulate home industry and Mormon self-sufficiency. This required him to give up his personal affairs and surrender family property as he helped manage the Pleasant Grove branch of the church collective.[46] After several years, the Browns (like most others who participated) emerged at the end of the experiment wiser but certainly no wealthier. But along with such sacrifices, the family also gained benefits through their association with prominent church leaders and other privileges that came through their membership in Pleasant Grove's religious elite.[47]

John's prominence in the community no doubt influenced his patterns of behavior toward his family; in particular, it seems to have reinforced his tendency toward strictness. Having given of himself unselfishly for his faith, for instance, he tolerated no criticism of the church or its leaders. Parental rigidity, a characteristic of Victorian family relations, when taken to extremes, in or out of Mormonism, could be highly destructive to family unity. But as remembered by his children, Brown tempered his firmness with good humor and constant affection. Believing strongly in self-control, he seldom raised his voice in anger or displayed his temper, practices that he deemed a waste of energy. He opposed corporal punishment and never resorted to it himself—an approach adopted by his children. Further, he made sure that all conflicts were handled privately so as not to become matters of public criticism or gossip. Brown encapsulated his life philosophy in a series of oft repeated aphorisms that were deeply imprinted on the minds of Amy and her siblings: "The man who cannot control himself will not be able to control others," "Temper outbursts harm the one who indulges in them more than they harm others," "Do not tell all you know," "Do not publish other people's faults," "Neither praise nor deprecate yourself," and perhaps most importantly, "Do not grieve over the past, but prepare for the future." In all, Brown set high standards for his children, but reportedly never expected more from them than he did from himself.[48]

Despite his much admired personal qualities and community prominence, John Brown was seen as somewhat old-fashioned by the children of his third wife. Above and beyond the normal generational divide, his case was unusual as he was in his late thirties when he married Margaret and was fifty-two when Amy was born. His younger children thought him overprotective when he refused to allow them to go unchaperoned in mixed groups to the nearby canyons for picnics, although as a more experienced adult, Amy, for one, saw wisdom in this. Yet, all in all, his children respected him for his common sense and unquestioned concern for their welfare, even if they occasionally bridled under his restraints.[49]

John, while closely involved in his children's lives, was often physically remote. It is thus not surprising that his children remembered him in somewhat idealized terms. As wives Elizabeth, Amy, and Margaret were left to carry out most of the day to day management of family affairs, including discipline, recollections of the Brown women seem more realistic. Margaret was no exception. With several children and an often absent and always shared husband, she sought to compensate by demanding absolute obedience—reinforcing what her children saw as characteristics stemming from her German heritage. In addition to the trials of her domestic arrangements, Margaret's tendency toward severity in her verbal chastisements might have been influenced by significant physical disabilities she endured as a consequence of her last two pregnancies that ended with complicated deliveries. Bedridden for five years due to a severely fallen uterus, even after a partial recovery, she "was never to be so strong again." Nonetheless, Margaret lived for another half-century and remained a dominant force in her children's day to day affairs as well as an important influence in the community. Even when reduced to invalidism she was seen as a local sage who "guided her family and almost the entire town from the realm of a four poster." With a keen mind and strong sense of sympathy born of her own suffering, many in the community came to her for advice, confident that they would receive a sympathetic hearing and straightforward counsel. She was especially remembered for urging young people to pursue their education and make something of themselves.[50]

The latter sentiments were taught as gospel in the Brown home where education was of central importance. Complementing John's interest, Margaret's parents came from a long line of teachers and civil servants in Germany. In her youth, Margaret had held high ambitions of her own not limited by her sex. When weaving homespun with the other girls of the community, some spoke of commonplace dreams, but she talked of becoming a doctor to help cure women of their ailments. Though these dreams became reality for some among the subsequent generation of Mormon women, at the time, such an ambition was unheard of, and, in the 1850s in frontier Utah, unattainable. But as conditions improved, Margaret was determined that her children have opportunities she had been unable to realize. She encouraged all of them to gain the best education possible and her voice was among the most vocal in Pleasant Grove calling for improvements in the schools. While commitments to progress through education were a hallmark of the age nationally, the accomplishments of the Brown family remain impressive, especially in Utah, where many schools lagged behind national norms.[51] Family records indicate that all the children received an education beyond the primary grades and several of the younger Browns even joined the then elite ranks of the university educated.[52]

Among the Brown children, Amy reportedly stood out as unusually energetic and intelligent. Perhaps, as the youngest daughter she received more attention from parents and older siblings. Or perhaps, due to the improving educational climate in the territory she enjoyed advantages not available to her older brothers and sisters. Whatever factors may have contributed to her later accomplishments, according to family and associates, Amy was also naturally endowed with exceptional ability. Family members used to joke that she had inherited all the energy and intelligence of both sides of the clan. Even as a young child she showed the directness and clarity of purpose that characterized her as an adult. After she wandered over to the church building one Sunday morning, a man standing at the door asked, "Well, little girl, who are you?" She quickly replied, "Amy Cassandra, three years old." Exhibiting a gift for leadership and self-confidence as a young teen, her fixed determination in pursuing goals earned her the nick-name "Ready-aim-fire" from other children of the community who sometimes admired and sometimes resented her take charge attitude.[53]

In addition to her family, the influences of community life helped channel the energies and interests of the youthful Amy. Observers at the time would have found an intermingling of secular and sacred in Pleasant Grove that was fairly typical of Latter-day Saint settlements. Life revolved around the church house where leaders provided counsel in all matters, spiritual and temporal. For Mormons of the era it was as much a religious obligation to dig irrigation ditches, cut and haul timber, weave homespun, or care for the poor, as it was to attend meetings.[54] It is thus not surprising that as adults, Lyman's generation often saw community problems through a lens of religious obligation—much like followers of the Protestant Social Gospel elsewhere in the nation.[55]

Situated in the shadow of Mount Timpanogos, which dominates Utah Valley, Pleasant Grove was laid out in a manner that formalized the primacy of religion. The churchhouse stood at the center of a grid of streets oriented reassuringly to the points of the compass. Like other Mormon settlements and similar to seventeenth-century Puritan villages, its homes were clustered in the town center with farm fields surrounding them. This layout was intended to foster the sense of community so vital to Mormon thinking and to avoid the isolation typically experienced by farm families on the frontier. Lining every street were ditches dug by collective labor through which flowed crystal streams of cold mountain water, divided carefully among the town's inhabitants for culinary or agricultural uses. Houses were set back from the street on large lots with gardens. Some were of log, others of stone or brick, but most were adobe, the ubiquitous material of choice for early Utah structures.[56] In the 1870s, a majority of the town's several hundred inhabitants were either old-stock Americans, or the children of immigrants who had already spent years in the eastern states. The architectural style of their dwellings reflected their sensibilities, being strongly reminiscent of the old Midwest.

Amy grew up in such a home. By the time of her childhood, John Brown's families lived in two modest story-and-a-half adobes clustered in Pleasant Grove's tiny town center.[57] Margaret's family shared two small rooms and a kitchen below with a sleeping loft upstairs. Nighttime saw the children climb up to the loft, their way lit with a carefully held homemade candle, that, for frugality's sake, was quickly blown out once their destination was reached. In winter, they hastened their journey through the unheated loft to the relative warmth of feather beds, often shared with a sibling. During winter days, extra layers of petticoats and woolen stockings, mittens and caps, kept the girls warm. In summer, the handful of Brown boys dressed relatively coolly while their sisters sweltered in calico and a few less petticoats. Meals were simple, with food limited for the most part to what the family produced themselves. Yet, later in life, with the knowledge gleaned through her years of social welfare work, Amy marveled at the well-balanced makeup of this humble fare.[58]

The course of life in Pleasant Grove did not develop in isolation, but was linked to the entire Mormon community, and that community, in turn, was linked to the larger nation. Despite Mormon intentions to form a semi-independent commonwealth in the remoteness of the Great Basin, Utahns were never completely cut off from other Americans. With its central position on the overland trails and, after 1869, the transcontinental railroad, the territory hosted large numbers of travelers on their way to or from the West Coast who brought with them news from the outside world. Brigham Young kept a keen ear attuned to such sources of information, alert for word of practical innovations that might strengthen Utah's economy as well as entertainments originating in the larger society that would uplift his people.

While Salt Lake City was no New York or even San Francisco, by the 1860s, even before the coming of the railroad, it was unusually cosmopolitan for a city of its size. Not only did it count among its twelve thousand or so inhabitants Mormon converts from Europe (nearly seventy percent of heads of households in Salt Lake County were foreign-born in 1870) and large numbers of missionaries well-traveled in distant climes, it also housed a small but growing population of non-Mormon merchants, miners, smelter workers, government officials, and military personnel. This increasingly diverse population supported a thriving theater company and orchestra—frequently patronized by Young himself—and regularly enjoyed lecturers, including such luminaries as Sir Richard Burton, and touring companies featuring Shakespearean plays performed by prominent actors. In addition, Salt Lakers organized their own array of literary, musical, scientific, and horticultural societies and supported several newspapers and magazines, both pro- and anti-Mormon.[59]

As Amy grew from infancy to young womanhood, Salt Lake began to look like other booming cities of the period as the single or two-story adobes of its downtown gave way to more substantial three- and four-story structures of brick that proclaimed the vitality of its commercial district. Meanwhile other faiths began to stake their claims in the territory, both to serve the needs of the growing "Gentile" population (as Latter-day Saints, who saw themselves as a modern Israel, referred to those not of their faith) and to save the souls of what non-Mormon religious leaders considered to be the deluded Mormons. During the same period, the landmark edifices of the LDS faith took shape; first the distinctive turtle-domed Tabernacle in 1867, and then, slowly, the Salt Lake Temple, commenced in 1853 but not completed for four decades. By the time Amy reached her teens, the walls of the latter had risen to eighty feet.

The small community of Pleasant Grove had no similarly imposing structures and only a modest business district of a few shops, including the one operated by the Browns. But like Salt Lake, it was not isolated. Located on the main north-south wagon road through the territory, those journeying to or from Salt Lake on business or for the church's great general conferences held in the spring and fall passed through bringing news from friends or family along with the latest gossip from outlying settlements. In 1870, the telegraph arrived and in 1873, when Amy was one year old, the Utah Central railroad, which connected residents with the transcontinental line and the rest of the nation. Together with newspapers and magazines, these represented important links to the larger world.[60]

For Amy, with her keen mind and driving curiosity, such connections to the outside must have beckoned toward new experiences and wider horizons. Did she ride in her father's wagon along the dusty road to Salt Lake City for conference? We do not know. Surely she had been to the neighboring town of Lehi where her father owned land. Possibly she accompanied him when he took her older siblings to study at the nascent Brigham Young Academy in nearby Provo, though this too is merely speculation. No doubt she rarely left the confines of Pleasant Grove during her early youth. But she did hear tales of the wider world. Her father had been to far away England and to the eastern states on church missions and both her parents had family in the East with whom they occasionally corresponded. Amy was aware of this larger world and though her mother and father had largely forsaken it, typical of her generation growing up in the isolated valleys of the far West, it called to her, and the road to Salt Lake City seemed a first step to solving the mystery of what lay beyond her own limited horizons.

Further feeding her curiosity, by the time of her youth recent converts from foreign countries had begun to arrive in Pleasant Grove and soon formed a large portion of its inhabitants. They no doubt contributed to Amy's knowledge of people and things while reinforcing her church-centered view of the universe by providing tangible evidence of the success of the Mormon gathering. Many of Pleasant Grove's immigrants joined the church in Great Britain. They shared a common language and heritage with American converts yet added a cosmopolitan flavor to the town. More, however, came from Scandinavia, so many in fact that for a time Pleasant Grove was known as Little Denmark. Their unfamiliar customs and strange language seemed exotic. While bound to the rest of the community through ties of religion, their cultural differences were pronounced enough to create strains while delaying their full assimilation into the mainstream.[61] Her own family became linked to some of these recent arrivals through marriage. These early experiences no doubt contributed to the sensitivity that, as an adult, Amy felt toward the challenges faced by immigrants.

Many years later, in a memoir written for the women of the church, Lyman described her childhood in idyllic terms: "As I think of it today," she recalled, "there could have been for me no more desirable place in which to be born and no better place which could have given me the environment and particular experiences . . . which I now prize so dearly."[62] In general she remembered the close-knit aspects of small-town life and emphasized happy school days, church socials and dances, and parades honoring those, like her father, who were among the original pioneers. Life, as she recalled it, was interesting. Returned missionaries recounted their experiences in foreign lands while traveling lecturers held their audiences in rapt attention and shaped collective memory with stories of early church history. Often in her recalled childhood work itself seemed less burdensome because of its communal nature; the weaving and sewing, the gleaning of fields for wheat, the gathering and drying of windfall cherries made lighter when shared among siblings and neighbors. In such reminiscences life seemed in harmony with heaven and earth.[63]

Yet other memories reveal that her childhood was not insulated from tragedy. In this era before mass vaccination, disease and death appeared regularly, upsetting Amy's sense of security and leaving lasting scars. Among the most frightening visitors was diphtheria, "the terror of my childhood," she remembered. One siege when she was eleven claimed three out of five children from a neighboring family. Amy vividly recalled their black, homemade coffins passed out of a bedroom window for a hurried trip to the cemetery. In another family five out of eight children were taken, the desperate parents so terrified that the scourge might spread to their remaining three that to stop it, they burned their home and all their possessions.[64] Rheumatic fever, though less common, was also dreaded. Though not usually fatal, it often left permanent health problems in its wake. The chronic heart and kidney conditions suffered by Amy and some of her sisters as adults were believed to be legacies of the disease. Measles also came regularly and it too often left behind death or disability.[65]

Not surprisingly, due to her long-standing interest in medicine, Margaret Brown sought to safeguard her children from the worst of these scourges through the best available advice. As was true for many other nineteenth-century families with little access to competent medical care, this meant self-treatment assisted by books published for the purpose. Margaret discovered one of the better ones—a popular volume by Dr. Gunn. Her exertions no doubt spared the Brown children somewhat. By following Gunn's advice, for example, she protected her family against smallpox using a needle and a scab secured from a successfully vaccinated relative. But not all of Gunn's recipes seem equally scientific. An example is found in the strong-smelling herb asafetida that the Brown children wore in bags around their necks to ward off diphtheria. Its only real value may have been to give them such an offensive odor that others would not get close enough to spread infection.[66]

Despite such precautions, death was not a stranger to their household. When Amy was eighteen, her twenty-three-year-old sister Margaret died of Bright's disease (this kidney malady likely the result of an earlier bout of rheumatic fever), leaving behind a grieving husband and an infant daughter. Perhaps even more traumatic, several years earlier, at the time of the terrifying diphtheria scourge, Amy's youngest brother, Lawrence Hoke, died of a burst appendix just a month before his eighth birthday. As the baby of the family and youngest boy, one of only two in Margaret's family, Hoke had been doted on by parents and older siblings alike. Amy, nearly four years his senior, had been especially close, watching over him like the proverbial mother hen. His death, after days of suffering, left an indelible mark on her soul. Perhaps significantly, she excluded memories of this event from her public writings, but privately, even in later years she and her siblings spoke of it often and remembered how helplessly the family watched his agony and lamented how, with just a little more knowledge, his death might have been prevented.[67]

Tragedy came in other guises as well. Until the arrival of modern medicine mitigated some of the consequences, childbirth commonly threatened women with death and debilitating injury. Amy's mother Margaret suffered for decades from just such causes and her invalidism served as a constant reminder of the perils of child-bearing. And despite her best efforts, other family members paid an even greater price for inadequate medical care. When Amy was ten, a half-sister, Laura, died of an infection borne by an unknowing midwife who also spread the bacteria to five other women with the same fatal results. Of course, the year before Amy was born, sister-wife Amy Snyder's death was similarly precipitated by complications of childbirth.[68] Yet in the Brown family such tragedies were not allowed to become sources of mere regret: as important as the deep impressions these occurrences left was Margaret's response to them. Not content with Dr. Gunn's advice, she was constantly on the lookout for new knowledge. As her children grew older, for example, she secured a teacher and organized a class in obstetrics and nursing for the women of Pleasant Grove and saw that all of her daughters were in attendance.[69]

These, along with the other occurrences of her childhood, were among the rich array of experiences that in her mature years Amy drew upon to inform her actions as a community leader and reformer. Looking back, she realized how, in her youth, she had witnessed not only searing tragedy and daunting community challenges, but a primitive social engineering laboratory, of sorts, through which her parents, family members, and others in her town sought through practical means and cooperative action to address such problems. From the vantage point of her youth she began to grasp the potential and limitations of trying to meet the needs of individuals while working toward larger social goals, ideas that would later find more coherent expression after her formal study of social issues. Colleagues later described her as a natural social worker. After considering the circumstances in which she came of age, her apparently innate abilities seem less surprising.

As important as these experiences were, others during Lyman's youth also revealed a great deal to her about the potential of organized action among women. In times of social crisis, women have often seized opportunities to expand their sphere of influence. Such an environment permeated Amy's youth due to the ongoing anti-polygamy crusade as well as other threats to Mormon separatism, specifically, the effects of the transcontinental railroad. Indeed, already in 1867, five years before Amy was born, the latter's approach led Brigham Young to enlist the aid of women to shore up the morals and economy of the Mormon community. As part of this effort, he authorized a reorganization of the Relief Society.

Established in 1842 in Nauvoo, the Society was in many ways similar to other women's benevolent organizations then emerging across the nation. But at its creation it obtained a unique status when Joseph Smith incorporated it into the heart of the church structure and organized it, as others later described it, "after the pattern of the

Priesthood." This granted it a status, in the eyes of Mormon women at least, parallel to that of the church's all-male lay priesthood quorums.[70] With the stamp of the prophet behind it, the Relief Society's activities carried great weight in the LDS community—seemingly more than similar groups of organized women enjoyed in communities across the nation. In subsequent decades Relief Society women carried out benevolent work, held their own meetings, regulated their spiritual and educational affairs, and even, after their reorganization by Young, orchestrated political activism in behalf of their people.[71]

They enjoyed this broad grant of authority in large measure because their activities served the larger aims of the church and its leaders.[72] In the period of the latter 1860s this resulted as Young came to see the Relief Society as a means to further his goals for LDS economic independence. Through it women were enlisted to take on less physically demanding economic responsibilities, which thus freed up men to do more of the heavy work required for his planned mining and industrial activities.[73] But in the process of using women to facilitate his goals for the church, Young opened wide the door Smith had unlocked that led to a sanctioned sphere of activity for women in economic and community affairs. If Young's empowerment of women was an imaginative refocusing of their talents intended primarily to further the cause of building the Mormon Zion, in subsequent years Latter-day Saint women showed themselves equally clever by remembering and repeating those parts of his public statements that were most advantageous to their circumstances. In particular they used his words to support their belief in Mormonism's divine role in restoring woman to her rightful place as the equal of man.[74]

To preside over this comprehensive reorganization of the Relief Society Brigham Young called upon a member of his large plural family, Eliza R. Snow. Reportedly one of the few women whose counsel he consistently respected and, unquestionably, the most influential Latter-day Saint woman of her generation, Snow proved extremely capable in any endeavor she undertook.[75] Noted for her keen intellect and deep spiritual insight—the latter quality earned her the honorific title of prophetess—she willingly complied with Young's directive and worked to strengthen the faith of LDS women and support home industry even as she used the same activities to further the interests of her sex.[76] Over the next several years she traveled by wagon or horseback along the dusty, primitive roads of the Great Basin to scattered settlements where she organized local Relief Societies. Frequently in company with one or more of the leading sisters, she repeatedly called upon women to act in new and wider spheres.[77]

Snow's priorities during the reorganization reflected not only the influence of earlier benevolent associations formed by American women, but also the emerging women's club movement with its emphasis on self-education and community improvement. Along these lines, the acquisition of public speaking and leadership skills headed her agenda for the rank and file.[78] She directed societies to meet regularly so local members could organize charity work, discuss religious or secular topics, and exercise gifts of the spirit. The latter included speaking in tongues and, perhaps more significantly, the gift demonstrated in the case of Margaret Brown, namely laying hands on afflicted sisters to bless them for the restoration of health, the alleviation of pain, or to prepare them for childbirth. Later generations would come to see the spiritual gift of healing the sick as strictly within the purview of male priesthood holders, but to these first generations it was part of a unique heritage of spiritual power which, alone among women, they felt members of their faith enjoyed.[79]

Relief Society women also demonstrated their collective power through the duties they assumed to foster Mormon self-sufficiency. To prevent the drain of capital from the territory, Young encouraged communities to create cooperative stores for the sale of locally produced goods and urged women, with their experience managing household expenses, to take charge of the enterprises. He encouraged them further to lend a hand in the manufacture of such products as hats, rag carpets, and homespun cloth. While not the most successful of these endeavors, perhaps the most impressive was the establishment of a silk industry which necessitated that women throughout the territory plant mulberry trees, carefully safeguard silkworms, and laboriously unwind cocoons to spin silk into thread that they then wove into cloth. As they did with other Relief Society projects, the women of Pleasant Grove, including those of the Brown family, joined the task. In February 1877, when Amy turned five, the town's branch of the society reported their purchase of three city lots "fenced and ready for planting mulberry trees."[80]

Such efforts represented a first step toward the broader economic and managerial role for women envisioned by Young and Snow. In their February report, Pleasant Grove women further revealed that they received "$115.57 ½" in income from "sundries, donation, and dividend from [a cooperative] store, of which they had $11.20 in cash." During the previous year they had paid $234.95 for plowing and fencing several lots they owned, dispersed $55.75 to the poor, donated $50.00 for construction of the Salt Lake Temple, and another $13.50 toward an organ for the local meeting house. In addition, they owned shares in the Pleasant Grove cooperative store totaling $515.38 and $118.00 in shares of another cooperative enterprise, the Provo Woolen factory, while their three lots were valued at $400.00. This represented an impressive amount of capital for women in small-town Utah, but it was not atypical for branches of the Relief Society at that time.[81]

Encouraged by such reports of initial success, Young called upon "wives and daughters" to assume an even wider role in the kingdom by preparing to work in banks, learn telegraphy, and even study law, medicine, or the sciences. A welcomed announcement, Young's words were long remembered, especially by second generation women like Lyman, who quoted such progressive sentiments well into the twentieth century. In practice, however, most women of the faith who moved outside of the household economy often gravitated to such "female" occupations as school teaching and, like their non-Mormon sisters elsewhere in the nation, generally renounced even such careers upon marriage. Yet, there were significant exceptions: while only a very few ventured into law, more moved into medicine. By the turn of the century, eleven percent of Utah's physicians and surgeons were women, a figure nearly double that of the nation as a whole.[82] Many more became nurses, some receiving training in practical nursing through classes organized by the Relief Society. Even the many Mormon women who did not take advantage of these opportunities pointed with pride to those few who did.

Additional responsibilities, such as a Relief Society grain storage program, while less radical departures, were more broadly assumed. Seeking to guard against famine resulting from the harsh and unpredictable environment in the Great Basin, in 1876 Young asked Emmeline B. Wells, a frequent contributor and soon to be editor of the *Woman's Exponent*, to encourage local Societies to gather and store grain.[83] At her urging, members of the organization gleaned fields for excess wheat and raised money to construct granaries, acquiring in the process expertise in management and fundraising.[84] Armed with new confidence gained from such experiences, they soon began to arrange for the construction of self-financed meeting halls.[85] Through the Relief Society, Mormon women thus engaged in a wide range of activities that broadened their skills and heightened their sense of self-esteem—qualities their non-Mormon sisters were then gaining in clubs and other organizations.

The Relief Society's expanding agenda benefitted not only mature women of the first generation, but also those coming of age, or about to, in the second. Role models among the leading sisters and local women—including their own mothers active in the society's work—expanded the coming generation's expectations of what women could accomplish. Lyman, like other girls and young women at the time, was surrounded by a cadre of such accomplished women who pointed her in the direction of greater opportunity. The senior Brown women, including Amy's older sisters, had been intimately involved in the Relief Society since its reorganization. Elizabeth Crosby Brown was president of Pleasant Grove's Relief Society and during Amy's youth the whole family was familiar with her "goings and comings" to visit the sick, help the needy, and supervise the storage of grain.[86] Similarly, Amy Snyder Brown and Margaret Zimmerman Brown served as visiting teachers in the organization who looked after the well-being of the women of the ward. As they matured, the older Brown daughters, among them Amy's half-sisters Paulina and Sarah (daughters of first wife Elizabeth), and her older full-sisters Rose and Lydia, also took up leadership positions.[87]

Though Amy would not become a member of the Society until after her marriage, like other young women, she was frequently involved in its activities. In her case this included the hard, tiresome work of gathering, drying, and selling peaches and windfall cherries. The tangible results of these labors became visible when the Relief Society used money raised in this manner to purchase additional wheat. Amy joined the curious throng of Pleasant Grove's children who often climbed atop the Society's large metal storage bins to gaze at the bounty inside, knowing they had played a small part in securing the well-being of the community.[88]

In addition to providing positive role models, first generation women created new organizations that prepared their daughters to assume their own roles in community affairs. The same year the Relief Society was reorganized, Eliza R. Snow helped form what came to be known as the Young Ladies Mutual Improvement Association (YLMIA). Like the Relief Society, it encouraged home industry, stimulated religious commitment, and guarded against negative moral influences. As was the case in its parent organization, with some adult guidance, YLMIA members governed their own affairs, conducted meetings in accordance with parliamentary procedure, prepared and taught lessons on religious topics, literature, and current events, and organized recreational and community service activities.[89] Though Amy was too young for some of the early activities in Pleasant Grove's YLMIA, her older sisters played active parts in the organization that followed an agenda of self-improvement and moral uplift. Like others so involved, they gained impressive experience as they carried out a variety of activities and entertainments—including a self-published newspaper.[90] In effect, the girls and young women of Pleasant Grove and elsewhere in the Mormon domain were paralleling the experience of club women across the nation even more closely than were their mothers in the Relief Society.[91]

Through such activities the YLMIA represented a self-conscious effort to prepare the younger generation to mobilize in collective activism. The results were impressive.

While membership figures are imprecise, it can be said with some safety that during the last decades of the nineteenth century somewhere between one quarter and one half of all Mormon girls and young women were enrolled as dues paying members of the YLMIA. This represented an impressive accomplishment, but it was not enough for Mormon leaders.[92] In 1878 Snow presided over the church-wide formation of the Primary Association, the last of the women's organizations of the church. Designed to instill community values at an early age, it included boys as well as girls and provided a venue where children could gain confidence participating in discussions and even speaking before mixed audiences.[93] Secretary of the local branch at age eleven, Lyman was responsible for taking attendance and keeping minutes. It was here that she gained her first practice speaking in public—a memorable if not entirely pleasant experience. After her address, she read a poem written by one of the local leaders that she was then to present to a visiting stake leader. Upon returning to her seat, however, she found that instead of presenting the poem, she had delivered a button that she had nervously twisted off her dress.[94] Such embarrassments were a rarity, however, as Amy gained a reputation for diligence and dependability that earned her abundant praise. As an adult, Lyman looked back to her time in the Primary for the earliest roots of her later self-confidence in the public realm. She also found important role models and mentors there, women of intelligence and ability who broadened her expectations of what she could accomplish. Among the most important of these was Mary Ann Winters who as a youth witnessed many of the formative events of Mormonism and drew upon these experiences while serving as Amy's Primary and Sunday School teacher. Winters exemplified not only abiding faith and a link to the past, but also demonstrated a commitment to community service and even women's rights.[95]

The benefits Lyman received from her youthful experiences in the church were not unusual. Because the women's organizations possessed similar structures and often shared an interlocking leadership they formed an ideal environment in which to develop networking and mentoring relationships for women and girls of all ages.[96] These relationships included the highest levels of the hierarchy. Snow, Wells, and other general leaders corresponded regularly with local women and often visited their meetings providing visibility and regular access to these exponents of a dynamic, empowered womanhood. In Pleasant Grove, the conferences presided over by the leading sisters were occasions not to be missed. This interaction, which occurred throughout the 1870s and 1880s, permitted local and general leaders of the women's organizations to develop a clear sense of the talents and abilities of the rising generation and to mentor those with special potential. Working together, the leaders of the Relief Society, the YLMIA, and the Primary Association thus initiated tens of thousands of Latter-day Saint women and girls into the developing activism of the late nineteenth century, including a surprising and impressive involvement in political affairs.

What energized Latter-day Saint women politically was the strident campaign mounted by eastern reformers to force Mormon compliance with national political, economic, and social norms.[97] But defending their religious liberties did not long remain the sole agenda of women of the faith. In January 1870 when a harsh antipolygamy measure was under consideration in Congress, LDS women organized a "Great Indignation Meeting." Aware that a woman's suffrage bill had just passed Wyoming's territorial legislature, one of the leading sisters, Bathsheba Smith, called the bluff of antipolygamy reformers, who saw Mormon women merely as victims of an oppressive patriarchy, by moving that the assembled women demand the right for their own franchise. Startled by their own boldness—for some this was the first time they openly voiced support for women's rights—they showed enthusiastic support for the motion. In response, church leaders secured a public relations victory when they quickly maneuvered a woman's suffrage bill through the territorial legislature, a measure soon signed into law by the acting governor. A few weeks later, a handful of Mormon women beat their Wyoming sisters to the polls in a municipal election, enabling them to claim bragging rights that they were the first in the nation to exercise the franchise.[98]

LDS leaders supported this quest for the vote in part because of benefits they thought it would accrue to the church. Indeed, women of the faith soon used the ballot to support their leaders, giving the lie to the idea that they were unwilling victims of oppression. But they also came to see the franchise as a right that was itself a vital part of the divinely ordained plan to restore the "fulness of the Gospel"; a plan they felt required the establishment of equal rights for women.[99] Once antipolygamy activists recognized the error in their assumptions they quickly reversed course and sought to strip away the franchise so recently granted. As they did so, their efforts were opposed by thousands of Mormon women inspired by real religious fervor to defend their newly won rights. Time and again they held meetings, circulated petitions, published tracts, and even sent representatives to Washington, D.C. to make their case. While these efforts ultimately proved unsuccessful, they gave birth to broadly based, transgenerational political activism.[100]

In this defense of religious and voting rights, the women of Pleasant Grove joined those manning the barricades. As in other communities, they organized protest meetings and drew up resolutions each time hostile legislation was debated in Congress. Elizabeth Brown presided over such gatherings and Amy's mother, sisters, and half-sisters, as well as family friends took prominent parts in defending Mormon beliefs and their own political rights. "We are much obliged to our neighbor sisters for their seeming sympathy," Amy's half-sister Paulina wryly observed at one such meeting in regard to the activities of anti-polygamy crusaders, "but would advise them to keep it till solicited."[101]

This assertiveness in the political realm also led LDS women closer to their non-Mormon sisters involved in the suffrage struggle once the link between the fate of suffrage in Utah and the larger struggle for women's rights became evident to both groups. As Louisa "Lula" Greene, Wells's predecessor as editor of the *Woman's Exponent*, astutely pointed out early on, those voting to disfranchise Mormons would be unlikely to support extension of the right to other American women, a view seconded by national suffrage leaders.[102] With alacrity, Mormon women took advantage of opportunities to enter the suffrage mainstream that soon led them into interaction with a wide range of women's groups. During a period of significant strain between Mormons and non-Mormons, the suffrage struggle created an important link that led to a process of reconciliation with many women in the larger society.

From the earliest days of such contacts, Latter-day Saint suffrage leaders kept even the most geographically isolated Mormon women informed about local, national, and international developments affecting their sex through the pages of the *Woman's Exponent.* Emmeline Wells, by far the central figure in Utah's long franchise struggle, used her position as editor and publisher of the newspaper not only to prod the faithful in the discharge of their religious duties, but to express her conviction that the church played a pivotal role in advancing the progress of women. "That greater liberty has been given to women in our Church than elsewhere is indeed true; that more equality of sex prevails is undeniable," she claimed in 1886. "That all this has been elevating in its tendency, and educational to women every careful observer must readily perceive."[103] If Mormon women in fact perceived events in precisely this manner, it was in large measure because Wells so successfully argued the point. Combining judiciously chosen quotations of church leaders with examples of remarkable accomplishments among women—Mormon and non-Mormon alike—she repeatedly highlighted the broad range of opportunities available to her sex even as she urged readers to be courageous in carrying out God's plan by defending their political rights and expanding their own sphere of usefulness.

Such ideas proved especially stirring to younger women who found further encouragement in the pages of the *Young Woman's Journal*, the official organ of the YLMIA, which first appeared in 1889. Edited by Susa Young Gates, a daughter of Brigham Young and a protégé of sorts of Wells, the *Journal* followed and sometimes surpassed the *Exponent* in its advocacy of woman's equality. To modern readers, its pages indicate just how far the second generation had internalized the ideas contained in prescriptive literature regarding broadened roles for women. "Our century," one second generation woman wrote, "marks in a striking way the intellectual renaissance of women." The modern woman, she continued, had been relieved by new labor saving technology "of the many tasks that her grandmother was forced to do." Thus freed, "she now studies music, literature, science and mathematics." Such observations might have been greeted with skepticism by readers not as privileged and still performing many of the tasks their grandmothers had been forced to do, as well as many new ones expected of them in that "modern" era, but they indicate, nevertheless, the higher aspirations held by younger women. Turning to the creation story of the Bible, another writer unabashedly declared: "Here is the first definition of woman's work: it was to hold dominion over all things, equal with man."[104]

The *Journal* also demonstrates that women's expectations for careers outside the home were on the rise. While most second generation women only worked until their marriage, given new realities, notably the public abandonment of polygamy after 1890, the leadership of the YLMIA recognized that marriage and homemaking were not to be the lot of all. As a result, they encouraged young women to prepare themselves for worthy professions, whether or not they expected to marry. In 1890 a series of articles examined possible career paths, ranging from less challenging options such as office work, to the skilled tasks of telegraph operator or "photo retoucher" and even to such demanding professions as lawyer, physician, and dentist.[105]

Overall, the *Journal* projected the image of women who were prepared to make significant contributions to society—both sacred and secular. When Inez Knight (Allen) and Jennie Brimhall (Knight) left for England in 1897 to become the first single female missionaries to serve in the same fashion as men—a matter of great pride to women of faith—the *Journal* followed their experiences through an ongoing series of letters.[106] Another group of articles tracked Latter-day Saint women attending medical school at Eastern colleges. Meanwhile, biographies of prominent women of the faith highlighted their educational and professional accomplishments alongside their church service.[107]

The *Journal* also devoted attention to meetings of national and international women's organizations, focusing on the activities of Mormon delegates so readers would recognize that LDS women stood in the forefront of the women's rights struggle.[108]

Such sentiments were shared by the women of Pleasant Grove and especially by those in the Brown household. Sister wives and daughters joined in the cause of women's rights with Amy's mother especially outspoken on the subject. An avid reader of the *Exponent* and then the *Journal*, Margaret regularly discussed their articles with her daughters and granddaughters, thus creating a family legacy of activism and a commitment to women's equality. In the late 1880s when Mormon women formed the Utah Woman Suffrage Association to petition for return of the franchise, not surprisingly, it was the Brown women who led out in forming the Pleasant Grove branch. At one meeting, chaired by Elizabeth, Amy's sister Rose spoke on "The Advancement of Woman" and pointed out the necessity of "striving for our just rights and fitting ourselves for any sphere we might be called to occupy." Another sister spoke on "Woman's Work," broadly defined. Indicating that such views were shared outside the walls of the Brown household, a neighbor gave a speech on the topic: "Woman's Mind Equal to Man's." When these efforts, joined with those of women throughout the territory, resulted in the inclusion of woman's suffrage in Utah's state constitution, the women of Pleasant Grove shared in the pride of accomplishment.[109]

Of course, Mormon women nevertheless enjoyed a sense of equality that was still limited in its sanctioned reach. While writers in both the *Exponent* and the *Journal* were unafraid to challenge those who opposed women's rights, even (in veiled terms) the rare church leader, they were careful to do so in a manner that reaffirmed their loyalty to the church—a necessity especially in the stressful decades of the latter nineteenth century when Mormonism was often under attack. This approach was sustainable because a sufficient number of church officials supported women's views that equality was part of the Gospel and looked favorably on the activities of women of the faith. Yet, when a question came down to a choice between loyalty to the cause of women or loyalty to the church, the church won out. With their sense of identity grounded in their membership and in the cause of building Zion, for Mormon women of both first and second generations there was little hesitation in such matters. However, they often pushed acceptable gender boundaries as far as possible before acquiescing, confident that in so doing their actions were serving not only the interests of their sex, but the larger cause of the church.

In her mature years, at the height of her activism when she could claim long experience interacting with leaders of national and international women's organizations, Lyman reflected on the contributions of the church to the equality of her sex. "With the advent of the gospel," she asserted, "came liberty and freedom for L.D.S. women." Not only had they long enjoyed the franchise in church and secular affairs at a time when these privileges were not generally shared by other American women, they had also attained unusual advantages through the women's organizations of the church. The Relief Society, the YLMIA, and the Primary, she maintained, "have, in addition to accomplishing much good, helped to develop and produce women who, in ability and leadership, compare very favorably with women leaders anywhere." "It is my conviction," she concluded, "that our church has given women and girls opportunities, the like of which no other church has ever given."[110]

For Lyman as an individual, and for her generation of women, the influences that emerged through the collective activism developed in the women's organizations of the church, together with those found in their home and community environments provided a solid sense of who they were and where their potential lay. For them, Mormonism was at the center of their universe and they had imbibed the idea that building the gospel kingdom was worth every sacrifice required. Securely rooted in this legacy, by the time Amy was sixteen she was poised to move beyond the confines of the world of her youth. Following the lead of her sisters, she then left home for study in nearby Provo to prepare for a planned career as a school teacher. Though she returned often to Pleasant Grove, her residency there was now effectively at an end. But while physically detached, she always carried in her memory the personalities and experiences that so decisively shaped her character and expanded her vision of what she and the women of her faith could accomplish through united endeavor.

2

WIDER WORLDS

> Women have ideas of matters in business and domestic life that are helpful and acceptable to men, why may they not have practical ideas of government and law-making?
>
> —EMMELINE B. WELLS[1]

> I want to see and hear a few more things before I sink into oblivion.
>
> —AMY BROWN[2]

In the fall of 1888, an old farm wagon piled high with luggage squeaked and rattled southward along the dirt road leading from Pleasant Grove to Brigham Young Academy, ten miles away in Provo. In it, both excited and anxious, Amy Brown sat next to her father, the latest of the Brown children to make the journey. Amy had looked forward with eager anticipation to this, her first extended foray beyond the narrow confines of her hometown, perhaps as much for the adventure it promised as for the heady atmosphere of learning she expected to encounter.[3] At the time, Provo was a town of some five thousand inhabitants with unpaved streets and an unmistakable rural character, but as the hub of business and church activities in Utah Valley, it seemed like a big city to sixteen-year-old Amy.

With this move she not only embarked on a personal adventure, but also joined the ranks of what was then the best educated generation of women in American history. By the 1870s, members of her sex had gained access in unprecedented numbers to institutions of higher learning, most, like Amy, at academies and teacher-training colleges. But doors were also beginning to swing open at four-year colleges and universities.[4] Women of Utah found this broadening of horizons thrilling, even if, as was the case with their sisters elsewhere in the nation, most were still limited in their opportunities.

This life-changing transition for Amy came at a difficult time for Latter-day Saints, corresponding as it did with the highpoint of federal pressure against plural marriage and church control in political and economic affairs. Congress had already passed laws that disqualified polygamists from holding public office in the territories, ending the political career of community leaders such as John Brown, and then moved to crush Mormon resistance through the seizure of church property and the disfranchisement of all Utah women.[5] Just two years after Amy's entry at the academy, LDS president Wilford Woodruff, convinced that he was saving the church from complete destruction, issued the so-called Manifesto, which officially terminated plural marriage and signaled Mormon willingness to accommodate to national norms.

Thus, as Amy moved from home, Mormons were entering a period of realignment in their religious expectations; they sought to retain as many of the core tenets of the faith as possible while they adjusted to the increasingly secular environment in which they found themselves. Though they would be compelled to publicly concede the practice of plural marriage, Latter-day Saints continued to value their communitarian ideals even as they increasingly embraced a capitalistic economy.[6] Such change naturally produced tension and anxiety, and some felt it sapped the ties that bound together the Mormon community.[7] Yet for Amy, these years were remembered more for the opportunities they presented than such threats. It was a time when she learned to blend ideas and strategies from the larger world with the religious beliefs and sense of community obligation instilled in her during her childhood. As she did so, she found that she shared much in common with her contemporaries across the country, a cohort that led the nation into a period of dynamic social and political reform.

At the time of her arrival, the academy consisted of a primary school, teacher-training institution or "normal school," and a preparatory department for students seeking university educations. Purchased by Brigham Young in 1875 as part of his campaign to counter the influence of secular public schools and sectarian academies in the territory, at Young's death, the institution was taken over by the church.[8] In 1888, the facilities were still quite modest, with classes held in a rented warehouse adjacent to the railroad tracks where learning conditions were less than ideal. Passing trains frequently drowned out instruction, Amy recalled, while older pupils—there for advanced work—found the younger children in the elementary and secondary schools rowdy and disruptive.[9]

Despite these drawbacks, Lyman was most impressed by the educational environment established there by Karl G. Maeser. A teacher in Dresden, Germany, at the time of his conversion to Mormonism, after his immigration to Utah he tutored the children of prominent LDS families until Brigham Young offered him the principalship of the academy. A man of formal bearing, Maeser set an old world ambience of serious study at the school. Appearing cold and distant to the uninitiated, he was, as students and friends soon discovered, kindhearted with a wry sense of humor—an illustration of which is found in an oft-told tale. Once, when Maeser was briefly called away, students coaxed a donkey into the classroom and placed it in his seat. Upon his return, he deadpanned: "You seem to have chosen the smartest among you to stand at the head of the class in my absence."[10]

A scholar who possessed a broad knowledge of history, languages, and geography, Maeser was regarded as a master in the field of pedagogy. As a follower of the Swiss educator Johann Pestalozzi, he shunned harsh discipline and sought to create a classroom environment where children learned through observation. Known for the high standards he set, he considered learning not an end in itself but a triumph of disciplined willpower that cultivated character.[11] Devoted to Mormonism, his goal was to send students forth from the academy with their faith strengthened. In Amy's case, Maeser's influence extended well beyond the classroom. Her father had arranged for her to board with the educator and his family and she became a favorite, more of a daughter than merely another pupil.[12]

When she arrived in Provo, Amy had already lost her youthful awkwardness and impressed her peers with her intelligence, energy, and beauty. Graced with striking brown hair and "flashing eyes," she made friends easily, loved parties and dances, and was fun to be around. "Gentlemen may prefer blonds," her close friend from this period, Alice Louise Reynolds recalled, "but in those days at Brigham Young Academy, they all preferred her."[13] Amy's friendship with Reynolds proved among her most enduring, lasting until the latter's death in 1938. In Alice, who was bright and self-assured in a way that made young men nervous, Amy found a kindred soul—someone fully her equal in intellect and range of interests. Like Amy, Alice was a child of polygamy and had suffered through federal efforts to crush the practice. But while John Brown fled to the underground, Alice's father, George Reynolds, was chosen by church leaders to serve as a test case to challenge the constitutionality of anti-polygamy legislation. In 1879, when Alice was six, his case reached the Supreme Court, which handed down a landmark decision stating that the Constitution, while guaranteeing the right to believe according to one's conscience, does not protect the right to act according to those beliefs. As a result, George Reynolds spent the next two years in the penitentiary.

Alice's upbringing differed from Amy's in other ways as well. When she was fifteen months old, a younger sibling was born to her mother and to ease the strain, her father's sister, Julia Reynolds, stepped in to care for young Alice. If Amy found some of her most important mentors in the women's organizations of the church, Alice found hers in an indulgent aunt who taught her a deep love of literature, art, and music. Even as a child, she stood apart from the crowd, earning the title "Princess Alice" in her Salt Lake City neighborhood. As she grew older, her father saw that she was given every opportunity to develop her keen mind, enabling Alice, after her time at the academy, to be among the elite few who traveled east to continue their education. In her case, this led first to the University of Michigan and in subsequent years to continued studies at the University of Chicago, Columbia, Cornell, the University of California, and even Queen's College in London. In addition, she was to travel extensively throughout Europe, visiting sites of historical interest and shrines to literature and the arts. She joined the faculty at Brigham Young Academy in 1890, and when it became a university, was the first woman to hold a professorship at a time when women in such positions were a rarity. She was also a prominent figure in church and community; she joined the leadership of the women's organizations and was a mover and shaker in Utah's Democratic party.[14]

Of course, the most significant relationship Amy developed at the academy was with outgoing, athletic, and intelligent Richard R. Lyman. If Amy was the belle of the school, Richard dominated campus life, both admired by the young men and reportedly "swooned over" by the young women. At six-foot-five, he literally stood head and shoulders above the crowd, with a booming voice and outgoing personality that made him the center of attention in any gathering. Confident and gregarious, he was class president, editor of the school paper, and involved in everything else of importance. Physically towering over Amy's five foot three inches, Richard, with his bluff manner, stood in sharp contrast to the equally energetic but ever discreet Amy. In many respects they seemed an unlikely pair, yet both were ambitious, eager to be at the center of things, and shared similar formative experiences.[15]

Born in 1870, Richard could claim an impressive Mormon pedigree. He was the son of church leader Francis M. Lyman and his second of two wives, Clara Caroline Callister. Clara was the granddaughter of John Smith, uncle to the prophet Joseph Smith. Francis's father, Amasa Lyman, had been a prominent player in Mormon affairs and had himself served as an apostle until his excommunication for doctrinal unorthodoxy the year of Richard's birth.[16] At that time, Francis was heavily involved in local ecclesiastical and political affairs in Fillmore, about one hundred twenty miles south of Pleasant Grove. When Richard was seven the family moved to Tooele, forty miles west of Salt Lake City, when Francis was called to be president of the stake; three years later, like his father before him, Francis was named an apostle. With his father often away on church or personal business, Richard, though still a young boy, was charged with looking after his mother and younger siblings. These responsibilities were interrupted when his father arranged for him, at age twelve, to attend Brigham Young Academy. He studied there intermittently for the next decade, alternating with periods at Brigham Young College in Logan and stints tending cattle, working in a sawmill, or bookkeeping—all part of his father's plan to inculcate intellectual skills and the value of hard work in his children.[17]

Such constant moving from place to place as well as the responsibilities entrusted to him at an early age might have been a crushing burden to most boys Richard's age, and they were undoubtedly difficult for him as well. But they also taught him to be confident in his abilities and judgment. His years tending cattle and sheep also made him much more a child of the frontier than Amy. Openly emotional, occasionally profane when making a pithy observation or telling a good story in select company, Richard had an affectionate demeanor that earned him ready friendships among men and women while ingratiating him to his elders.[18]

When the two first met, Amy saw a charming and handsome young man from a good family who seemed to be going somewhere. Richard, in turn, saw a pretty young woman who was full of life, possessed a keen mind, and, like him, held views she was not afraid to express. Strongly attracted to one another, Richard soon wrote John Brown asking permission to court his daughter. Brown, who had worked alongside Richard's grandfather and father as a missionary, pioneer, and territorial legislator, and had come to think very highly of the family, replied that he was "not displeased" by the request.[19] With this paternal approval, Amy and Richard soon reached an understanding about their eventual intentions.

It would be seven long years before this understanding culminated in matrimony. Amy was only seventeen and Richard nineteen at their first encounter. At the time, both believed they were too young to marry, but within a year or two began to think differently. Aware of their intense feelings, Richard's father encouraged them not to delay. Born in 1840, he had married his first wife when he was seventeen. Perhaps reflecting broader views regarding women present in the Mormon community when he was a young man, Francis Lyman pointed out that Amy could continue to work after their marriage and contribute to the family income until Richard completed his education. John Brown, however, rejected such ideas. A full twenty years older than his long-time friend, John responded in a more "old fashioned" manner, making it clear that Amy must wait to marry until Richard finished his education and was established in his profession.[20] Ultimately, Brown's views prevailed and for the time being the couple maintained their separate educational and career paths. But their courtship continued, though often limited to the exchange of correspondence, as long distances frequently separated the lovers.

In the fall of 1889, Richard returned to Brigham Young College in Logan, where he continued his studies and worked as an assistant teacher. The following year, he was back at the academy. Meanwhile, Amy completed her normal training in June 1890, and, at the request of Karl Maeser, joined the faculty as a teacher-trainer in the primary department, a position she held for four years. It was an opportunity accompanied by restrictions. At eighteen, Amy, newly freed from the constraints incumbent upon her as "the bishop's daughter," now had to adhere to the code of staid behavior and dress set for faculty members—unwelcomed limitations for a young woman who, as she recalled, loved dances, parties, and pretty clothes, including the elaborate fashions of the time.

Amy often recounted one occasion when her feelings of frustration boiled over. In what served as the event of the season in Provo's modest society, she had been invited to a costume ball hosted by one of the town's elite families. Maeser made it clear that while she might attend the party, like other faculty members she was expected to forego dressing in costume and would have to watch the festivities from a respectable distance. Uncharacteristically, Amy challenged the principal in his decision and even cast aside the rigid control of emotions so valued in her family. She pled with him to change his mind, and recalled that she even "shed a few tears about it." As a bishop's daughter, more had always been expected of her, she explained, and she had always been "held back" from the freedom other young people enjoyed. Now that such restrictions were placed upon her again, she felt it was almost more than she could endure. Maeser, however, refused to yield and Amy, true to her upbringing, at last brought her emotions in check and followed her sense of duty. While her girlfriends arrived dressed and masked for the occasion, a heartbroken Amy watched the fun from the "bald headed row" with other faculty members.[21]

Such circumstances, disappointing as they were, tempered Lyman's self-mastery. Nor were they so traumatic that they marred her memories of the academy. Instead, she recalled the period as one of growth and rising expectations—thanks in part to Benjamin Cluff Jr., who assumed the principalship in 1891 when Karl Maeser became commissioner of church schools. Cluff joined the faculty in 1882 but by the time Amy arrived in 1888, had recently departed to continue his education at the University of Michigan. His decision to study in the East illustrated a growing divide between some first and second generation Latter-day Saints in their attitude toward the outside world. Typical of the former, Maeser, having fled Babylon to build the Mormon Zion, opposed sending students to eastern institutions, fearing the intellectual environment there would undermine their faith. Cluff, on the other hand, saw only benefits in such a course, believing that much was to be gained and little to be feared in the East.[22] Not alone in his thinking, he proved a pioneer in a small but growing wave of Latter-day Saint students seeking better educations than Utah could yet offer.

Upon his return in 1891, Cluff set to work using what he had learned. As yet, there was no standardized teacher training program in the territory, therefore one of his first goals was to create a more rigorous curriculum to make the academy a suitable training institution for all church schools. In 1892, his plans were accelerated by the move to a newly constructed building in central Provo, where for the first time the institution enjoyed accommodations expressly designed for educational purposes. Coupled with Cluff's innovations in course work, this development brought increased prestige to the institution. As a result, the number of students in attendance swelled and almost before the new building was completed the academy outgrew it, prompting the construction of two more imposing structures over the next decade.[23]

Growth in the student body also required a larger faculty and Cluff sought to ensure that new teachers were of the highest caliber. To this end he encouraged current faculty and talented students to follow his lead by going east to continue their studies.[24] His glowing reports of the University of Michigan no doubt influenced young Richard Lyman, who left in 1891 for Ann Arbor to study civil engineering.[25] At Cluff's urging Alice Louise Reynolds soon followed to study English literature.[26] In 1894, after Cluff approached Amy about joining them, she broached the subject with her father. While committed to the value of higher education for his daughters, John Brown, like Karl Maeser, was reluctant to expose them to the moral dangers he feared they would encounter outside the territory.[27] Though disappointed, Amy acceded to his wishes and for the time being gave up plans for further study.[28]

By then Amy had been at the academy for six years, first as a student and then as a faculty member. She had taught her own courses in the primary department, led classes in needlework and physical education, joined and supervised campus clubs, and contributed articles to the school newspaper. Despite her youth, she had even served briefly as school matron.[29] Yet, while innovative programs were being developed at the institution, with Richard and Alice in Ann Arbor and other friends moving on, she was growing tired of Provo and looking for a change. Her opportunity came when Dr. J. F. Millspaugh, superintendent of Salt Lake City schools, visited the academy to observe the new teacher-training techniques Cluff had adopted. Deeply impressed with what was being accomplished at the institution, Millspaugh also noted Amy's superior teaching skills and offered her a job in Salt Lake. She accepted with alacrity.[30]

In the early 1890s Salt Lake City's fifty thousand inhabitants made it by far the largest city in the territory. Economically it was heavily dependent on railroads and the mining industry that continued to attract large numbers of non-Mormons to the area. Ethnic and economic divisions came with urban growth, adding to growing tensions based on religion: Mormons and their growing numbers of Gentile neighbors clashed regularly, especially over political matters. When federal legislation disenfranchised most Latter-day Saints, the anti-Mormon Liberal Party took the majority of offices in the 1890 election, including seats on the board of education.[31] To many, the new board seemed to advocate blatantly anti-Mormon policies when it reorganized the district and fired nearly all its teachers, most of whom were Mormons. When Amy started work in the fall of 1894, the lion's share of the district's more than two hundred teachers had been brought in from outside the territory and only a handful were LDS.[32]

In later years Amy vividly recalled these tensions, but at the time she seems to have been more interested in the opportunities that the move to Salt Lake City opened to her. Though watched over by the "good Mormon family" with whom she boarded, for the first time in her life she was free to pursue activities of her own choosing. Moreover, her starting salary of $100 per month seemed a fortune, even after she sent a portion home to her parents, especially when compared to the $40 per month she had received at the academy, where one third was in cash and two-thirds in tithing script.[33] Better still, the social world of Salt Lake City awaited with its many cultural amenities.

As Amy started in her new position, Richard began his final year at Ann Arbor. Anticipating his return to Utah, she began to have second thoughts about their relationship—feelings reinforced by her new social environment. Frequently invited to parties, church dances, or the theater, she was flattered by the attention lavished upon her by the attractive sons of some of Salt Lake's well-to-do families.[34] At this point she was undoubtedly grateful that her father had limited her to an understanding with Richard, as she was only now beginning to gain a fair view of her options in the choice of a marital partner. Amid such considerations, Richard's imminent return seemed more of a threat than a long-hoped-for event. Baffled by these conflicting emotions she seemed "indifferent" to Richard during his visit home during the Christmas holidays.[35] Queried a short time later about her impending marriage, she admitted that she was "not ready at all for 'the event,'" adding that "I want to see and hear a few more things before I sink into oblivion."[36]

Amy's fears that as a married woman she could look forward to few opportunities outside the home were certainly not unfounded. Eastern reformers who had successfully pressured Latter-day Saints to abandon many of their distinctive social practices did so believing they were freeing women of the faith from the oppression of patriarchy and polygamy. In fact, the results were mixed. While the trials of polygamy must not be minimized, many Latter-day Saint women had obtained a degree of autonomy in this distinctive Mormon environment and enjoyed opportunities that most non-Mormon women did not. As with women in other minority groups forced into the national mainstream, those in the Latter-day Saint community found that assimilation often diminished rather than expanded the legitimacy of their public roles in society.[37]

As Mormons adapted to changing circumstances, they developed a number of conflicting ideas about women. Many felt the precedents established in past decades should serve as a pattern for the future, while others embraced the more constrained gender norms characteristic of American society during the Victorian Era.[38] Some among the latter accepted the theories of self-proclaimed experts who warned of dire physical and emotional consequences for those women who violated traditional roles and moved into the public sphere.[39] Amy's future father-in-law, on the other hand, rejected such views and advised that if she wished to continue teaching after marriage, she should be free to do so as marriage would only make her a better teacher. However, this perspective was not shared by Amy's father or her mother, who, based on her own experiences reinforced by the opinions of prominent Victorian physicians, advised Amy to give up her career in the classroom before she "ruined her health."[40]

Like other LDS women of her generation, Amy had been prepared to expect something more than the straitjacket of a Victorian marriage. Yet, in common with other educated and ambitious American women of the time—typified most notably by prominent reformer Jane Addams—when she came of age she faced a personal crisis. Her education had given her glimpses of wider horizons, yet now she was expected to give up all such possibilities in order to fulfill the role prescribed for her: that of wife and mother. Addams, like many of her generation, solved this dilemma by foregoing marriage and a family and instead took on the broader tasks of social reform and community betterment. In the Mormon realm, with its family-centered theology, such paths were not easily followed and indeed this was not the path Amy chose or seemed to want.

But, in addition to a family, Amy clearly desired to have a role beyond the walls of her own home and struggled to find a way to combine the two. In a letter she wrote during this period she protested that as a working woman her health was certainly no worse than that of many of her married friends who had given up their careers.[41] Yet concerns lingered in the back of her mind, leading her to see each injury or illness as a possible threat to her long term well-being. As she pondered her marriage and all it would bring, she could not help but recall her mother's long years of suffering as well as the death of two sisters from illnesses contracted in childbirth. Such realities were not easily rationalized away. Even without concerns about "oblivion," they must have given her pause. Nature and society, it seemed, were forcing her into a difficult choice: on the one hand, family, but with it, possible oblivion or, even worse, death or long term disability. On the other hand, a path possibly traveled alone, to dreams whose fulfillment might destroy her health. Under the circumstances, Richard's impending return seemed to force her to confront a dilemma she would have preferred to avoid.

Although conflicted in her feelings about Richard, Amy seized the opportunity occasioned by his graduation to "see and hear" a few of those things in the larger world about which she was so curious. Invited by Francis M. Lyman, she agreed to accompany the family to Ann Arbor for commencement ceremonies in June 1895. As her departure date neared, she exchanged a series of letters with Will Hayes, the widowed husband of her sister Margaret, who was then completing a church mission in the Midwest. In these communications she quietly arranged to meet Hayes after the graduation to begin a tour of the East.[42]

These letters provide fascinating insights into Amy as a young women. Full of life—at times seeming very girlish, even occasionally a flirt—she reveals herself as both audacious and practical. Knowing that her plans pushed the boundaries of propriety and might meet with the same resistance from her parents that had thwarted previous efforts to travel east, she swore Hayes to secrecy until all arrangements were made. The strategy brought success. With the completed plans laid before them, and in consideration of Hayes's status as a member of the family, her parents granted their approval. At the last minute, however, Hayes contracted typhoid fever, and while he eventually recovered, his illness threw everything into chaos. Characteristically, Amy responded with resolve rather than panic and, even as she departed for Richard's graduation, began to reconstruct her itinerary with new traveling companions.[43]

Her adventure really began in Ann Arbor where she attended a series of balls in honor of the graduates. Although she had taken great pains to update her wardrobe before she left home, she felt provincial in comparison to the "stylish" Michigan co-eds, especially after noting how they lavished their attention on Richard.[44] A few days later, with Richard safely shipped off to Utah, she recuperated from the commencement festivities and resumed the task of securing suitable traveling companions for the remainder of her trip that included stops in several eastern cities. For the first leg, which took her to New York City, she joined a group of buyers and their families from the church-owned

ZCMI department store.[45] In later years she returned several times, seeing the great metropolis through the eyes of a social worker, but on this first occasion she experienced its wonders as a tourist. While missionary work had taken many Mormon men out of the territory, this was not yet the case with Latter-day Saint women, for whom such an excursion was a significant treat. Amy was no exception, later declaring that it "would be difficult to explain how thrilling New York was." The elevated trains and subways were "equally mysterious" and the theater district and shops "marvelous." Linking up with family friends, she then traveled to Boston, Washington, D.C., and then Chicago by way of Niagara Falls, and finally spent a few days on her own with her father's family in southern Illinois. Although she was warmly received, as the daughter of John Brown's third wife she was no doubt viewed as an exotic product of the unusual religion and lifestyle he had followed. Returning to Utah as a skilled traveler, she took satisfaction in the fact that she had seen something worth remembering, even if, as she feared, she was never to leave the territory again.[46]

Teaching once more in the Salt Lake schools during the 1895–96 academic year while Richard served as principal of the high school at the academy, Amy discovered that closer proximity soon pushed aside her doubts. The couple's understanding now became an official engagement and on September 7, 1896, they were married in the recently completed Salt Lake Temple. Presiding was Richard's second cousin, apostle Joseph F. Smith, nephew of Mormonism's founding prophet and himself soon to rise to the church presidency.[47] A reception followed at the home of Richard's sister, Annie, who was wife of then judge and future congressman and senator William H. King. The events and personalities surrounding her marriage thus symbolized Amy's entry, through Richard, into the highest reaches of the Mormon elite—a status that would bring the new Mrs. Richard R. Lyman significant opportunities.[48]

Amy and Richard began their life together in a small rented house in Salt Lake City near the campus of the University of Utah, then located on Fourth North and Second West, where Richard had recently begun work as professor of civil engineering. For her part, Amy gave up her teaching position and focused on her new role as housewife. Though both had lived in the city before, this move marked their real initiation into urban life. Recalling just how much of an adjustment they still had to make, Amy noted that as they hauled her trousseau and a load of furniture from Pleasant Grove to their new home, tied behind their wagon was a cow, a sure sign of the couple's roots. "Being country bred," she later observed with some amusement, "we could not conceive of a real home without at least a cow and some chickens."[49] They were soon to learn that such holdovers from Salt Lake City's agrarian past were becoming rarities.

Salt Lake, like Utah as a whole, was changing rapidly as the pioneering generation passed away and a younger, native born generation was coming into its own. Amy had to look no farther than her own family for evidence of such change. After a long decline, her father died just two months after her marriage, while her mother was increasingly unable to care for herself.[50] The year of Amy's marriage also marked another passage: the culmination of the long struggle for Utah's statehood. Significant concessions on the part of the Mormon people in their religious practices had been required to bring this about, as had similar changes in the political arena, where the church disbanded its own political party and encouraged members to align themselves with the Democrats or Republicans.[51] For women, statehood also represented an opportunity to reclaim their rights. After a new flurry of organized activism, they helped win passage of a constitution reinstituting the franchise and granting them the right to hold public office. But political matters soon brought new stresses into the communal nature of Mormon society, from which women of the faith were not immune. Partisan political activities divided the electorate and women, in a foreshadowing of the experience of their counterparts in the nation a quarter century later after passage of the Nineteenth Amendment, diluted their influence as they divided their loyalties between political parties. This led to bitter feelings between those previously united in the suffrage cause, while male political leaders soon recognized and exploited such divisions to effectively neutralize the political power of women.[52]

Political developments were not the only significant changes of the 1890s. In previous decades the railroad had provided access to new markets for Utah's agricultural bounty and mineral wealth, but in the international depression known as The Panic of 1893, Utah paid a high price for this integration into the economic mainstream. Salt Lake City, heavily dependent on the hard-hit mining and railroad industries, suffered most with an unemployment rate estimated as high as 48 percent.[53] Church leaders and local governments sought to alleviate the hardship through a variety of stop-gap measures. Foreshadowing ideas advocated decades later during the early years of the Great Depression, they urged unemployed urban dwellers to move back to farms in rural areas where they might be able to live with relatives and provide for their own sustenance. For those unable to relocate, church and municipal leaders opened vacant city lots for garden plots. The church went even further, in a kind of proto-Keynesian measure, spending well beyond its means to expand a number of enterprises to provide jobs for the unemployed.[54] Supplementing these efforts, civic groups and prominent individuals organized soup kitchens and other relief activities, yet unemployment and attendant suffering continued largely unabated until national conditions eased in the late 1890s.[55]

Industrialization and urban growth also affected public health and municipal services. In the later nineteenth and early twentieth centuries rapid strides in scientific knowledge, especially in regard to the spread and prevention of infectious disease, led towns and cities across the nation to reexamine their safeguards to public health. In Salt Lake City an inadequate supply of safe drinking water, coupled with a nearly nonexistent sewage system raised red flags among community leaders, prompting them to warn of possible epidemics of typhoid fever. Statewide outbreaks of smallpox and diphtheria raised similar concerns among civic officials and public-minded citizens, which created a chorus call for the mandatory vaccination of children. Meanwhile, an 1890 report noted that there were only five miles of sewer pipe along 275 miles of streets in Salt Lake City, even as unpaved streets in urban areas spawned choking dust in the summer and thick mud during the rainy season. At the same time, smelters scattered throughout the Salt Lake Valley spewed forth a choking haze that damaged crops, injured livestock, and even turned washed clothes yellow on the line.[56] Complicating matters, urban growth also contributed to ongoing social strains even as it taxed existing services. By 1890, over a third of the territory's population lived in cities or larger towns, a rate of urbanization that, like other areas of the West, exceeded the national average. This trend was accelerated by new arrivals from southern and eastern Europe and Asia looking for jobs in Utah's mines and smelters.[57] In this chaotically expanding urban, industrial environment, crime rose—particularly vice and juvenile delinquency—the latter exacerbated by inadequate public schools. In short, Utah experienced many of the maladies afflicting urban and industrial areas across the nation and lagged in its efforts to ameliorate them.

Scholars describe the late nineteenth century as the beginning of what came to be known as the Progressive Era. Throughout the industrial world "progressives" sought to harness the kinds of advances in scientific knowledge that had stimulated the growth of industry to control the abuses and waste of laissez-faire capitalism. With roots stretching far back into the American tradition of moral and social reform, progressives were not an organized, unitary group, but pursued a variety of reforms through shifting coalitions of interested parties who sometimes found common ground on one issue, but were poles apart on another. Progressive measures were thus spearheaded at different times by a wide range of disparate interests including big business, middle class men and women, politicians, women's clubs, organized labor, and Evangelical Protestants. The result was an unprecedented era of reform lasting through the First World War, during which initiatives at the local, state, and national levels tackled such issues as political reform, protective legislation for men, women, and children in industry, and a host of public health measures.[58] The developing ideas and activities of progressives resonated with many Utahns seeking to address problems arising in their own communities. For Mormons, whose concepts of religious obligation linked to social well-being were deeply rooted, the practical and common sense approaches advocated by many progressives found broad appeal.[59]

Amy was no doubt aware of the political and social problems developing in Utah, but, as with other tensions of the period, her few surviving letters indicate no broad concerns beyond friends and family. When Utah women were fighting for the vote in the state constitution, her mother and sisters, long active in the Utah County Suffrage Association, followed events closely, but Amy, who was then making arrangements for her tour of the East, makes no mention of the suffrage struggle, the economic turmoil so evident in Salt Lake City during the early 1890s, or developing movements to deal with social problems.[60] Insulated from serious want—first by her job as a teacher and then by Richard's position at the university—not surprisingly, she seems to have focused on personal matters, concentrating after her marriage on her husband's career and her new family responsibilities.

In regard to the latter, such responsibilities proved fairly broad. Immediately after their marriage, Amy's brother and Richard's sisters stayed with them for extended periods and other family members soon followed. Many came because the Lymans lived conveniently close to the university, others because circumstances, such as the severe illness or death of a parent, made it necessary for them to leave home for a time. But for whatever the reason, over the course of their long marriage Amy and Richard seldom lived without siblings, nieces, nephews, or eventually even grandchildren in their home.[61] This was of great benefit to their guests, who saved on room and board and lived in a hospitable atmosphere.[62] Such practices, which were not particularly unusual for the time, also provided a number of benefits for Amy and Richard. Deeply in debt from Richard's years of study, the couple found that boarders provided a modest amount of help with household expenses. The additional assistance such guests provided in housekeeping was also greatly appreciated, especially given the onerous burdens resting upon Victorian housewives.[63]

The couple's family obligations also extended beyond the walls of their own home. Richard's mother had died while he was attending the University of Michigan, but upon his return, his father charged him with looking after the welfare of his siblings. Richard took his responsibility seriously and in 1916, after the death of his father, assumed the position of de facto patriarch of the extended Lyman clan. As for Amy, her widowed sister Rose took on the lion's share of caring for their semi-invalid mother, but Amy and Richard assisted financially and helped with household tasks as well. Amy's take-charge attitude when assisting with housekeeping chores during her frequent visits to Pleasant Grove sometimes grated, and earned her the nickname of "the regulator" from her mother. And, though the youngest girl of the Brown clan, like Richard, Amy became in time something of a family matriarch, always ready to dispense sound advice—whether solicited or not. But despite her straight-shooting manner, she was known for her good intentions and overarching compassion and when a crisis arose or a difficult job needed to be done, it was "aunt Amy," to whom family members most often turned for help.[64]

Amy's responsibilities soon expanded in other ways as well. She loved children and after a lengthy courtship was eager to begin her family. Pregnancy is a time of joy mixed with anxiety, and this was certainly the case for women in the Victorian Era. Amy had to look no further than her own family to see the reason for the latter.[65] Her first pregnancy apparently was not too difficult and she remained active into her last month, sewing not only bed gowns for her "confinement," but a dress for a boarding relative as well. She even assisted in the family's move to a home closer to the university just three weeks before her delivery. Keeping busy held her anxieties in check, but as she neared full-term her worries increased, sending her in search of both practical assistance and spiritual reassurance. As was common for the time, she planned to deliver at home and asked her mother and sister Rose, the latter an experienced nurse and prominent member of the Woman's Hygienic Physiological Society of Utah, to join the doctor attending her. For spiritual reassurance, she turned to her father-in-law who, along with two other apostles, gave her a special blessing promising comfort and health. Further comfort came when she was "washed and anointed" in preparation for childbirth by two prominent church women who then blessed her and told her she "would get along o.k."[66] As was the case with the other Brown women, Amy's delivery seems to have been difficult, but ultimately all went well. With considerable relief and joy, she greeted the arrival of Wendell Brown Lyman on December 7, 1897.

Amy now seemed destined for a role as a supportive wife and mother who would devote her spare energy to church work in her local YLMIA and Primary Association. In her free time, she expected to take an occasional class in history or literature at the university. Yet, within weeks of Wendell's birth, her options suddenly expanded. In January 1898, two well-known Latter-day Saint women, Rebecca N. Little and Jane Kingsbury, invited her to join the Authors Club.[67] Her acceptance of their invitation set her on a new journey, one that would lead her to prominence in the Utah community and beyond.

By the late 1880s, the club movement had swept the nation with local, state, and even national coalitions such as the General Federation of Women's Clubs formed, as women in individual clubs sought to coordinate activities aimed at improving conditions in their communities.[68] In Utah, however, clubs languished until the early 1890s, largely due to Mormon-Gentile animosity. Utah's first woman's club—the Ladies Literary League, founded in the 1870s—banned Mormon women from its membership for more than two decades. As for Latter-day Saint women, the Relief Society's wide-ranging activities had first claim on their energies, leaving little time or inclination to join other groups.[69] However, social changes soon undermined the Relief Society's hold on the rising generation.

As church leaders continued to shift their goals from establishing a semi-independent commonwealth to gradual assimilation into the economic and social mainstream, many Relief Society activities, particularly those aimed at fostering home industry and economic independence, seemed increasingly anachronistic, especially to younger women. At the same time, the culmination of the suffrage struggle stripped an item from the organization's agenda that had unified first and second generation women in common cause. Meanwhile, Utah's increasingly wage-based economy forced many Latter-day Saints to leave their homes in small communities to seek employment in urban areas. While older Mormon women formed bonds of sisterhood during long years of shared struggle in small communities, younger LDS women, forced to be more mobile than their mothers, often found themselves feeling left out of established Relief Society networks in their new homes. Finally, and perhaps most important, as the local and general leadership of the organization aged, a generational divide emerged. Many in the second generation came to see the Relief Society as the domain of aging women who emphasized old-fashioned testimony meetings where oft-repeated stories intended to promote the faith were shared by those whose days of dynamic innovation seemed long past. For younger women confronting a modernizing and increasingly secular society, such features seemed to have little relevance or appeal.[70]

Despite some ongoing tensions, animosities between Mormons and non-Mormons were also fading, leaving the second generation, already curious about the larger world, increasingly receptive to ideas originating beyond the limits of LDS settlement. By the 1890s even some older women, such as Emmeline B. Wells, then in her sixties, felt a need for new venues in which to broaden their intellectual development. Indeed, it was she who blazed the trail into club work, forming two of her own, the Utah Woman's Press Club in 1891 and Cleofan, a study club, in 1892. In the pages of the *Woman's Exponent* she published her own clubs' minutes and noted the creation of others throughout the territory as well as the accomplishments of club women nationally and internationally. Inspired by such accounts, thousands of Latter-day Saint women began to organize scores of clubs in cities and towns throughout the state.[71]

As Mormon women embraced the club movement, a debate arose over whether the agenda and techniques of club work should be adapted for the use of the women's organizations of the church. Once again, responses fell along generational lines. The YLMIA had taken an early lead in moving toward the agenda of club work and so managed to retain the loyalties and energies of its second generation women, whether or not they were involved in clubs. But the aging leadership of the Relief Society was much more reluctant to embrace the club agenda that would have required the women of the organization to reach out beyond the LDS community. Yet, as would prove true for Lyman, it was precisely the broadness of club work that held the greatest appeal for younger women. Failing a change in Relief Society, many simply declined to "move up" into the organization, remaining in the YLMIA, often as teachers of younger women.[72] Those seeking to address the challenges posed by Utah's increasingly secular society supplemented their MIA work by moving directly into the world of clubwomen. Clubs, as a result, claimed the energies of the most talented and ambitious women in their communities—the same kinds of movers and shakers flocking to club work across the nation.

For LDS women, club work brought some notable departures. For the first time, they were entirely free to set their own agenda. While motivated by Mormon ideas about building Zion as well as a generalized desire for community betterment, they now moved firmly into the secular arena of what came to be termed "municipal housekeeping." "The true mother," Authors Club member Rebecca N. Little observed in a May 1890 meeting of the Utah Congress of Mothers, "will consider the welfare, not only of her own child alone, but will be interested in improving the condition of all children in her locality."[73] Using terms and ideas that linked women's public activism with their roles as women and mothers—an ideology scholars have designated "maternalism"—as elsewhere, this female assertiveness in the larger community met with a mixed reception. Emmeline Wells reported hearing some grumble that while women's involvement in community affairs, even politics, had been a necessity when Mormons were trying to build an independent society, now that circumstances had changed, there seemed little reason to continue that pattern. Wells countered such views, which she saw as reactionary, by noting astutely that some men praised the "eternal womanly," in order to discourage the "fairer sex" from exercising influence in their communities. "As if," observed the politically active Wells, "it were not womanly and dignified in any case to try and better the conditions of the city, county or state where one resides." "Women have ideas of matters in business and domestic life that are helpful and acceptable to men," she added, "why may they not have practical ideas of government and law-making?" Especially, she observed, when these ideas involved the well-being of mothers and children.[74]

In this atmosphere of developing activism, the Authors Club emerged. Its founders, Rebecca Little, May Booth Talmage, Augusta Winters Grant, and Martha Hughes Cannon, were all prominent women who had traveled to Chicago in 1893 as part of the Utah delegation to the Congress of Representative Women held at the World's Columbian Exhibition. Organized to commemorate the four hundredth anniversary of Columbus's discovery of America, the exhibition was a long anticipated combination of world's fair and celebration of American progress. Large numbers of Utahns visited the fair, gazing at the new technical wonders of the age, including the ferris wheel and the White City with its vision for the future of urban life. Utah women attending sessions of the Congress gravitated to the Woman's Pavilion, created through the tireless efforts of Chicago club women, where they watched their sisters from across the nation and around the world conduct large meetings, deliver impressive speeches, and manage roundtable discussions that addressed human betterment and women's empowerment. Mormon women themselves presented an entire session (May Talmage was one of the featured speakers) which garnered a great deal of positive attention for the women of the church.[75] Like so many visitors, Little, who was in her early forties, Grant and Cannon, in their mid-thirties, and Talmage, in her latter twenties, returned home inspired to take up the banner of club work in their own communities and determined to "improve themselves through study and application."[76]

These founding members of the Authors Club already claimed wide ranging and impressive accomplishments. Rebecca Ellen "Nellie" Mantle Little, the club's life force in its early years, was born in 1852. Among the oldest members, she nevertheless shared experiences typical of Mormonism's second generation. After receiving normal training at the University of Deseret (the future University of Utah), she taught school in Salt Lake City until her 1881 marriage to Feramorz Little. A widower, whose first two (polygamous) wives had died, Feramorz was also a well known church and community leader. After his death due to typhoid fever just six years after their marriage, Nellie, while devoting herself to raising her two young children and to her work in the church and community, simultaneously continued her education in literature and the arts, receiving a degree at the now renamed University of Utah in 1898. Her prominence in community affairs and advocacy of higher education soon earned her a seat on the board of regents of her alma mater. A leading suffragist and a guiding light in Utah's free kindergarten movement, she was also among the first presidents of the Utah Congress of Mothers. The latter was affiliated with the National Congress of Mothers, predecessor of the Parent Teacher Association. Its members sought, in the progressive spirit of the age, to draw upon developing "scientific" knowledge to assist women in their roles as mothers amid the challenges of a modern, industrializing society. At the same time, they advocated a broad range of community reforms to address the same issues.[77] In 1902, Little would become prominent in church affairs as well when she joined the general leadership of the Relief Society.[78]

May Booth Talmage was similarly active. Born in 1868, she attended Brigham Young Academy where she met her husband, James E. Talmage, who became a prominent educator and church leader.[79] The mother of eight children, she nevertheless found time for suffrage work and, like Little, played an active role in the free kindergarten movement. In 1892, she was asked to join the general board of the YLMIA, where she served for nearly forty years.

Augusta Winters Grant was the daughter of Amy's teacher in the Primary Association back in Pleasant Grove. Augusta had herself been the long-time friend of Lyman's older sisters and an admired and beloved principal in Pleasant Grove's school when Amy was in the eighth grade. It was she who seems to have recommended Amy for Authors Club membership. A plural wife of apostle and future church president Heber J. Grant (who, because of the deaths of his first two wives was a monogamist by the time he assumed the church presidency, leaving Augusta as the most visible of his spouses in the eyes of church members), and a worker in the YLMIA, she shared the experiences of Little and Talmage through her own service in the territorial suffrage association.[80]

Of the four women who traveled to Chicago, Dr. Martha Hughes Cannon had the most impressive credentials. After graduating from the University of Deseret with a degree in chemistry, she traveled to Ann Arbor where she studied medicine at the University of Michigan. Upon her return, she entered polygamy as the fourth wife of Angus M. Cannon, prominent civic leader and president of the Salt Lake Stake for twenty-eight years. In 1886 she fled the state to spend time on the underground to avoid federal prosecution, eventually traveling all the way to England. But she returned to Utah in time to play a prominent role in the suffrage struggle. When statehood came, she was elected to the state senate as a Democrat—the first woman in the nation to hold such an office—beating out a field of candidates that included her Republican husband. In the senate she sponsored a number of important public health measures including one that established a state board of health.[81]

A number of other accomplished women were invited into the club as charter members. Like Cannon, Alice Merrill Horne was one of a handful of women to achieve prominence in Utah politics soon after statehood. Elected to the legislature in 1898 when she was in her early thirties, she supported Cannon's public health agenda and successfully pushed through her own measure creating a state arts commission. Together the two women self-consciously played the suffrage card. Horne even threw a bouquet of yellow jonquils (yellow then being the suffrage color) on the desk of a male legislator speaking against one of their measures. The other lawmakers in the room understood immediately the meaning of the gesture—the threatened loss of women's votes in the next election—and laughed good naturedly, even as they refrained from supporting their male colleague. Prior to her legislative career, Horne, like her counterparts, had been involved in a number of civic activities and was prominent among those supporting the free kindergarten movement. She was the granddaughter of leading sister Bathsheba Smith, who was named general president of the Relief Society in 1901, the same year Horne found herself in the organization's leadership as a member of the general board.[82]

Other Authors Club members, though somewhat less prominent, were similarly active and accomplished in community affairs.[83] They, like their better known sisters, sought solutions to Salt Lake's growing juvenile delinquency problem while working for such civic improvements as the construction of playgrounds, the paving of city streets, and cleaner air and water. In all these activities, club members proved effective advocates. Like Lyman, all were advantaged as well-educated second generation women who had married men whose names signified power and prestige.[84]

At its meetings, the Authors Club maintained a strict schedule of study and discussion. Books and articles were formally reviewed by members on a rotating basis followed by critiques of the presentations. Reading selections ran the gamut from literary classics including the Bible, and the works of Shakespeare and Milton, to provocative modern works such as *The Crux*, a fictionalized treatment of the consequences of venereal disease by the noted advocate of reformed gender roles, Charlotte Perkins Gilman. The many former teachers among them expected the highest quality in these presentations. When an inappropriate word was used, or one was mispronounced, the official critic would note it in her commentary. If such criticism was unsparing, it accomplished what was intended—teaching members to speak in public correctly, effectively, and easily with or without prepared texts, thus preparing them for their roles as community leaders.[85] Discussion also involved current events and women's roles in society. It even faced gender roles head-on through an array of topics such as "Should a girl receive a college education?" and "What girls should read." They sought to stay away from purely political discussions, which proved divisive, but numerous topics touched on government, national and local, including "President Roosevelt, his qualifications and policy."[86] Also discussed were the women's own activities to reform society. For Lyman, this proved an important period of schooling in community activism and exposed her to her friends' wide-ranging efforts to address problems in Utah society.

The activities of other women's organizations were also a focus of discourse, as the club served as a link to other clubwomen through its membership in the Utah, Salt Lake, and General Federations of Women's Clubs. Through these connections, the Authors Club joined in the quest for municipal reform and responded to calls for action from nationally prominent women and organizations. Its members also had opportunities to interact personally with influential figures, both in Utah and nationally.[87] The older generation of Mormon women had forged ties to these larger networks through the suffrage struggle; now, second-generation women were building on these ties and extending them into areas of their own interests and activism.

If Amy's marriage to Richard provided entrée into the Mormon elite, Authors Club membership solidified her position as she made new friends and explored new worlds of actions and ideas with some of the most accomplished and well connected women in Utah. She was flattered to be associated with them, but reciprocally, they sensed in her a kindred spirit of promising talent and intellect. Just a few years after joining the club, she was appointed permanent critic of the weekly presentations, and shortly thereafter became secretary of the group.[88] Meanwhile, Lyman took her own tentative steps into the larger realm of community affairs. In 1899 Rebecca Little, then president of the Utah Congress of Mothers, discovered that Amy held strong views about child rearing and invited her to join the list of speakers addressing that year's annual meeting of the organization. Though a mother for only a year and a half, Amy accepted. In her remarks, which were titled "Obedience without Severity" and later published in the *Woman's Exponent*, she elaborated on the views of "experts" about the need to avoid corporal punishment.[89]

Club work was not the only experience that profoundly influenced Lyman's involvement in community affairs. During the early years of their marriage, Amy and Richard focused on repaying the $2,500 loan with interest made to Richard by his father, a task they accomplished in 1902. Once free from this debt, Richard arranged to continue his education.[90] Accepted into the graduate program in civil engineering at Cornell University, one of the premier institutions in the field, he took a leave of absence from the University of Utah and packed up his family—including his two younger sisters—for what would become a new phase of their lives, one that soon exposed Amy to the full range of challenges facing society and the most up-to-date techniques used by reformers to address them.[91]

Their first stop was at the University of Chicago where Richard and Amy arranged to attend a summer session. While this stopover was of minor importance to Richard's career, Amy found it a pivotal event with major implications. Reflecting interests refined in the Authors Club, at Chicago she enrolled in classes on Shakespeare and the Bible as literature. But curious about what, by all accounts, was the most popular class on campus, she also decided to sign up for a course taught by George Vincent on the subject of sociology.[92]

Vincent was one of the developers of this relatively new field. He had joined others inspired by the explosion of knowledge in such areas as physics, biology, and chemistry, who sought to apply the scientific method to the analysis of society. Unlike Social Darwinists who used theories of organic evolution to justify a laissez-faire approach to social policy, pioneer sociologists adopted the empirical approach of the "hard" sciences to better inform their intervention in social issues. They began by amassing data that illuminated the underlying causes of unemployment, dependency, delinquency, and problems in public health, then used this information to devise solutions. Subsequently their ideas were utilized by individuals, charitable organizations, and government officials. In Vincent's class, Lyman not only learned concepts that seemed similar to the ethos of communal responsibility imbibed during her youth in Pleasant Grove, but was exposed to innovative strategies to deal with the problems of a modern society. While Vincent's lectures held her spellbound, she was even more fascinated by a field assignment that took her to the already famous social settlement of Hull House.[93]

Headquartered in an old family mansion located in a densely populated immigrant community on Chicago's south side, Hull House was founded by Jane Addams and her friend Ellen Gates Starr in 1889. Addams, like other educated women of her generation, had been searching for meaningful outlets for her energies, but discovered the most interesting avenues closed to her because of her sex. During a tour of Europe, she had visited the pioneering social settlement of Toynbee Hall where university men from Cambridge and Oxford lived among, and provided services to, the working-class community in London's East End. With a model in hand, she returned to the United States where she and Starr started the settlement as "an experiment in doing good." They created in the process new vocational opportunities for themselves and other like-minded women.[94]

Addams wanted Hull House to foster a sense of community among its working-class neighbors by serving as a focus of education, entertainment, and activism. Staffed by well-educated, generally middle-class, and most often female residents who stayed for periods ranging from a few days to many years, the settlement counted among permanent residents and visitors a veritable who's who of American social reform. These included such notables as the Consumers' League's Florence Kelley; Alice Hamilton, a pioneer in the field of industrial medicine; Julia Lathrop, who would be the first head of the Federal Children's Bureau; and her successor in that office, Grace Abbott. Abbott's sister Edith, an influential sociologist, was also a long-term resident. Periodic visits from prominent reformers, intellectuals, and labor leaders—both men and women—enriched the intellectual milieu. The noted philosopher and educational reformer John Dewey was a frequent guest, as was reform lawyer and future Supreme Court Justice Louis Brandeis. While Hull House was unquestionably the premier institution in the settlement movement, dozens of others in major cites and even rural areas across the nation performed similar roles, providing liaisons between local and national reform movements and creating practical learning and vocational opportunities for such figures as Eleanor Roosevelt and future New Dealers Frances Perkins and Harry Hopkins.[95]

By 1902 when Lyman first visited Hull House, the settlement had expanded well beyond the original Hull mansion into a sprawling complex of buildings covering a full city block. Providing a growing list of services including a kindergarten for working mothers, a coffee house and café (alternatives to the saloon), rooms for lectures, classes, social gatherings, and political meetings, a labor exchange, and social clubs for children and adults, it hosted a steady stream of the interested and curious.[96] Addams, whom Lyman met after a lecture given by the famous settlement worker, must have liked her young Utah visitor, as she invited her back several times to continue their interview. For her part, Lyman was so impressed by what she learned that she decided to put the concept of "scientific" social work into practice by volunteering for two weeks with Chicago's city charities.[97]

It was a life-changing experience for Lyman. She found in Chicago dedicated reformers who not only tried to alleviate the misery of the poor, but more importantly, attacked the roots of poverty by initiating changes that extended well beyond the limits of the windy city. The implications for her Utah community were unmistakable. It was, she would later recall, as if a curtain had suddenly been drawn in her mind to reveal a whole new perspective. After Chicago, she would never again see the world in the same fashion. Yet, as profound and far-reaching as these influences would prove, several years would elapse before she could put them into practice.[98]

Once in Ithaca, Amy was again preoccupied with the duties of a mother and student's wife, although with Richard's sisters as baby-sitters, she was able to attend some classes of her own as well as occasional lectures delivered by prominent visitors to the community. Richard's student colleagues also proved intellectually stimulating. Nora Stanton Blatch, granddaughter of Elizabeth Cady Stanton, and daughter of Harriot Stanton Blatch, was especially impressive. A strong-willed and outspoken advocate for women's equality, Blatch was destined for a successful career as a civil engineer in New York City. What Lyman found most remarkable about her was her willingness to challenge men in any activity, most memorably, a five-mile swim across Cayuga Lake with Amy and Richard joining others following along behind the competitors in motor launches.[99]

There were less congenial memories as well, such as a frightening outbreak of typhoid fever during the winter of 1903 that no doubt reawakened Amy's childhood fears of disease. The first cases were reported in the middle of January and by the end of March, when the epidemic was over, 681 cases had led to 51 deaths, among them, 13 Cornell students. At the time, the outbreak was blamed on workmen doing construction upstream on the city's waterworks, one of whom was reputed to have had walking typhoid. Subsequently, however, it was thought to have more likely occurred through contamination of well-water by outdoor privies. Whatever the truth, these hypotheses raised concerns about the purity of the water supply to a fever pitch, which, in turn, led to construction of a new municipal water works and filtration system serving both college and community. For Lyman, the epidemic was a long-remembered object lesson on the necessity of safeguarding public health.[100]

Lessons of a different sort came soon after the typhoid epidemic during a new outbreak of anti-Mormon sentiment. While antagonism towards Latter-day Saints had decreased markedly in the wake of the 1890 Manifesto, information arising out of new Congressional hearings reawakened animosity toward the faith. The catalyst was the 1903 election of LDS apostle Reed Smoot to the United States Senate. Several years previously, B. H. Roberts, a high ranking church official (one of the First Council of the Seventy), and husband of another Authors Club member, Dr. Margaret Curtis Shipp Roberts, had been denied his seat in the House of Representatives because he was a polygamist. Smoot, a monogamist, was accepted into the Senate chamber, but for the next four years had to fight to keep his seat as the Committee of Privileges and Elections conducted what has been termed "the most wide-ranging investigation of a religious organization in American history."[101]

Testimony from Smoot and other high church leaders, including the new church president, Joseph F. Smith, revealed that a significant number of aging polygamists had been unwilling to give up their plural families after the Manifesto. Smith himself admitted that he had fathered children from plural wives after 1890. More damaging still was the admission that each year since 1890 a small number of plural marriages had been solemnized or authorized by church leaders.[102]

This reluctance by some to completely surrender the practice was perhaps understandable in light of the tremendous sacrifices made to carry out a principle that the faithful believed to be divinely inspired, not to mention the loyalty and affection plural spouses felt for one another. But in the eyes of many outside the fold, such behavior demonstrated a duplicity and lingering un-American strain in the Latter-day Saint community. As troubling were allegations during the hearings that church leaders continued to dictate to members in political, social, and economic affairs. If this were the case, those on the investigating committee wondered, did Smoot, as an apostle of the church, owe his allegiance first to the Mormon prophet and secondarily to the nation for whose well-being he was responsible as a member of the Senate?[103] Smoot ultimately held on to his seat, no doubt as much for the political influence he could deliver through a strong Republican machine in Utah as for the resolution of concerns about Mormonism. But the consequences of the hearings reached far beyond the Senate. The embarrassment it caused to the church led Joseph F. Smith to take decisive action in the church's April conference of 1904 (immediately after his grilling in the Senate) where, in the so-called "Second Manifesto" he spoke out strongly against those still contracting or solemnizing plural marriages. While Utah's constitution had made plural marriage illegal in the state since 1896, in the wake of the Smoot hearings Smith would eventually make it church policy that Mormons who entered into the practice faced excommunication as well. As recent scholarship has demonstrated, by hastening a final termination of the practice, the hearings also led to a far-reaching realignment of emphasis in Mormon doctrine and concepts of group identity.[104]

The church's belated actions did little, however, to quell a new and lingering wave of anti-Mormon sentiment. In Ithaca, Lyman encountered this animosity when she was invited by non-Mormon friends to hear a visiting "woman lecturer," who attacked her faith and accused her people of being "ignorant, illiterate, and immoral." The lecturer asserted further that "there were no public schools in Utah" because of the machinations of church leaders. Lyman's friends took part in refuting the charges, noting the high caliber and morality of the Latter-day Saint students attending Cornell, while Amy pointed out that she had taught for two years in Salt Lake City's public schools.[105] She did not recount how the exchange ended. Occurring, as it did, in an age of strong, and often violent prejudices, this incident seems relatively mild, but it clearly made a deep impression on Lyman, as would similar encounters in the future. As a member of the second generation, she had hoped Mormons would find greater acceptance after the Manifesto. In Ithaca, she discovered that the actions of church members would continue to be closely scrutinized and that the reputation of her people would take a very long time to recover. In years to come, as she began to associate with women outside the LDS community, perhaps because of her concerns about the stigma of the past, she became something of an over-achiever, working hard to gain acceptance in the larger world for herself and her faith.

Amid these dramatic events, the time in Ithaca was marked by less spectacular but extremely important family milestones as well. Richard completed his education and obtained not only his master's of civil engineering in 1904, but his doctorate the following year. In addition, he developed contacts that served him well in years to come even as he published papers that began to establish his professional reputation.

Meanwhile, young Wendell fell into a cistern and injured his back. At first the injury seemed minor, but continuing pain led to growing concerns about his long-term prognosis. After the family's return to Utah, he was placed in a full cast for two years and had to sleep in traction. To allow for growth, the cast was changed periodically; a hook mounted on the wall facilitated the procedure. Amy taught him at home for a time, bringing him huge stacks of books from the library, but after a year or so he began to attend public school, pulled there in a wagon by willing classmates. Not long thereafter the doctors pronounced his back healed and the cast was removed.[106] Wendell nevertheless continued to suffer some lingering effects from the injury and his health remained a matter of family concern. On the happier side, after a great deal of difficulty conceiving a second child, in September 1903, Amy gave birth to a daughter, Margaret.[107]

In 1905, with Richard's studies completed, the family returned to Salt Lake City where he resumed his position at the University. The Lymans soon purchased what would be their permanent home—a modest two-story located in the Avenues section of Salt Lake City, not far from Richard's father and within walking distance of the new campus of the University of Utah on Salt Lake's east side. It was also conveniently close to the homes of Amy's sister club members.[108]

At the university, Richard was a popular educator, although known for a somewhat overblown lecture style that earned him the nickname "Windy Dick." He also was considered slightly eccentric, having his students align their desks to the points of the compass, for example, to give them a better sense of spatial relationships.[109] But he rose rapidly to the rank of full professor and was soon chair of the Department of Civil Engineering. On the side he ran a very successful consulting business. While the income produced by the latter was a boon to the family, the work had a downside as well, leading Richard to spend extensive periods away from home that proved hard on everyone.[110] For her part, Amy settled into the now familiar routine of a professor's wife and mother—roles that required a busy social calendar in addition to her usual church work. A leader in the making, she took on major responsibilities, accepting prominent positions in the local YLMIA and Primary. Intellectual stimulation came with renewed participation in the broad-ranging activities of the Authors Club and the recently organized Daughters of the Utah Pioneers. As she became immersed in the social world of Salt Lake City, the experiences of Chicago and Ithaca seemed increasingly remote. Yet, after four years, this relatively simple, family-centered existence was exchanged for another in which her experiences in the East would assume renewed relevance as Lyman became involved in unexpected new challenges and opportunities.[111]

3

REINVENTING THE RELIEF SOCIETY

> It was a mistake in thinking that none but elderly sisters should belong to the Relief Society.
>
> —*WOMAN'S EXPONENT*[1]

> The most imposing group of women I had ever seen at such close range.
>
> —AMY BROWN LYMAN[2]

"It becomes my duty to notify you officially of your election to membership in the Board of Directors of the National Woman's Relief Society." So began a letter dated October 5, 1909, to Amy Brown Lyman from Emmeline B. Wells, Relief Society general secretary. "I feel honored," Wells continued, "to have this opportunity of congratulating you on your becoming a member of this Quorum (so to speak)." Wells further expressed her conviction that "The work will no doubt appeal to you, as it has to most of us, who have enlisted in this worthy cause of uplifting humanity."[3] Lyman was stunned by this brief but momentous communication that had come to her without warning. The call to service it tendered was as an honor, but one that promised to completely upend her life. Not surprisingly, she remembered her first response was to shed "tears of anxiety."[4] As she well knew, general board members were expected to accept regular travel and speaking responsibilities. Intimidating in its own right, she was also fearful that the demands of the work might adversely affect her children, who were now eleven and seven years old.[5]

As a member of the board she would also become a public person whose every action would be scrutinized—no small consideration for one who had struggled in her youth to live up to community expectations incumbent upon her as the bishop's daughter. Adding to her reservations, several friends warned that the organization had become the realm of "old women." If the thirty-seven-year-old Amy had larger ambitions, they advised, then club work or the YLMIA would present better venues for achieving them.[6]

Yet Lyman remained true to her upbringing. Taught to accept all calls to church service, she held fears in check and pushed resolutely, if anxiously, forward to enter the inner circle of what was still the most prestigious of the Mormon women's organizations.

When Lyman embarked on what became a lifetime of Relief Society work, she joined an organization struggling to define its role in a changing community. As her friends indicated, younger women often found the old guard at the head of the society out of touch with issues of the day and—it seemed to some—more focused on the past than on blazing a trail through contemporary problems. Feeling thus left to their own devices, the younger generation struggled to determine what it meant to be Mormon and female in an increasingly secular society. Unlike many of their parent's generation, the great majority were not self-defined as polygamists working to create a separatist society, but, what then was their new role to be? What was their relationship to the larger society in Utah and the United States? Many had found fulfillment through club work, but was there still a role for them as an organized body of *religious* women? If so, how would they fit into Progressive America and how far would they go in embracing the strategies of reform-minded men and women across the nation?[7] These questions were at the heart of a mighty struggle threatening to engulf the Relief Society as Lyman spent her first years in its leadership.

It was in this environment, filled with sometimes wrenching adjustments, that Lyman learned the ropes of administration. In so doing, she honed her familiar skills and discovered new talents even as she gained greater insight into the world around her and joined others in the Relief Society leadership in finding new ways for Mormon women to fit in. Ultimately these first years Lyman served on the general board marked a time when the society's leaders reclaimed for the organization its preeminent status as they channeled the energies of a new generation into an unprecedented era of accomplishment.

As Amy was pulled into this new period of her life, she emerged from circumstances with which she had grown quite contented. Richard's career as a professor and consulting engineer had brought the family status and financial security while she found further satisfaction in local church and club work. Personally charming and socially popular, she remained attractive, quick paced, determined, and opinionated. Through her years of teaching, traveling, and work in the YLMIA and the Authors Club, she had grown poised, well-informed, and nearly dauntless—though not completely—as speaking before large groups and new social situations continued to cause her trepidation.[8] But the requirements of her new calling forced her to fill these chinks in her armor fairly quickly.

In fact, Lyman immediately confronted such fears when she attended her first meeting of the general board. As she "timidly" walked in, she found herself among "the most imposing group of women" she had ever seen at close range.[9] They represented the Relief Society's past glories and future hopes. Presiding was eighty-five year old Bathsheba Bigler Wilson Smith, president of the organization and the last surviving charter member from Nauvoo. A first wife and widow for more than four decades of George A. Smith, long serving counselor of Brigham Young—Bathsheba had loved and supported her husband as he took several plural wives. After the Utah reorganization of the Relief Society she had been closely involved in all its activities, including the extended struggle to obtain suffrage for women. Seated beside her was Emmeline B. Wells, herself a plural wife and widow of Daniel H. Wells, another counselor of Young and a prominent figure in Utah politics and church leadership. Now, at eighty-one, Wells remained the still-vigorous editor of the *Woman's Exponent*. She was a close associate of prominent women across the nation and an unswerving advocate for Mormonism, suffrage, and equal rights. Next was Emily S. Richards, a mere fifty-nine and a monogamist, with a still living and very supportive husband, Franklin S. Richards, who was chief counsel for the church. Along with Wells, she had been a moving force in the successful struggle to regain the vote at statehood. Other similarly accomplished veterans of the first generation were positioned around the table.[10] Lyman had not known these older women well, but through the Authors Club and the ties that grew out of it, already enjoyed close association with several younger members in the leadership. Undoubtedly it was one of them who had put forward her name when a vacancy arose on the board.[11] Among this younger group, Amy grew especially close to fifty-year-old Clarissa Smith Williams, a step-daughter of Bathsheba Smith who already counted decades of service in the YLMIA and the Relief Society.[12]

Often linked by birth or marriage to elite families and bound together by social and kinship ties, these leaders were in turn separated by generational differences in experience and outlook.[13] Most of the older women were plural wives who had spent the balance of their lives building the semi-independent Mormon community in the West. Openly religious, they were millenarian in outlook and freely exercised spiritual gifts, such as speaking in tongues or laying on of hands for healing of the sick, which they considered fundamental fruits of their faith. As Utah's society became more secular and modern, some of these founding mothers found it difficult to adjust. Younger board members, by contrast, were monogamists who came of age during the period of accommodation to national norms. Accustomed to the increasingly secular environment, like Lyman, most were more reserved in their religious behavior and tended to be post-millennialist in their expectations: they saw it as their task to perfect the world in preparation for the Savior's second advent—something they expected to occur at an indefinite date in the distant future. In this regard, they had much in common with other Americans of the progressive generation, especially adherents of the Social Gospel who sought to adapt Christ's teachings to solve the societal problems of the day.[14]

Many of the generational differences among Relief Society women were bridged through the common commitment both groups shared to the church and its leaders. However, some of the most important divisions that remained involved administrative reorganization, a task that had become pressing due to the growth of church membership. Yet, as divisive as it eventually became between these generations of women, when Lyman first encountered the issue it had actually produced a unified response: wariness.

By the turn of the century, expanding numbers had placed strains on the informal administrative structures and personal ties, characteristic of the territorial period, which had linked local members and leaders to the general authorities of the church. As they sought to resolve these strains, priesthood leaders drew upon new organizational practices developed to meet the needs of America's growing corporations.[15] While such innovations were adopted without much resistance in the priesthood quorums and auxiliaries like the Sunday School and the Mutual Improvement Associations, several Relief Society leaders saw them as weakening valued traditions of local autonomy in their affairs while they threatened the organization's distinctive position in the church structure. Specifically, Relief Society leaders saw the organization, while functioning under the leadership of the church president, as uniquely empowered by Joseph Smith as a parallel to the priesthood quorums. This was a concept already in peril by the turn of the century as priesthood leaders had already begun to assign the Relief Society a lesser status, as simply one among several church auxiliaries. In 1913, church president Joseph F. Smith went further, making a definitive statement affirming the society's status as an auxiliary. He then noted that none of the auxiliaries "were independent," and continued "nor can they exercise any rights in their organizations independently of the Priesthood." Smith's statements should be seen as part of his efforts to reorganize the affairs of a growing and increasingly complex church organization, but in decades to come this change would have profound implications for the Relief Society and the control it exercised over its own agenda.[16]

Lyman joined the board just in time to witness the conclusion of a rather involved but telling lesson related to the shifting status of the Relief Society in the church. By the early years of the twentieth century, Salt Lake City was aspiring to achieve the standing of a great city. Substantial multi-story buildings were filling its downtown that boasted, among other advantages, a first-class electric streetcar system with rail links stretching north and south along the Wasatch Front. While religious tensions had flared in the wake of the Smoot hearings, only a few years later church and community leaders put aside their differences to work together to create a more efficient municipal government and enhanced community services, including street paving and modern sewer and water systems. Part of the church's contribution to this process was a plan to redevelop the Tithing Block. A site of historic importance directly east of the Salt Lake Temple that included the storehouse and tithing barn of the Presiding Bishop (where contributions in kind to the church had been stored), it seemed increasingly out of place with the growing aspirations church leaders had for downtown.[17]

As they worked out their plans, church leaders soon found themselves at odds with previous commitments they had made to the women's organizations. For years the leadership of the Relief Society, the YLMIA, and the Primary had met in private homes or in the offices of the *Woman's Exponent*. After repeated petitioning, the president of the church had promised the women a building of their own to be constructed on the Tithing Block. The one condition was they had to raise half the cost of construction, roughly $20,000, before title to the property would be handed over to them. The women moved with alacrity to begin the process of raising the needed funds, although progress toward their goal proved painfully slow.[18] But as church leaders later mulled over the prospect of redeveloping the Tithing Block, they concluded that the cost for construction and maintenance of the type of structure now deemed suitable for this prominent location was too much for the women to manage alone. In 1907 the Relief Society and the other organizations were therefore asked to contribute their combined funds toward a larger structure to be known as the Bishop's Building. In addition to the women's organizations it was also to house the offices of the Presiding Bishopric and the Young Men's Mutual Improvement Association.

Both generations of leaders in the women's organizations reacted with stunned astonishment at the news (Bathsheba Smith reportedly fainted), not only because of the change in plans, but because it had been made without consulting them. While they eventually adjusted their expectations to the less prominent accommodations offered, the affair seemed to affirm the older generation's fears of declining status and served as a warning to the younger generation of the challenges that lay ahead.[19] All this was fresh in the minds of Relief Society leaders as Amy joined the board shortly before the move to the permanent offices in the newly completed Bishop's Building.

The move into the new offices in 1909 also marked a sort of generational changing of the guard—a fact poignantly obvious to the older women in the leadership. From the *Exponent's* offices, then located in the Templeton Building across from Temple Square, Emmeline Wells had watched some months previously as the bishop's storehouse and barn on the old tithing block were taken down to make way for the new structures. "[O]ne who has seen these old places in the course of construction," she mused with a touch of melancholy, "can call up the moving pictures of the men who figured conspicuously in public matters; and recall such scenes and events as strike deep at the fountains of feeling in the human heart." Most of those men and women were now gone, and with the redevelopment of the Tithing Block, so was the setting for many of the important events of their lives. As Wells reflected wistfully on the vanished buildings that once symbolized the hopes and accomplishments of her generation, she expressed a desire that the structures now taking shape—including the new Bishop's Building—might fill a similar role for the rising generation.[20]

In contrast to Wells's mixed emotions, Lyman and the women of her generation came to embrace change. For them the construction of impressive new edifices on the site only reinforced their views that they lived in an era of progress. But in this eagerness to accept the new, some in the first generation, with insight gained from decades of experience, saw a danger that younger women would unwittingly surrender some of the hard-earned advantages of the past.

While such concerns loomed over the future, at the time many saw the establishment of the new headquarters for the Relief Society as marking a coming of age for the organization. For Lyman, the building was to become the center of her professional life for the next thirty-five years. It sat on the west end of the old Tithing Block, just north of the Hotel Utah (then under construction). It shared space with the campus of the LDS University to the north, Brigham Young's Beehive and Lion Houses to the East, and, after 1920, the Church Administration Building.[21] Across Main Street to the west, was the Temple Block, spiritual heart of the church. On its east side, then facing the Bishop's Building, the site is still dominated by the Salt Lake Temple. Farther west, the Tabernacle holds sway. With seating for five thousand, it then housed the great conferences of the church. To the south of the Tabernacle stands the smaller, neo-gothic Assembly Hall where many of the Relief Society conferences were held.[22] Three miles to the east of all this, on Third Avenue, was the Lyman home near the end of the streetcar line. Despite all her travels during her decades of church service, these few sites remained the heart of Lyman's universe, with its nexus being the second floor of the Bishop's Building where the Relief Society offices were located.

The Relief Society held its first meeting in its new quarters in December 1909, just two months after Lyman joined the board.[23] However, the change in venue did not, as yet, bring a consensus to the board about an updated agenda for the organization. In fact, the issues of administrative reorganization and the modernization of goals and practices at times sharply divided Relief Society leaders. Bathsheba Smith and other senior women were forced to admit that new circumstances required new directions, especially as younger women had been staying away from the organization in droves. But they were not yet willing to diminish their commitment to past agendas nor eager to usurp the autonomy of local leaders by imposing a host of new programs from above. In defense of their position, they could point to significant contributions that long-running programs continued to make to the Mormon community, especially in rural areas where some still lived under primitive conditions. In such places activities like grain storage retained their practical applications as did the Relief Society's well-established training program for practical nurses.[24] The board also maintained strong ties to larger networks of women involved in reform activities including the ongoing national suffrage struggle and a growing international movement for world peace—causes seniors leaders felt were of interest to all generations of Mormon women.[25] And, of course, the organization remained a place for religious uplift, gospel scholarship, and charity work. Yet, for younger women, including Lyman, such arguments in favor of the status quo were not convincing. Indeed, Emmeline Wells's biographer, Carol Cornwall Madsen, concluded that the nursing classes were "floundering" and grain storage was "scientifically archaic and financially inefficient."[26] As for Relief Society meetings, to younger women they seemed hopelessly out of date, while such spiritual gifts as speaking in tongues, were increasingly out of place in their modernizing world. Trained in the YLMIA and women's clubs in parliamentary procedure and public speaking, these younger women wanted a whole new approach from the Relief Society; most of all meetings that were more focused and to the point as well as organized around topics relevant to their lives.[27]

For some time before Lyman joined the board, younger members had sought to establish a standardized educational curriculum prepared by experts in a variety of fields. They hoped this would invigorate meetings and increase attendance.[28] Senior women in the leadership recognized in principle the need for such a move, but, concerned about impinging on local autonomy, hesitated to implement the recommended changes.[29] Younger members, led by Bathsheba Smith's counselors Annie Taylor Hyde, daughter of former church apostle and president John Taylor and the mother of eight children, and Ida Smoot Dusenberry, a teacher at BYU's training school and a mother of two, nevertheless achieved a victory of sorts when, in 1901, the *Woman's Exponent* began to publish sample lessons submitted by local Societies on a then widely-appealing topic: motherhood education. In practice, however, the content of these lessons fell far short of their proponents' goals—most of the lessons tended to be sentimental rather than practical in tone and often ignored topics of pressing interest to younger women, such as nutrition and health care. But these lessons would prove an opening wedge that eventually allowed innovations in Relief Society curriculums and activities of the kind that began to slowly draw younger women back into the organization.[30]

Greater change, and continued tensions, came soon after Bathsheba Smith's death in September 1910. In a break with precedent, rather than selecting her successor himself, as had been the practice, church president Joseph F. Smith asked board members to submit nominations for her replacement. In accordance with their recommendations, he called Emmeline B. Wells to assume the presidency of the organization and named Clarissa Williams as one of her counselors.[31] Though eighty-two, the still vigorous Wells remained strong-willed and independent, traits she displayed through an increasingly bohemian style of dress: she often appeared in public wearing long, flowing pieces of tulle, which, coupled with her petite frame, made her look somewhat ethereal. Yet, in the early years of her presidency there was nothing ethereal about her grasp on power. Though reluctant to advance at too swift a pace, she nevertheless moved the organization inexorably forward in its efforts to address issues of interest to the rising generation and of importance to the modern age.[32] As she did so, she turned increasingly to younger women on the board to carry out her plans. Among the most important of these trans-generational relationships was the one she formed with Lyman. The older woman quickly recognized Lyman's drive and potential and came to rely heavily upon her. In turn, Lyman found in Wells a significant mentor and role model, although, like some of her peers on the board, she eventually bridled at the older woman's reluctance to adapt to emerging realities.

At the beginning of Wells's administration in October 1910, a new church policy that prohibited individuals from holding concurrent church responsibilities forced the departure of several women from the board who were also serving in ward and stake leadership positions.[33] The reorganized general presidency and board thus found an immediate opportunity to add several younger women to its ranks. Influenced more strongly than ever by second generation women, Relief Society leaders moved quickly on a number of pressing issues, including the expansion of an employment exchange and the establishment of a home for working girls in Salt Lake City. They also considered lending support to community efforts such as the free kindergarten movement, the juvenile court, and Salt Lake City's own social settlement: Neighborhood House. As it considered these steps, the general board signaled it was preparing to embrace causes relevant to the lives of younger women of the faith.[34]

These first steps toward a revitalized Society were carried out in urban terrain, but not long after Wells became president, Lyman had an experience that greatly enhanced her understanding of the challenges women still faced in rural areas. During the summer of 1911, Richard decided to homestead on public lands that opened up near the town of Delta, a farming and ranching community in Utah's western desert where members of his extended family lived. He had designed an irrigation dam on the Sevier River that flowed through steep cliffs below the tract and thought this would be a good opportunity to benefit from his labors by investing in land made more valuable by a reliable water supply. Indeed, Richard would eventually develop the land by building several houses on it.[35] As he had ongoing obligations in Salt Lake City, it fell to Amy and the children to maintain the required residency during the work week leaving him to come out "when he could" on weekends.[36]

Perhaps due to childhood memories of the Raid, Amy was fearful of being alone at night. She was also deathly afraid of snakes and mice—both "a plague" in the area. Richard, therefore, arranged for one of Amy's nephews, Jean R. Driggs, to accompany the family to provide companionship and protection. After plowing out his 120 acre tract at the stroke of midnight on opening day, Richard joined with the family to construct a tent cabin with a canvas top and wooden sides that served as a home for the next two months.[37]

Though Amy was the daughter of pioneers, by the time of her birth her family was already well established and enjoyed living conditions, which, albeit simple, were reasonably comfortable. In addition, for the last two decades, her standard of living had continued to improve. Since the birth of her children she had not been without electricity, a telephone, or indoor plumbing. Now she found herself with none of these so-called luxuries. Richard attempted to provide the tent with all the amenities possible under the circumstances: a double roof for cooling in the desert heat, screened windows to keep insects out while maximizing ventilation, a fuel oil stove for cooking and heating during the cold desert nights, and an adequate supply of drinking water. Yet his efforts proved far from adequate. "We soon found," Amy recalled, "that it would not protect us from the simoons or sandstorms which blew up often in this treeless, and except for the sagebrush, practically verdureless plain." The storms sent dust seeping through cracks, coating everything with a fine grit and requiring the whole family to join in a thorough cleaning after each occurrence. For someone as scrupulous about cleanliness as Amy, this must have been an enormous challenge. The desert wind also prevented the stove from drafting properly, sent black smoke billowing into the tent, extinguished the fire, and required Amy to cook outside on a metal plate over a shallow trench. Water, a scarce commodity, was delivered once a week by wagon and emptied into a barrel half-buried in the sand to keep it cool. But the family "did not relish" it very much, because it "was never very cool nor appetizing" as the water was drawn from the Sevier River and tasted heavily of alkali. To make matters worse, the family adopted a "homeless, half-blind stray" dog that was sick and one week, soon after a visit by the water wagon, Amy's daughter Margaret dipped the dog's dirty dish into the barrel to fill it. Amy tried to spoon off the contaminated water, but they had to make do for nearly a week until the next delivery, boiling it when they could to assuage their concerns about sanitation.[38]

Despite these hardships, perhaps the most difficult aspect of the experience for the sociable Amy was the isolation. Neighbors were far away and visitors were few. When it was necessary to stock up at the general store, the whole family went on the three mile walk through the summer heat as no one wanted to be left alone at camp. Among the rare visitors was Mary M. Lyman, an older relative of Richard's, who came in the capacity of a Relief Society teacher to see how the "city folk" were coping with desert life. Well read in history and literature, she and Amy enjoyed long, stimulating conversations that relieved the otherwise dull monotony of the experience.[39]

After two months, their claim uncontested, Richard purchased the plot for $1.25 an acre and Amy and the children returned home to the city. In later years she would often laugh about the adventure and rib Richard about the "convenient" obligations that kept him comfortably at home while the rest of the family battled dirt, heat, and loneliness.[40] But her experience exemplified the great diversity in living conditions for Westerners—and Americans—during the era. Not only was there an enormous divide between the privileged middle and upper classes and urban laborers, but farm families also struggled, often suffering in extremely primitive circumstances. Her time in Delta thus provided an invaluable reminder—one she would not forget—of the real hardships women in outlying areas still faced as they tried to maintain their own physical and emotional health and that of their families. It also reaffirmed for her the value of the Relief Society in providing companionship and a sense of community for women coping with the realities of rural life.[41]

Upon her return, Lyman resumed her growing Relief Society responsibilities. Wells frequently asked her to assist with secretarial duties and in August 1913, named her general secretary of the organization when the previous secretary resigned.[42] This placed her at the center of activity, in the offices nearly every day where she managed routine duties and answered correspondence from wards and stakes regarding problems or questions of procedure. Sometimes these queries could be both perplexing and humorous. In later years Lyman would often chuckle about a letter she received in 1913 from a bewildered (and brand new) stake Relief Society president in a small Utah community who was struggling to know how to record the value of a "a beautiful pair of ducks" donated by "a very poor lady" to the charity fund. The donation had been made "in kind," a practice quite common during the territorial period, but largely restricted to rural areas as Utah modernized. Despite the best efforts of local leaders, the ducks did not sell at a Relief Society bazaar and, greatly complicating the matter, while trying to figure out what to do next, hawks killed one and the other swam down the river and was lost. The question was, the befuddled stake leader asked, how, according to proper practices, should they credit the donation to the good sister and still account for the lost ducks in the records? "But say," the president added, "we do feel bad about the ducks." With her sensitivity to the plight of her rural sisters heightened by her recent homesteading experience, Lyman responded to the women with kindness. But the letter, though humorous, was a potent reminder of the variety of circumstances affecting Mormon women of the time, and the challenges that faced Relief Society leaders as they struggled to address their needs.[43]

Most problems were more routine and easier to resolve, but even as Lyman helped address the circumstances that arose in the day to day affairs of the organization, she also served as an informal bureau of information to out-of-town visitors.[44] In these capacities, Lyman—now functioning as a public face as well as a voice of the Relief Society—quickly became familiar with every aspect of the organization and most of its local leadership as well, thus developing a breadth of knowledge and a network of contacts that proved extremely useful in years to come.

Emmeline Wells also spent most of her days at headquarters, but unlike Lyman, sometimes even stayed the night in her office, sleeping on a couch. In their long hours together she tutored Amy in the intricacies of Relief Society leadership and "took great pains to pass on her almost limitless knowledge" of the history of the organization. The latter preserved a reservoir of institutional knowledge that buttressed a sense of continuity and helped ground the organization during what would be a period of rapid change.[45] As Lyman traveled to local Relief Society conferences with Wells and accompanied her to meetings of national women's groups, the young, vigorous Lyman and the aging Mormon matriarch bonded emotionally. In 1911, Wells chose Amy to accompany her to Chicago for a meeting of the executive council of the National Council of Women. This experience opened a new world to Lyman and marked the beginning of her thirty-five year association with that organization.[46]

Established in 1888, the National Council was affiliated with the International Council of Women, and like it, grew out of the movement for women's rights. Its founders, the leading lights of the suffrage struggle, intended that it would bring together representatives of national women's groups to further the advancement of their sex. Mormon women had been associated with the Council since its inception and notables such as Emily Richards and Brigham Young's daughter, Susa Young Gates, had each held positions in its leadership. Foremost among those associated with the council, however, was Wells herself, who held an honored position due to her long years of work in behalf of woman's suffrage.[47]

In the years around the turn of the century, many Latter-day Saint women began to lose interest in the National and International when both councils considered passage of anti-Mormon resolutions during the controversy over the seating of B. H. Roberts in the House of Representatives and, again during the Smoot investigations. Wells, however, saw the value in continued association, and, soon after she became president, worked tirelessly to return the Relief Society to full participation.[48] Other church leaders, including Smoot himself, saw the wisdom in this move and strongly supported her initiative. Here was a long-running association, they agreed, that was still of considerable value to the Relief Society and its members.[49]

Lyman, having heard about the Council from older board members, eagerly anticipated her first meeting. Arriving in company with Wells and YLMIA board member Ardella W. Eardly, she was not disappointed, finding the program filled with interesting and informative speakers on such timely topics as public health, morality, and even—a popular topic of the day—eugenics. Interesting as well were the brief reports by member organizations such as the National Council of Jewish Women and the National Board of the YWCA, which gave her valuable insight into their activities and agendas.[50] A high point came when the delegates were invited to a luncheon at Hull House where Lyman renewed her acquaintance with Jane Addams and listened attentively as the famous reformer explained the ever-growing activities of the settlement. Of particular interest to Lyman were efforts aimed at child welfare and infant health.[51]

Other experiences in Chicago also left their mark, including one that occurred even before the first meeting was held. As soon as she and Wells checked into their rooms at the hotel, a number of newspaper men asked for an interview. Lyman was impressed by the aplomb with which Wells handled the crowd of reporters with their repeated queries about "the place of Latter-day Saint women in the Church" and the attitude among Utah women "toward polygamy and the seating of Reed Smoot in the United Sates Senate in 1904." With her decades of experience in journalism and her own interaction with the leaders of suffrage and women's organizations, Lyman described the diminutive eighty-three-year-old Wells as clearly in her element, "holding her own with ease and composure, to the great amusement of these husky, aggressive young newshawks." In the process Wells won over the group as she fielded their questions, presenting an example of serenity under pressure that Lyman would strive to emulate.[52]

Yet another incident served as a potent reminder of the challenges that still confronted Mormons. The council's vice president, Kate Waller Barrett, a longtime friend of Latter-day Saint women, informed Wells and Lyman that a delegate from the National Christian League for the Promotion of Purity—then at the forefront of an effort to exclude Mormon women from the council—was trying to secure a resolution protesting supposed polygamous practices still ongoing in Utah and deploring the Senate's seating of Smoot. Barrett arranged for a Relief Society representative to sit in on the next session of the resolutions committee so the motion could be blocked before it came before the whole convention—a development that surely would have embarrassed the Utah women. Showing the trust Wells placed in her young protégé, Lyman was chosen for this delicate assignment. Though anxious, she performed her role well, and, with the help of well-placed friends, the motion was defeated in committee.[53] After the close of the meeting, the representative of the Purity League invited Lyman to her room where she expressed "with great earnestness her regret that I, as a young woman, was not more enlightened regarding religion and morals." "She was not surprised," she told Lyman, "at the attitude of the older Mormon women, who had not known better, but it was too bad that the promising young women of our Church were not better informed." She then offered to kneel down with Amy to pray for her enlightenment. "We parted on friendly terms," Lyman related, "though I did not accept her offer."[54] As in Ithaca, this experience left a lasting impression and increased her resolve to dispel misconceptions about the Latter-day Saints and their faith. In the larger sense, it also revealed the formidable barriers that confronted those who sought to build a unified national and international woman's movement.[55]

Back once more in Utah, Lyman's sphere of influence in Relief Society affairs continued to broaden as she took her turn traveling to stake Relief Society conferences and speaking at the organization's annual and semi-annual general conferences, tasks she at first found daunting but at which she soon excelled.[56] Stake and ward leaders who had become acquainted with her through correspondence now saw first-hand her keen intellect at work as she delivered well-crafted addresses and handled questions with clarity and wisdom. Still others among the rank and file with whom she had previously had no interaction came to know her, appreciate her sociability and sound judgement, and so joined her growing network of contacts.

That she was able to take on this heavy load was due in no small measure to the assistance she received from her husband. Despite his own daunting schedule as college professor and increasingly prominent consulting engineer, it was Richard who took up much of the slack at home when she was occupied with Relief Society business. An unusually involved father for the time, he looked out for the welfare of the children, served as both father and mother when Amy was away, and—aided by a series of nieces and nephews who boarded with them for months or years for varied reasons and by "hired girls"—he managed household affairs in her absence. Emotionally Richard was her rock as well as her biggest booster, reassuring her with words of effusive praise (extended family recalled that "he was always bragging on her")and regular tokens of his love.[57]

In an example of the latter, one day when Amy had been on the general board for a only a couple of years, she reluctantly turned away a traveling salesman from her front door who had been peddling the multi-volume *The Historian's History of the World*. With her inherited thirst for knowledge and love of reading, the beautifully bound and well written books were hard to resist, especially as they would be wonderful sources for her presentations at the Authors Club. But their exorbitant cost was well beyond her budget and so "heroically" she marshaled her self-discipline to maintain unsullied her practice of frugality. As she recounted the experience with the family over dinner that night, she expressed pride in herself for doing the right thing, noting however, how hard it had been to do so. Much to her consternation, however, a month later, the entire set of twenty-five books was delivered to the house. Amy was alarmed and angry at the salesman who she felt had deceived her and sent the books against her wishes. She was nearly beside herself as she pondered how difficult it would be to resolve the situation. Over dinner as she unburdened herself to Richard in the presence of the children and the current crop of visiting nieces and nephews, he replied simply, "Don't worry about it. I ordered the books as a surprise for you, and they're all paid for." Such acts, coupled with the continuous and unstinting support he gave, provided her the confidence and sense of security that enabled her to move forward with her work in the Relief Society despite the many hours away from home and family it required.[58]

It was about this time, at Amy's initiation, that an important change came to the Lyman's marriage. This is something that would have remained strictly a private matter except for the long-term consequences that grew out of it. Though Amy loved and desired children, she had always had difficulty conceiving.[59] When she reached forty, perhaps in light of her own deliveries, which, like those of the other Brown women, seem to have been lengthy and complicated, and no doubt with the harrowing disabilities in mind that her mother suffered due to the last two pregnancies she had experienced—pregnancies that occurred after Margaret Brown herself reached forty—it seems Lyman prudently concluded that her childbearing years were at an end. Consequently, she apparently decided the only appropriate course was to draw upon her iron willpower and cease marital relations.[60]

In considering her decision, a number of factors must be considered. While a small but important movement extolling romantic and erotic aspects of marriage was emerging among some Americans at the time, such trends were not widely followed until the 1920s and not broadly promulgated at all in the Mormon community in the early twentieth century. Instead, far more visible and influential were concepts of Victorian morality current in society as Amy came of age. In popular marital guides of the time, women were repeatedly urged to maintain an absolute standard of purity before and after marriage. Both on the basis of religious ideology and the belief that to surrender to "man's passions and instincts" would only delay one's "higher spiritual attainment," sexual relations were depicted as an evil necessitated by procreation. From this perspective, the ultimate marital relationship was a platonic one.[61] Such views seem to have been widely—though certainly not universally—held in the Mormon community where conversely, as in the larger society, birth control, even where it was legal, was generally frowned upon and labeled "race suicide."[62] For Lyman to have cut off physical intimacy once her family was complete would not have been unusual for the time either in or out of the Mormon community. Of course, many other factors could have contributed to her decision. In a day when such intimacy was not openly discussed, even among spouses, physical or emotional incompatibilities with Richard or insensitivities on his part, seemingly quite common among men at the time, could have become intolerable for her, significantly contributing to this move. Family lore provides information on the timing and indicates that Amy initiated the move, but the details of why she reached this decision and Richard's initial reaction to it remain unknown and unknowable. Ultimately he acquiesced and the couple began to sleep in separate rooms.[63] In the long run, however, Richard found this too hard a course to follow, with serious consequences resulting for them both.

As for Amy, as her energies were now freed to focus on Relief Society work, new responsibilities soon came her way. When Joseph F. Smith set her apart as general secretary in 1913, he charged her with three tasks that in many respects set the stage for her subsequent accomplishments in the organization. First, she was to update the record keeping and business practices of the society, bringing them into line with the modern methods used elsewhere in the church. Second, she was to make a thorough study of welfare work so the Relief Society could adopt the highest standards of efficiency in its own charitable activities. Third, she was to join with the entire board in finding ways to bring more young women into the organization.[64]

The first of these directives was the most pressing and long overdue. While an outstanding personality in many regards, as Amy recalled her, Emmeline Wells was the first to admit that she was not a business woman—indeed by this point in her life she hated the detail work required to run the business affairs of the Relief Society. Consequently, when Amy joined the board, the organization owned no equipment common to a modern office of the period, not even a typewriter or file cabinet. Nor did it employ a secretary or bookkeeper. Lyman moved quickly to remedy such inadequacies, securing requisite equipment and necessary personnel.[65] Updating the record-keeping practices of the organization took more time as there had previously been no uniformity in ward and stake records. But by 1916 she had distributed a ward record book, containing not only a set of standardized forms with space for rolls, minutes, historical notes, statistical data, accounts, and yearly reports but also, influenced by her experience handling queries from local units, a statement of standard procedures for Relief Society workers. Two years later she produced a similar book for the stakes. Together, these produced records that greatly facilitated the job of tracking the progress of the organization in a variety of areas.[66]

Soon after beginning her secretarial duties she joined two committees that focused on the third charge given to her by Smith: declining membership, not just in the Relief Society, but in other church auxiliaries as well. Both committees saw their most important recommendation being a call for administrative modernization and, in particular, standardization of church curriculums.[67] While such standardization had been rejected during the administration of Bathsheba Smith, and Wells herself had been strongly adverse to embracing it, by 1913 several new members of the board were adding their voices to the chorus calling for change.[68] Most prominent among them was the formidable Susa Young Gates, daughter of Brigham Young. Then fifty-seven, she had founded the *Young Woman's Journal*, served as its editor for eleven years, and worked closely with Wells in the National and International Councils of Women.[69] She gained support from another new board member, forty-seven-year-old Jeannette Acord Hyde, who had long experience working with younger women in the YLMIA and was deeply involved in community affairs and issues ranging from charity work and home economics, to politics and reform.[70] Lyman became another ally in the cause, as did Wells's counselor, Clarissa Smith Williams.[71] Working determinedly, these four now led others in the fight to bring about the changes their generation had so long sought. Shaped by their own experiences in club work and community activism—and well aware of the power still lying dormant in the Relief Society—they agreed that a new agenda should include not only spiritual uplift, but items such as public health, home economics, and self-improvement. These, they felt, would serve the needs of the women in the society better than the dated pursuits of the previous generation.[72] Faced with pressure both from her board and from priesthood leaders, early in 1913, Wells reluctantly agreed to move toward a standardized curriculum.[73]

Caught up, as they were, in the cause of revitalizing the society, second generation women did not fully realize the import of Wells's reservations. As she saw it, when the board infringed on the prerogatives of local units, it strengthened a trend toward centralized control in the church. While beneficial in many respects, as this trend progressed it would ultimately weaken the autonomy of the Relief Society itself.[74] To be sure, at this time the organization still retained a great deal of freedom over its own affairs. Despite growing priesthood oversight, Joseph F. Smith, himself a supporter of the creation of a centralized curriculum, had refrained from dictating in the matter, leaving it for the society to decide.[75] Yet, with her decades of experience in church affairs, Wells knew something was at work here that the younger women did not fully comprehend: though Smith was reluctant to impose his will on the organization at this time, the innovations sought by second generation women would make it easier for future church leaders to directly intervene if they were inclined to do so. Still, she acquiesced to the will of the majority, hoping such forebodings would not materialize.[76]

As the newly standardized curriculum took shape, Wells was worried as well about the secular nature of the topics covered in the lessons. "[I]n these outlines," she told the board, "we are getting too far away from the spiritual side of our great work."[77] While her comments undoubtedly reveal nostalgia for a world already vanishing and for the values shared by her own fast-dwindling generation of women, like her previous reservations, they also reflected legitimate concerns. In particular, Wells feared that if the society became more secular in its programs, the distinctive character of the organization would be threatened which, in turn, would undermine the foundation stone of its own empowerment. And from her perspective, there was abundant evidence that this was already taking place.

Wells was certainly no stranger to pursuits that could be considered secular in nature. And to be sure, the power of the Relief Society had been frequently manifested through the political, economic, and social achievements of Mormon women mobilized in common cause. Wells herself had been a leader in these moves, and few, if any, could match her involvement in community affairs and the struggle for women's rights, either in or out of the church. But as Wells was acutely aware, the organization had been built on a foundation of shared spiritual experiences. And it was this characteristic that set the Relief Society apart from other women's organizations of the period. And prominent in the spiritual legacy of the organization was something Wells held especially dear: the exercise of spiritual gifts.

Common during the Second Great Awakening of the early 1800s, such manifestations formed a central thread in the religious experience of many Americans during the years in which Mormonism came into existence.[78] Latter-day Saints continued to emphasize spiritual gifts during their exodus to the West and the early decades of colonization, even as the wave of religious fervor subsided elsewhere in the nation. But in the last decades of the nineteenth century, as Mormons accommodated their practices to the demands of reformers and their society became more secular, their practice of spiritual gifts began to fade there as well. As a group, second generation women were increasingly reluctant to engage in such manifestations of the faith. Speaking in tongues was the first to fade from common appearance, and, by the later 1910s, Wells and others were lamenting that even the simple testimony, fervently borne in Relief Society meetings, was seen as "old fashioned."[79] Among the most powerful—and empowering—spiritual gifts was that of blessing the sick or afflicted through the laying on of hands. Lyman's generation was among the last to seek blessings from other women at childbirth, in sickness, or simply at times of special spiritual need, though the practice would linger for a generation more in some rural areas and indeed, in parts of Salt Lake City itself. Wells herself continued to give blessings throughout the remainder of her life but this seems not to have been continued by her successor. And once fallen out of the realm of common experience, as Wells had feared, the privilege first became tightly regulated, then, at last, was lost, with the laying on of hands falling within the exclusive purview of the male priesthood.[80]

Wells could see the declining emphasis on spiritual power manifest in other ways as well, including such simple means as the titles claimed by successive presidents of the Relief Society. Eliza R. Snow had been known as "Presidentess, High Priestess and Prophetess" due to her official responsibilities presiding both over the Society and the women's work in the temple, and in consequence of her innate spirituality. When Snow died, her successors were not generally known by the honorific title of prophetess, though Zina Young and Bathsheba Smith, both of whom oversaw the women's temple work, bore the dual titles of president and high priestess. Wells, who focused exclusively on the Relief Society, was known simply as president.[81] Apparently, younger women, like Lyman, were not especially troubled by what was to them merely a change in semantics, nor did they seem to notice the declining status it implied. They looked instead for empowerment through the college educations many had received and through closer linkage to (secular) American society, made possible through club work. This change of outlook was illustrated by the terms used to introduce speakers at general Relief Society conferences. Women had previously been introduced as "sister," or, if an older woman, as "aunt," the latter perhaps a legacy of the extended family relationships of polygamy. But by the 1910s, borrowing the more formal methods of secular women's clubs, they were introduced as "Mrs." or "Miss."[82] Only to later generations would the full consequences of these changes become clear.

Relief Society leaders announced at the 1913 October conference that, in addition to theology and testimony, the new centralized course of study would include lessons on genealogy—the special concern of Susa Young Gates, and, with its growing religious importance to Mormons, the only lesson to be required—as well as optional material on art, architecture, literature, gardening, and home economics. Soon to follow was material on health, nutrition, and civic improvement. Following the pattern of club work, each of the new lessons was to begin with a brief discussion of current events in the community.[83] With change came continuity: in accordance with long-standing Relief Society practice, one week during the month was devoted to sewing or other handicrafts and the discussion of local Relief Society affairs in lieu of a lesson.[84]

Having determined the lesson content, board members now had to work out methods of circulation and financing. They decided to distribute monthly twelve thousand copies free of charge in a sixteen page pamphlet known as *The Relief Society Bulletin*, edited by Susa Young Gates. Jeannette Hyde and Lyman, as business managers, assumed responsibility for raising revenue to cover costs, estimated at $175.00 monthly.[85] Their efforts were initially greeted with skepticism by businessmen reluctant to pay for ad space in a new publication, especially one managed by women. But Lyman and Hyde were able to lay to rest these apprehensions and secured the needed revenues even as they simultaneously established the foundation for long-term business relationships. Finances, however, were extremely tight and only by watching every penny, even commandeering their children to wrap and mail the *Bulletin*, were the two women able to come in on budget.[86]

The response from local Relief Societies was extremely positive. Most wards adopted the entire standardized curriculum, affecting dramatically the content of meetings, their frequency, and the level of instruction. Given these successes, despite the continued reluctance of Wells, the general board moved in 1915 to make mandatory what increasing numbers of local societies were already doing voluntarily: requiring local units to teach one of the new lessons each week.[87]

It light of this success, the board decided the next year to expand the *Bulletin*. Appearing in January 1915 with a new name, *The Relief Society Magazine*, it contained forty-five pages of text, formatted to fit "in a ladies handbag," with additional material of interest to women and a subscription price of one dollar. Like mainstream publications such as *The Ladies Home Journal*, the *Magazine* carried short stories, poetry, household hints, current events, and accounts of accomplishments of women.[88] But it also offered distinctly Mormon material such as conference reports, news of the church, and discussions of Mormon history and theology. In many ways it was similar to the *Woman's Exponent*, yet packaged in a manner more in tune with the times.

Lyman remained closely associated with the *Magazine* for over thirty years, as business manager, sometimes editor, and frequent contributor. From 1915 until 1928, she wrote a monthly column, "Notes from the Field," that highlighted the activities and achievements of local Relief Societies and helped set the agenda for the organization. She described the publication as "a dearly beloved child." If not a "beloved child," like the *Woman's Exponent* before it, the *Magazine* was to three generations of Mormon women something more than a journal: it was their door to a larger world, their tie to their community, their entertainment, their inspiration, and their voice.[89]

The publication of the *Magazine* represented a significant marker in Lyman's career development, symbolizing the end of her apprenticeship as a Relief Society leader. She had joined the board rather timidly, overwhelmed by the responsibilities she faced and overawed by the personalities she encountered. Her early years had been ones of apprenticeship especially to Wells, and to others who had seen her potential and provided intensive mentoring. Amy's abundant skills and the force of her personality ingratiated her to the organization's president, which led to even greater opportunities for growth, including association with national organizations of activist women. Added to these important experiences were others that enhanced Lyman's understanding of the challenges that faced the rank and file, such as her visits to stake conferences and her own harrowing adventure as a homesteader. Her determination in using these insights as she carried out new responsibilities demonstrates that the pluck she showed during her "Ready-aim-fire" days had been carried with her and was now being turned to the advantage of her sisters in the Relief Society.

Lyman's ability to help translate two of Joseph F. Smith's charges into reality had already marked her as a force to be reckoned with in the Relief Society's affairs. Now, as she prepared to address Smith's third charge, she was moving toward a position of even greater influence. She was also about to begin the greatest work and the most productive period of her life.

4

A REVOLUTION IN CHURCH CHARITY

> Save the children. It is easier to maintain them in health than to heal them from sickness.
>
> —ELIZABETH WILCOX[1]

> Mrs. Lyman pointed out that the watchword of the Relief Society is "Charity" in its highest and most practical sense, based upon the inter-dependence of mankind.
>
> —*RELIEF SOCIETY MAGAZINE*[2]

As Amy Brown Lyman and other like-minded Relief Society leaders moved toward the task of modernizing church charity practices, they did so gradually, again looking to the activities of club women to find ways to expand the organization's agenda. They were particularly interested in matters related to public health and social welfare—concerns that, when adopted by the Relief Society, made it a leader in progressive reform. Arising in an age of optimism and expanding scientific knowledge, progressives believed that social problems could be solved through a combination of careful study and disciplined common sense. In Utah, men and women, Mormons and Gentiles alike worked together to use legislative means to address a wide range of problems afflicting their communities. These resulted in the creation of a state board of health, protective legislation for women and children, the establishment of mandatory public schooling, education for the deaf and blind, regulatory commissions for utilities and workplace safety, workman's compensation laws, widows' pensions, and even state prohibition. In sum, by the 1910s, Utah ranked high among those states enacting progressive measures.[3]

That much of this legislation passed into law was in no small part due to intense lobbying on the part of women. Like their counterparts outside of the state, Utah women showed themselves especially adept at addressing issues linked to what scholars denote as the maternalist agenda: a set of strategies that allowed women to utilize gender stereotypes (namely of their supposed natural roles as mothers and nurturers) to legitimize an expanded sphere for themselves in community affairs. As guardians of the home, in other words, women had a compelling reason to address community ills that might impinge on the well-being of families. Utilizing such concepts, progressive women, often operating within the framework of voluntary associations or women's clubs, were especially successful in addressing issues relating to the welfare of mothers and children.[4]

Emmeline Wells and the majority of the board supported most of these measures and had even lent the organization's endorsement to several. By the early 1910s they became more outspoken, even using Relief Society General Conferences to urge women to become more involved in bettering their communities, including recommendations that they exert their influence through the political process.[5] Some, including Lyman, would go still further, encouraging Relief Society cooperation with community groups and public agencies in a variety of maternalist activities.

In taking these steps, Relief Society leaders locked arms with women's associations and clubs across the nation seeking reform. One result of such collective endeavors was the establishment in 1912 of the Federal Children's Bureau in the Department of Labor. Commissioned to gather and disseminate information about the status of mothers and children in the United States, the bureau championed protective legislation, improved education and health care for women and children, the prohibition of child labor, and the enactment of the so-called "living-wage" for men that would free women to stay at home to care for their families. Under the able direction of Hull House alum Julia Lathrop and her successor, Grace Abbott, the bureau tapped into the very organizations that helped create it to become the center of a widespread network linking social science and public health professionals with organized women involved in community betterment.[6]

Over a period of several years, seemingly small steps taken by Relief Society leaders in the interest of maternal and infant health led them into ever greater involvement in this national movement. In 1913, at the behest of board member Alice Merrill Horne, the Society helped sponsor a series of milk depots on Salt Lake City's poorer west side.[7] These "milk stations," as they were also known, had first appeared in New York City in the 1890s and, by the turn of the century, reformers were utilizing them in many urban areas across the nation. Their purpose was to provide fresh, pasteurized milk, especially during the hot summer months when, physicians observed, infants and young children experienced a much higher rate of death from illnesses linked to impure or spoiled milk.[8] Horne, who had lost a child of her own due to illness, made the milk depots her special cause. During the months the depot was in operation, nurses gave away 800 quarts of milk, sold 300 more at wholesale prices, and dispensed care and instruction to nearly 330 visitors while making more than 1,000 home visits.[9]

Lyman stood next to Horne in championing the stations, convinced that this initial effort had saved many lives. But others on the board, including Emmeline Wells, viewed the expenditure of what they saw as the Society's sacred funds, to provide funding for the milk depots, as a diversion from their sanctioned task of building the gospel kingdom. For the time being, such objections carried the day.[10] In 1916, however, Lyman and other supporters of the depots presented their case so compellingly that the board appealed to the First Presidency for guidance. Seeing this as a useful opportunity for Christian service that also built bridges to the larger community, priesthood leaders not only granted their approval but even promised financial assistance from church revenues. For Lyman and like-minded women on the board, this was a real victory, albeit limited in scope as the depots directly involved only a handful of Relief Society women.[11] By this time, however, other public health activities were already drawing in growing numbers of the organization's members. In 1914 and 1915, for instance, the board urged cooperation with local and national "Swat the Fly" campaigns.[12] This created a link to the Civic Improvement League's effort to clean up Utah cities. In a related move, the board obtained fifteen thousand circulars from the State Board of Health on eye care for children. These were then mailed to Relief Society women along with the *Bulletin*.[13] Such moves accelerated a trend toward enhanced cooperation with non-Mormon agencies, women's associations, and civic groups concerned with public health. But for those, like Lyman, who had a vision of the Relief Society's full potential, this was not enough.

At this juncture, national efforts provided the ideal stimulus Relief Society modernizers needed to move the organization decisively forward. In May 1914 Congress passed the Smith-Lever Agricultural Extension Act that provided matching grants to states—an important innovation—to subsidize extension courses for farmers at agricultural colleges. Intensive lobbying by women of the National Home-Economics Association resulted in amendments to the bill that encouraged colleges to expand their existing home economics programs to include new extension work aimed at improving family health and nutrition.[14] Consequently, land grant colleges soon began to play a role in the dissemination of up-to-date information about healthy foods, proper cooking techniques, and the prevention of disease. With the enthusiastic support and cooperation of women's groups, agricultural extension agents organized informational "roundups," made presentations in local communities, and formed clubs to teach women and girls the skills of proper household management. All this provided a powerful if unlikely pathway toward female empowerment in community affairs.[15] The Relief Society's experience with Smith-Lever activities illustrate both its importance for women and its impact on public health.

For years, Mormon women had followed the developing home economics movement in the pages of the *Exponent* and watched as clubwomen, such as those in the Authors Club, successfully lobbied for its inclusion in high school curriculums. But passage of Smith-Lever moved the Relief Society from an observer to a participant in the movement, a development especially appealing and beneficial to younger women. The first step took place in the summer of 1915 when Utah State Agricultural College (USAC) president (and future apostle) John A. Widtsoe wrote Emmeline Wells to propose that the society adopt the home economics disciplines of home science, home art, and gardening in its standardized curriculum. In turn, he promised the college would send teachers and trained lecturers to its meetings to provide expert instruction. For Wells, eager to attract younger women into the organization, spicing up lessons with experts speaking on interesting topics must have seemed tempting. Yet, she hesitated, again constrained by concerns about straying from the proper role of the organization as well as the specter that such cooperation might lead to a loss of organizational autonomy and identity. This latter point was a matter of special import to Wells as church president Joseph F. Smith had made explicit his own concerns about this issue. Her wavering led Widtsoe to observe that, if the Relief Society was not interested, he might be forced to establish home economics clubs, as had been done elsewhere in the nation. This, of course, might have drawn younger women *away* from Relief Society activities rather than *toward* them. Widtsoe knew his correspondent well. Faced with such a choice, Wells accepted the plan.[16]

As this cooperation developed, first in Utah and then with state agricultural colleges in several western states, Jeannette Hyde, head of the Relief Society's home economics committee, and Lyman, a committee member, along with other Relief Society leaders were invited as delegates to the convention of the American Home Economics Association held at Cornell University. This trip, which allowed Amy to renew ties with friends and acquaintances in Ithaca, was a productive one: while there the Relief Society delegates listened to presentations on nutrition, health, clothing, housing, hygiene, and even promotion of the extension work. They contributed frequently to roundtable discussions and made important contacts with national leaders in the movement. In light of her recent homesteading experiences that had provided stark reminders of the need for up-to-date information on health and nutrition in rural areas, Lyman took an abiding interest in the work. But it was her close friend Hyde, already an experienced veteran of the movement, who was most outspoken in championing the cause and who took the lead in supervising Relief Society women in home economics activities. With the assistance of the USAC faculty and a broad assortment of government literature, Hyde soon had the women of the organization studying such topics as household management, health and nutrition, and the care and feeding of infants and children.[17] All of this information was of real benefit to women, not only in rural areas, but in growing urban communities as well. It also provided a further solution to the problem of declining membership: "The guide lessons are greatly enjoyed," Lyman reported in the *Magazine* in July, 1916, "and are bringing into the Society the young married women in the communities."[18]

In the nation's capital, leaders of the new Children's Bureau kept close watch on what was being accomplished through the Smith-Lever work and began to tailor programs of their own built on the concept Smith-Lever pioneered: namely federal sponsorship of health and nutrition work. Other than as a precedent-setting example of federal matching grant provisions, little scholarly attention has yet been given to the influence Smith-Lever had on the Children's Bureau.[19] Little noticed as well, those guiding the agricultural extension work were themselves influenced, in a reciprocal relationship, by the developing agenda of the Children's Bureau. As the Bureau's activities brought greater attention to the topics of maternal and infant health, administrators of Smith-Lever readjusted their own activities to address these new areas of concern. Consequently, the agricultural extension work eventually expanded to include sponsorship of so-called "well-baby clinics" that provided diagnostic care for infants and school-aged children. Smith-Lever thus played an extremely important role in anticipating later federal welfare efforts, even as it broke new ground for cooperation between government and private groups.

Despite the evident success of this growing home economics agenda, no doubt mindful of Joseph F. Smith's admonitions in this regard, Wells remained reluctant to broaden the society's cooperation with outside organizations, although at the request of local public health officials, the organization did participate in the Children's Bureau's "Day of the Child" in the spring of 1916.[20] Yet, her resistance could not prevent what had already become an inexorable shift toward greater interaction with other social work agencies. Lyman's own expanding involvement in social welfare matters helped drive this trend. In 1916, she was invited to join representatives of the city's private and public charities on the board of Salt Lake's Charity Organization Society (COS).[21]

The Charity Organization movement developed in the last decades of the nineteenth century to coordinate the activities of community charities with the goal of preventing wastage of scarce resources through duplication of aid. Much of the scholarship on the movement has focused on its early opposition to direct or "outdoor" relief (in favor of better controlled "indoor relief" administered in county poor houses or poor farms) and its efforts to separate the deserving poor (those destitute due to illness or misfortune that was no fault of their own) from the undeserving poor (paupers who were seen as victims of their own moral failings). However, by the time of Lyman's involvement, Salt Lake's Charity Organization Society, like others nationally, had broadened its approach to become a strong advocate for a full range of modern social work methods.[22] Lyman found the meetings of the COS especially beneficial because they provided her with detailed insight into the rising tide of social problems locally and the strategies used by other organizations to address them. In this setting she served as a liaison between the Relief Society and public and private welfare agencies in the community. As with the society's association with the National Council of Women, this interaction implied a certain acceptance and respect for the Relief Society even as it signaled the society's move further away from its strict focus on serving its own members and toward its greater involvement in issues affecting the entire community.[23]

No doubt because of such evidence of her growing prominence in social welfare matters, church leaders called Lyman to work under Apostle Stephen L. Richards in leading a new committee designed to address rising rates of vice and delinquency among LDS youth. The Social Advisory Committee, organized late in 1916 and staffed by representatives of the various church auxiliaries, sought to deal with rising social problems by developing a program of so-called preventative social work. Amy was a strong believer in approaches like these that included the elimination, where possible, of corruptive influences—at the time thought to include new modes of dress, dance, and music (she voiced at one point fears about the corruptive influences of jazz)—and the simultaneous creation of positive alternatives into which the energies of young people could be productively diverted. As part of its efforts, the committee produced a series of recommendations for the wards and stakes even as it worked with community and business leaders to address these issues.

In many ways, this represented a continuation of activities long pursued by the Relief Society and other auxiliaries in the church.[24] The committee's path also was strongly reminiscent of that laid out in previous decades by Protestant Social Gospelers who advocated vigorous youth programs such as those found in the Young Men's Christian Association, to counteract negative influences.[25] But rather than merely following well trodden paths, the Social Advisory Committee also formulated a more systematic and unified response to confront growing social ills. As it pressured recreation areas in the local community to provide wholesome environments for young people and worked to coordinate an aggressive program of youth activities in the wards and stakes, the committee also advocated educational measures, such as anti-tobacco and prohibition campaigns. In addition, recognizing that ignorance and curiosity often led young people into dangerous situations, it even lobbied for the adoption of a public school curriculum covering the fundamentals of sex education. As its agenda continued to broaden, the Social Advisory Committee eventually embraced all aspects of preventative social work and then turned its attention to remedial measures to deal with existing problems. Until its dissolution in 1922, Lyman found the committee a useful forum for the interchange of ideas with other church leaders and a valuable platform from which to coordinate her own growing social work agenda with those developing in the other auxiliaries.[26] Yet even as the Social Advisory Committee was in its formative stages, the First World War was propelling the Relief Society toward still greater involvement in social welfare work.

Like other Americans, most Utahns had been happy to steer clear of the conflict that was laying waste to a generation of European fighting men. In 1916, the state helped reelect Woodrow Wilson, the man who "kept us out of the war."[27] Progressives (including women's organizations) were especially happy to avoid the conflict they saw as a waste of manpower and resources. Yet only a few months later when the United States entered the war, American's (including Utahns) generally supported the move. Most progressives did as well, hoping for some domestic gains through wartime reform; even the majority of women's organizations were supportive. All joined together in response to Wilson's call to "make the world safe for democracy."[28]

With many of their number long involved in the international peace movement, like a significant portion of other American women, Relief Society leaders were somewhat reluctant to throw their support behind the war effort.[29] Ultimately, however, they gave in to their patriotism and joined the mainstream of American women, and even attained some national prominence in the process. The Relief Society's own Emily Richards, for example, held a position among "One Hundred Selected Women" that joined the National American Woman Suffrage Association's Carrie Chapman Catt in offering President Woodrow Wilson the services of two million members of their sex.[30] In joining in this national movement, Mormon women also aided both the larger cause of equal rights and furthered the ongoing quest for the acceptance of Latter-day Saints as loyal citizens. American participation in the conflict also brought Mormon women opportunities to bolster their sense of collective identity and to strengthen ties to the national community. As reported in the *Relief Society Magazine* the general board was "besieged with letters and inquiries" regarding possible participation by local Relief Societies in Red Cross activities. At Wells's direction, Relief Society leaders worked out plans for local units to contribute one week of Relief Society meetings in four to war work.[31] Relief Society women were soon rolling bandages, making bedding and hospital gowns, and collecting other items for troops at the front. Integration into the national service mainstream was furthered when Utah's governor appointed Clarissa Williams head of the Woman's Committee of the Utah Council of National Defense. Williams's special responsibility was to bring Mormon women on board. To help stimulate their participation she authored a monthly "Patriotic Department" for the *Magazine* and urged members to take nurses training classes, can fruit and vegetables from their home gardens, and give generously to bond drives. Women of the faith responded enthusiastically with impressive results.[32]

Reformers also saw opportunities in the war to promote improvements in maternal and infant health, a matter that proved of special interest to Lyman. In May 1917 the Children's Bureau sponsored a national "Baby Week" campaign to weigh and examine infants and young children across the nation; part of an effort to gain a more accurate picture of the unusually high rates of infant and maternal mortality that existed in the United States. Early studies by the bureau revealed that in 1916 more than sixteen thousand mothers died of complications of pregnancy or childbirth, a number that increased to twenty-three thousand in 1918. The infant death rate was even more striking: available statistics indicated that two hundred and fifty thousand died each year. All this in a nation where advice or trained care was received by only twenty percent of women. Among twenty nations where mortality statistics were available, the United States ranked seventeenth.[33]

Before the war, many had believed Americans were immune from the health problems of other industrialized nations and conservatives had portrayed the Bureau's proposals to improve the health of mothers and children as unnecessary and dangerous expansions of government. But with the onset of the conflict and the subsequent draft, reformers found a new tool to strengthen their case: the surprisingly high rejection rate of inductees, upwards of thirty percent, due to physical or mental disabilities. With Americans now dependent on the strength of their youth to maintain their security and that strength decidedly lacking due to poor health, Bureau officials saw an opportunity. Somewhat disingenuously (as Julia Lathrop and others in the bureau had hoped to avoid the war), they argued that the best way to ensure future security was to improve the physical well-being of the nation's children. Cleverly, they thus turned the quest for improved child health into a test of patriotism, a move that negated opposition and resulted in a new groundswell of support for this part of their agenda. Indeed, the work of the bureau soon became linked with that of the Council of National Defense.[34]

The cause of improving maternal and child health held great appeal for women of the Relief Society. Given her own family history in which she had witnessed the death of her youngest brother due to a ruptured appendix, that of an older sister as a result of complications arising from a childhood bout of rheumatic fever, and the loss of a half-sister because of illness brought on because of unsanitary conditions during the birth of her child, not to mention the long-term disability of her mother due to inadequate gynecological care, Lyman was especially interested in the cause. The same was true for Clarissa Williams, herself the mother of eleven children. The two formed a partnership to orchestrate the Society's full support for the Baby Week campaign. Williams asked stake and ward leaders to plan activities where "capable and enthusiastic speakers" provided parents with "intelligent and authentic advice with regard to the care of children."[35] Lyman gave such calls to action prominent attention in the *Magazine*, a practice she continued when the Bureau initiated the next phase of its agenda.

In April 1918, Julia Lathrop asked the Women's Committee of the Council of National Defense to begin an educational program as part of its Children's Year activities. Williams used her column in the *Magazine* to wholeheartedly endorse the work and showed herself as clever as the leaders of the Children's Bureau in linking this new initiative to larger causes. In particular, Williams noted the symbolic import for Mormons of the beginning date for the program: April 6, the anniversary of the church's organization. She then urged Relief Society women to support this new effort not only as a patriotic duty, but as a religious one as well.[36]

With such support at the highest levels, members of the organization in nearly every LDS community participated in a variety of Children's Year activities, especially the sponsorship of clinics where vital statistics of young children were gathered and information on maternal and infant health was distributed. Local branches also utilized Bureau pamphlets in educational work.[37] Like the earlier Smith-Lever activities, these new activities set an important precedent for future cooperation with government agencies. In conjunction with the Red Cross work, these projects also involved large numbers of LDS women, enhancing a sense of collective power for a growing proportion of the Relief Society's membership. But another aspect of Red Cross work, in which Lyman played the leading role, soon set the stage for even more impressive developments in the post-war period.

In the spring of 1917, federal officials asked the Red Cross to organize a corps of social workers to assist servicemen and their families with financial and emotional needs anticipated to arise due to American entry into the war. On the one hand, government leaders and social workers were concerned that the disruptions caused by the massive mobilization of troops would leave many families in disarray as wage earners and heads of households were called into national service. At the same time, they feared that post-war adjustments, particularly for disabled veterans, might overwhelm traditional family coping skills. In both these circumstances, social workers believed positive intervention might preserve the economic and emotional stability of families.[38]

Over the years, scholars have pointed out a number of benefits that grew out of these "Home Service" activities, as they came to be known. Perhaps most important was the part they played in helping to de-stigmatize family and child welfare work. In the public mind, the developing field of social work had previously been associated only with charity cases—a group often perceived as undeserving of assistance. Now, through this war-related effort, it became linked to the well-being of servicemen and their families, who, as a group, were widely viewed as "deserving." In consequence, the profession and the aid it rendered gained in stature. As social workers began to organize volunteers through the auspices of the Red Cross, the instructions they offered their recruits reveal how this de-stigmatization took place: "The work of civilian relief is not to be considered as charity," Lyman herself would record. Rather, it was "legitimate aid" to families who had given husbands or sons for the safety of the nation.

Some social workers objected to the plan because they feared its use of quickly trained lay volunteers would undermine the status and standards of the still emerging profession. But not seen by them at the time, and little noticed today, was the role this Red Cross work played as a catalyst for the expansion of modern social work practices and with it, higher standards. This was especially significant in places like Utah that previously had been isolated from modern currents in the profession.[39] Lyman's involvement in the administration of the Red Cross relief thus warrants close scrutiny, as it led to important changes not only in LDS charity efforts, but in public and private agencies in several Western states.

Her initiation into this aspect of Red Cross work began in June 1917 when, as a member of Utah's delegation, she joined volunteers and community leaders from across the nation in attendance at the annual meeting of the National Conference of Social Work held in Pittsburgh.[40] Red Cross leaders there announced plans for a series of regional conventions where volunteers were to receive training on the proper use of up-to-date social work techniques. Most important among these new methods was casework, the focus of which was not to render merely short-term aid, but to assist those in need to develop the skills and abilities that would enable them to become self-reliant. A pioneer of this approach was Mary Richmond.

Born in Illinois in 1861, but raised by relatives in Baltimore, Maryland, after being orphaned at an early age, Richmond represented an important strand in the fabric of Progressive reform. Working through the Charity Organization Society movement and then based at the Russell Sage Foundation, a pioneering think-tank for the study of social problems, for more than three decades Richmond had worked tirelessly to improve the effectiveness of her profession. She did so by convincing social workers to view their charges not as the undeserving poor out to cheat the system, but as "clients" in need of counseling and services to get back on their feet. By 1917, her methods, which had by then been largely accepted by her peers, were codified in her best-known book, *Social Diagnosis*, published that year. It laid out the process social workers were to follow in investigating the roots of dependency and clarified what resources, including medical and psychological care, were available to assist clients in developing their capacity to help themselves. It was she who had coined the term "Home Service," in reference to the Red Cross war work and it was she who, along with another noted social worker, Karl De Schweinitz, wrote the manuals used to teach basic techniques to Red Cross volunteers. Lyman became acquainted with both Richmond and De Schweinitz at subsequent meetings of the National Conference and relied heavily on their writings when developing her own social work philosophy.[41]

This Pittsburgh meeting marked a turning point in the development of social welfare work in Utah where public relief agencies, if they existed at all, were tiny, backward and inefficient. Even the LDS Church, which remained the dominant charitable organization in the state with programs and resources far more extensive than other private or public agencies, relied on an antiquated and increasingly inefficient system created in the territorial era.[42] Lyman's experience at the National Conference was no doubt representative of that of many of the delegates drawn by the Red Cross work. Often ignorant of developments in the profession when they arrived (or like her, simply eager to learn more about this rapidly changing field) by the time they left, most had become strong advocates for comprehensive training in modern methods. When Lyman returned to Utah she summed up such feelings when she told reporters: "I think delegations from all social institutions throughout the country should be sent to these yearly gatherings," and added, "there is so much good that can be obtained from the ideas put forth."[43]

Lyman made sure her time in Pittsburgh was put to the best possible use. In addition to attending as many sessions as possible related to the war effort and new social work practices, she managed to squeeze in a host of other activities, including visits to local Relief Society meetings. She also renewed her contacts with old friends of the society, most notably with radical feminist and reformer Charlotte Perkins Gilman. Gilman had a long acquaintance with Mormon women as a result of their mutual work in the suffrage struggle, and had grown to admire them. Gilman was a frequent visitor to Salt Lake City and Lyman had first met her there in 1912 at a reception in honor of the prominent activist hosted by the Relief Society. The two women subsequently met briefly several times. Now a featured speaker at the National Conference, when she was feted at a special dinner, Gilman invited Lyman as her special guest to accompany her.[44]

When Lyman returned home and reported her experiences to Relief Society and church leaders, she secured their support for the next phase of the Red Cross work. In late October, she traveled to Denver with Clarissa Williams and joined over five thousand delegates in a three-day seminar where they were given an overview of the

Home Service work.[45] At the conclusion of the seminar, Lyman returned only briefly to Salt Lake (where she left her husband in charge of domestic affairs—somewhat less demanding than before as their son Wendell was now nineteen and daughter Margaret fifteen), before returning to Denver where she joined a much smaller group that received six weeks of training at a "social service institute" hosted by the University of Colorado. Under the direction of the Denver Bureau of Charities and Corrections, the attendees were given academic instruction and mentored in actual fieldwork. In addition to Lyman, four other Utah delegates, three representing the Relief Society, were present.[46]

Directing this institute was Gertrude Vaile, who had headed the Denver Charities before her recent move to the leadership of civilian relief work in the Red Cross's Mountain Division. A graduate of Vassar and the Chicago School of Civics and Philanthropy as well as a veteran of the United Charities of Chicago and the Russell Sage Foundation, Vaile was well connected to the vanguard of the social work profession. Upon her arrival in Colorado five years previously, she had taken the unprecedented step of incorporating casework into the Denver Bureau, the first time any public charitable agency had adopted these modern methods. This accomplishment earned Vaile national prominence in social work circles. In 1916 she was asked to address the National Conference on her Denver activities; ten years later she rose to the presidency of the organization.[47] Florence Hutsinpillar, a protégé and friend of Vaile's, headed the Denver office after Vaile assumed her Red Cross responsibilities and, like her, worked closely with the volunteers.

The Utah women impressed both Vaile and Hutsinpillar with their seriousness and ability. Lyman, in particular, stood out. At this first session seeds were sown for a fast and long-lasting friendship between the three women, a friendship that would have important consequences for social work in Utah. In subsequent years as she developed the Relief Society's own social service agency Lyman repeatedly availed herself of the two women's advice and assistance.[48]

After the completion of their time in Denver, Lyman and the other Relief Society representatives returned to Salt Lake where they reported to church leaders. President Joseph F. Smith, in particular, displayed a keen interest in their work. This was not a recent development: before her trip to Denver Smith had given Amy a special blessing signifying that he considered her efforts a sacred trust.[49] As Lyman focused on her demanding new responsibilities as chair of the Family Consultation Committee of the Salt Lake Red Cross and supervisor for the work involving Latter-day Saint families, Smith followed her activities closely and made plans of his own.[50] In the middle of March he called her to his office and expressed his feelings that it was time to adopt the modern methods Lyman was using to the church's advantage. "If there was anything in the Church that needed improvement," Lyman recalled him observing, "it was the charity work." To bring this about, he offered to provide funding for a modern social service agency to be administered by Lyman through the auspices of the Relief Society.[51]

Smith's concerns were rooted in his recognition that the church's existing system of aid had become woefully inadequate in the increasingly urban environment of the West. Developed by Relief Society and priesthood leaders in small, relatively stable communities during Utah's territorial period, it was dependent upon local leaders' intimate knowledge of personalities and circumstances. As large numbers of Latter-day Saints migrated to urban areas in search of employment, such techniques were rendered impractical.[52] For these reasons, bishops and Relief Society presidents who ministered to increasing numbers of often transient newcomers with whom they were often unfamiliar, found it daunting to assist even the so-called "worthy members" especially given the limited amounts of cash and commodities available for the task. Such problems were particularly acute in Utah's three largest urban centers where in-migration was the heaviest: Salt Lake City, which by 1910 had swelled in population to nearly one hundred thousand, and Ogden and Provo, which between them counted around thirty-five thousand residents.[53]

Smith, well aware of these demographic changes and their ramifications, supported some of the cooperation that had already taken place with groups in the larger community to coordinate demands for aid.[54] But he was taken aback by an article in the nationally influential social work magazine, *The Survey*, that praised Salt Lake City's Mormon bishops for their willingness to turn to the local COS for routine investigations of families seeking aid and for assistance in counseling difficult cases.[55] Like others of the faith, Smith took pride in the church's heritage of self-reliance and was disturbed that local leaders had to look to outsiders for help in resolving confidential matters. If the bishops needed an agency to clear cases or deal with complicated situations, he felt that the church ought to provide it through the Relief Society.[56]

Though agreeing with Smith's assessment, Lyman, aware of her own lack of preparation, informed him she needed more training. In particular, she wanted to return to Denver for additional supervised work. Indeed, the idea of Lyman heading a social service department after just six weeks of formal instruction was the very thing many social work experts most feared might result as a consequence of the Red Cross Home Service work. But Lyman's response undercut their argument that the war work was thus counter-productive to their quest to raise the standards and prestige of the profession. Rather than simply shying away from the challenge, or worse yet, blundering in unprepared, Lyman recognized her weakness and saw the solution in further training.[57] If the Red Cross work had stimulated the desire of Joseph F. Smith to turn modern social work methods to the benefit of the church, it was Lyman, with this decision, who charted a course that led to ever-higher standards of proficiency.[58] On the national level, those behind the Home Service work had hoped that wartime upgrading of social services would leave a lasting legacy after the conflict was over. In the Relief Society's case, the decisions of Smith and Lyman ensured that this vision became reality.

As Lyman's activities with the Relief Society intensified, other developments were already complicating her life. In April 1918, two years after the death of his apostle father, Amy's husband Richard was called to fill an opening in the church's Quorum of the Twelve. Completely taken aback at this unexpected development, he gave up his position and most of his commitments at the University. At the advice of Joseph F. Smith, however, he continued his consulting work to help the church's bridge-building efforts with the larger community.[59] Now, in addition to professional obligations that continued to take him far afield, Richard assumed a schedule of church related travel even more intensive than Amy's. Though he remained supportive of her efforts, the couple's increasing responsibilities added significant strains to what was already, in essence, a two career family.

The Home Service work kept Amy preoccupied while she adjusted to these changes. In fact, the demands of Red Cross work soon grew to such an extent that another worker was employed to assist her. This was Beth Bradford, a young stenographer in the Relief

Society offices chosen because of her intelligence and interest in the work. Lyman and Bradford continued to divide their time between the Red Cross and the Relief Society offices, taking a small first step towards forming an independent social agency when they created a confidential registry of families receiving aid. They then used this record to coordinate their efforts with other charity agencies in the county to prevent duplication of aid, a process known as "clearing cases." Soon after her employment, Bradford was sent to Denver to receive training at a second social service institute; upon completion of the course, she accompanied Lyman to Kansas City, where the pair joined another large Utah delegation—including representatives of the Social Advisory Committee—attending the 1918 meeting of the National Conference of Social Work. There, they were appraised of the status of the war work and exposed to the reform agenda social workers expected to pursue in the post-war period.[60]

The following November, however, after renewed prodding from Smith, Lyman pulled herself away from her responsibilities to return to Denver for additional training.[61] By then, the worldwide flu epidemic of 1918, which cost more American lives than the war, had stricken several of the Denver workers and left the office seriously understaffed.[62] This misfortune worked to Lyman's advantage: Hutsinpillar gave her far greater responsibility than planned, including supervision of office and field work in one of the districts.[63] Impressed with Lyman's abilities, Hutsinpillar and Vaile judged her a "natural" whose intelligence and temperament allowed her to grasp the fundamentals of the work quickly. In their view, this talent more than compensated for her comparative lack of formal training. As a social worker, Lyman was to gain the reputation of being compassionate but clear-headed, an ability that enabled her to find the way to the root of any situation. Though she continued to learn and develop her technique, these weeks at Denver really marked the completion of her apprenticeship as she began to sense her readiness to carry out Smith's vision for Mormon charity work.[64]

Not long after her arrival in Denver, the belligerent powers signed the armistice that ended the First World War, an event that sent Salt Lakers, like other Americans, into the streets in celebration. But a week later these celebrations were muted among Latter-day Saints when Joseph F. Smith succumbed to influenza. With his passing, the plans he and Lyman had made for church charity work were called into question. Smith's successor, Heber J. Grant, was a successful businessman, who, as president, focused his attention on shoring up the shaky finances of the church. Under his leadership, all requests for funds were now subject to careful scrutiny, an approach that forced Lyman to scale back the plans she and Smith had made. Nevertheless, Grant gave permission for the unveiling of a more modest Social Service Department in January 1919 and, over time, proved a strong supporter of most of Lyman's efforts.[65]

Deteriorating economic conditions in Utah combined with a lack of public resources made the department's services more important by the day. Much of the nation experienced a comparatively short economic downturn in the postwar period, but like other Western states heavily dependent on mining and agriculture, Utah remained economically depressed throughout the decade of the 1920s. These conditions exacerbated already chronic unemployment created by streams of young people who left the countryside to compete for scarce jobs in the city.[66] For Lyman, this demographic shift meant a rapid and steady increase in her activities even as her responsibilities with civilian relief continued unabated after the war was over. Adding to her workload, the Social

Service Department soon took on additional commitments, including responsibility for LDS families at the Community Clinic, the Salt Lake County Charity Department, the county hospital, the city and county courts, the county jail, the police, the Salvation Army, the Traveler's Aid Society, and the YWCA. Other important services in these early years included an employment bureau and an adoption agency. This avalanche of demands on the department indicated not only a lack of public agencies in the area at the time, but also the inadequacy of previous church social welfare practices.[67]

To meet these needs, Lyman gradually increased the department's staff, eventually employing half a dozen caseworkers. This modest increase in personnel, however, continued to lag behind the accelerating pace of the department's workload. Making matters worse, the absence of large numbers of trained social workers in Utah forced Lyman to scramble to meet even these minimum staffing needs. Many of her early employees had some college education but, like Bradford, were otherwise qualified only by an interest in the field and a disposition compatible to the work. Lyman herself took responsibility for training these apprentices in the rudiments, but encouraged those with potential to seek additional education through more established channels. She drew upon her growing contacts among national social work leaders to bring this about. No doubt influenced by the advice of Vaile and Hutsinpillar, Lyman saw that her social workers followed a path that combined applied experience and formal study. For a profession still coming of age in standards and requirements, this was not unusual for the era. The experience of the department's first caseworker illustrates how this worked.

In October 1919, Lyman sent Bradford to New York City for an apprenticeship with the Red Cross. From there, assisted by a Red Cross scholarship, she attended the Boston School of Social Work for six months with the expectation that she would return to the Relief Society's employ at the conclusion of her study. Unfortunately for Lyman, in what was a very frustrating but not uncommon occurrence among the young Mormon women drawn to the department, once trained, Bradford married her fiancé who was an officer in the army, and departed with him to the Philippines, leaving behind her social work career.[68]

Despite such disappointments, Lyman trained other workers by following a similar course that mixed apprenticeships at social settlements like Lillian Wald's Henry Street Settlement or Mary Simkovitch's Greenwich House in New York City, with extended periods of study at such institutions as the New York School of Philanthropy and the School of Social Work at the University of Chicago.[69] Lyman's department benefitted tremendously from this exchange, while she contributed some of her own skilled workers, including a few who rose to prominence, to public and private agencies, not only in Utah and other western states, but even in New York City and Washington, D.C.[70]

As an administrator, Lyman was tough and demanding, one who sought the highest standards from her workers. Her sometimes brusque manner could be off-putting, and she was not one to beat around the bush when something was wrong: her social workers always knew exactly where they stood with her. Yet her employees often expressed not just admiration, but real affection for her, explained in large measure because of the unbridled concern she showed for them and for their personal development. She used her unusual powers of perception to sense their needs and potential; she challenged them all to do more than they thought they could, mothered those who needed it, and used her links to social work leaders to facilitate their growth.[71]

In addition to drawing upon her connections to nationally prominent reformers to facilitate the training of her workers, Lyman also drew upon such ties to rally support for the development of social welfare work both in the church and in the state.[72] She encouraged church and civic leaders to attend meetings of the National Conference of Social Work and orchestrated their visits to established social agencies where they could learn the benefits of properly organized social services. She also used her influence to motivate public officials to fulfill their legal obligations for welfare matters. In this regard she was later to note: "It has been the constant aim of the Relief Society to point out to the County its responsibility in caring for its indigent families."[73]

Lyman also sought to improve charity work not only at the central offices but also at the local level by immersing the Relief Society rank and file in the rudiments of modern social work. But here she met an impediment to her plans. Some on the general board strongly resisted the adoption of modern methods—in particular, the use of trained workers to provide skilled services in lieu of the informal aid and compassionate service of the kind long provided by women in Mormon communities. Foremost among the opposition was Susa Young Gates.

Gates, sixty-three in 1919, represented a formidable presence in the Relief Society offices beginning with her call to the board in 1913, not the least because her editorship of the *Relief Society Magazine* placed her in position to shape priorities and practices. That she was strong-willed was not unusual for members of the board (Lyman was certainly no shrinking violet by this time), but Gates could be extraordinarily determined and was accustomed to getting her own way. She was also known to be less than tactful. As general secretary, Lyman interacted regularly with Gates—who was at the senior end of Mormonism's second generation, while Lyman was at the junior end—and generally deferred to her. "Aunt Susie," as she was often called, had an office at one end of the Bishops Building, while Amy's was at the opposite. A long hallway that ran the length connected the two. When Gates wanted something from the general secretary she simply stepped out her door into the hallway and loudly called "Aimee!" as if she was summoning in the cows. At such times Lyman would trot down the hall, notebook in hand, to see what was needed. Outwardly, the women interacted well with one another and continued to do so even after they were privately locked in a determined struggle over the fate of the organization.[74]

At the heart of Gates's concerns was her fear that modernization would marginalize older women less able to adapt to the rigorous standards for delivering aid that Lyman was advocating. Somewhat ironically, in light of her earlier confrontation with Emmeline Wells over the standardized curriculum, Gates was also anxious that the spiritual side of the work would be lost in a quest for "scientific" expertise.[75] In voicing such concerns, Gates spoke not only for LDS women who might be adversely impacted by Lyman's plans, but for an entire generation of charity workers across the nation who saw themselves being pushed aside by the rising tide of professionalism.[76]

For Gates, an especially troubling development was an experiment in Utah Stake (which then included all of Utah Valley, located south of Salt Lake) that seemed to establish a precedent for the full professionalization of all church charity. In a move that revealed both the dearth of adequate public services and the still fluid lines separating church and state in the 1910s, stake Relief Society president, Inez Knight Allen—together with her counselor, Annie D. Palmer, a veteran of Home Service training at

Denver—organized a community welfare department. Following the lead of the Red Cross, they established an institute for sixty stake and ward charity workers and gathered commodities and funds that, with the aid of local bishops and Relief Society women, they distributed to both Mormon and non-Mormon families in need.[77]

The Relief Society General Board encouraged the Utah Stake effort, as did local and general priesthood leaders, and all followed its progress closely. If this experiment had been taken as a prototype for future LDS charity work, it would have represented a realization of Gates's worst fears. In light of these threats to the status quo, she worked tirelessly behind the scenes to prevent the Utah Stake experience from serving as a template for further innovation. Adding to her alarm was an address delivered by Lyman in November 1919 to the Colorado Conference of Social Work on the topic "Permeating an Established Relief Agency with Modern Case Work Methods."[78] Though advised to let the matter alone by first counselor Clarissa Williams, who was by then handling many of the day to day affairs of the Relief Society due to Emmeline B. Wells's declining health, Gates attempted repeatedly to sway both the general board and the president of the church to her view and even went so far as to solicit support for her position from prominent figures involved in charity work nationally.

Seeking to resolve this brewing conflict before it completely boiled over, Williams called a special committee of the general board to look into the matter. When this committee failed to find a resolution, Williams referred the dispute to President Grant.[79] The meeting with Grant must have been memorable. Lyman was convinced of the superiority of her plans and believed further that she was carrying out the commission of the late Joseph F. Smith. Gates was equally sure that she was saving the soul of the Relief Society by holding on to its traditional methods. Unable to resolve the conflict, Grant sent Lyman and Gates back to the board, where the matter was left to cool.[80] Whether the two women ever worked out a formal compromise is unclear, but the Utah Stake example was not followed by the entire church. Perhaps this was due to Gates's concerns, but there were doubtless practical and philosophical reasons as well, relating to financing and questions of church-state separation.[81] What Relief Society leaders developed instead relied on professionals only to provide specialized services on a limited basis, primarily for assistance of the Salt Lake stakes. But this compromise hardly represented an unqualified victory for Gates. With the support of the majority of the board, Lyman organized a program to train several women in each stake in the fundamentals of modern social work technique and to prepare them to recognize when the resources of a central agency were required. At the same time, the board commissioned a set of lessons that appeared in the *Relief Society Magazine* as part of the standardized curriculum that provided an introduction to the basic aims and methods of social welfare work. Meanwhile, Williams, Lyman, and others presided over extensive discussions of social work topics at Relief Society conferences. In October 1919 for example, Lyman delivered "a scholarly and exhaustive talk," in which she defined terms such as casework and explained the value of preventative and corrective social work. In the same address she emphasized the need to strike at the roots of dependency through reform in the larger society.[82]

As moves to carry these plans forward began to take shape, Gates could do little more than watch with dismay. All this she came to see as steps along a path leading to her own marginalization. She reached a breaking point when Lyman's authority was extended to the *Magazine* and Gates, as editor, was required to submit all articles and copy either to Lyman or Williams for their approval. In the fall of 1921, Gates submitted her resignation as a member of the Relief Society board to Heber J. Grant and told him to use it when he felt best. She was released early in 1922 although her interest—and involvement—in the affairs of the Relief Society did not end.[83]

By that time Lyman had already held what was to be the first of many of her own social service institutes. It took place in 1920 during a six-week summer session at Brigham Young University. The summer school was part of a church-wide effort to improve the training for leaders of church auxiliaries. Sessions included course work in such areas as social and recreational leadership, teacher training, and, most important from Lyman's perspective, charity and relief work.[84] Representatives from sixty-five stakes attended the latter sessions that Lyman supervised. The curriculum included readings and lectures on sociology supplemented by field trips to the state mental hospital, the state industrial school, the Salt Lake Community Clinic, Salt Lake City's own social settlement (Neighborhood House), and the Salt Lake County Hospital and Infirmary.[85] As a highlight, Lyman arranged for a series of lectures by nationally prominent social worker and reformer Edward T. Devine, whom she had met at the previous year's meeting of the National Conference of Social Work. In what proved only one among several visits to assist Lyman with her training activities, Devine drew his lectures from his book, *The Normal Life*, a popular volume written in highly accessible style that Lyman felt ideally suited for initiating the rank and file into the rudiments of the work.[86]

More such institutes were held in coming years. By 1928 forty-three, ranging from two days to six weeks, had been convened in communities throughout Utah and Idaho, where over twenty-nine hundred students were introduced to the practical application of the case work method. Because of the Relief Society's need for the informed support of bishops and stake presidents in carrying forward this work, Lyman saw that local priesthood leaders were invited to these institutes as well.[87] The "social service aids," as graduates of these institutes came to be called, represented a veritable army of paraprofessionals devoted to advancing Relief Society charitable work. Upon their return home they continued to study methodology while gaining first-hand experience in the field. They also organized their own institutes where they taught the rank and file what they had learned. The general board supplemented these local measures with an impressive array of lessons and articles treating such topics as health and nutrition, public education, family life, and delinquency. Relief Society leaders encouraged women to use the methods taught when managing problems within their own homes and when seeking to improve conditions in their communities.[88]

In consequence of this wide-ranging program to modernize charity work, for the first time since the run-up to statehood the full resources of the Relief Society were again directed at a common task. The results were spectacular. Though all were certainly not experts, a large share of the vast body of the organization became well-informed advocates of modern social work techniques, not only in the church, but in the community at large. As a result, Relief Society women began again to exercise noticeable influence in the affairs of their towns and cities.

A noticeable spike in membership growth during these years testifies to the appeal these programs had for younger women. And, as word of the Relief Society's accomplishments in social welfare work was passed along by such figures as Devine and Vaile, its activities drew the attention and praise of national social work leaders. In July 1921, an editor of *The Survey* even invited Lyman to report on Relief Society activities for the journal—something she undoubtedly found a matter of great satisfaction.[89] But more important to her was the realization that she was creating a corps of women armed with the tools to significantly improve the lives of individuals in communities throughout the Intermountain West. Commenting in Relief Society conference on the growing assertiveness that resulted from this heightened consciousness of social issues, Clarissa Williams noted that reports were indicating that "Relief Society women everywhere are being regarded as powers in the local communities, as is proper they should be."[90] At a time when other American women in clubs and associations were organizing to improve conditions in their communities and across the nation, Mormon women thus represented an especially cohesive and powerful force.

Also impressive was the way the Relief Society was able to do something most women reformers were not able to do—namely, bridge the chasm between charity volunteers and professional social workers. While a few, like Susa Gates, remained unreconciled to change, most women of the faith found a role in the new system. Those skilled in spiritually oriented compassionate service were not marginalized but utilized in cases of temporary hardship. Furthermore, they were trained to know when to draw upon the services of professionals and trained paraprofessionals who were able to assist in more difficult cases. As a result of this broad and multilevel participation in social welfare work, the needs of the community were met more effectively than either a professional agency (with its limited staff and funding) or a lay volunteer force could have managed alone.

While all this was occurring in the realm of social work, there were several other competitors for Lyman's time and energies. One was her growing association with national women's organizations, in particular, the National Council of Women. Through a developing friendship with Eva Perry Moore, head of the National Federation of Women's clubs, and then president of the Council, over the next decade Lyman found herself shepherded into positions of leadership in the National Council. She served first as recording secretary, then auditor, and finally as third vice-president.[91]

Changes in the Relief Society leadership brought Lyman more responsibilities as well. By 1921, the ninety-three-year-old Emmeline B. Wells was increasingly disengaged from the daily affairs of the organization.[92] In declining vitality, for some time her main contribution to the Relief Society conferences had been her simple but fervent testimony of Joseph Smith and the gospel restoration. Yet, as her predecessors in office had served for life, Wells soldiered on, to the despair of some on the board who felt she was holding the organization back.[93] Aware of these frustrations, in March 1921, Heber J. Grant stepped in and notified Wells that he had decided to honorably release her from her duties as Relief Society president. Wells was devastated and in a pathetic scene tried to change Grant's mind by reciting the history of the Relief Society from its beginnings.[94] However, he would not be swayed and Wells's release was announced at the Relief Society conference a few days later, with first counselor Clarissa Williams named as her successor. The aged former president failed rapidly thereafter and died, heartbroken, before month's end. Her passing severed one of the last remaining bonds to the Relief Society's origins in Nauvoo, and, less evident at the time, signaled a further step toward the diminished autonomy of the organization. Never again would a Relief

Society president enjoy, like the apostles and church president, life-long tenure at the helm of the organization. It is indeed ironic that Wells who had worked so hard to preserve the authority of the Relief Society should end her service in a manner that weakened it. A similar irony lies in the fact that the desires of younger women to strengthen the organization instead weakened the independence it enjoyed within the larger church organization.

In contrast to the diminutive and somewhat pessimistic Wells, her successor Clarissa Williams, now sixty-two, was a physically large woman, known for her compassion and optimism. This daughter of Mormon leader George A. Smith was seen by her peers as possessing the wisdom and perspective gained through two decades of service on the general board and as the mother of a large family. As leader she lost no time changing the course of the Relief Society, clearing the way for rapid change by replacing older members of the board and further revealing her generational outlook by referring to the organization as the "club of the Church."[95] One of her most significant innovations came when she placed Lyman in charge of the day-to-day affairs of the organization, granting her additional responsibilities and unprecedented authority. Lyman, according to Williams was now to be "'directing manager' of all activities and departments" and was to be considered a third counselor rather than just general secretary of the organization.[96]

Williams's move, though revolutionary in terms of administrative practice, was a logical step. Lyman had grown into a self-confident, well informed, and well connected leader even as she took a preeminent role in overseeing the increasingly complex agenda of the organization. In her new capacity she continued to cultivate close ties with local Relief Society leaders who admired her now impressive abilities. No one had a surer hand on the pulse of the organization than she.

By 1921, most of the questions that had confronted Relief Society at the time Lyman joined the board had been answered. While women of the society had maintained their own identity and religious focus, they had begun to work with other reform-minded groups and had accepted significant portions of the progressive agenda as their own. In so doing, they reshaped their relationship to their communities and accomplished long-standing tasks in new ways. In this manner, they became acknowledged players in the mainstream of social welfare work and community betterment and gained for themselves a renewed sense of their collective power and potential. While all this was occurring, Lyman had developed a clear vision for the future of the society. Armed with the full confidence of the new president—and her own natural tenacity—she would not be easily deterred from pursuing it. In 1921, with the unwavering support of Williams and other like-minded women on the board, Lyman was poised to guide the Relief Society through one of the most dynamic periods in its history.

5

SAVING MOTHERS AND CHILDREN

> You may ask, "Would not the men . . . have done the same?" I shall only answer you by asking: "Have they done it in the past?"
>
> —JEANNETTE HYDE[1]

> Self preservation is basic and fundamental, and it is only to be expected that women, especially, will be interested in working for those things which tend to the preservation of their own lives.
>
> —AMY BROWN LYMAN[2]

Like other progressives, Lyman had hoped that wartime measures addressing social problems would be carried on or expanded in the postwar era. As she noted with apparent approval in the *Relief Society Magazine* in 1918, a division of the National Conference of Social Work went so far as to present an ambitious list of priorities for future federal legislation that included a minimum wage, health insurance, unemployment benefits, and tax policies that would lead to greater funding of social programs. But rather than continued progress, the gains made during the war disappeared in a conservative backlash initiated by businessmen and politicians eager to cast off government regulation. This took place in the context of a fear of anything smelling of radicalism that swept across the nation during the so-called Red Scare that followed the Russian Revolution. However, after seventy years of organized struggle, in August 1920 the Nineteenth Amendment to the constitution was ratified, which granted all American women the franchise. With women wielding new power at the ballot box, not surprisingly, politicians became more sympathetic to matters thought especially important to them. In unison with their sisters across the nation, Utah women used this (all too brief) period of respect for their electoral clout to initiate a new era of political activism that lasted throughout much of the 1920s.[3] Standing, as she did, in the forefront of the reforms of the time, the decade produced important opportunities for Lyman, making it the most productive of her career. One such opportunity came in recognition of Lyman's growing expertise in social welfare work.

By 1921, Utah faced a number of serious social welfare problems and was one of only three states nationally without a permanent welfare board directing its charitable activities. At that time, Governor Charles R. Mabey appointed a twelve-member commission to review public welfare needs and make recommendations for further action. Perhaps motivated as much by the desire to ingratiate himself with the female electorate as by her qualifications, Mabey named Lyman vice-chair.[4] After a lengthy investigative period looking into the needs of Utah's population, the commission presented its findings that included recommendations for several new state agencies to serve the indigent and disabled. Among the most pressing items on the commission's agenda was its desire to improve funding for the state board of health to facilitate its cooperation with new federal measures aimed at reducing rates of infant and maternal mortality in the United States.[5]

As they had with the earlier Children's Week and Children's Year activities, the women of the Relief Society had followed with interest the development of these federal programs that had been initiated by Children's Bureau chiefs Julia Lathrop and her successor, Grace Abbott. Early in 1921 the efforts of Lathrop and Abbott came to fruition when Congress, mindful of the female vote, passed the Federal Maternity and Infancy Act. Better known as the Sheppard-Towner Act, this measure, which provided matching grants to the states to support educational work and the establishment of clinics for the benefit of expectant mothers and young children, came to stand nearly alone as a beacon of progressive achievement in the 1920s.[6]

After passage of the Nineteenth Amendment, as had been the case in Utah after women regained the franchise with statehood, national political leaders not only sought to draw women to their party standards through their support of maternalist legislation, but also by inviting women into the highest reaches of the party apparatus. Democrats and Republicans both took this course and two of Amy's closest friends were among the elite, if token, few. Alice Louise Reynolds, an active party worker, was named a member of the Democratic National Committee and in 1920 gave seconding speeches for the presidential and vice presidential nominees at the party's convention in San Francisco. Jeannette Acord Hyde, a long-time Republican activist, served as secretary of her party's Chicago convention then joined the delegation traveling to Ohio to inform Warren G. Harding of his nomination. In an aside, Hyde, like Lyman, strong-willed and opinionated, gained attention at this time in Eastern papers because of her finesse (and firmness) in dealing with another female delegate with anti-Mormon views.[7]

The account of the episode recounted in the *New York Sun* and copied in the *Relief Society Magazine* in August 1920, is worth repeating at length because of what it reveals about the ongoing prejudices with which Mormon women were confronted, and also captures the strength of intellect and personality that characterized members of the Relief Society General Board, and in particular, Lyman's close friend. "A most interesting event occurred in the private committee meeting held of all of the women delegates to the convention," the *Sun* account began. As measures and resolutions were proposed "suddenly Mrs. Hyde was made the subject of an attack by Mrs. Emma Bush, [a delegate from Michigan] in connection with the resolution brought forward . . . denouncing

'Mormonism,' Senator Smoot, etc., etc., and calling for an order in the convention which would prevent any 'Mormon' from taking part therein." The chair of the session, Mary Garrett Hays, then called on Hyde to answer the charge while "expressing [Hays's] own admiration at the same time for 'Mormon' women and for Mrs. Hyde in particular." "Instantly," the account continued, "the delegate from Michigan was on her feet" and then "sharply" asked Hyde: "Do you believe in polygamy?" Hyde replied: "Yes, I most certainly do." This created a "hubbub," which Hays quickly quieted. Bush then repeated her question and Hyde repeated her answer, "frankly and without reservations except the explanation that the principle is not practiced today nor has been since the issuance of the manifesto, in 1893 [sic]." Hyde then continued on by "explaining that she supposed the gathering was a political one and not a religious one." "She did not feel called upon," she further explained, "to inquire if any of the women believed in the signs and crosses of the Catholic faith, nor Christian Science, nor any other religion, but left every woman to worship as she pleased." Instead, she felt "that a common ground for all good will be found in the principles of freedom upon which this government was founded." The account concluded by noting that "Mrs. Hyde's independent and frank reply won instant admiration of all members present and she was showered with social attentions all the time she was in Chicago." Back home, her Relief Society sisters took pride in her spirited defense of their faith as well.[8]

Meanwhile, state and local party leaders sought out women willing to run as candidates for office, a development with important consequences for Lyman. Though her father had sided with the Democrats, since her marriage to Richard, Amy had been a staunch Republican. In September 1922, Jeannette Hyde approached her about allowing her name to be submitted to the party caucus for nomination to the legislature. Having never envisioned herself as a candidate, Lyman was flattered but also anxious about running. However, she was mindful that as a legislator she might be able to further the cause of social welfare work, in particular, by pushing through enabling legislation accepting matching-grant provisions of the Sheppard-Towner Act. Easily gaining the nomination, she soon learned the responsibilities incumbent upon her as a candidate; in particular, she was expected to go wherever sent "both early and late in the day, to speak before political meetings." This she found very difficult, especially when she discovered she "was expected to point out the virtues of one party and the weaknesses of the other and to answer questions and arguments of all sorts."

Not comfortable with the normal "rough and tumble" of a political campaign and feeling herself "not very well informed with respect to politics and political procedures," or, for that matter, the main issues of the race, Lyman decided to talk about something she *did* know about: "I decided," she recounted, "to talk mostly about women." She noted, practically, that leadership was always in short supply, and in the wake of the increase of that supply with the emancipation of women, "we should look among women's groups for new leaders, especially in certain fields." In further making the case for women in political office, she then succinctly expressed the case for maternalist reform. Due to their experience as mothers and homemakers, "women are a great asset to any humanitarian cause because they have a special and different viewpoint." Women are particularly needed in legislative bodies "because of their special knowledge of human needs and humanistic rights." Because of the need of men to provide for their families, they are naturally interested in "lands, mines, flocks, herds, property ownership and rights and property protection." Women, she argued, are different. They "are inclined to think more about education, health, recreation, morals, and character." In addition, she continued, "most of the social legislation of late years had behind it the influence of the mothers of the nation, and therefore legislative bodies should not be made up entirely of men; that there should be enough women to foster and secure necessary humanitarian and social action."[9]

Her arguments must have been convincing as she won handily in the general election and, as Republicans controlled the statehouse, at the onset of the 1923 legislative session was appointed chair of the public welfare and education committees. Lyman did not particularly enjoy her time in the statehouse and would decide not to seek a second term; especially galling to her were the pressure tactics and outright dishonesty of lobbyists—one of whom offered her a bribe. Lyman was particularly upset about lobbyists from the mining industry who threatened massive job losses in the state if desired legislation was not passed. Again showing her mettle, she faced them down and urged fellow legislators to ignore their tactics.[10] Her steadfast honesty and refusal to be intimidated earned the respect of her peers. She was also highly effective. She introduced several public health measures, as well as a measure to help secure pensions for the faculty of the University of Utah and the Utah State Agricultural College. And, as she had hoped, she played a key role in facilitating the passage of the enabling act accepting the provisions of the Sheppard-Towner Act.[11]

Her growing prominence in community affairs and social work activities also brought her attention in other venues, including the National Council of Women, where she had remained involved and a regular attendee at its biennial conventions and regular board meetings representing the Relief Society. At its biennial meeting in the fall of 1923 held in Decatur, Illinois, Lyman was asked to deliver an address on the citizenship work of the Relief Society. She recounted the organization's recent course of study that had been prepared by Dr. Arthur Beeley at the University of Utah. Its lessons on citizenship dealt with everything from recent proposed and enacted legislation—locally and nationally—to issues such as public health, child labor, and immigration. "The result of the course was a great awakening in all phases of community and public welfare," she observed, that "inspired the members of the organization and community to greater activity," while shaping public opinion. Indeed, Lyman also reported that as a member of the legislature she had found that Relief Society women trained by these lessons were vital in creating public sentiment throughout the state that resulted in the passage of a number of important measures, including, especially, the Sheppard-Towner Act. "I had the great honor of introducing the provision for the acceptance of the national Sheppard-Towner act, which passed both houses without a dissenting vote," she reported with pride. She noted further her belief that Utah's state legislature was the only one completely united behind the measure, a fact she implicitly attributed to the work of the Relief Society.[12]

Lyman's own efforts in behalf of Sheppard-Towner, in combination with the lobbying work of Relief Society women, thus ensured that Utah joined an important national experiment: For the first time federal monies were parceled out to the states explicitly for social welfare work. In particular, these funds were intended to address the unusually high rates of maternal and infant mortality in the United States—the highest in any industrialized nation of the time. Though it moved far beyond the Smith-Lever Act, like aspects of that measure, it subsidized educational programs that covered nutrition and health care for mothers and children and provided support for clinics where infants and young children could be screened for health problems. And by using matching-grant provisions similar to those of Smith-Lever, Sheppard-Towner stimulated cooperation between the federal government and the states, and, further, between charitable organizations and public agencies at all levels.[13]

The pages of the *Relief Society Magazine* charted the progress of Sheppard-Towner as it moved through Congress and toward implementation at the state level. None in the organization watched these developments more closely than Lyman and Clarissa Williams, both of whom knew through experience the dangers inadequate medical care posed to expectant mothers and young children. Anticipating ultimate victory for the measure, the pair did not wait to make plans to intensify the Relief Society's own involvement in maternity and infancy work. Specifically, they sought to address the lack of access to quality medical care, especially in childbirth, experienced by many women in both urban and rural areas. Even before Sheppard-Towner passed through Congress, they secured the permission of the First Presidency to use Relief Society monies for an experimental move to fund a maternity home in Salt Lake City. At a subsequent meeting of the general board, Lyman expressed hope that this be considered the first step in "a movement in the interest of maternity and motherhood throughout the Church."[14] Members of the board were united in their support for the idea. From this time forward, Lyman added the supervision of this new child welfare work to her growing list of responsibilities.

In the October conference of 1921, a month before Sheppard-Towner was signed into law, Williams announced that the general board desired "to inaugurate a movement throughout the Church in the interest of maternity and motherhood." She then introduced tentative plans for "some form of maternity nursing service for the rural communities." According to Lyman's records of the conference, the stake leaders in attendance heartily favored this step and responded by recounting "the great needs in the various communities for just such help as this would supply."[15] By the following April, general Relief Society leaders were poised to move forward with their program as they eagerly waited for the act's enabling legislation to make its way through the 1923 legislature allowing them to begin cooperative work with the state and federal governments.[16]

To fund their own efforts, the society's leaders found a surprising source: the long-running wheat storage program. From the program's beginnings in the 1870s, the Relief Society continued to gather and store grain until 1919 when church leaders sold the wheat (without the Relief Society's knowledge or permission) to the government to alleviate the post-war famine in Europe. The money received in payment was held for the organization in a separate account by the Presiding Bishopric's Office. Now, the board proposed the interest on the account be used, under its supervision, to supplement local revenues in carrying forward maternity work.[17] As Sheppard-Towner's direct federal funding for social welfare activities denoted a milestone for the welfare state, so the use of the wheat interest to support local projects was a turning point for the Relief Society, facilitating activities previously too expensive for wards and stakes to manage themselves. On the other hand, by maintaining control over disbursement of the interest, the general board further tightened its hold over local units, thus accelerating the process of centralization with all its pros and cons.

In a similar fashion, Sheppard-Towner represented—albeit modestly by today's standards—a significant expansion of federal authority. Intensive lobbying on the part of organized women had played an important role in the creation of the Children's Bureau and had been similarly important in the passage of Sheppard-Towner. It is somewhat ironic then, that the legislation resulted in diminished influence for lay women in social welfare matters. Historians and political scientists have argued that the Children's Bureau's maternity and infancy work was the opening wedge for a larger agenda advocated by professional social workers to build a comprehensive system of social services in the United States—what is referred to by scholars as the welfare state. Sheppard-Towner served these ends, not only by creating rudimentary programs to address a major area of concern—the well-being of mothers and children—but also by requiring states to possess a minimum apparatus of public services in order to receive federal funds. At the same time the act expanded public control by placing private agencies cooperating in its sponsored activities under the supervision of these same state agencies. In each of the forty-five states that participated, private and volunteer agencies such as women's clubs, the Parent-Teacher Associations, the Red Cross, and in Utah's case, especially the Relief Society, were invited to join in the maternity and infancy work, but only if they agreed to work under the supervision of their state divisions of child hygiene. This development, thought necessary in order to insure the highest standards for the maternity and infancy work and ensure efficient use of resources, resulted in a corresponding reduction of influence for women's organizations as independent actors, even as the public sector grew in strength.[18]

It was years before these implications became clear, however. In the meantime, the energies of Relief Society women were focused on the task before them. Long before the first Sheppard-Towner funds reached Utah, Lyman and Williams were shaping the organization into a more effective vehicle for improving infant and maternal health. This became the primary focus of general and stake conferences and, on occasion, all but crowded out discussion of religious themes. Similarly, the pages of the *Relief Society Magazine*, which already highlighted social welfare work, began to feature articles and lessons on such Sheppard-Towner related topics as nutrition and breast feeding. Given the varied conditions in Mormon communities, Williams and Lyman were reluctant to mandate a standardized program for the wards and instead encouraged local women to develop a wide range of responses to their needs. But, reflective of concerns on the national level, to ensure the effective use of funds and resources they asked stake and ward leaders to submit their plans to the board for approval.[19] As these local efforts developed, Lyman gave them exhaustive coverage in her "Notes from the Field" column and highlighted them in conference reports in the *Magazine*. In this manner she sought to ensure that every possible strategy to improve the health of mothers and children was brought to the attention of the rank and file.[20] Working with its new editor, Lyman's old friend Alice Louise Reynolds, Lyman thus transformed the *Magazine* into a clearing house for information and ideas related to maternity and infancy activities.

Local Relief Society women eagerly took up the task. In comparatively affluent areas closer to the urban core, more elaborate projects were put in place. In Cottonwood Stake, south of Salt Lake City, Relief Society president Amanda Bagley was already known as a leader in maternity work, having been one of the first to organize health lectures under Smith-Lever. Now, she was selected by the general board to carry out its plan to establish a maternity home. In 1922, using general funds, she purchased a large home and converted it for use as a maternity hospital where, for $40, women could receive up to two weeks of care. In its first year of operation, over one hundred patients utilized its services. In the wake of this success, others sought to follow Cottonwood's lead. In addition to providing maternity care, Cottonwood's facilities operated clinics for pregnant women and young children and dispensed advice on health and nutrition.[21]

While leaders in urban areas in Utah were better able to carry out more elaborate measures such as these, Relief Society women in rural districts throughout the state and in nearby areas of Nevada, Idaho, and Arizona, had far fewer resources to draw upon. For them, securing the aid of doctors or even trained nurses was exceedingly difficult, while raising funds sufficient to establish a maternity home was impossible.[22] Significantly, one of the goals of Sheppard-Towner's framers was to reach into just such locales where the need for information and aid was greatest.[23] This became a priority for Relief Society leaders as well. "We hear reports of lamentable conditions in the outlying communities which are far removed from medical help," Williams noted in the 1922 October conference, adding, "We hope that we will be able to alleviate some of this suffering and distress."[24]

With the encouragement of the general board, projects within reach of even the poorest of regions were taken up by local societies to attack the gravest threats to mothers and children. In counties too poor to support a health department or even a public health nurse, Relief Society leaders sought to aid women by sponsoring itinerant health conferences organized in cooperation with the state board of health under Sheppard-Towner auspices.[25] Preventative measures were also adopted: as elsewhere, infection caused by unsanitary conditions during childbirth—the condition known as puerperal fever that had taken the life of Amy's half-sister so many years before—was still the largest single cause of maternal mortality in the nation. To facilitate a clean, safe, environment for women in areas without access to hospitals or maternity homes, the general board urged local societies to stockpile sterile bedding and instruments necessary for safe childbirth. The *Magazine* carried plans for maternity closets that could be set up in Relief Society halls where such items could be stored, along with lists of instruments to be included and instructions, which Lyman secured from the state board of health, for proper sterilization techniques. Local societies provided these supplies at minimal or no cost to those in need who then returned them for re-sterilization and reuse.

Within a few years, Relief Society women had stocked such closets in nearly every community in Utah. Physicians serving rural areas discovered that these supplies met "their every need," and, as Lyman recorded in her "Notes" column, some even required their maternity patients have them at the ready for their delivery.[26] While most beneficial in sparsely settled districts, they also proved useful to physicians in larger towns. Of the 163 maternity cases reported in Brigham City between January and November, 1924, for example, 75 used Relief Society maternity bundles.[27]

Julia Lathrop, Grace Abbott, and other backers of Sheppard-Towner had been convinced that relatively simple measures could work a revolution in infant and maternal health in America. Through local initiatives such as these maternity closets, Relief Society women working under the direction of the general board began to bring this vision to reality. Yet this marked only the beginning of the society's contribution. Such volunteer efforts remained essential to states like Utah and its neighbors that lacked the resources to address fundamental heath care needs in a comprehensive manner, even with Sheppard-Towner monies. States such as Pennsylvania and New York, on the other hand, already possessed rudimentary systems of public health. Coupled with their larger populations, which brought a proportionately larger share of Sheppard-Towner funds, much of the maternity and infancy work in these areas could be managed by state employees alone.[28] But in Utah's case, a small population made it eligible for a maximum of only $13,000 annually in federal funds. Its small tax base also meant that state and local initiatives to provide public health services were necessarily limited.[29] For this reason, the volunteer work of the Relief Society proved absolutely critical to Sheppard-Towner's success.

State officials in Utah involved in Sheppard-Towner's administration came to rely on local Relief Society volunteers to perform a number of tasks, including the organization of conferences. These women arranged for locations, often in schools where mothers and children could be examined and counseled, and did the necessary publicity and preparations to make sure clinics and classes ran smoothly. Utah's relatively small cadre of state workers especially valued these Relief Society volunteers because they grasped the work quickly—perhaps due to their studies of related issues in their educational curriculum. Inasmuch as these volunteers were also well acquainted with local women, including their fears and prejudices, they were able to explain effectively matters of concern to those in attendance. In fact, understaffed and stretched thin themselves, state-employed public health nurses soon learned that with a little additional training Relief Society women could be counted on to run conferences even in the absence of paid professionals.[30]

Relief Society women also helped address many of the health problems discovered at these conferences. Children during this period routinely confronted a variety of debilitating or life-threatening diseases. Some, like diphtheria or smallpox, could be prevented through vaccination; others, like goiter or rickets, cured with proper diet. Often, problems like poor vision were not as debilitating if diagnosed and treated in a timely manner. When attending physicians or nurses spotted such maladies, Relief Society women worked to see that follow-up treatment was provided and even helped with financial arrangements when necessary. In addition, they kept records of examinations and gave "health talks" stressing nutrition, hygiene, and vaccination. State officials deemed their contributions extremely valuable as they allowed them to make the most of limited resources and freed public health nurses to develop follow-up work in selected areas.[31]

Even before Sheppard-Towner monies became available, the pioneering Cottonwood Stake under President Amanda Bagely's direction, and under the watchful eye of Lyman and the board, took the lead to demonstrate what could be accomplished through such cooperative work. In January 1922, Cottonwood's Relief Society women secured the services of an assistant county physician and began holding a weekly clinic. The following year, after their affiliation with the state board of health under the new federal provisions, they received literature on pre-natal, infant, and child care, which they then distributed to prospective mothers in their locality. Representatives of the state board assisted their efforts as they provided training to Relief Society officers and made periodic visits to the clinic themselves. Cottonwood Stake women also secured the support of the examining physician of the Salt Lake City Board of Education, and through him, a school nurse. In addition, eight local physicians volunteered their time, in pairs, for three month rotations. By October 1926, when Williams and Lyman asked the stake Relief Society president to report on their efforts at a special conference session given over entirely to the maternity and infancy work, Mary P. Lindsay, the new stake Relief Society president for Cottonwood revealed that a total of 793 children had been seen for initial exams with 2,623 follow-up visits—an important tally.[32]

At the same October conference Lyman asked Electa S. Dixon, the new Relief Society president of the Utah Stake to report on her own impressive experiences. Working under the direction of the state board of health and assisted by local physicians serving on a voluntary basis, she joined with other Relief Society women to organize health conferences and clinics in each of the five stakes in the county. Aware of the need for a public health nurse, these women successfully petitioned county commissioners to secure the necessary funding. At this point, however, a dispute arose between the physicians and the state board, resulting in the withdrawal of the doctors and the resignation of the nurse. Undaunted, local Relief Society leaders drew upon their growing expertise in government affairs and contacted the state head of maternity work, who advised that a county health unit be established, staffed by a full-time doctor and nurse and funded by the state and county.

As subsequent events make clear, when necessary, Relief Society women learned to shift effortlessly from organizers of conferences to lobbyists. Despite conditions in which heavy expenditures and a limited tax base already strained county budgets, Relief Society leaders of the five stakes, after soliciting the support of civic groups and club women, achieved their goal. Under the new arrangement seventeen health conferences were held each month. From January to September, 1926, over 2,300 expectant mothers and young children received initial examinations. Over 560 had follow-up exams from the county health care professionals through which nearly 4,000 health defects of various kinds were found. In those cases where the problems were correctable and where families themselves were unable to meet the costs, the stake Relief Societies arranged for low-cost services or used local donations and central maternity funds to cover expenses. In this manner the organization supplied medical treatment or surgery for sixty-six cases during the first nine months of 1926.[33]

Full-time health units such as these were possible in the more populous areas of the state, but, as with maternity closets, Lyman wanted Relief Society women in sparsely settled regions to recognize they had less costly options to meet their needs. Competent health care, she documented, could be had by drawing on the voluntary services of physicians and the cooperation of state or local officials. In her "Notes" column she highlighted developments in the Box Elder Stake Relief Society in Brigham City, where, late in 1923, members joined local women's groups and the state board of health to host a demonstration health center where 106 children were examined by doctors and dentists volunteering their time. The stake Relief Society then helped sponsor follow-up work two months later and weekly clinics thereafter. Lyman also noted that about the same time a stake in Bingham, Idaho sponsored its first free clinic for mothers and children. Women then resolved themselves to "advocate aid financially and educationally for maternal and infant welfare."[34] Such services were welcomed by families concerned about the health of their children, but often without resources to pay for the services on their own. In 1925, Millard Stake, headquartered in Fillmore in central Utah, reported periodic clinics held in five of its largest wards and noted that in one "all families, where there were small children, save three, attended." "All wards seem interested and are prepared to hold a clinic every three months," Relief Society leaders observed.[35]

Government reports back up Lyman's observations about the success of this work with statistics indicating a willingness on the part of families throughout Utah to avail themselves of health care provided through Sheppard-Towner work. Though rated fortieth by population, Utah consistently ranked high among those states examining the most children under the act. For the year ending July, 1924 (the first for which figures are available), Utah, with 7,094 children examined, ranked within the top quarter of all participating states. Within two years, state public health officials assisted by local volunteers saw 8,599 children, placing Utah within the top five or six states in the nation.[36]

The Relief Society's role in these figures can be illuminated by comparing them to subsequent years. In the fall of 1926 Lyman and other Relief Society leaders, fearing a slackening of energies among the membership, sought to "stir up interest in the Maternity and Infancy Act" by devoting the entire October conference to Sheppard-Towner. In attendance were women representing all ninety-four of the geographic divisions into which the state had been divided by the board of health, as well as delegates from several other western states.[37] After listening to accounts of what had already been achieved, as well as admonitions for greater future action, these women returned home determined to redouble their efforts. The results were dramatic. By December, the number of children attending health conferences had already increased significantly, and by the end of the administrative year in July 1927, a total of 10,558, had been seen by medical staff—an increase of twenty-three percent. For the remainder of the life of the act, over 10,000 children were examined yearly in Utah.[38]

Through her "Notes" column and when organizing and reporting on Relief Society conferences, Lyman made sure that the benefits of these efforts in local communities were readily apparent to Relief Society women. In 1925, for example, she highlighted the comments of Carbon Stake leaders. Living in eastern Utah's coal mining region they spoke for many when they reported with eloquent understatement: "A great deal of good has resulted from the health centers."[39] As recorded by Lyman a year later, the Utah Stake Relief Society president Electa S. Dixon succinctly summed up the value of the educational work made possible through the unique partnership of the Relief Society, the state, and the federal government through Sheppard-Towner. "Our health centers have been invaluable in helping us to discover people in sore need of health opportunities," she noted. "Women who suffered almost constantly and were dependent because of it, have been freed from their ailments and made happy and self-supporting." As for children, the "defects" of the ill and handicapped had been corrected and "they have been put on an equal footing with their associates."[40]

Infant and maternal mortality figures support these anecdotal accounts. By the first year of the act, infant mortality rates in Utah (including those of non-Mormon women), previously reported at 69 per 1,000 live births, began to decline noticeably to 59 per 1,000, where they would hover for the duration of Sheppard-Towner. As Clarissa Williams reported in conference, the decline in mortality rates for the children of Mormon women throughout the church—those most affected by the full range of Relief Society health work—was even more impressive: from 53 per 1,000 in 1921 to 39 per 1,000 in 1923. By 1929, Utah was one of nine states with the lowest infant mortality rates in the nation, with only four states reporting lower levels. During the same period, maternal mortality declined from 59 to 49 per 10,000, with only Iowa attaining a lower rate.[41] The verdict was in: Utah, understaffed and underfunded, had achieved one of the lowest combined rates of infant and maternal mortality of any state in the nation, a matter of great pride to Relief Society women.

As Utah continued its move from national pariah (religion), it now became something of a national model (maternal and infant health) and its low combined rate of infant and maternal mortality attracted the attention of Children's Bureau officials who highlighted its progress in bureau reports on Sheppard-Towner activities. In a 1926 visit, the bureau's chief, Grace Abbott, praised local efforts, noting that Utah stood "very high in child welfare work."[42] Abbott had for some time recognized the "unique features" of the state's success, having invited H. Y. Richards, director of Utah's Bureau of Child Hygiene, to address a 1925 conference of Shepherd-Towner administrators on the topic of "Cooperation of Lay Organizations in Maternity and Infancy Work." At that time, Richards noted that each local Relief Society had been told "to do everything in its power to assist the state board of health in this field" and credited the organization with much of the work's success.[43]

Abbott's esteem for the Relief Society led her to establish professional and personal ties with Lyman as well. During her 1926 visit, the society hosted a reception in her honor at the Hotel Utah and Lyman invited her afterwards to her home to meet informally with workers from the social service department. In subsequent years the two women carried on a correspondence centering on professional matters, but venturing into personal affairs as well. Both Grace and her equally prominent sister Edith, who headed the school of social work at the University of Chicago, came to hold Lyman in high esteem, counting her an important member of their national network of reform-minded women. Relief Society Social Service Department workers seeking further training at the University of Chicago could count on being asked about Lyman, and hearing her accomplishments much praised.[44]

The Abbotts were not the only national figures who had taken note of Lyman, her co-religionists, and her state's accomplishments. The year after Abbott's visit Dr. Blanche M. Haines, director of the Division of Maternity and Infant Hygiene of the Children's Bureau, toured the Rocky Mountain West to evaluate local administration of Sheppard-Towner, making quite clear her particular interest in observing firsthand the activities of Relief Society women.[45] "I saw a great deal of your work," she wrote to Utah's state health commissioner after her return, "and it impressed me as being very fine child hygiene work." Its high quality she attributed to the extensive cooperation between state administrators and voluntary organizations, especially the Relief Society. "Your relations with the Mormons and their wonderful organization," she observed, "certainly has made it possible for you to do much that other States are not able to do."[46]

Relief Society leaders agreed. "We feel that some of the credit for the decrease in infant mortality is due to the efforts of the Relief Society women," Clarissa Williams noted in the April 1925 conference. But, not content to reflect on past accomplishments, she reminded her listeners that there was still much to do, and urged them to "go on assisting in the work which will further decrease the death rate of children."[47] Under her orders and Lyman's direction, the general board did everything in its power to continue to facilitate and advance the impressive work being carried out by the rank and file.

Amid all this recognition in the world of social welfare in which Lyman was now ensconced, a number of significant developments also arose in her personal life. Amy and Richard had continued along their path as a two career family, of which, it seemed Amy's was now the most demanding. Despite Richard's position in the highest reaches of the church hierarchy and his ongoing prominence in the field of civil engineering, Amy also appears to have held the highest profile. This occasionally led Richard to be ribbed by friends and close associates. When Amy was elected to the state legislature, for instance, at a social function hosted by a group of wives of the general authorities, one member read a poem in which Richard purportedly lamented his wife's travels, and "grieves night and day,/To have her making laws which he's forced to obey."[48] Although, one can only wonder if there might not be at least a touch of resentment behind his humor, to all appearances, he seems to have adjusted to his wife's prominence good naturedly, even introducing himself occasionally at stake conferences as "Amy Brown Lyman's husband."[49]

These years were also eventful ones for the Lyman children, now young adults. Margaret had taken up undergraduate work at the University of Utah, alternated with summers at the Juilliard Academy of Music in New York City. Twenty-two in the fall of 1925, she was enjoying a lengthy period of study in France when she fell in love with another young Mormon studying music, Alexander Schreiner, who would one day become the renowned organist at the Tabernacle on Temple Square. The couple became formally engaged upon their return to Utah and married in June 1927.[50] Wendell, meanwhile, after serving a proselytizing mission, had completed a business degree at the University of Utah and at age twenty-six married Rachel Ballif in June 1924. They were an extremely popular couple on campus, and theirs was, by all accounts, a very happy union. In April 1925, a daughter, Amy Kathryn, was born. Amy and Richard grew very close to Rachel and socialized frequently with their son and daughter-in-law. The events that unfolded at the end of 1925 were therefore all the more devastating to them.[51]

At that time, Wendell and his wife were living in an apartment near Temple Square that they shared with Rachel's father. On New Year's Eve, Wendell went out to do some last minute shopping, leaving Rachel behind to get ready for a party the couple was to attend that night. Around six o'clock, her father walked into the kitchen to find her seemingly unconscious on the floor, the baby in its crib nearby. In a panic he summoned a doctor—several, actually, including Amy's brother John—but was unable to locate Wendell. Amy and Richard were then living in the Hotel Utah, having recently closed up their home in the Avenues to be nearer to work during the winter months. Thinking Wendell might be with them, the senior Ballif called and told Richard to bring Amy right away as "something terrible has happened." Leaving Amy behind because she was too sick with the flu to get out of bed, Richard rushed over, wondering what possibly could have occurred.

When he arrived, he found Rachel's father pacing back and forth holding the baby while Rachel lay stretched out on the floor. Pressing his ear to her chest, he thought he could hear a heartbeat, but shortly thereafter the family physician arrived, followed by Amy's brother John, and another physician friend. After brief examinations, each shook their heads grimly, recognizing that she was, in fact, dead. It was into this scene that Wendell finally arrived, carrying a bouquet of flowers under his arm and holding a just-purchased phonograph record of one of Rachel's favorite pieces of music. As he entered the room, his bride lay lifeless on the floor nearby, her new dress and shoes placed nearby ready for the New Year's celebration. "Not even in story have I known such a tragic situation," reflected Richard.[52]

Amy found the shock was almost more than she could bear. Despite her lifelong practice of keeping her emotions in check, when she called her secretary, Vera White (Pohlman) soliciting help to notify family members of the tragedy, her voice was so choked with tears that she could barely be understood.[53] Soon recovering her composure, Lyman remained outwardly in control throughout the rest of the crisis. Wendell followed his mother's example and suppressed his emotions before and after the funeral. When it came to caring for his infant daughter, however, not surprisingly for a man of the era, he confessed to his mother that he was completely at a loss. After some discussion, the family decided it would be best if Amy and Richard moved back to the house on Third Avenue where Amy's namesake, little Amy Kathryn, and Wendell could join them. Amy arranged to do some of her work from home and employed domestic help to look after the baby when responsibilities required her to be absent. While Wendell remained involved with his daughter, from this point on Amy and Richard raised Amy Kathryn as their own.[54]

Wendell's outward self-mastery earned him high praise from his father who admired his "manly" way of dealing with the tragedy. Inwardly, however, he did not handle his grief nearly as well. Though his mother had taught him the Brown family maxim that things that could not be changed must be put in the past, this proved a tragedy from which he never recovered.[55]

Amy, on the other hand, summoned her own enormous emotional strength, looked resolutely forward, and found solace in meeting the needs of her granddaughter and in her demanding schedule that included an ever-increasing number of responsibilities. Her work with the National Council of Women had continued and reached a new highpoint in 1925 when she began serving as recording secretary of the organization, which required significant commitments of her time and energies. In that year as well she was also honored to be named a delegate from the National Council to the triennial meeting of the International Council of Women held in Washington, D.C., a meeting she attended with a number of Utah women, including her sister Rose. She also remained well connected in social work circles; she attended meetings of the National Conference of Social Work and the newly formed Utah State Conference of Social Work, of which she had been a founding member and was currently secretary. She was also closely associated with the work of the National Association of Business and Professional Women, which was dedicated to workplace equality for women.[56] In addition to the intellectual stimulus and satisfaction these activities gave her, they also provided practical insights and contacts that could prove beneficial to the work of the Relief Society. But Lyman's activities in these organizations proved significant as well in shaping public perceptions of the church and its members. As she later observed in regard to the participation of Relief Society and YLMIA women in the work of the National and International Councils, "these contacts have furnished rare opportunity for presenting to others the work of their organizations and also the work of their Church, which has been so misunderstood."[57]

In the Relief Society itself, in addition to supervising and promoting the Sheppard-Towner work, she was heavily involved in a number of other activities related to the Social Service Department. Most demanding was her supervision of casework in the department and management of the social service institutes for training stake aids. In addition, she was involved with the department's employment exchange and with long-term efforts to build the department into the adoption agency for the church. Among other noteworthy endeavors during these years was her oversight of a Relief Society program for malnourished youth from urban areas that placed them in homes in rural communities for the summer. All of this, of course, was in addition to her normal labors handling correspondence with local units as well as her share of regular travel to stake conventions throughout the West.[58]

But perhaps the most important issues she faced during these years were those linked to the drive to renew federal funding for the Sheppard-Towner Act. The last year of Sheppard-Towner's five-year appropriation was 1926 and, despite progress nationally, the maternity and infancy work was still on a very tenuous footing. Nowhere was this more true than in Utah where only three counties had been able to assume full responsibility for health units while the Division of Child Hygiene, which oversaw all efforts in the state, remained dependent on Sheppard-Towner funds. "We still have a lot to accomplish," H. Y. Richards, Utah's Director of the Bureau of Child Hygiene observed in 1926 with notable understatement. Supporters both in the state and Relief Society agreed, and they saw the extension of federal funding for another five-year period as imperative.[59]

However, despite Sheppard-Towner's impressive achievement in lowering infant and maternal mortality, a serious fight arose over the renewal of funding. Nationally, opposition was spearheaded by physicians, many of whom saw the clinic work as a threat to private practice and a first step toward socialized medicine.[60] Utah physicians were as divided as their counterparts elsewhere. In places like rural Smithfield, stake Relief Society authorities could report that "doctors very willingly give their help and support to the work." But in other areas physicians were "not quite converted to the idea."[61] In addition to ideological objections, disputes over technique or professional autonomy could ruffle feathers and lead doctors, even those who initially cooperated, to turn against the work. This had been the case in Utah County, where the dispute described above led the Utah County Medical Society to pass a resolution that "practically prohibited any of its members from affiliating with [the] health centers."[62]

Relief Society women often reacted with righteous indignation in such circumstances: one group in northern Utah even published a resolution stating that they "resented the attitude of an individual or organization who would sacrifice the life of a mother and child for material gain."[63] But Lyman and other general leaders recognized both the immediate necessity of securing the cooperation of physicians for the local success of the work and the long-term danger if doctors as a group opposed the clinics. Their advice to local leaders was to smooth over sources of conflict whenever possible. Speaking in conference, Clarissa Williams noted that the potential threat to their livelihoods was the biggest source of friction involving doctors and recommended that Relief Society women explain to local physicians that "the opening of clinics is not designed in any way to interfere with private practice." "These health centers and clinics are supposed to make examinations only," she continued, "and refer all work to the family physicians," thereby increasing, rather than sapping their clientele.[64] While such mollifying tactics sometimes succeeded in Mormon communities, nationally many doctors remained antagonistic. That the American Medical Association emerged as one of the most adamant opponents to Sheppard-Towner sent out warning signals that extension would meet with stiff opposition in Congress.[65]

By the fall of 1926, much to the surprise of the Act's supporters, extension won easy approval in the House of Representatives. Like other organized women, Relief Society leaders, including Lyman, breathed a sigh of relief. In the October 1926 conference, Lyman even went so far as to opine that Sheppard-Towner's funding "will no doubt pass the Senate and will then be brought to the state legislatures early in the new year." At that point, Lyman continued, "Knowing, as Relief Society women know, the value of this work, it is to be earnestly hoped that every woman will use her influence to have the work continued." With that in mind, she observed "Our state legislators should therefore be urged [by Relief Society women, she clearly meant] to pass the necessary legislation for the continuance of the work."[66] Emphasizing state action, however, proved to be a serious misreading of the situation, not only by Lyman, but by social welfare advocates across the nation, as it was in the Senate that Sheppard-Towner met with determined and stiff opposition.

Nationally, women's groups like the Relief Society had provided support critical for Sheppard-Towner's passage and implementation. While the measure had enjoyed relatively broad approval not limited by sex, it was not universally applauded, even in the Mormon community where some opposed it on ideological grounds. This is not surprising, positioned as Sheppard-Towner was, along one side of a divide that had rent American society from the very beginning: the issue of an expansionist versus a strictly limited government.[67]

But other issues were at play as well in stirring up opposition. Efforts to block its renewal were spearheaded by such groups as the male dominated American Medical Association (many of whose members saw Sheppard-Towner as a threat to their professional status) and the ultra-conservative (and formerly anti-suffrage) Woman Patriots. Given that the measure represented the successful efforts of women empowered in the leadership of the Children's Bureau and many hundreds of thousands more active in women's organizations and at the ballot box (all of which represented challenges to "traditional" subordinate roles for women), it is perhaps not surprising that their opponents made use of rhetoric heavy with misogyny.[68] Among the worst offenders in the Senate was James Reed of Missouri, who mounted a vitriolic attack on the Children's Bureau and female social workers in general. Sheppard-Towner, in his view, was "a menace" put forth by "endocrine perverts [and] derailed menopausics."[69] Surprisingly, Utah's own Senator William H. King was also one the most outspoken critics of Sheppard-Towner's renewal, despite the benefits that had accrued to his state under the measure. In a Senate speech he termed its supporters "neurotic women . . . social workers who obtained pathological satisfaction in interfering with the affairs of other people."[70] King, whose first wife had been Richard's late sister, was well acquainted with Lyman and she must have wondered if his harsh words might have, in part, been directed at her.

Hoping to save the legislation, Grace Abbott contacted Lyman to enlist the Relief Society's aid in changing the Senator's mind. After meeting with her onetime brother-in-law, Lyman advised Abbott that he would not be swayed, with gross understatement concluding that he "certainly has very little appreciation for welfare work."[71] King's opposition led him to filibuster against the measure, and he yielded the floor only after he was offered a compromise that allowed for a one-time, two year extension of the act after which it would be automatically terminated.[72]

Despite this setback, Relief Society women continued their successful cooperative work while they hoped, like progressives around the nation, that in 1929, a more sympathetic Congress would reverse course and agree to an extension. Some among the organization's leadership did their part to make this possible and even worked to unseat King when he came up for reelection in 1928. Lyman's close friend and sister board member Jeannette Hyde, by then living most of the year in Honolulu where she held a patronage position as custom's collector, helped pay for a full page advertisement in the *Salt Lake Tribune* that denounced King's record as "One of OPPOSITION to Utah's Welfare." The ad further stated in bold type: "King against the Welfare of Utah Mothers and Babies." But the maternalist ideology that had united Relief Society women so effectively in pursuing practical maternity and infancy work was not strong enough to prove decisive in the realm of politics. Both nationally and in Utah it took politicians little time to learn what an earlier generation of Utah politicians had discovered thirty years before: women's issues could be safely ignored. As women joined men in again splitting their votes along party lines, King easily won reelection to the Senate where he rejoined those in opposition to Sheppard-Towner's renewal.[73]

Nationally, the story was much the same: when Congress reconvened in 1929 the extension of Sheppard-Towner again went down to defeat. Grace Abbott sought the aid of Lyman and the Relief Society once more in 1931 when another brief attempt was made to revive the maternity work, but again, the effort proved futile.[74] Some aspects of the measure were taken over and maintained by a number of the states, but not until the 1935 passage of the Social Security Act would major portions of the program be reinstituted on a nation-wide basis.

For the women of the Relief Society and for Lyman in particular this loss represented a sobering reminder of the limitations on women's influence as a force for change. As was the case with national coalitions of women, the Relief Society's power was predicated upon pursuing issues of such overriding import that carrying forward their agenda superseded other considerations that might weaken their unity and dilute their effectiveness as an interest group.[75] The widely popular Sheppard-Towner work seemed to have been just such an issue, but in the end, other factors influenced women's voting patterns and decided the election. The results at the polls and the subsequent defeat of Sheppard-Towner also made it clear that gains in the realm of social welfare often prove as transitory as political gains, so intertwined is the fate of the one with the other. Nevertheless, under Williams's direction and Lyman's supervision, the Relief Society's contributions to the Sheppard-Towner work were indeed impressive and not only resulted in a dramatic decrease in infant and maternal mortality, but laid a foundation for improved public health as well.

As was the case in other areas around the nation, the effect of Sheppard-Towner's termination on Utah was not immediately apparent. The federal effort had, to a degree, met its framers expectations by initiating a movement that survived—in a weakened form—even after its demise. As for the Relief Society, the organization continued to work with state and county officials in the interest of women and children, and did so, albeit with declining emphasis, even after the reforms of the New Deal.[76] However, the Sheppard-Towner work did more than benefit public health. By providing Mormon women another legitimized focus for activism, it drew them firmly into a national network of female reform in which they garnered recognition and praise. Unfortunately, as subsequent events revealed, finding another issue of such obvious import that both united women and justified their organized public activism was difficult.

This was only one of several major challenges that confronted the Relief Society in subsequent years. For the moment, however, maternity and infancy work had put the organization at the apex of its influence and prestige. Grace Abbott reportedly told the director of Utah's Department of Health during her 1926 visit to Salt Lake that "There is probably no group of people in this country where this Sheppard-Towner law . . . can be more satisfactorily administered than it is in the 'Mormon' communities."[77] At a time of minimal spending for public welfare the Relief Society's cooperation in the federally sponsored program stretched scarce dollars to extend the benefits of modern medical and nutritional information to women and children in every community in Utah, and indeed to communities throughout the West. Simultaneously, it created important and valued opportunities for women to become agents for change, thus allowing Latter-day Saint women to solidify anew their role in the public sphere.

In her report of the Relief Society's April conference for 1923, as federal efforts were just getting started in Utah, Lyman recorded her friend Jeannette Hyde's reflections on a long list of recent accomplishments by Mormon women, all of them aimed at improving conditions in their communities. Not the least of these was the recent lobbying effort to ensure passage of Sheppard-Towner's enabling legislation in the statehouse. Aptly, Hyde summed up the importance of the contribution made by LDS women—working through the Relief Society—to the social reforms of the period: "You may ask, 'Would not the men . . . have done the same?' I shall only answer you by asking: 'Have they done it in the past?'"[78]

At the center of these reforms and pivotal to their success was Lyman. The formidable level of her energy and the full range of resources at her command enabled her to mobilize her troops for an unprecedented, decade-long era of activism. Taken together with her contributions through the Social Service Department, she must have experienced great pride in the role she had played in improving the health and well-being of individuals and families throughout the West. No doubt she noted with satisfaction, as well, how her actions had served to reinvigorate the Relief Society. Satisfying also was the national recognition she earned for herself and the Relief Society through the Sheppard-Towner work, with the organization—and Lyman—now recognized as important contributors to the cause of social reform.

Despite the impending demise of the Maternity and Infancy Act, Lyman thus had good reason to be optimistic about the future. She did not know, however, that arguably her period of greatest accomplishment was already coming to an end. Important opportunities still awaited her, but none that would bring such far-reaching results as those she had just achieved. For while the Relief Society had fully exploited the potential of maternalist activism in the 1920s, the following decade proved more important in revealing the limits of such rationales based on differing gender roles.

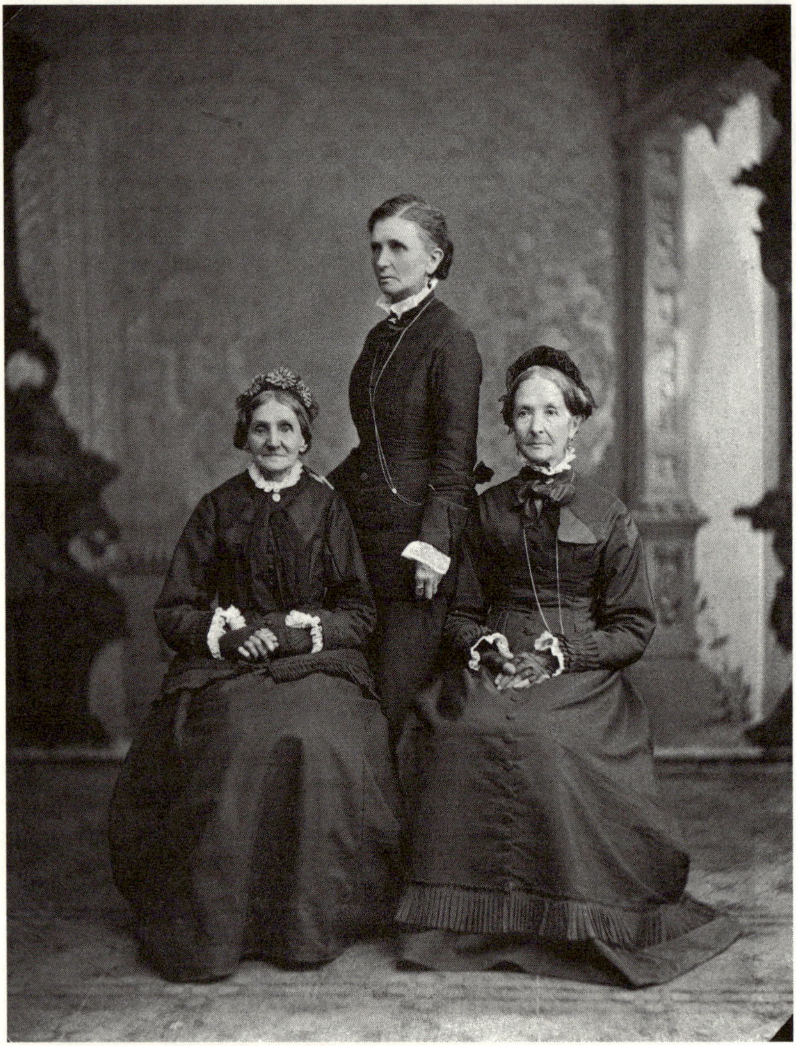

Leading Sisters Elizabeth Ann Whitney,
Emmeline B. Wells, and Eliza R. Snow.
(LDS Church History Library)

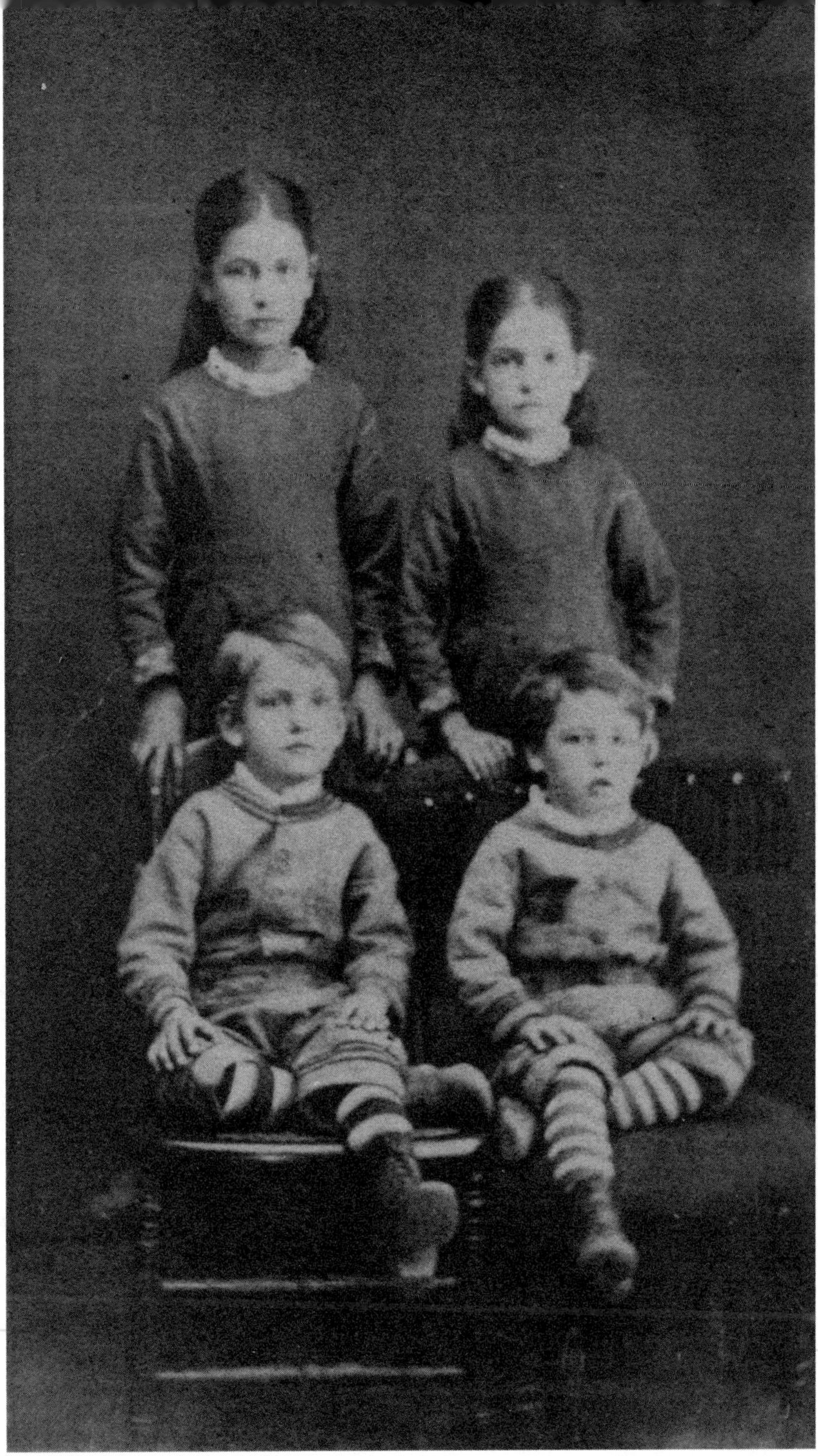

Youngest four children of John and Margaret Brown. Clockwise from bottom left: John Zimmerman Brown, Susan Elizabeth Brown, Amy Cassandra Brown, Lawrence Hoke Brown. (Author's collection, courtesy of Amy Lyman Engar)

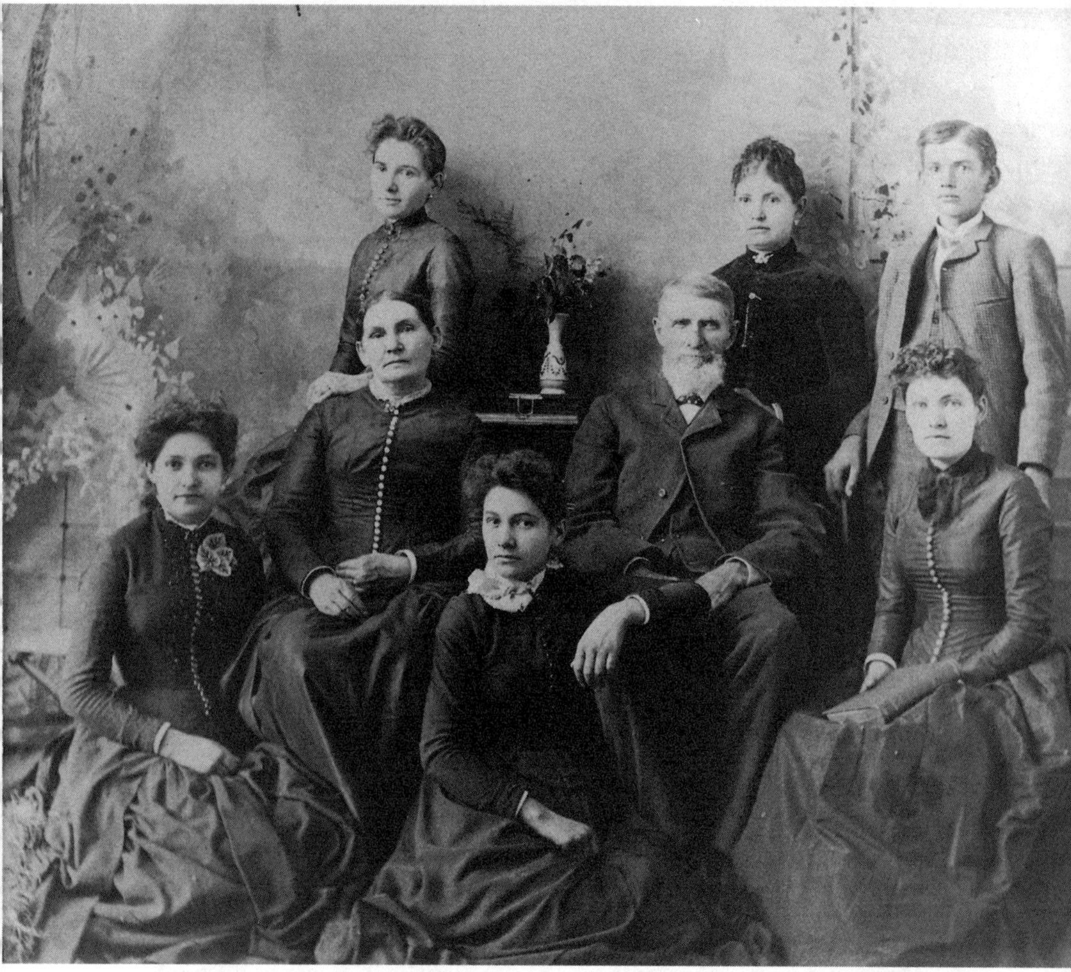

John and Margaret Zimmerman Brown family. Seated in center: Margaret Zimmerman Brown, John Brown. Children clockwise from far left: Amy Cassandra, Margaret, Rose, John Z., Lydia, Susan. (Author's collection, courtesy of Amy Lyman Engar)

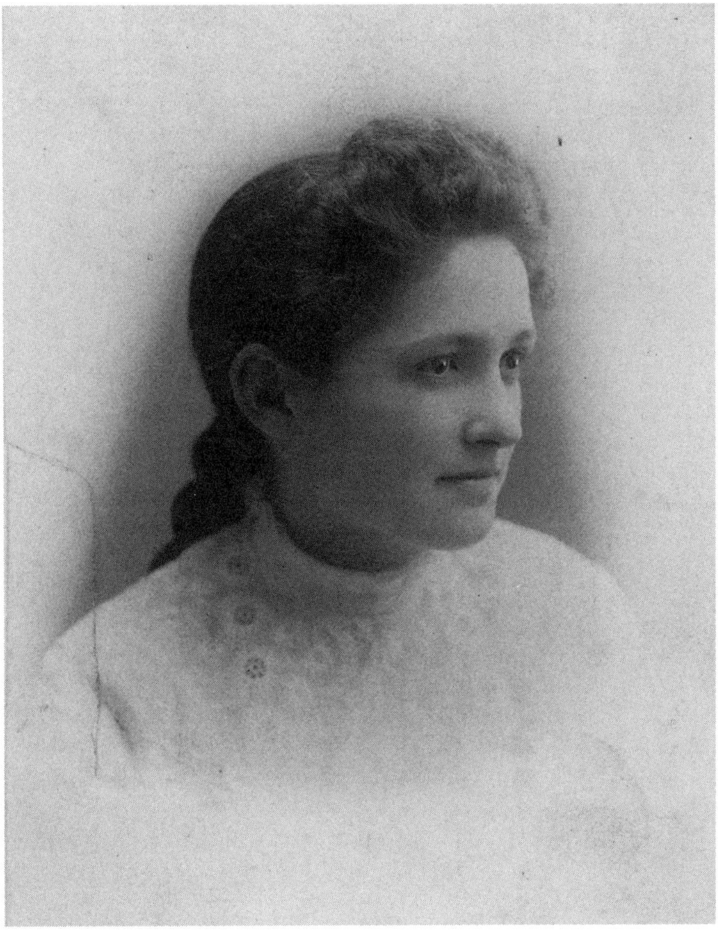

Amy Brown about fifteen years old. (Author's collection, courtesy of Amy Lyman Engar)

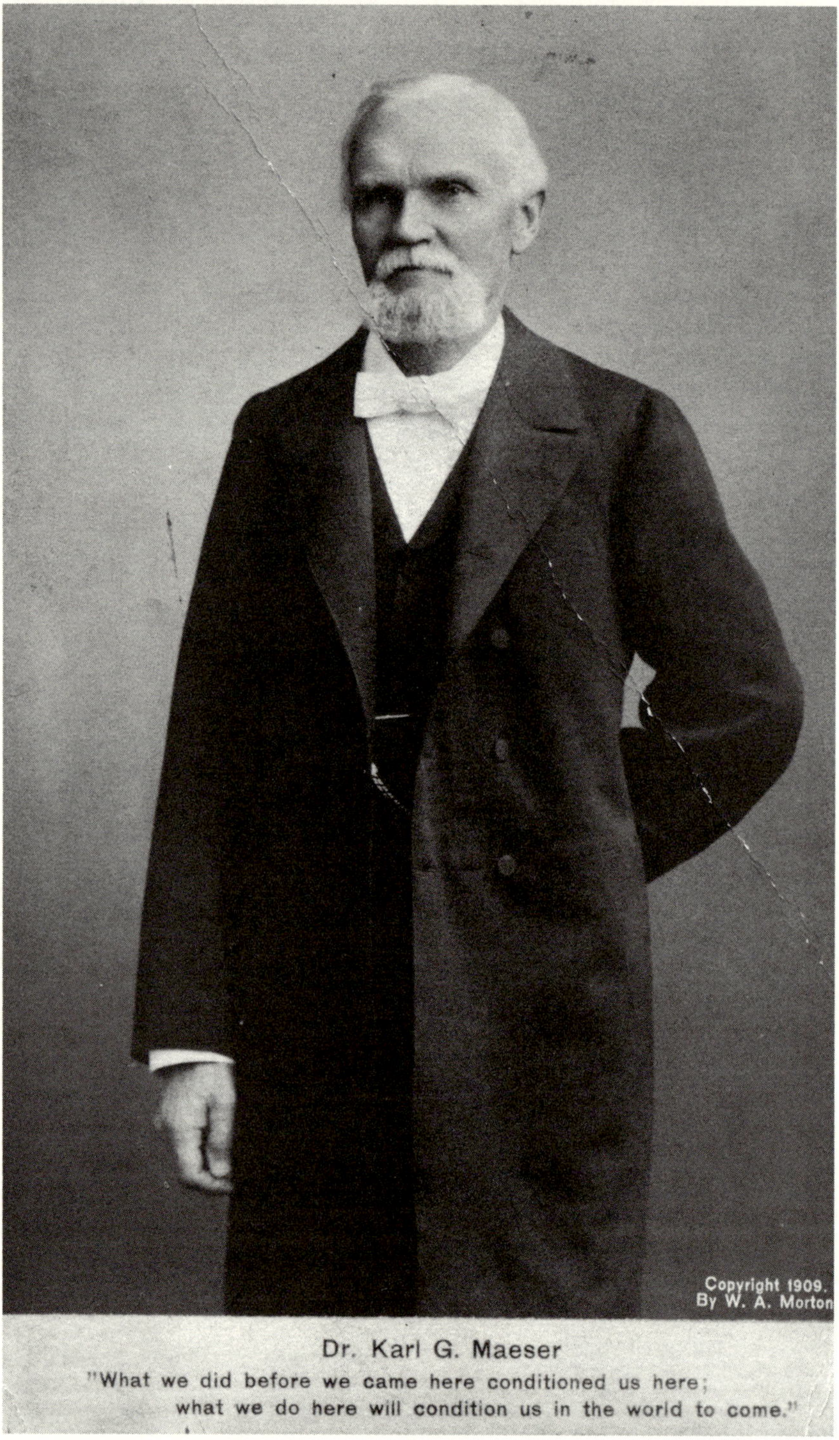

Karl G. Maeser. (Author's collection, courtesy of Vera W. Pohlman)

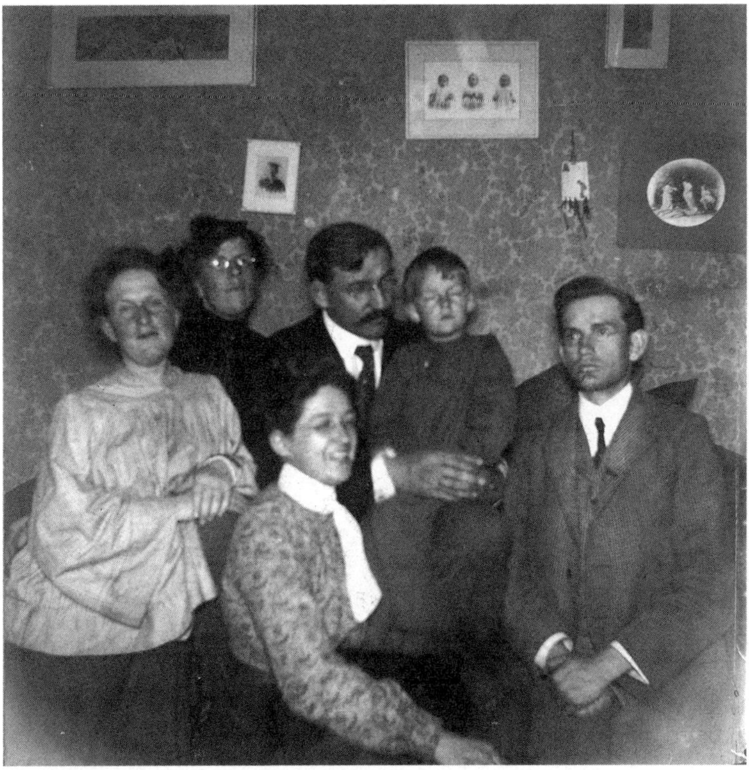

Amy and Richard R. Lyman and son Wendell, with Amy's brother John Z. Brown on far right of photo and his wife Alice Driggs Brown on the left, and unidentified woman in the center. (LDS Church History Library; courtesy of Engar family)

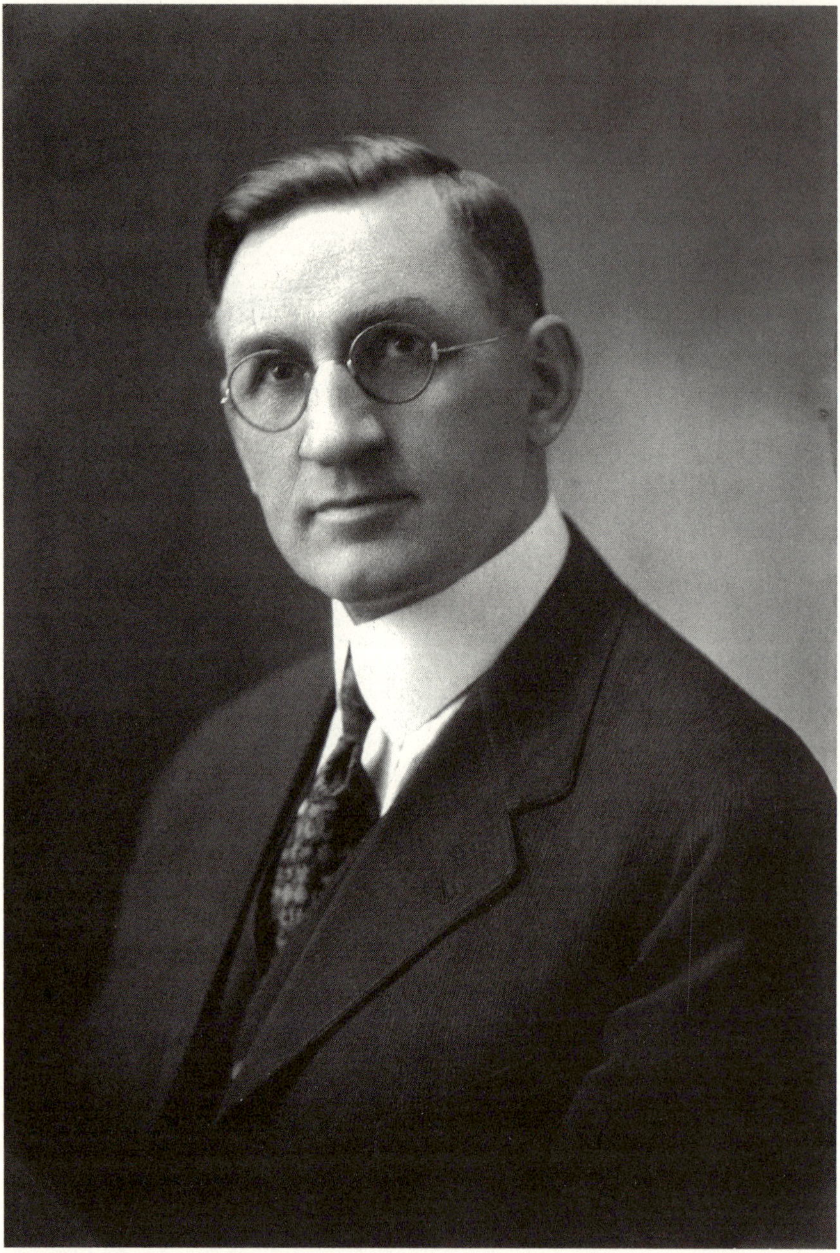

Richard R. Lyman, early 1900s.
(LDS Church History Library; courtesy of Engar family)

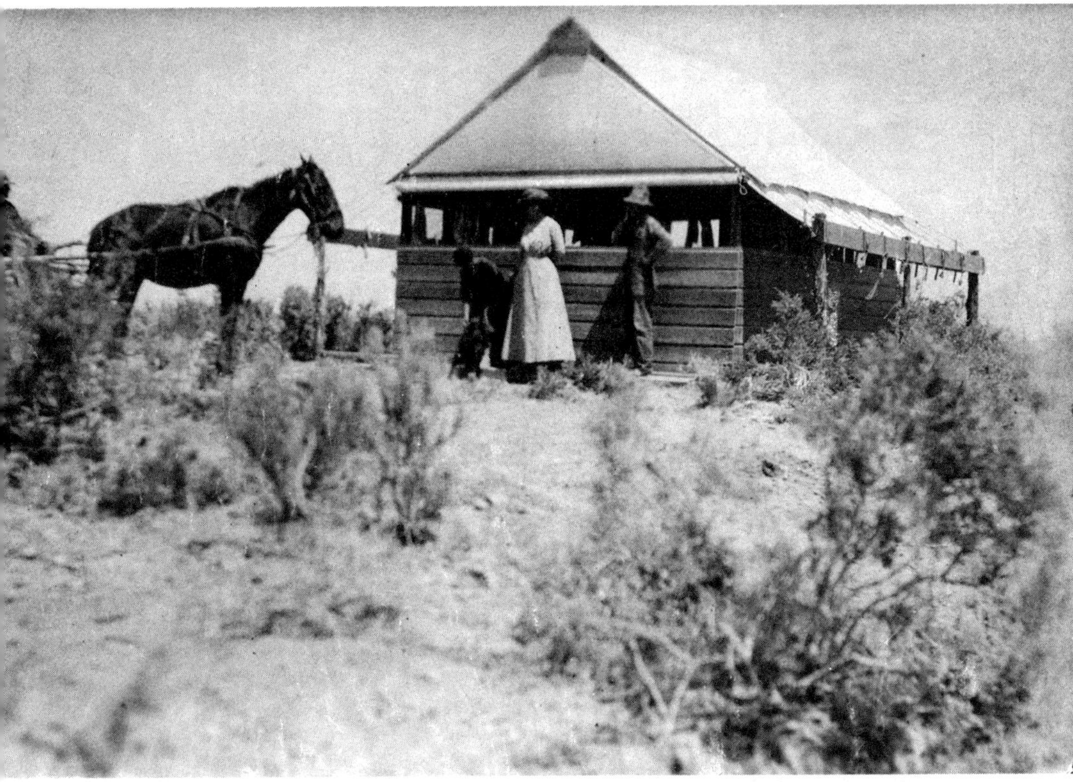

Tent cabin where Lyman and her family lived while homesteading in Delta, Utah, during the summer of 1911. From left: Wendell B. Lyman (in cart), Margaret Lyman (Schreiner), the dog, Amy Brown Lyman, and cousin Jean R. Driggs. (LDS Church History Library; courtesy of Engar family)

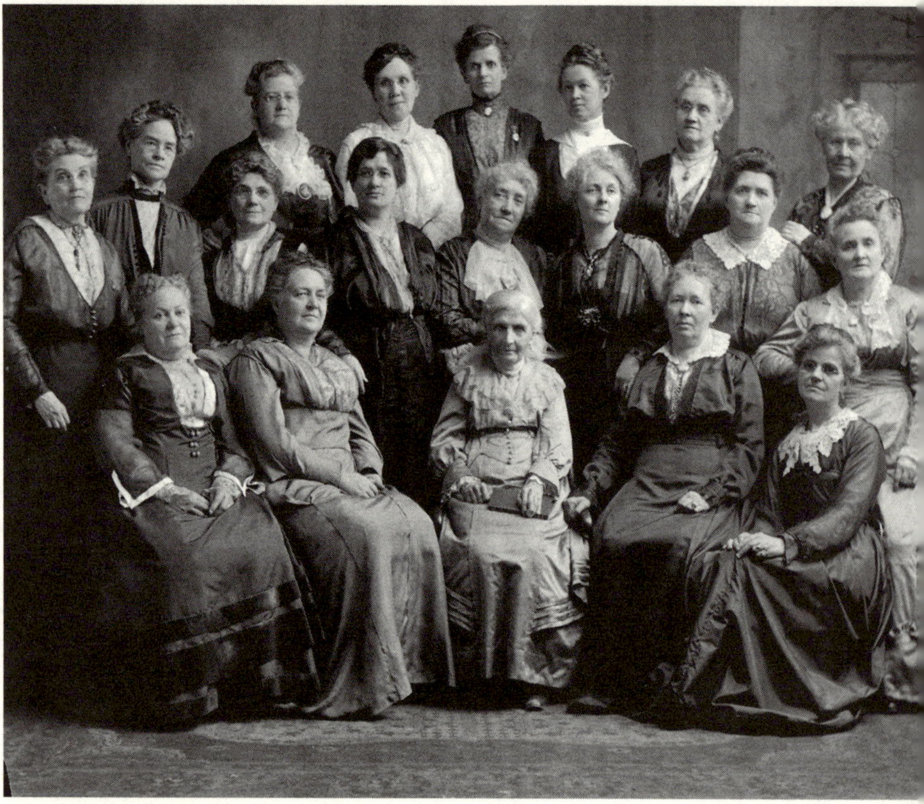

Emmeline B. Wells and General Board of the Relief Society, 1916. Lyman is standing in the middle of the second row between the seated Wells and Clarissa S. Williams. Standing third from right in the second row is Alice Merrill Horne. Standing at the left of the top row is Jeannette Acord Hyde. Second from right in the top row is Susa Young Gates. (LDS Church History Library)

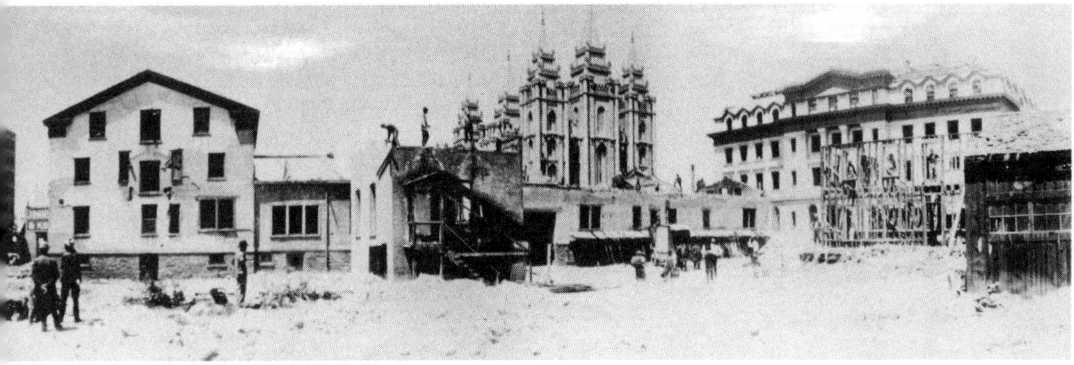

The old Tithing Block, with the completed Bishop's Building (headquarters of the Relief Society) on the far right across the street from the Temple, and the old tithing barn and bishop's storehouse being demolished to make way for new construction. (LDS Church History Library)

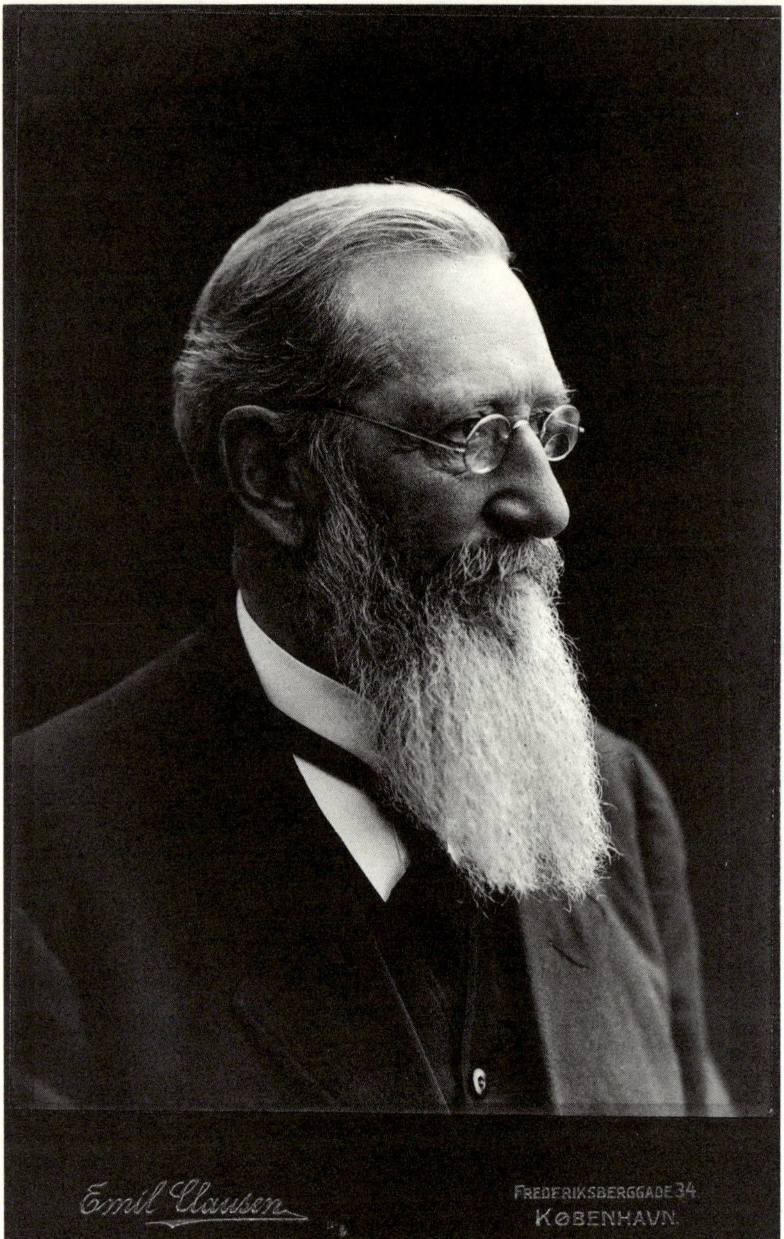

Church President Joseph F. Smith.
(LDS Church History Library)

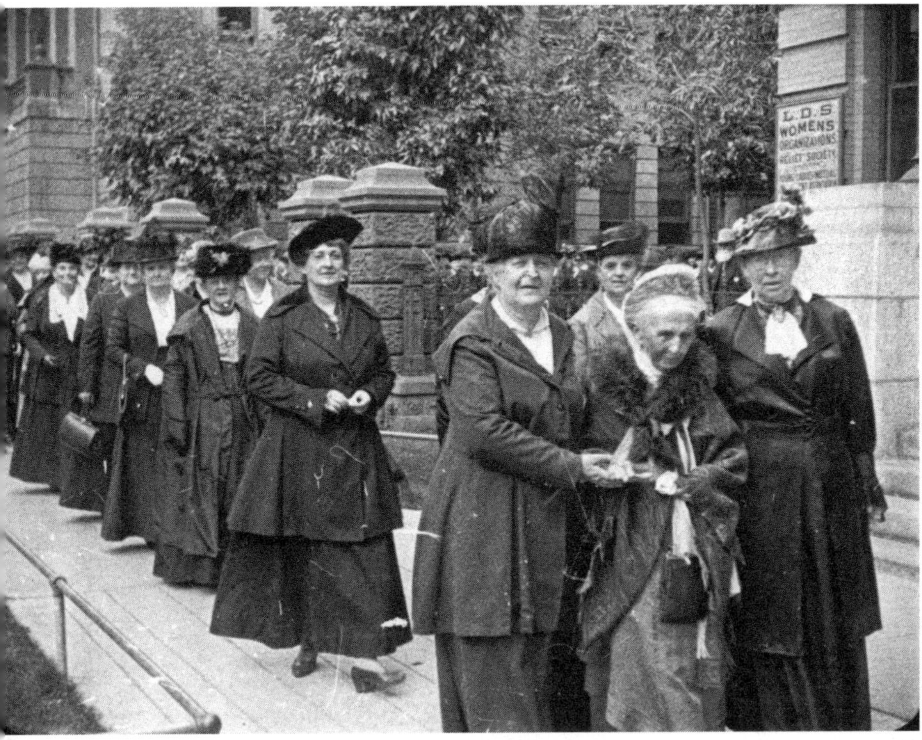

Members of Relief Society General Board entering the Bishop's Building, with Emmeline B. Wells being assisted by counselors Clarissa S. Williams and Julina L. Smith. Lyman can be seen walking directly behind. (LDS Church History Library)

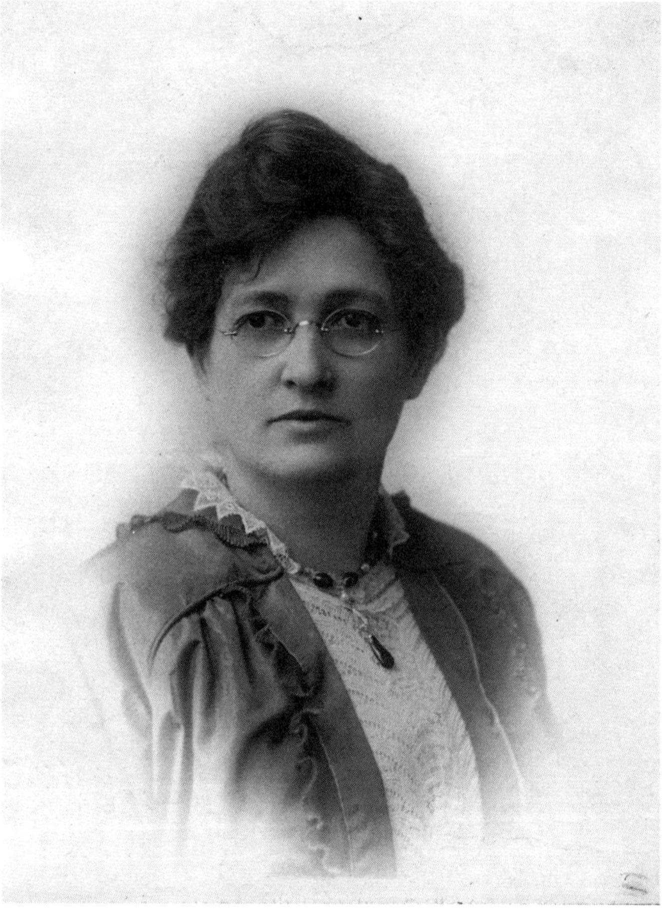

Amy Brown Lyman, early 1920s.
(LDS Church History Library)

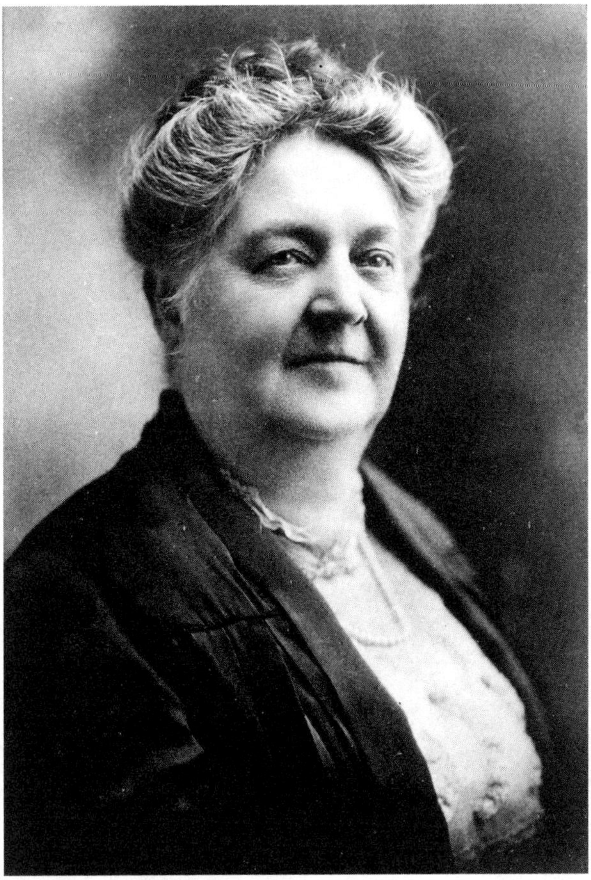

Clarissa Smith Williams as General Relief Society President. (LDS Church History Library)

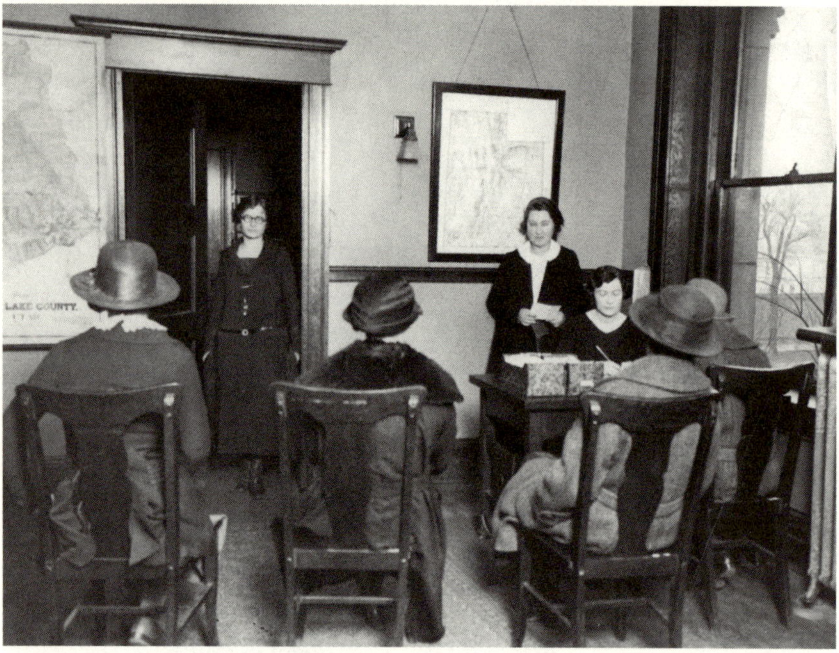

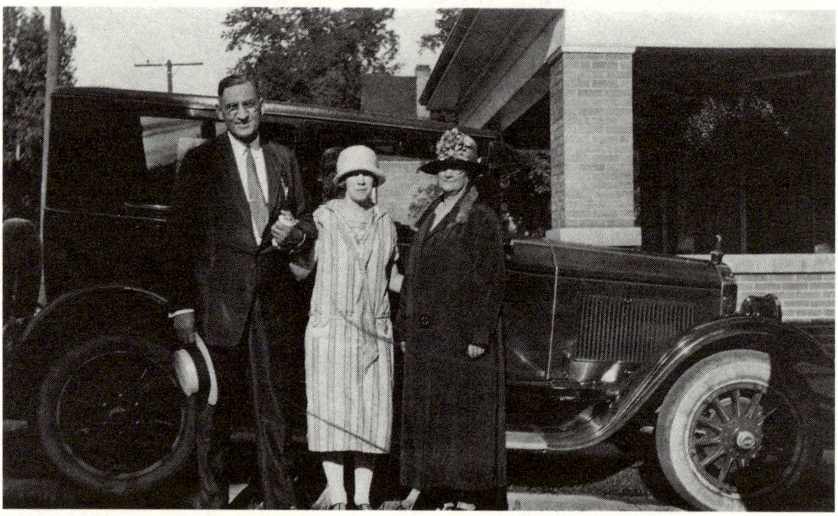

TOP Relief Society Employment Bureau in Bishop's Building 1920s. Vera W. Pohlman is standing in doorway, Mary Schindler Nielsen is standing to the right of the door. Department social workers are posing as clients. (Courtesy of Vera W. Pohlman)

BOTTOM Richard R. Lyman, daughter-in-law Rachel Baliff Lyman, and Amy Brown Lyman. (LDS Church History Library; courtesy of Engar family)

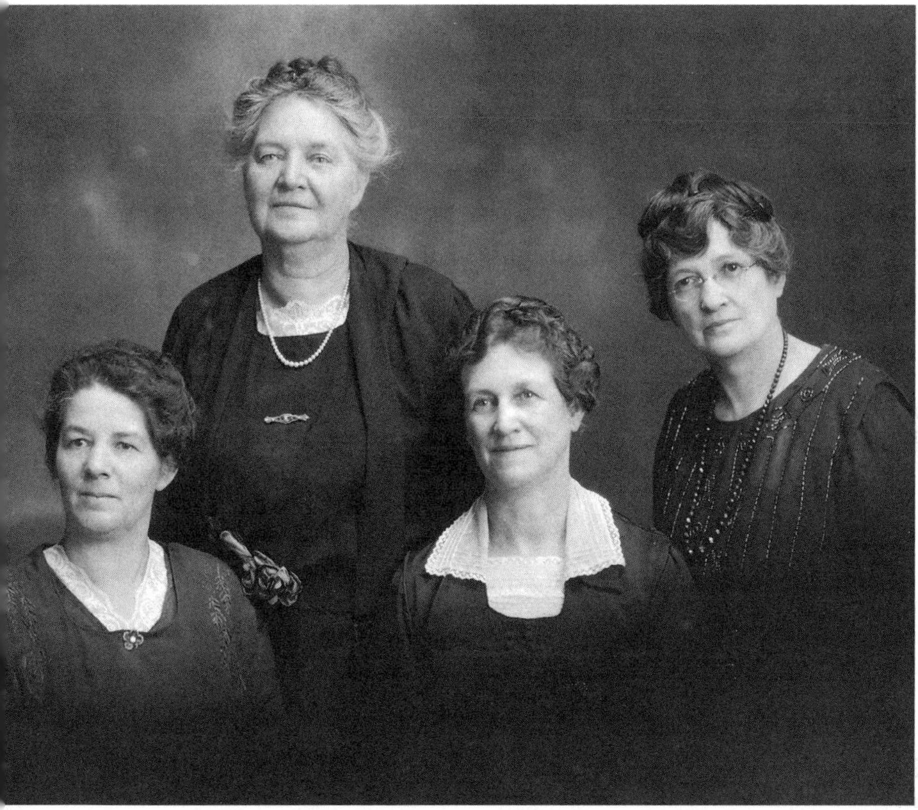

Clarissa Smith Williams, standing center, with her First Counselor Jennie Brimhall Knight, seated on the left, Second Counselor Louise Yates Robison, bottom center, and General Secretary-Treasurer Amy Brown Lyman on the right. (LDS Church History Library)

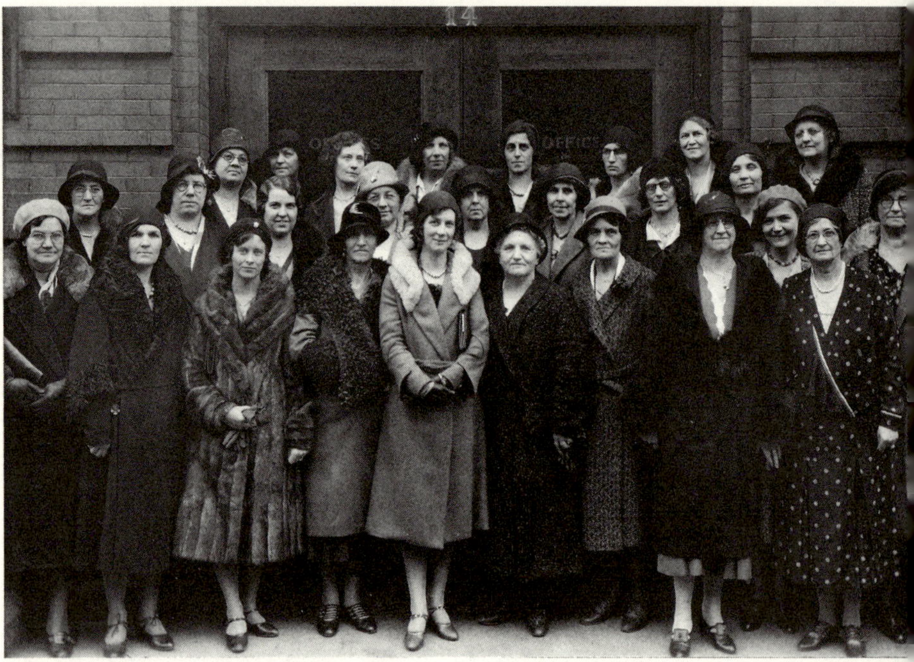

Amy Brown Lyman and class for Social Service Aides, 1932. Lyman is in bottom right of photo with Relief Society President Louise Y. Robison immediately to her left. (LDS Church History Library)

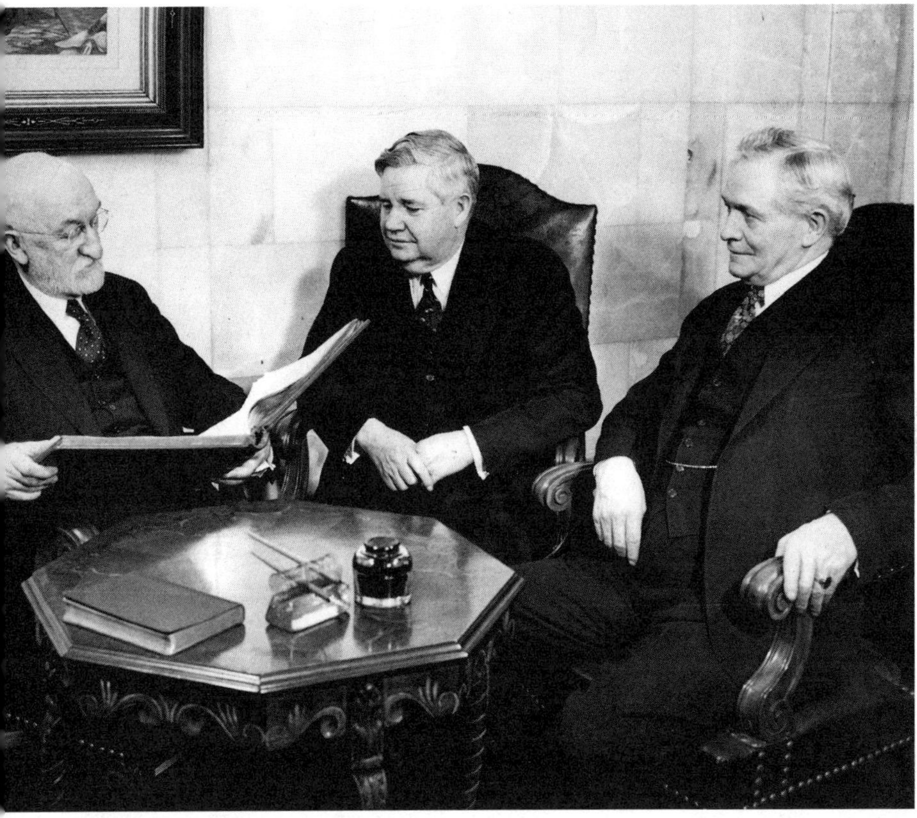

First Presidency of the Church of Jesus Christ of Latter-day Saints, 1935. On left, President Heber J. Grant, center, First Counselor J. Reuben Clark, right, Second Counselor David. O. McKay. (LDS Church History Library)

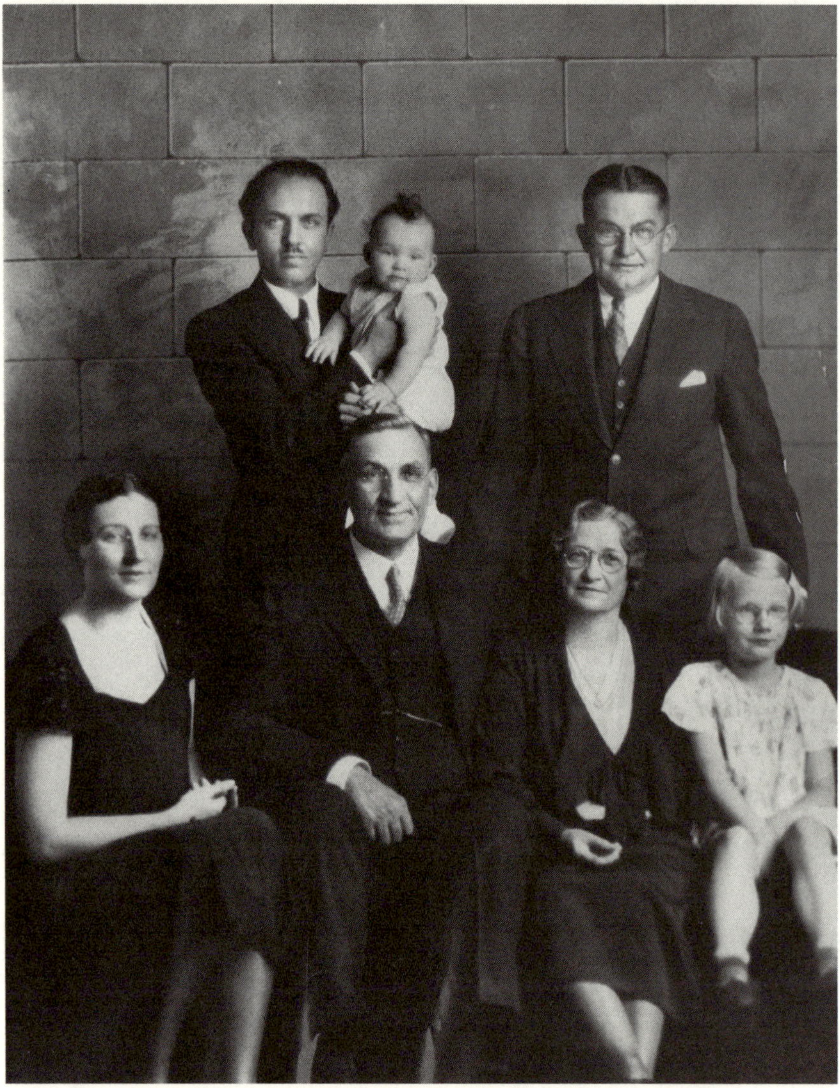

Lyman family portrait, 1932. Seated from left: Margaret Lyman Schreiner, Richard R. Lyman, Amy Brown Lyman, Amy Kathryn Lyman. Standing: Alexander Schreiner, holding Richard Lyman Schreiner, Wendell Brown Lyman. (LDS Church History Library; courtesy of Engar family)

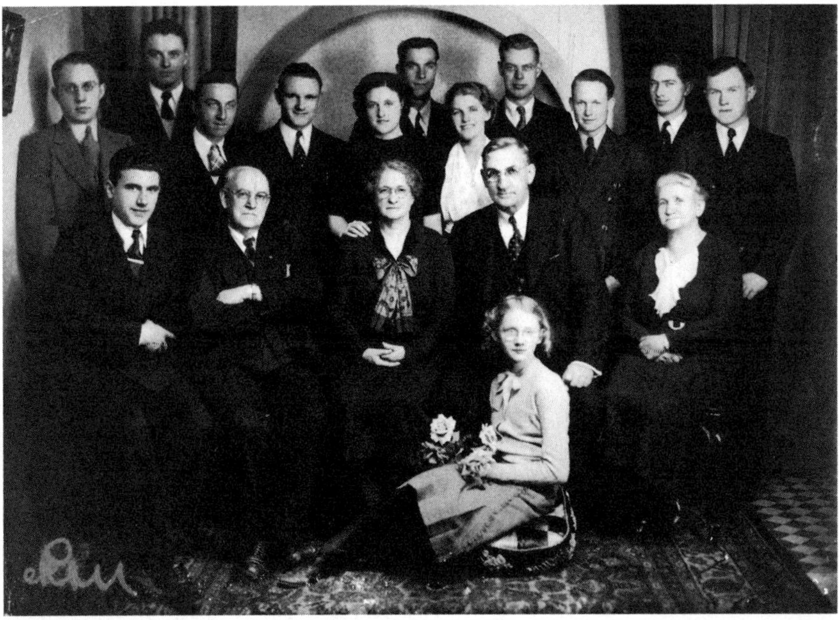

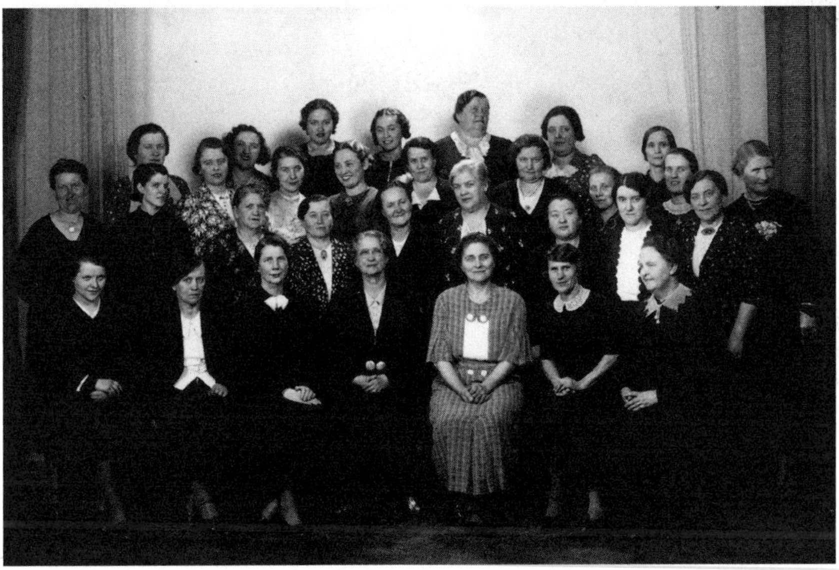

TOP Lymans with missionaries of the French Mission, 1938. Seated to the left of Amy Brown Lyman is Mission President Octave F. Ursenbach, on the right of Richard R. Lyman is his wife, Hannah Ursenbach. The Lyman's granddaughter Amy Kathryn is seated on floor in center. (Courtesy of Jocile Ursenbach Nielsen)

BOTTOM Amy Brown Lyman with members of the Prague, Czechoslovakia Relief Society. Seated to the left of Lyman is Martha Sharp Toronto, wife of Wallace Toronto, president of the Czechoslovakia Mission. (LDS Church History Library)

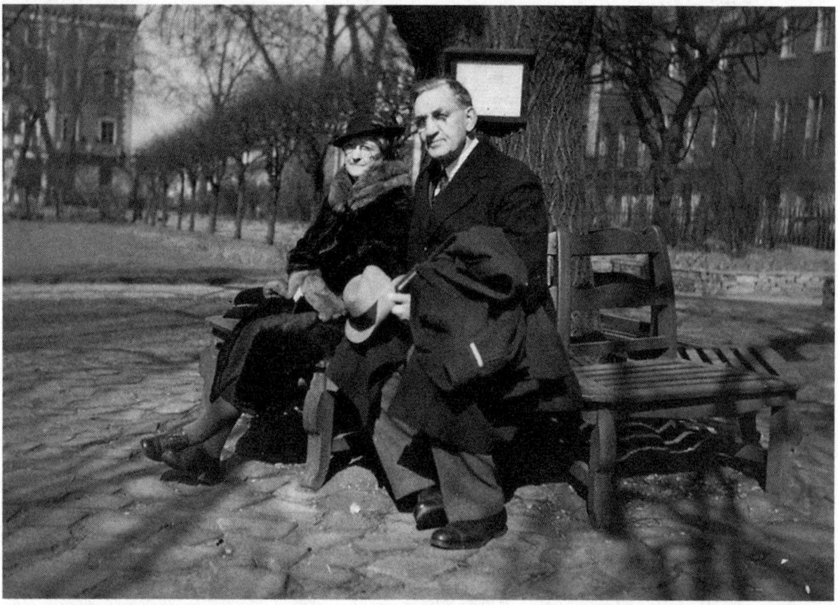

Amy and Richard R. Lyman touring on mission business. (LDS Church History Library; courtesy of Engar family)

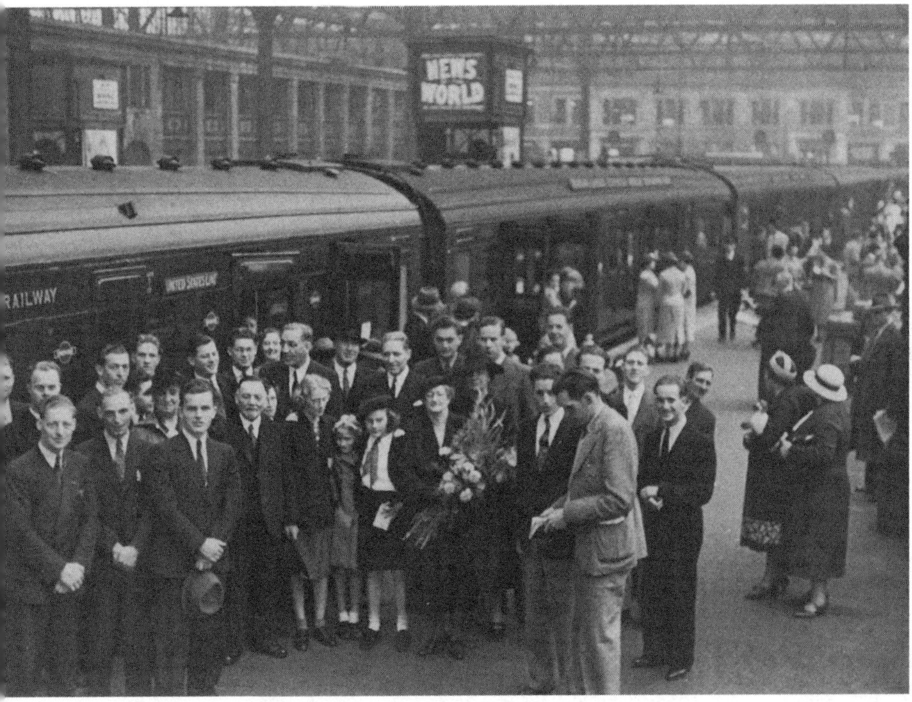

Lyman family with group of missionaries at their departure for home in September 1938. (LDS Church History Library; courtesy of Lyman family)

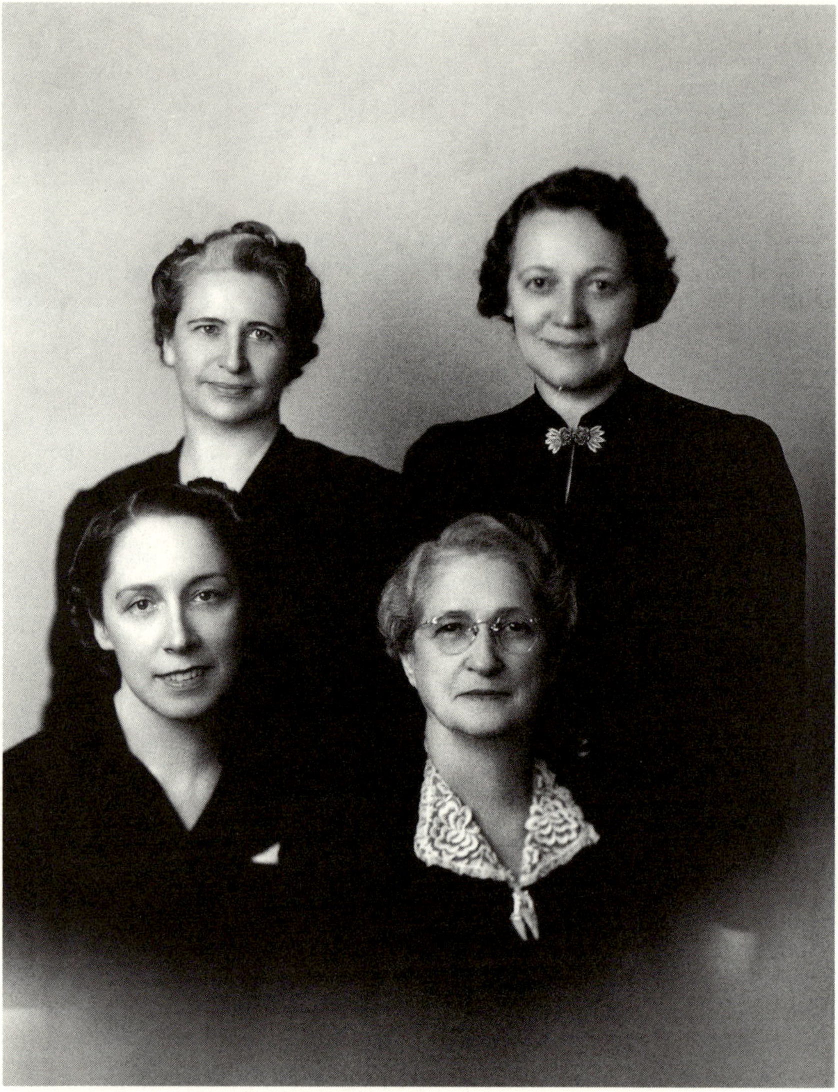

Lyman and her presidency. Below, left, First Counselor Donna D. Sorensen, top left, General Secretary-Treasurer Vera W. Pohlman, top right, Second Counselor Marcia K. Howells. (Lignell and Gill photographers; LDS Church History Library)

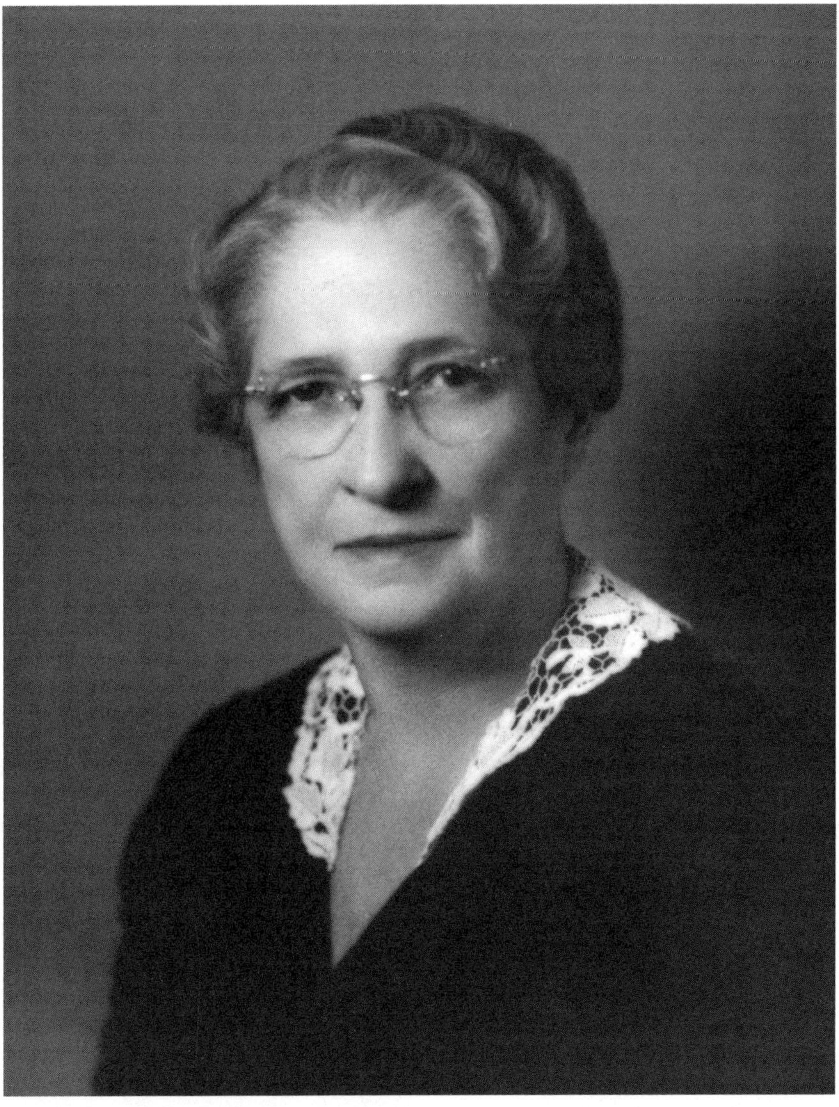

Official portrait of Amy Brown Lyman as Relief Society General President. Vera W. Pohlman felt this photo revealed Lyman's inner character and deep compassion. (Blackstone Studios; LDS Church History Library)

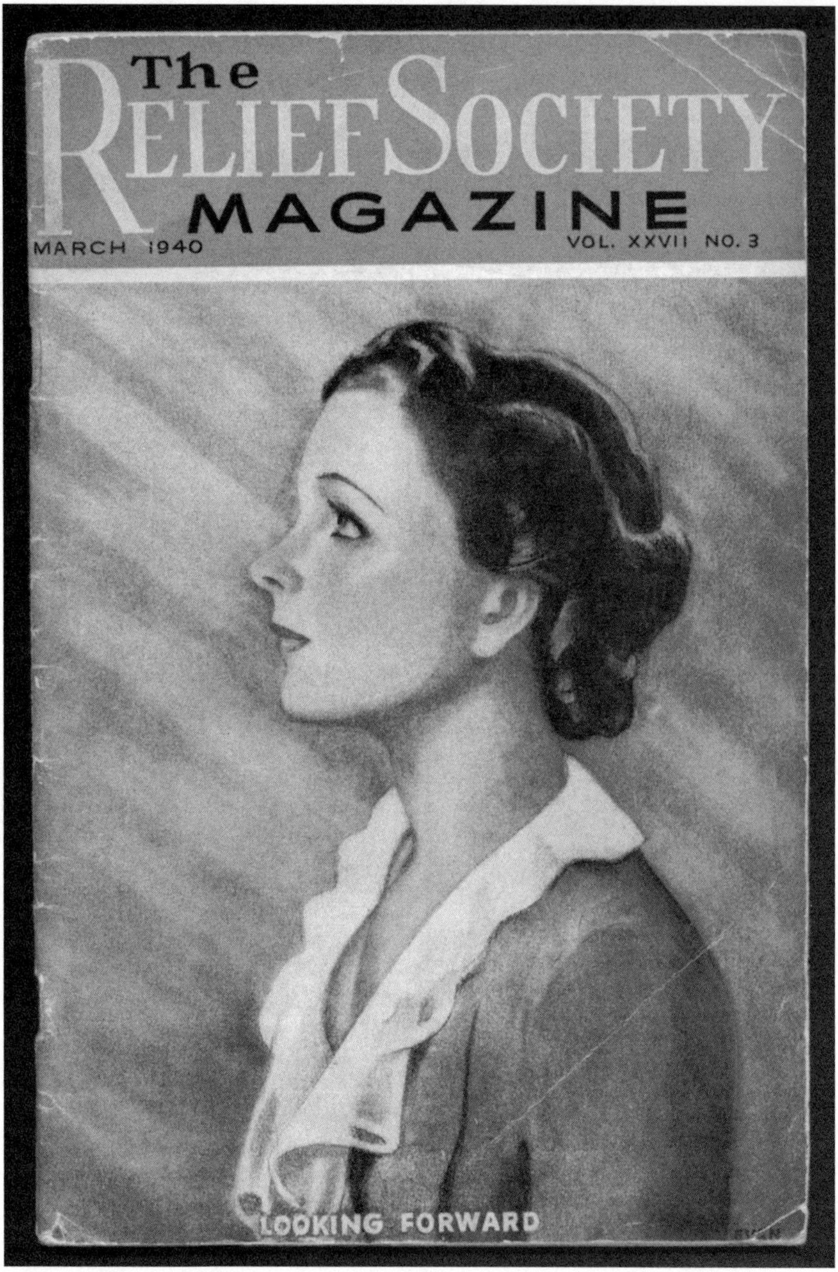

Cover of March 1940 *Relief Society Magazine* that contained Lyman's agenda for her administration. (Author's Collection)

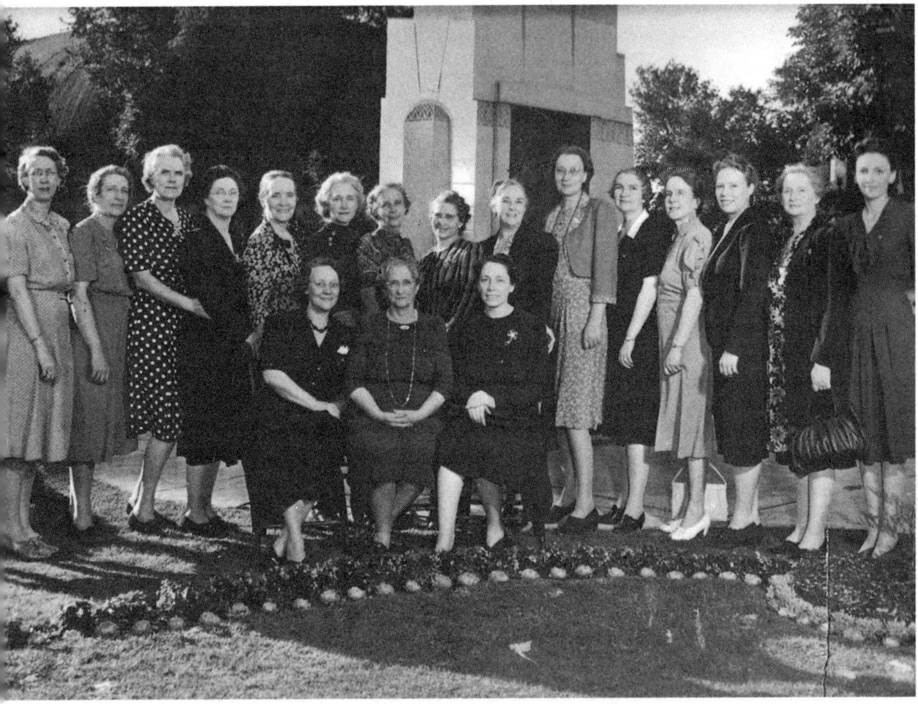

Amy Brown Lyman and her presidency with General Board of Relief Society, ca. 1941, with arch representing membership drive for Relief Society Centennial. Edith Smith Eliott stands on the far left of the second row, Mary Grant Judd sixth from right, Gertrude Ryberg Garff, third from right, and Leona Fetzer Wintch far right of the second row. (Author's Collection; courtesy of Vera W. Pohlman)

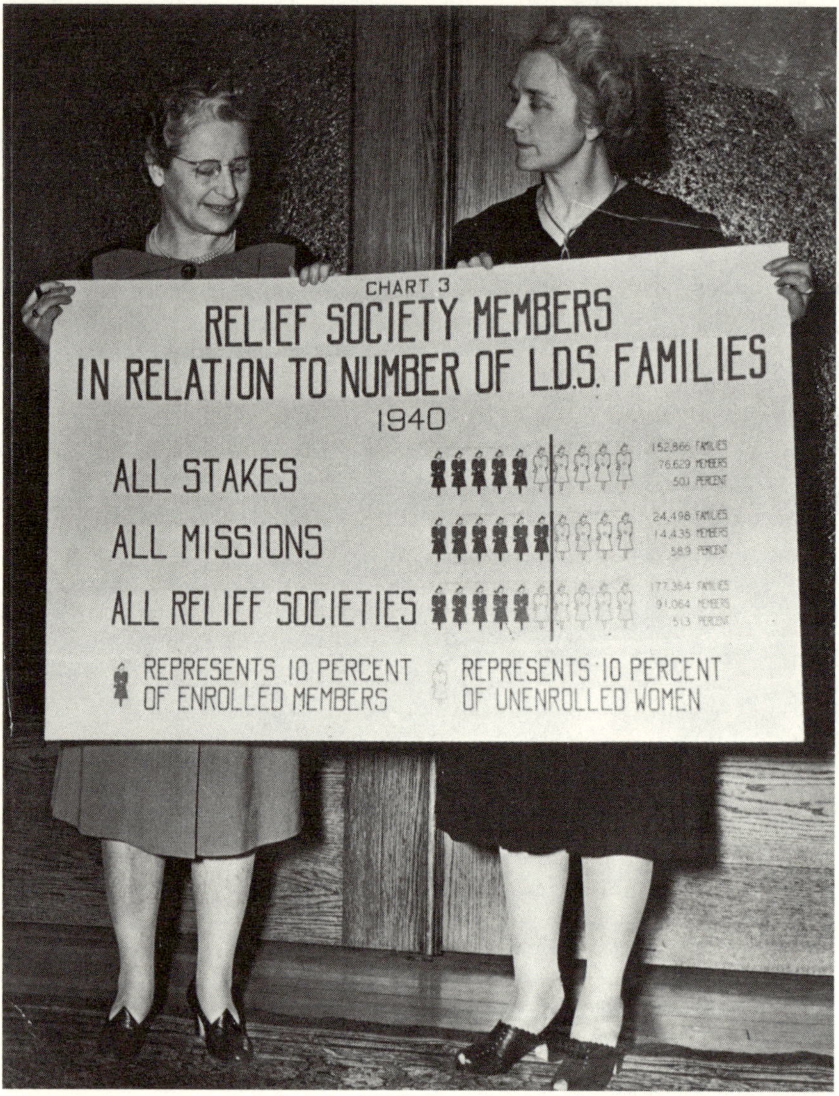

Vera W. Pohlman and general board member Rae B. Barker with poster for Relief Society centennial membership drive. (Lignell and Gill photographers; courtesy of Vera W. Pohlman)

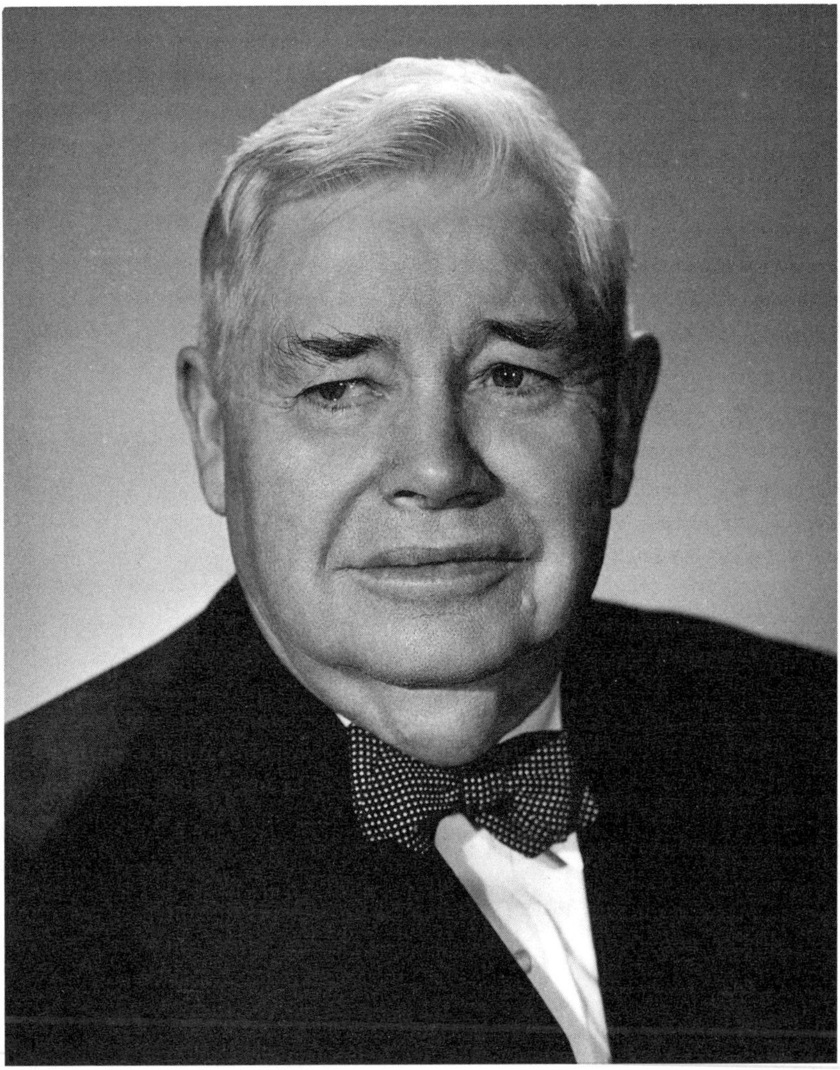

First Counselor in the First Presidency, J. Reuben Clark. (LDS Church History Library)

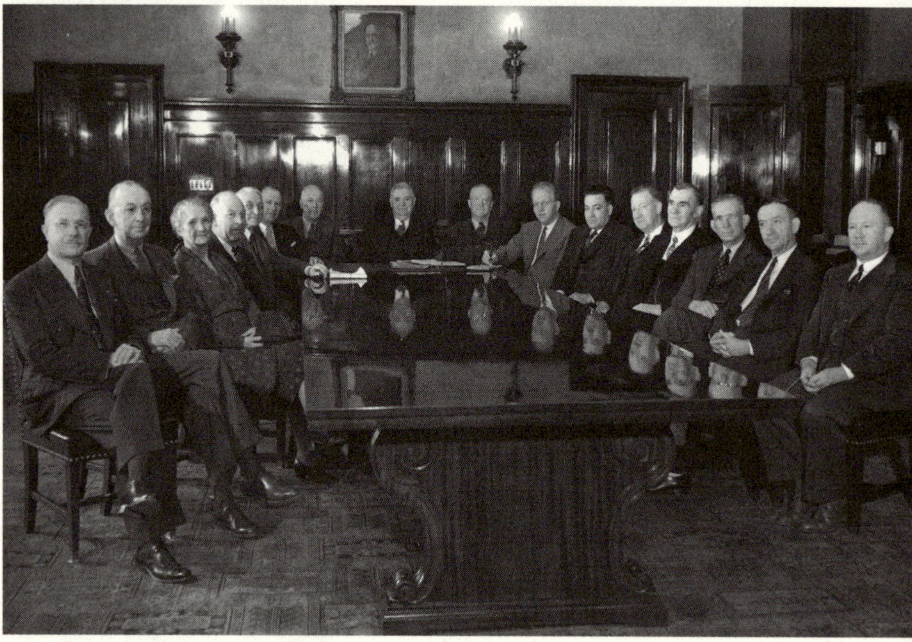

General Church Welfare Committee, 1940. Lyman is the only woman in the photo. (LDS Church History Library; used with permission of the *Salt Lake Tribune*)

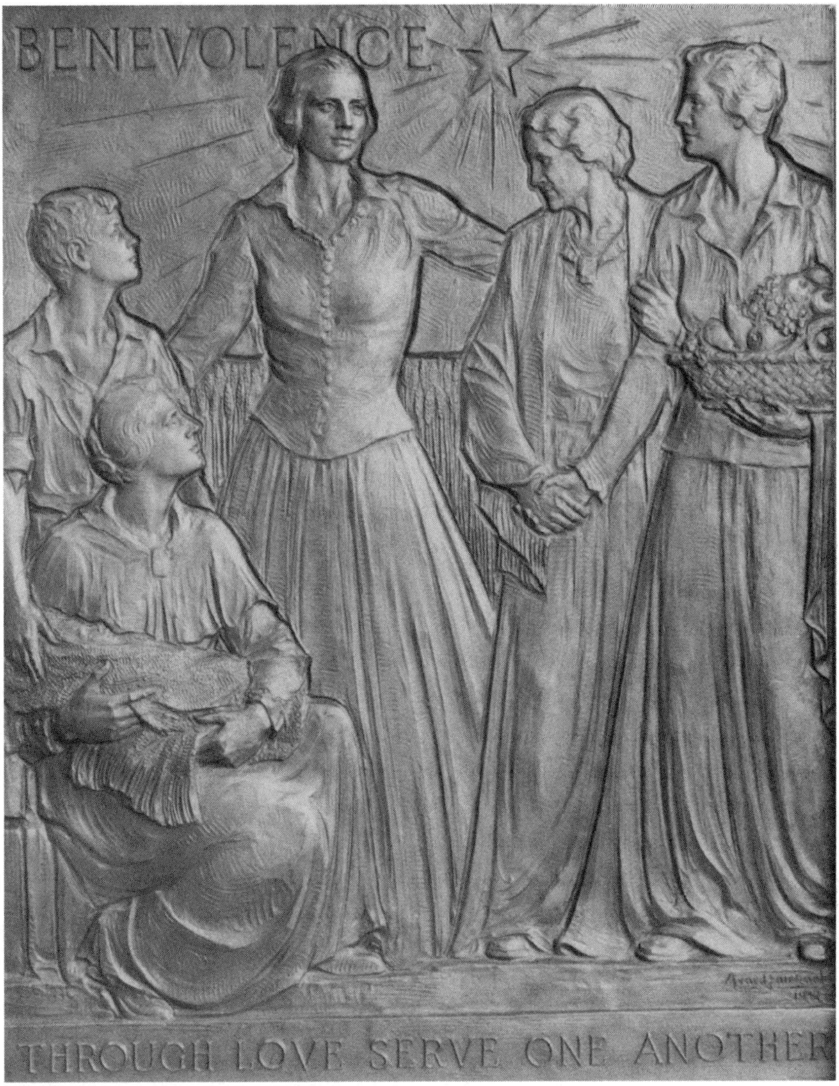

Bas relief panel by noted sculptor Avard Fairbanks from Relief Society Campanile. (LDS Church History Library)

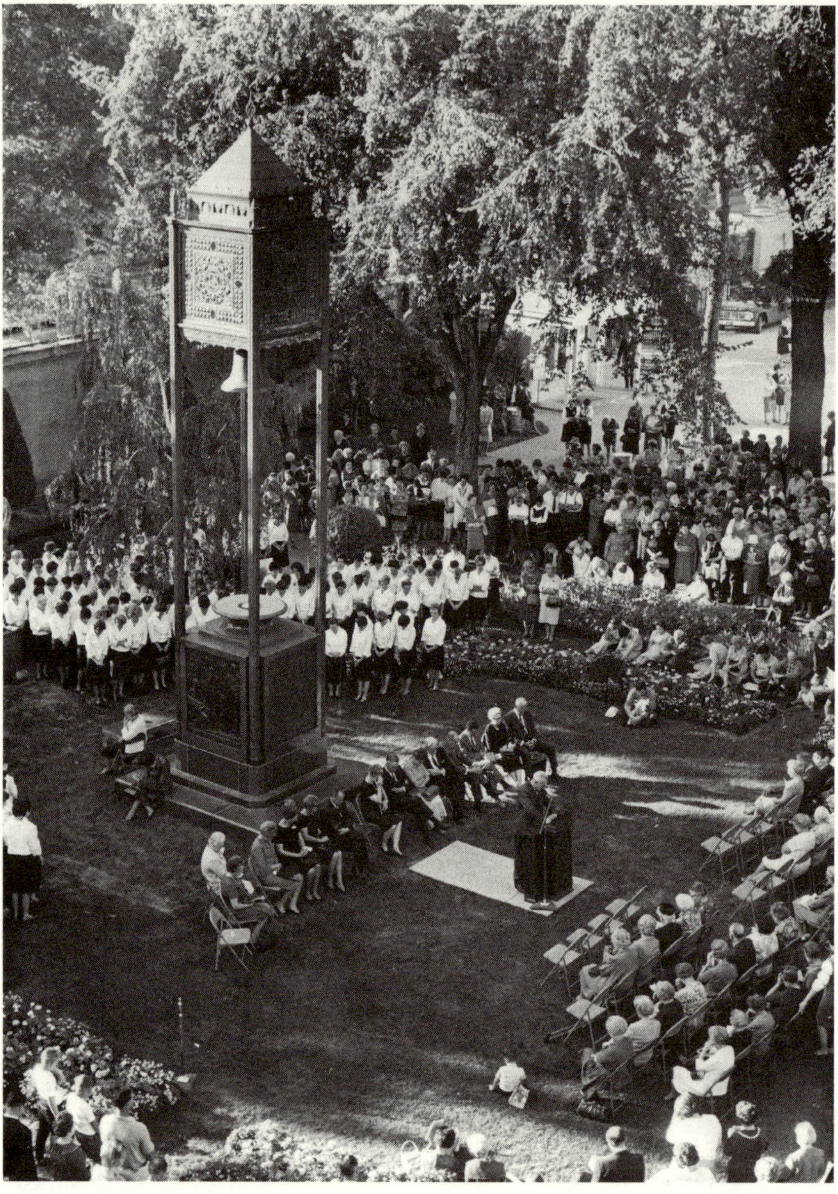

Campanile at the time of its dedication by Belle S. Spafford, 1967. (LDS Church History Library)

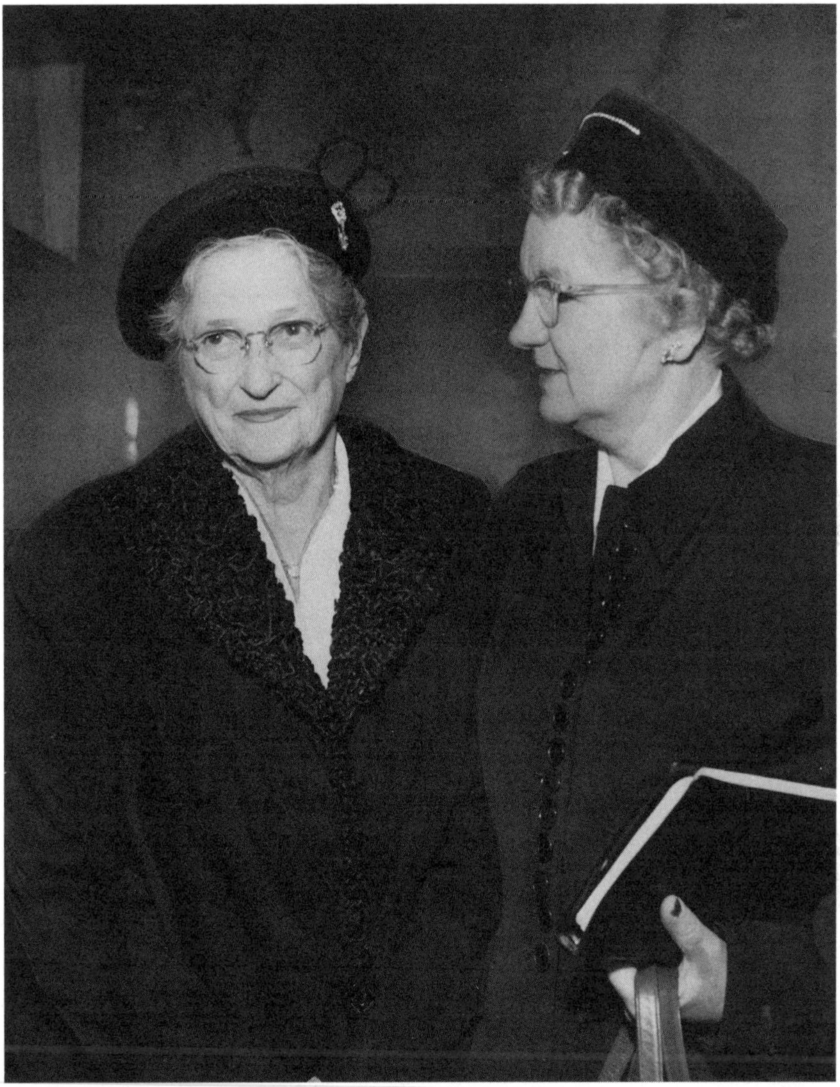

Amy Brown Lyman and General Relief Society President Belle S. Spafford, 1951. (LDS Church History Library; used with permission of the *Salt Lake Tribune*)

6

TRYING TO HOLD ON DURING THE GREAT DEPRESSION

> The effectiveness of the Government measures depends largely on our general understanding of what is being attempted, and how it may be worked out.
>
> —MARCIA KNOWLTON HOWELLS[1]

> You know women have a definite viewpoint, and wherever human welfare is involved we think there should be a woman's viewpoint.
>
> —AMY BROWN LYMAN[2]

By the latter 1920s, Amy Brown Lyman had grown into a highly effective leader of a far-flung organization, an experienced social worker, reformer, and skilled lobbyist. Perhaps the best-known and best-connected LDS woman of her generation, no one in the Mormon community was better positioned to deal with the great economic crisis about to descend on the nation. Yet, at the very time her talents were most needed, Lyman faced a failure, not of vision or determination, but of opportunity, one that left her unable to marshal effectively the now formidable resources of the Relief Society. Lyman's relative powerlessness was rooted both in larger trends affecting all American women involved in social welfare work and also in factors uniquely impinging on the Relief Society. Together these trends meant that for Lyman, rather than finding new peaks of achievement, the last years of the 1920s and the decade of the 1930s more frequently produced frustrations.

Scholars have noted that during the latter nineteenth and early twentieth centuries, women carved out a niche for themselves in social welfare work and so dominated a field that most men, who enjoyed access to more promising avenues to power, found uninteresting. The Mormon community was no exception. During the Great Depression, however, social welfare work became a matter of national import that required the close attention of political leaders and a growing share of community resources. Initially, this brought significant gains to female social workers who found opportunities to move from often poorly funded private agencies with few advancement opportunities to more lucrative and influential positions in the burgeoning public sector. But in the long run, women, even seemingly well positioned ones such as those in the Children's Bureau, lost influence over the development of welfare services as male politicians and community leaders, sensing new sources of power, seized control of the process.[3] Lyman and the women of the Relief Society lost ground as well, not only through the shift from private to public sector relief, but also as male church leaders began to exercise much greater priesthood oversight over LDS charity and relief activities.

Even before the end of the 1920s, however, Mormon women had begun to encounter obstacles to a continuation of the influence they had previously exercised. The most important of these was an eroding sense of unity and direction due to changes of leadership within the Relief Society, a circumstance not unique to that organization. In her 1926 presidential address to the National Conference of Social Work, Lyman's friend Gertrude Vaile, for example, noted the passing of a generation. "In the past we have had great leaders," she observed, and singled out such social work pioneers as Jane Addams, Mary Richmond, Florence Kelley, and Julia Lathrop. "They stood out in the public mind," she continued, "identified with their cause and inspired a host of followers who carried it forward." Now she wondered pointedly about the kind of leaders who would—or could—replace such figures. As Vaile correctly perceived, competent administrators arose, but there were few who could match these powerful, charismatic icons of the profession's heroic age.

While such iconic figures might not have be as critical to the survival of what by then had become a well-established profession as they had been to its earlier development, Vaile astutely observed that something was lost with the arrival of new leaders whose skills lay more in management and less in inspiring further quests for change. What was needed, she opined, was a core of leadership diffused throughout the charitable community committed to promoting social work as an ongoing matter of vital public concern. A lack of such devoted leaders, Vaile warned, threatened the vibrancy of entire organizations.[4]

The kind of diffusion of leadership Vaile was calling for in the mid-1920s is precisely what Lyman and other like-minded Relief Society leaders had worked to accomplish since the 1910s. While they had achieved impressive results, the fruits of their efforts were soon called into question. By the latter 1920s several dynamic second-generation leaders who had previously helped chart the Relief Society's course through the difficult waters of administrative reorganization—even as they held onto and expanded upon much of their inherited legacy of organized womanhood—departed or were about to depart the stage to make way for successors less openly committed to ongoing activism. The choice made by Lyman's close friend and sister activist, Jeanette Hyde, is an early example that stands out. In 1925 Hyde accepted a patronage position as collector of customs in Hawaii (where her daughter lived) and largely withdrew from active service on the Relief Society General Board.[5] Lyman and a few other like-minded peers remained, but found their influence waning. As a result, it became an open question whether the Relief Society could hold onto its broadened agenda or even if it could transfer its legacy of activism to a new cohort of women.

By this time, the Relief Society's role in helping shape the gender expectations of Mormon women had become especially critical as it appears that the leaders of the other women's organizations, the Primary and the YLMIA, had given up much of the broad rhetoric of equality that had characterized their official discourse in previous decades even as they largely abandoned efforts focused on mentoring girls and young women for roles in community affairs.[6] Now, despite the desires of Lyman and others like her on the general board, new leaders in the Relief Society soon began to shy away from that organization's activist agenda as well, which left the future of LDS women's involvement in community affairs and social reform very much in doubt.

This highlights a question: Did the hierarchal structure of the Relief Society and its status as an official auxiliary strengthen or limit the options available to the Mormon variety of organized womanhood? Official standing had bestowed legitimacy on the society's activist agenda, but had also constrained its options. In 1921, and again in 1925, for example, concerns voiced by priesthood authorities led Relief Society leaders to recant their public support for measures advocated by the Children's Bureau such as the eight hour day for women and the proposed child labor amendment. While they complied with priesthood counsel, some privately expressed regret "about not being permitted to express ourselves over pending legislation in which women and children are affected."[7] A related question involved the relative advantages of the Relief Society's own hierarchal structure: on the one hand, it facilitated the ability to achieve impressive results under a unified leadership, but, on the other, it threatened to stifle innovation by the rank and file. On occasion, it even resulted in inaction when its president was unable to chart a clear course or its board was sharply divided. Such had been the case during the last years of Emmeline Wells's presidency. In contrast, Clarissa Williams's administration showed just how effective the organization could be when clearly focused under firm leadership. But her years at the helm were nearing an end.

For some time Williams had been in declining health, suffering from chronic heart problems complicated by bouts of nervous exhaustion, the latter worsened in measure due to the recent deaths of both her husband and mother. By 1928 she was physically and emotionally strained to the breaking point.[8] Concerned about her increasing inability to perform her duties and anxious not to create the kind of deadlock that marred the last years of Emmeline Wells's presidency, she tendered her resignation to church president Heber J. Grant immediately following the final session of the October conference.[9]

As Williams's right hand at the center of Relief Society activities, many expected Lyman to be the next president of the organization—she seems to have anticipated this possibility herself. But her strong administrative style had aroused animosity and jealousy among some board members while her intense focus on social welfare work had led a few to express concerns to church leaders, including Heber J. Grant, about a perceived lack of balance in the society's agenda. In the summer of 1928, Grant told Annie Wells Cannon(the daughter of Emmeline Wells), who was perhaps the most agitated on the subject, that he shared her concerns, agreed a change was necessary, but, reluctant to interfere in the internal workings of the society, "how to go about it he did not quite know."[10] Williams's resignation gave him the desired opportunity. Rather than repeating the process that brought Emmeline Wells to the presidency, Grant took no vote of the board, but named First Counselor Louise Y. Robison to the position.[11]

Like Williams, Robison was the mother of a large family, but she was more conservative in her outlook toward women than her predecessor. She came relatively late into the leadership of the organization, had not expected to find herself as president, and shy and rather self-conscious about her small town origins and lack of educational attainments, never seemed entirely comfortable in the position.[12] Some of those working under her found her a capable and dedicated, if not overly imaginative administrator, generally willing to maintain but not expand the society's agenda. As events proved, she was also unable or unwilling to lead the organization into a repeat of the dynamic activism that characterized Williams's administration.[13] Instead, she emphasized the social (as opposed to social welfare) and spiritual aspects of the society's program. In a further, albeit symbolic, distancing from the agenda of the 1920s (and the professional world of women to which it was linked), it was during her administration as well that forms of address at Relief Society conferences changed back to "sister" from Mrs. or Miss.[14]

But the choice of a new president did not signal an immediate change for the organization as, much to the chagrin of Annie Wells Cannon, Robison chose the experienced Lyman as her first counselor.[15] Perhaps motivated by jealousy over Lyman's rise to unparalleled influence over Relief Society affairs under Cannon's own mother and then to an even greater extent under Clarissa Williams, Cannon confided with anxiety in her journal "I hope [Robison] does not get under matched with her subtle advisor."[16] Cannon sought to counter this possibility by working behind the scenes to prevent Lyman from dominating the new administration as she had the old. Unsettled by what Cannon and a few others on the board told her, Robison was unsure as to whom she should trust. Lyman's personality seems to have worked against her here. By forcefully—and perhaps impatiently—expressing her own strongly held views, Lyman played into the hands of her detractors. Robison sometimes found her overbearing and this formed a wedge that began to divide the determined Lyman from the more retiring and somewhat insecure Robison. Over time, the relationship between the two women noticeably deteriorated.

Of course it must be admitted that Robison was in a very difficult position, overshadowed, as she was, by her more accomplished and better connected counselor to whom public honors continued to come. In June 1930, for instance, Lyman was named to the board of the Western Branch of the Public Health Association, a matter given some attention in the *Relief Society Magazine*.[17] For whatever the cause, while Lyman continued to enjoy the support of several on the board, this increasing (and increasingly obvious) estrangement from Robison eventually restricted her influence in Relief Society affairs.[18]

That being said, one should not think that Lyman's influence disappeared entirely, nor should her ongoing contributions, especially in the Social Service Department, and Robison's support for many of them, be ignored or understated. Neither should it be thought that the change in administration resulted immediately in a dramatic shift in focus for the society. Social work, for example, remained an ongoing topic of emphasis in conferences as well as in the *Relief Society Magazine*—as late as January 1931 an entire issue was given over to the subject—though with diminishing emphasis over time. However, Lyman's genius was not only in administration but also in innovation, and it was here that a gradual but clear change was apparent. What Lyman wrote about Clarissa Williams in a piece published in the *Magazine* after Williams's death in March

1930, and then again in Lyman's own autobiography a decade later, speaks volumes: when reflecting on Williams qualities as a leader, Lyman pointedly noted the late president's willingness to move the organization forward into progressive directions.[19] As for her self-appointed rival, Annie Wells Cannon, once having broken Lyman's hold over the organization's agenda, it appears she was less able to influence Robison in developing an alternative vision that matched Lyman's in its dynamism or appeal.

Thus, on the verge of some of its greatest challenges, the leadership of the Relief Society was plagued by division and at least a few felt, operating with an unsteady hand at the helm.[20] From Lyman's point of view, things must have seemed much worse because she was also cut off from her main avenue of communication with the rank and file. With her call as first counselor she turned over to the new general secretary her "Notes from the Field" column that she had used as a clearing house for ideas related to social welfare work. Not only had Lyman recognized singular accomplishments in her column, she had used it to stimulate a competitive spirit among the women of the church, inspiring them to greater achievement in community activism and social welfare work. The new secretary, Julia A. F. Lund, on the other hand, seemed to share Robison's more genteel views about womanhood, with the result that accounts of maternity and infancy work or social activism slowly disappeared, replaced by expanded coverage of local leadership changes, social events, and the passing of long-time leaders: items unquestionably of interest to Relief Society women, but not calculated to prod them toward greater social action. Exacerbating this shift, Alice Louise Reynolds, Lyman's long-time friend and ally who had edited the *Magazine* for seven years, was released from her position in October 1930. Like Lyman and Williams, she had promoted a progressive vision for Mormon women.[21]

For some women of the faith, already strained by activities of the 1920s and soon to be confronted by the depression's widespread hardship, the Relief Society's shift from the center of action no doubt represented a welcome respite. But for others, attuned to an agenda aimed at community betterment, the move away from the activities of previous years proved distressing. For no one more so than Lyman. Indeed, in coming years it even led her to engage in a rare indulgence: that of second guessing her choice back in 1921 to serve as general secretary rather than counselor to Clarissa Williams, when, she speculated, the latter position might have placed her in a better position to succeed Williams instead of Robison.[22]

Other factors also contributed to Lyman's growing inability to influence the organization; among the most important were her physical ailments. Despite a minor heart problem linked to a childhood bout of rheumatic fever, for the most part, Lyman's health had been good, though she suffered the aches and pains—as well as the weight gain—of middle-age. These developments had given her little cause for concern, although early in the 1920s, the latter had led Amy to solicit Richard's accompaniment as the two joined in a short-lived attempt to get into better physical condition by walking the three miles from their home to their offices. But by the end of a decade of intense exertion and stress linked to her social service and Sheppard-Towner activities, chronic kidney problems—another legacy of childhood illness—began to flare and ultimately became quite debilitating. Already forced by then to work as much as possible out of her home to help care for her granddaughter, her afflictions sometimes led her to work out of bed as well. Office staff summoned to take dictation or to run errands for the department in the latter twenties would often find her there, propped up with pillows and using a hospital tray for a desk.[23]

As her condition deteriorated, she sought expert help, on one of her trips east on business, even detouring through Rochester, Minnesota to consult physicians at the renowned Mayo Clinic. They recommended that one of her kidneys be removed—at the time a rather risky procedure. News of the surgery was kept strictly confidential and none but her most intimate relations were aware that in December 1927, after attending a meeting of the executive board of the National Council of Women, she entered the clinic for the surgery. Fearing the worst, before the operation, she wrote her daughter Margaret with instructions for the care of Amy Kathryn and the distribution of some money and family heirlooms. In reality, the surgery went well, and within weeks she was back on her feet and beginning to resume her busy schedule. However, full recovery took much longer than Lyman had anticipated and a year later she was still feeling the effects.[24] During a period when relationships and areas of authority were developing within the administration of Louise Robison, Lyman's lengthy convalescence may have contributed to the diminution of her influence with the new president.

This situation was exacerbated by long health-related absences occasioned by severe bouts of asthma suffered by her granddaughter. These were especially troublesome during the winter months when temperature inversions over the Salt Lake Valley trapped in choking clouds of smoke from smelters and coal burning stoves. Amy's son, Wendell, remained interested in his daughter, but was largely uninvolved in her day to day care. Richard, of course, was busy with his own church and career responsibilities. The family employed a housekeeper during these years, but Lyman did not wish to turn over the care of her granddaughter to hired help, no matter how trustworthy. Consequently, while bearing very heavy responsibilities of her own, early in 1930, even as the economic climate in Utah began to deteriorate, she took the first of several lengthy trips to California with her namesake.[25] Young Amy Kathryn remembered these as happy times, marked by long walks on the beach at Santa Monica where her grandmother seemed free from normal concerns.[26] Yet for Amy, these must have been anxious periods, knowing, as she did, that she was unable to influence the developing dynamics in Relief Society affairs and aware that her talents were desperately needed back in Utah. Having already struggled to balance career and family with her own children, she once again faced the challenge with her granddaughter. But for now, at least, her granddaughter needed her more. Anticipating the lot of future generations of professional women, she thus gave up important opportunities for career advancement in order to meet family obligations.

Though internal power dynamics coupled with health and family concerns denied her much of her former influence in the organization, Lyman kept any frustrations largely to herself. Publicly she supported Robison despite their disagreements and she remained unshaken in her commitment to the church and the Relief Society. Yet, when possible, she aggressively pursued those options that remained open to her and achieved some notable results.

One of the most significant accomplishments of Robison's administration was in consequence of just such an opportunity exploited by Lyman. Begun before Williams resigned the presidency, it was a push to create a state training school for the mentally disabled. During the second half of the nineteenth century and into the twentieth, reformers had advocated improvements in treatment for individuals with mental disabilities, which today, when emphasis is placed on bringing them into the mainstream of society, may themselves seem backward and even barbaric. Yet compared to the conditions that prevailed at the time, these efforts represented real progress. Those with mental disabilities had long been seen as a negative reflection on their families, a circumstance that had not improved during an era when concepts such as Social Darwinism and eugenics had come into vogue. Ideology and such stigmas aside, lacking social support networks, a "feeble minded" relative, as they were then denoted, required a degree of care that few families at the time were capable of providing. As a result, even in Utah many were locked away in attics or spare rooms in an effort to keep them out of public sight or simply under control.[27]

In the mid-nineteenth century, some reformers began to advocate the creation of special institutions to house the mentally disabled. By the turn of the century the emphasis was shifting from warehousing to education for productive labor. In the 1920s, special "training schools" were preparing thousands for productive roles not only within the walls of state institutions, but even for some, as self-supporting members of the larger society.[28]

All this had been a matter of concern for Lyman since her service on the State Welfare Commission in the early 1920s when she came to recognize that Utah lagged significantly in relation to other states in this matter. By early 1928, inspired by the Relief Society's successful Sheppard-Towner work, Lyman and Williams felt the time was ripe for the organization to press forward with efforts aimed at creating such an institution. The keynote was sounded when Dr. Franklin G. Baugh, director of the Colorado Psychopathic Hospital addressed Relief Society women at their spring conference and urged them to mobilize in behalf of proper care for the mentally disabled. Lessons added to the Relief Society curriculum began to make the case as well, and the following fall members of the general board spoke in stake conferences on the subject.[29]

It was at this juncture that Clarissa Williams resigned, but because the effort was already underway, Lyman was able to secure the somewhat reluctant approval of Louise Robison in moving it to the next phase: a mass mobilization of Relief Society women in a petition drive aimed at securing state funding for the institution. Illustrating her reservations about broadening the organization's agenda, Robison prefaced a December 1928 circular letter to local leaders regarding the collection of signatures with the statement: "As you know the Relief Society is very conservative in its activities, but this is in reality a piece of follow-up work upon our convention program, and we feel that the need sought justifies all our efforts."[30] In light of this statement, one is left to wonder if Robison had been paying close attention to the kinds of activities the society had been pursuing over the previous ten years. Her seeming ambivalence notwithstanding, Mormon women throughout Utah moved with alacrity, lobbying lawmakers, and soon gathered over fifty thousand signatures that they presented to the legislature on the opening day of its session. Faced with such overwhelming support, legislators enacted measures that provided funding for a commission to select a site for the institution, oversee its construction, and provide ongoing oversight of its activities.[31]

As testament to her dynamic involvement in the creation of the training school, Lyman was among the select group appointed by the governor to serve on the commission. Within a year a site for the school was selected in American Fork, a community in Utah Valley, not far from Pleasant Grove, and the legislature had appropriated another

$300,000 to begin construction of the facility. Lyman remained closely involved with the institution and its development for more than a decade. Mark Allen, son of general board member Inez Knight Allen, was resident psychologist at the training school and for years observed Lyman's activities. Allen recalled her actions when she served as a member of the institution's supervisory board that was composed of equally strong-willed and committed individuals. Even in this context, Allen remembered, she held her own as a prominent player in steering the development of the institution. Though not always right, Allen recalled, she always had the best interests of those attending the school at heart. And, when employees neglected their charges, Lyman could be outspoken and heated in her indignation as well.[32] All in all, the story of the training school marked another triumph for the Relief Society. It was also one that signaled a highpoint in its political influence—one for which Lyman was largely responsible although she herself loyally gave the credit to Robison.[33]

In regard to the Relief Society's political sway, as demonstrated through its successful efforts to create the school, speaking at the October 1929 General Conference of the organization, Presiding Bishop Sylvester Q. Cannon observed: "I do not believe you really know how powerful your influence is." Commenting that many believed the Relief Society even had the power to "put over elections," he noted that such views, whether true or not, show "that many people think that the Relief Society has political as well as moral influence."[34] Lyman no doubt took great satisfaction in the success of the Training School legislation. Although she did not know it at the time, it represented one of the last significant organized forays by Relief Society women into the political process.

As important as were these achievements, other developments were already overshadowing such strictly local concerns. Throughout much of the seemingly prosperous 1920s, important sectors of the nation's economy had remained weak. As the decade neared its end, unsold inventories began to pile up in factories, layoffs were increasing, and other signs were indicating the beginning of a major downturn. Most Americans remained blissfully unaware of the impending crisis until the stock market crashed in October 1929. Even then, the magnitude of the emergency would remain largely unrecognized for months. Estimates indicate that by the end of the year 1.5 million Americans were unemployed. By the end of 1930, that number had swollen to 4.5 million, and a year later to 8 million. By the winter of 1932–1933, 12 million Americans would be unemployed, a total equaling nearly one quarter of the workforce. Wages fell from $50.4 billion to $30 billion over the same period while over 300,000 businesses failed.

Some areas were hit harder than others: unemployment in industrial cities like Detroit and Chicago, for example, hit fifty percent by the end of 1932. During the same time, unemployment in Utah, which was heavily dependent on the hard-hit mining and agricultural sectors, was approaching an astonishing thirty-six percent, while per capita annual income shrank to a meager $300. Some areas of the state were hit even harder. In light of such circumstances nationally, economists already familiar with ideas about counter-cyclical spending advocated aggressive action, but most of their colleagues felt little could—or should—be done other than to wait out the crisis.[35]

As for the workers themselves, the jobless faced not just humiliation, but without unemployment insurance or adequate public relief—reforms social scientists had been calling for since the 1910s—they often lost their homes through foreclosure or found themselves on the streets when evicted from their apartments. Meanwhile, their families were left ill-clothed and undernourished. The American Dream had promised that if you worked hard, you would get ahead. Many did so during the 1920s and saw their success as a natural outcome of their good character. Now, hard-hit by depression, they saw in their economic distress evidence of some personal moral failing, adding to the emotional burden they carried.

As the United States had no tradition of national responsibility for relief, Americans had looked to city and county governments or private charities to assist the unemployed. But the deepening crisis soon revealed the limits of these local resources, leaving politicians and charity workers scrambling for innovative solutions. Heeding a December 1929 call by President Herbert Hoover to create what would later be termed an economic stimulus, many municipalities and some states stepped up scheduled public works programs, taking on extra workers to build roads, sewers, and government buildings. Local governments and charities also cooperated in attempts to create work, while Community Chests mounted spectacular drives to raise relief funds.

Yet, despite the best efforts of public agencies and private organizations, the cities were awash in a flood of unemployed and each day the distance between need and available resources expanded further. Unable to find adequate assistance from local government or charitable agencies, the increasingly desperate numbers of the unemployed turned to a variety of strategies to cope. Some went from business to business day after day relentlessly seeking any kind of available job. Others hit the road, looking for work far afield or sought assistance from relatives. In some areas a few even tried to help themselves by forming cooperatives or barter economies to provide the necessities of life. These measures most often proved inadequate. A few, strained beyond their ability to cope, simply gave up. Back in Salt Lake, Lyman and her social workers witnessed a steady stream of such case-studies of despair.[36]

Circumstances were no better in rural areas where drought mixed with plunging agricultural markets forced thousands off their farms and into the growing army of unemployed. In Smithfield Utah, for example, by 1932 one half of the town's families were receiving relief or some form of charity. Faced with this widespread economic collapse and the attendant suffering, President Hoover claimed that at least no one was starving. Social workers knew better. They had seen school children who fainted from hunger in classrooms, or simply wasted away by inches, their faces grown gaunt and their eyes sunk into their sockets. In big cities, gangs of unemployed were so desperate they even fought over garbage for scraps of food.[37]

Tasked with confronting this economic hurricane, existing social agencies, such as the Relief Society Social Service Department, were flooded by large numbers of a new clientele—formerly prosperous and industrious, now thrown out of work by the great upheaval and unable to find new employment. As the Home Service work of the First World War had helped remove some of the stigma from social work, the presence of these former members of the respectable middle-class among the unemployed eventually played an important role in changing societal attitudes towards the causes of dependency. With joblessness cutting such a broad swath through the workforce it became clear that something more than simply personal failure was involved.

The shift in character of those who desperately sought aid at the height of the crisis was captured early in 1932 in a poignant article in the *Relief Society Magazine* written by long-time social worker Annie Palmer. "In the hurry of this winter's office intake, practically all rules have been suspended and most methods subjected to undesirable modification." Gone was time for careful counseling; clients could expect only a quick evaluation of their cases followed by a hurriedly filled-out order for a small amount of food and perhaps some coal before they were rushed out and the next case hustled in. In addition to the changing pace of work, "They who come to the Relief Agency are now so different!" No longer the chronically unemployable, the "weak or sick or unfortunate," many now were "strong and determined and defiant." Young men, clean, well dressed, "*demanding* that their dependents shall not suffer," and "sturdy men of middle age who weep because of rents unpaid and credit houses threatening." Most never thought to find themselves seeking help in a social agency. As caseloads swelled, and resources remained limited, social workers could hope only to stave off starvation for a short time while attempting during their brief interviews to buoy sagging spirits, perhaps, Palmer hoped, giving their clients enough courage to last until the crisis passed.[38]

As elsewhere in the nation, breadlines and soup kitchens became a fixture in Utah's cities. Meanwhile, large numbers of the unemployed wearily walked the streets searching for work while sidewalk vendors and door-to-door salesmen appeared selling everything from apples to Fuller brushes. Though the suffering in Utah's urban areas did not equal that of the great Eastern industrial centers, unemployment and economic hardship in the state consistently remained above the national average, with Salt Lake City especially hard hit.[39]

As they tried to find adequate solutions to these truly daunting challenges, political leaders and social workers in the West turned to methods employed elsewhere. By the fall of 1930, Utah's cities were supplementing county efforts with emergency work programs such as snow shoveling or wood cutting. Due to her ongoing role with Salt Lake's Central Council of Social Agencies and her ties to state programs and officials, Lyman played an important part in organizing these efforts. She helped as well when Salt Lake's mayor arranged for a municipal warehouse to be stocked with food and commodities provided by the city, the church, and the Community Chest for distribution to the needy. In a testimony of Lyman's foresight in preparing for just such an eventuality, the Social Service Department and social service aids were critical to this effort as they carried out a survey of needy residents and wrote about one-half of all the food and commodity orders.[40]

Clearly, despite being sidelined in some aspects of Relief Society work, Lyman remained the public face of the church in relief matters. The respect she had earned over the previous decade-and-a-half from public officials and the heads of private charities won her appointments to several local and statewide boards formed to deal with the crisis, including the governor's committee on unemployment.[41] Meanwhile, when church leaders decided to stretch limited charity funds by centering LDS relief efforts at the local level where social service aids served on a volunteer basis rather than by increasing the paid employees at the central offices, it was Lyman who facilitated this plan with a new round of social service institutes during the summer of 1930 and the winter of 1931.[42] Yet, despite such vigorous efforts, Lyman was still largely cut off from the rank and file of the organization and unable to mount any broad moves of the kind that characterized the 1920s.

Meanwhile, individual members of the Relief Society—like women across the nation—faced daunting challenges of their own as economic insecurity reached into their homes and forced some into the workforce for the first time. They worked because they needed to support their families and sometimes found positions when their husbands could not. Yet, their presence in the office or storefront left them vulnerable to charges they were stealing jobs from men. Women, like immigrants, thus became scapegoats for worsening economic conditions. The federal government even began to fire some women to open positions for male heads of households and several states tried to pass laws prohibiting married women from holding public sector jobs, especially if their husbands also worked. In Utah, Lyman's former secretary, Vera Pohlman, then a public employee, helped head off such a move in the legislature.[43]

Even as Relief Society women faced challenges in their own lives, they were advised by their leaders to be on the alert for others in need of assistance and called upon to be generous in their monthly contributions to the Relief Society charity fund. They gave, but with their personal resources already stretched thin, there was little chance that they could keep up with the steadily expanding magnitude of need.[44] Human resources were strained to the limit as well. Among local Relief Society women the ward presidents were the most overburdened. Laboring alongside their bishops, they faced a truly impossible task of feeding and clothing an ever-growing number of ward members, often while confronting hardship themselves. Desperate to do something to assist the needy, some Relief Society presidents joined stake priesthood leaders in the development of self-help programs similar to many springing up elsewhere in the nation. The six stakes of Salt Lake City achieved particularly impressive results: priesthood and Relief Society leaders there created a city-wide employment exchange, planted crops on vacant land, share-cropped for local farmers, purchased food and fuel in bulk to be sold at cost or distributed free of charge to the needy, and even created small enterprises where locally produced commodities could be sold. Hundreds of LDS families were helped in this manner.[45]

While such efforts provided important and valued supplements to meager public funds, they were far from sufficient. By the end of 1931 it was becoming evident all across the nation that the resources available to private agencies as well as local and state governments were grossly inadequate in the face of the growing crisis. In 1932, sixty-seven percent of all non-federal public monies were spent on relief and still the most basic needs of millions were left unmet. As for voluntary efforts, one commentator noted they were "bucket brigades fighting a skyscraper fire."[46] Some ideologues continued to insist that relief should remain a matter of local concern, requiring only better use of available resources and a recommitment by the unemployed to find work. Such prescriptions ignore the obvious reality that finding work for all is impossible when the number of unemployed greatly outnumber the supply of available jobs, but they reveal equal ignorance of a simple equation: at times of greatest need local sources of aid decline because fewer people can afford to pay taxes or make donations to local charities. That even the Mormon Church, well organized and practiced in caring for its needy members and experienced in working closely with local officials, was unable to deal successfully with the crisis, provides convincing evidence that such views were out of touch with reality.

For Lyman and the employees of the Social Service Department, a compelling illustration of the magnitude of suffering came in the spring of 1931 when an army of unemployed marched on the capital seeking greater state action. As they moved past the windows of the Bishop's Building, Lyman called over her workers to watch the procession silently shuffle by. Showing no anger, this disheveled army with their hollow eyes devoid of hope or emotion, presented a pathetic tableau of men broken by circumstances they did not fully understand.[47] Despite the power of the scene, the calls of the marchers for state action were largely unheeded; the Utah legislature would do little until compelled by later federal action.[48] This was not unusual. Among state governments, most focused shortsightedly on balancing budgets. This, in turn, led to layoffs of government employees making the depression still worse. In contrast only eight had taken meaningful steps to aid the unemployed and they soon found themselves burdened almost beyond the breaking point.[49] By the following spring of 1932, Lyman was telling the general board about a shift in thinking among charity workers and politicians: faced with state governments unwilling or unable to take action and with local sources of relief largely exhausted, among knowledgeable observers, she noted, "it was the feeling now and general among the agencies as well as the lay people, that the only source of relief in the future will be through federal channels." This was because "the States and local communities have just about exhausted their resources."[50]

By then, even President Hoover had been forced to this conclusion. Ideologically opposed to most direct interventions on the part of the federal government, he had sought to orchestrate cooperative endeavors by individuals, industry, and banks. But when these non-governmental solutions proved all but fruitless, Hoover dramatically expanded the federal role. An example is found when he asked Congress to create the Reconstruction Finance Corporation (RFC), which he signed into law in January 1932. This measure was designed to shore up the nation's financial system with two billion dollars in loans to "banks, building-and-loan societies, railroads, and agricultural stabilization corporations."[51] Though revealing remarkable flexibility on the part of a man known for his devotion to principles, this step, too, proved inadequate. By spring, many in Congress were calling for even more aggressive action—specifically, direct federal relief to needy Americans.[52] Confronted with grim economic realities, Hoover agreed in July to compromise legislation that allowed the RFC to finance $1.5 billion in public works projects while loaning up to $300 million to states, counties, and municipalities for direct relief.[53]

Like other states, at this time Utah had few reliable figures on the extent of joblessness. Anticipating the arrival of these new federal funds, public officials initiated a survey to determine the extent of need. When state officials turned to the church for help, it was Lyman who gathered statistics and collected sample case histories; all this was presented as evidence at hearings held at the capital to document Utah's requirements for assistance.[54] By late summer 1932, when the first RFC funds arrived in Utah, Lyman aided in their distribution as a member of the Governor's Committee on Emergency Relief.[55] In keeping with its already established policy of cooperation with government in social welfare matters (and at a time when the separation of church and state was not as sharply drawn), the church welcomed these new funds and even praised the move in the *Deseret News*. Eventually, one in four Utah families received aid through the RFC, a percentage well above the national average.[56]

These federal monies, however, were far from adequate in meeting relief requirements in the state. Making the situation worse, they spawned a false hope that the crisis was now being effectively addressed and that the federal government was shouldering the lion's share of the relief burden—a view, some historians believe, that may have accelerated a decline in Relief Society charity donations during this period.[57] Similarly, the arrival of federal monies also led at least one of the six Salt Lake City stakes to shut down its self-help efforts. Charity workers, too, seemed to have misread the situation, with even Lyman seemingly caught up in the moment. In the October conference of 1932 she observed that in the past the church had "assumed more of the burden of caring for those in need than it can carry." But, with the arrival of these new federal funds, it was "cooperating with other agencies and groups in placing responsibility where it rightfully belongs," namely, with county governments.[58] However, private agencies, including the Relief Society, continued to render service by clearing cases and assisting in the distribution of these new monies. As a result, rather than becoming more manageable, the workload of the already overburdened Social Service Department continued to increase.[59]

At this already trying juncture Lyman suffered an unexpected setback when Annie Palmer, her right hand in directing the affairs of the department, died while undergoing surgery in the summer of 1932. An experienced and valued social worker as well as a close friend, Palmer had worked with Lyman since they trained together with the Red Cross during the First World War. She had gone on to be a key player in Utah Stake's efforts to create a community welfare department and, in 1924, it was Palmer who assisted public officials in providing aid to families hit by the Castle Gate mine disaster in eastern Utah. Since that time, she had served alongside Lyman in the Social Service Department, supervising case workers and assisting with the social service institutes. In a moving eulogy in the *Magazine*, Lyman paid tribute to her friend, describing her in a manner that provides insight not only into the qualities Lyman valued in her social workers, but reveals, according to those who knew her well, much about Lyman herself. Lyman praised Palmer for her "fine intellect," a mind "not cluttered up with disconnected odds and ends," and a straight-forward demeanor characterized by "rugged honesty." Yet she also possessed "an ever ready sense of humor and a playfulness which relieved tension and stimulated social intercourse." Often "blunt and frank in her speech," she could claim "a heart as tender as a child's," though importantly, Lyman noted, "her sympathy did not get the better of her judgment," a quality "often misunderstood by those less disciplined in their ministrations."[60]

As Lyman adjusted to the loss of Palmer, she faced another obstacle: the move of her most experienced personnel to the public sector. In September 1932, the Salt Lake County Charity Department, swamped by applications for aid, put out a desperate appeal for experienced workers. In response, Lyman sent over half-a-dozen of her most capable employees.[61] Now facing a critical shortage of her own, Lyman circulated word that the Relief Society was willing to accept unskilled volunteers. She took charge of the necessary training herself, including rigorous course work and on-the-job experience. As compensation for the long hours of work and study these recruits could expect little in return, some at first being paid only in bus tokens for their ride to and from the Social Service Department offices. Leona Fetzer (Wintch) accepted an apprenticeship position at such terms around this period. A few months later, with some on-the-job experience under her belt, Fetzer received a meager $25 per month in salary. This was raised to $60 three months later with the advent of the federal minimum wage. Yet despite these modest financial rewards, enough workers were drawn in by the opportunity to see the department through this latest crisis.[62] In the meantime, the departing professionals played a pivotal role in the developing public sector, demonstrating a further link between the private and public relief efforts during the period.

These adjustments were taking place during an election year in which Herbert Hoover was seeking a second term as president. After four years of depression, Hoover's policies seemed ineffectual and his energies spent. What course his opponent, Franklin Roosevelt, would take remained largely unknown, but as governor of New York he had been one of a handful of state executives to initiate meaningful action during the unemployment emergency. This, combined with his self-confident demeanor—a seeming beacon of hope to a demoralized nation—led to his landslide victory in November. But as the fourth winter of the depression began and the months between the election and the March inauguration dragged on, the nation found little to celebrate as the economy continued to slide and the banking system headed for total collapse.[63]

During this interregnum, the Relief Society again cooperated with the county and the Community Chest in distributing supplies from a commodity warehouse partially funded by RFC monies. Yet, as economic conditions continued to worsen, frustration and despair began to boil over among the unemployed. In the Salt Lake County charity offices clients rioted, throwing the cans of peas they had received in commodity orders at social workers. Lyman's former secretary, Vera Pohlman, by then a county employee, witnessed one agitated client try to strangle the director.[64] At about the same time farmers massed in Salt Lake City to block sheriffs' sales of farms due to delinquent taxes or unpaid mortgages.[65] As tempers and unrest flared, RFC funds neared exhaustion and it was clear that something more had to be done—and soon. In February, faced with these grim developments, two members of the general board presented a plan calling for immediate action by the Relief Society to initiate a comprehensive program of church relief. It is not known what Lyman thought of the plan, but the board voted to table the proposal because it was too limited in scope. It served notice, however, of just how desperate circumstances were perceived to be.[66]

Lyman had long believed that the work of the Relief Society in social welfare matters required a two pronged approach. First was the rendering of aid by professionals in the central offices assisted by trained volunteers in the stakes and wards. Second was disciplined activism aimed at convincing political leaders to address the roots of societal problems. Though she remained heavily involved in the first, her estrangement from Robison prevented her from marshaling the Society's continued activism in the latter arena. But now, seeing opportunities in the national political scene, Lyman tried once again to rally Relief Society women to push for more effective government measures. In the April conference of 1933, even as President Roosevelt took his first steps to address the crisis, she called on the women of the organization to work for the establishment of a state department of public welfare. This was a reform she considered a necessity if local resources were to be efficiently drawn upon and the federal funds anticipated from the new administration adequately administered.[67] In fall conference she went even further, speaking in favor of national unemployment insurance—a measure already present in most industrialized nations—as part of a well-rounded program to deal with cyclical economic downturns.[68] In the 1920s through such calls from the pulpit she had repeatedly organized the women of the Society in collective endeavor. But then she had spoken with the full confidence and support of the organization's president. Now, it seemed, she was speaking only for herself.

Lyman was certainly not the only member of her sex to suffer such a dilemma: in the radically altered environment of the 1930s many American women discovered that maintaining a meaningful role in community affairs required such a high level of dexterity in adapting to rapidly changing conditions that the likes of a Jane Addams or Florence Kelley would have been challenged. Lyman was one of the rare individuals who possessed the ability to take up the gauntlet in such circumstances. Her calls to action, if heeded, might have significantly contributed to the shaping of the welfare state in Utah. But while her words made headlines in Salt Lake City papers, without the support of Louise Robison, no new waves of collective action by Relief Society women developed in response. Consequently, at this time of crisis (and potential opportunity that came with it) the organization's influence in the community waned.

While Amy faced daunting challenges in the department and mounting frustrations over her inability to spearhead efforts in the larger community, as to her own family situation, the Great Depression tightened but did not seriously constrain the Lyman's financial circumstances. In addition to Richard's modest living allowance that he received as an apostle, he was also involved in a number of business ventures as well as occasional consulting work as a civil engineer. Throughout the period the Lymans were secure enough to be able to employ domestic help. However, while spared economic hardship, they were not immune from tragedy.

After their daughter-in-law Rachel's death, their son Wendell had not adjusted well. He spent lengthy periods at his old fraternity house at the University of Utah where he began to smoke, drink, and was a frequent party-goer. Though he had girlfriends, including some serious relationships, he did not remarry. For employment he helped manage a car dealership in Salt Lake in which Richard had invested, but his business decisions were called into question while his intemperate habits angered not only his father, but partners in the venture as well. As to Amy, her concerns are implied in a number of conference addresses she delivered during the period in which she talked of the need to face difficulties head-on and the importance of religious faith and of following LDS standards of behavior.[69] Despite their anxiety over Wendell's struggles, Amy and Richard seem to have maintained a close, albeit at times strained relationship with their son. They repeatedly urged him to pull himself together, to put the past behind him and move ahead, but he found this impossible to do.[70]

Apparently, by April 1933, the situation had deteriorated to the point that Richard and his business partners had forced Wendell out of his job at the car dealership. In the middle of the month Richard and Amy had a lengthy discussion with their son during which he was told that in order to regain his position he had to get his life in order.[71] It is unclear at this point how Wendell responded, but nearly a month later, on Saturday afternoon, May 13, Richard arrived home from a business luncheon to be startled by Amy running into the house in "hysterics." Back from her own morning's work at the Social Service Department, she had just found Wendell in the garage lying dead underneath his still-running car. The newspaper accounts indicated that he had been working in the rain and was asphyxiated by the carbon monoxide fumes. Reportedly he had been found with a wrench still in his hand.[72]

For the Lymans the loss was almost unendurable. Here was their only son whose health had been the center of so much concern early in her marriage, whom Richard had mentored to follow him into business and in whose early accomplishments they had taken such pride, now gone in a tragic manner. Especially grievous was the unsettled nature of their relationship with him. Yet, true to form, somehow, to all appearances they suppressed their regrets and grief—a coworker remembered Amy looking down stoically but composed during the funeral—and focused instead on helping their young granddaughter through the crisis, who, as she herself pathetically observed to a close relative, now truly was an "orphan."[73]

Under these circumstances both Lymans must have welcomed the diversion provided by their responsibilities. And for Amy, at least, there was a mind-numbing amount of it to claim her attentions as the first of Roosevelt's New Deal programs, the Federal Emergency Relief Act of 1933 (FERA), was implemented. The FERA extended federal participation in relief for two years, changed its nature from loans to direct grants to the states, and provided additional work relief through a host of New Deal sponsored projects.[74] Utah benefitted from all aspects of the measure. During the winter of 1933–34, for example, twenty thousand in the state found employment through the Civil Works Administration.[75] Yet despite this growth, federal assistance remained far from adequate and ongoing contributions by private charities like the church remained vital in addressing even the most basic relief needs of the army of unemployed and their families.[76]

Once again, not only were donations of cash and commodities required, but manpower as well. In August 1933, for example, the federal government ruled that public funds must be spent by public agencies and set a December deadline to achieve this goal. Public officials across the nation went into panic because, as yet, few local or state governments had the necessary organizations or staff to handle the massive caseload about to be shifted to them. In Utah, as elsewhere, this resulted in a temporary "federalization" of private agencies that allowed them to assist with the distribution of relief during a transitional period while adequate public agencies were built. As the result of negotiations between church, county, and federal officials, the Social Service Department was designated District 7 of the Salt Lake County Department of Public Welfare, with special responsibility to continue its oversight of relief needs for LDS families.[77] In order to meet manpower requirements, one trained social service aid from each of the Salt Lake Stakes was brought into the Social Service Department offices. Working closely with bishops, they determined the needs and sources of aid for families seeking relief and filled out appropriate assistance orders. Faithful and active Latter-day Saints could receive aid from a stake warehouse, whereas public funds were used to provide for less active members. To complicate matters, the church sought to provide for all needy active members regardless of their circumstances, but federal aid was to provide only for the unemployed—not the widowed or disabled. Again, the already oppressive workload of the department swelled dramatically. One social worker in the department reported that the number of cases for which she was responsible rose from a pre-depression average of seventy-eight to well over seven hundred.[78]

As this was taking place, church leaders decided to divide the department into two sections, one providing public relief and aid for transients, the other responsible for training caseworkers and social work specialists in the stakes and wards. Lyman assumed responsibility for the latter and moved quickly to organize another round of social service institutes. She also began to send out a monthly newsletter to social service aids to provide ongoing updates on relief matters.[79] Typically, her concerns about training took in the "long view," as she often phrased it, one that extended beyond current needs to the larger goal of upgrading the department. To this end, for example, she continued to encourage talented employees to seek education at the best social work schools in the nation.[80]

Lyman's encouragement to her workers reflected her keen judge of character and ability, and often had profound impact on their lives. Leona Fetzer (Wintch), who began work as one of Lyman's largely unpaid volunteers, remembered fondly the role Lyman played in her own development. Her mother's lengthy illness and eventual death had hindered her studies at the University of Utah while higher education in the depths of the depression was considered an unwarranted luxury by her father and step-mother. Lyman recognized her natural abilities and sent Fetzer to discuss continued study with her close friend, Dr. Arthur Beeley who headed the school of social work at the University of Utah. After examining her academic record, however, he bluntly told her that she showed no potential. A short time later, when Beeley asked Lyman to send someone to lecture to one of his classes on social work, she sent Fetzer. Upon her return, Amy asked her wryly, "Well, do you feel vindicated now?" She did, and soon went to the University of California where she graduated with honors in social work and then continued her studies at the School of Social Work and Philanthropy at the University of Chicago.[81]

Locally, Lyman's change in responsibilities also allowed her time to prepare a rising generation of new workers through a series of classes in social work at Brigham Young University. Here again, the words of a former associate provide valuable insight into Lyman's personality. Writing many years later, one of her students, Virginia Brand Smith, recalled that Lyman's was a class "not to be missed." "Barely getting there on time, in a rush from Salt Lake, she came each week," Smith recalled, "with lots of books and papers." Lyman would then come to the front of the class and "with a little hop (she was not tall), she'd perch on the desk, and begin to talk." As she did so, Lyman's teaching mastery took over: "We were as one as she wove a spell over us," Smith continued. "Delightful, insightful, funny, tremendously earnest, she opened the range of the Church social work programs, and how they applied to us and our future assignments or work opportunities." Again, in this setting, Lyman had a touch for reaching out to the individual: "We felt she saw and recognized each one of us." After class she visited briefly, answered questions, and then "off again in a little whirlwind." But she left behind lasting memories: "Warm, witty, kind, fun, knowledgeable, and an excellent teacher, she added a fresh dimension to my life," Smith observed, and then concluded, "AMY BROWN LYMAN is a person one does not forget."[82]

While updating her approaches toward long-standing goals, Lyman did not ignore the other part of the social work agenda: adding to the voices calling for reform. Despite a lack of support from Louise Robison for her most recent efforts to rally the rank and file, whenever an opportunity presented itself Lyman continued to call upon Relief Society women to become more involved in public affairs. Recognizing that collective moves were unlikely for the time being, she urged them as individuals to support new federal measures. Lyman knew that in these early years of the New Deal important precedents were being established that would have consequences for years or even decades. She thus thought it imperative that Relief Society women use their experience and influence to shape the developing welfare state along the most constructive lines.

Despite her own Republican leanings, Lyman favored much of Roosevelt's agenda. He was vigorous and willing to experiment. He was willing to DO SOMETHING, to innovate at a time when old solutions were ineffective and something dramatic had to be done and soon! In the Relief Society's April conference in 1934 she praised those who supported "the government loyally in its heroic efforts it is making in untrodden paths to correct economic and social evils and to restore opportunity and security." "No government," she continued, "has ever tried harder to meet a situation than has ours, and many remarkable things have already been accomplished." After listing a broad range of New Deal programs aimed at addressing unemployment and societal problems, she then urged the women of the organization to remain interested participants in the political process.[83] Again the following October, she voiced anew her support for national unemployment insurance, then quoted the assertion of Secretary of Labor Frances Perkins that had such measures been in effect in 1929, they would have "put a bottom to the fall of depression and unemployment." Lyman used her time further to recommend that Relief Society women study such social issues as child labor, wage and hour legislation, and national health insurance. And rather than just talking about problems and passing resolutions, Lyman called for more: "We can create public opinion; we can act as well as talk; we can vote." She even encouraged the assembled women to work for the election of qualified women—as well as men—to public office. "Until we support our words by action we won't be able to help much," she continued, adding as a final admonition: "Let us be more active."[84]

A year later Lyman commented on additional opportunities for action she saw in local welfare agencies developing under the auspices of the New Deal. "A great many County Welfare Boards have been appointed recently," she observed, "and we are very much surprised to find so few women on such Boards." "We are wondering if our Relief Society Stake Presidents could not do something about it," she continued, "if you could not remind citizens in your communities that there are fine women everywhere who have spent a great deal of time in the interest of welfare work, and would make valuable members on such Boards." She then recommended that a goal be set that every six member county board include at least two women. "I believe that if we will make a little effort in this direction we will be able to accomplish something."[85]

Despite the growing influence of federal measures, Lyman also recognized an ongoing need for direct participation by the Society in relief matters. In June 1934, Roosevelt responded to pressures from the grass roots calling for more government assistance by appointing a committee on economic security to study the issue of social insurance. In early 1935, the committee made recommendations that eventually resulted in the passage of the Social Security Act that included not only old age pensions, but, among other items, provisions for disability benefits and unemployment insurance.[86] Soon a new work-relief program, the Works Progress Administration (WPA) was putting larger numbers of Americans back to work in government building projects. Taken together, federal efforts were now coming closer to meeting the expectations voiced for them early in the New Deal: they were at last shouldering the lion's share of the nation's relief needs.

With the end of "federalization" of the Social Service Department, which came at this time, and the transference of the bulk of its relief responsibilities to newly improved public agencies, the burden carried by Relief Society caseworkers was at last beginning to subside. Yet, despite these new federal measures, some unemployed Latter-day Saints qualified neither for federal work projects, nor for benefits under the Social Security Act. Lyman joined Louise Robison and other church leaders in recognizing that the Relief

Society still had a responsibility to provide aid to such individuals, as well as to church members reluctant to accept federal assistance on ideological grounds.[87] Furthermore, while details of the Social Security Act were still being worked out, many social workers thought that relief for unemployables—considered unable to find steady work due to chronic physical or emotional disabilities—might be shifted completely back to the states. If this occurred, Relief Society women might again be called upon to assist with a daunting relief burden.

In light of such circumstances, in October 1935, when she presided over conference sessions when Robison was absent due to her husband's critical (and ultimately fatal) illness, Lyman urged local leaders to remain involved in welfare matters. As she did so she also let slip some of her frustration regarding the general board's recent lack of initiative. "I have often wondered why, during this depression, when so many men have been out of work, somebody did not mobilize them in the interest of community improvement," she opined. "I hope that by next Spring we in the Relief Society will have some plans for this work."[88]

Yet, even as Lyman was advocating her own vision for church relief complementing the efforts of government, it was about to be superseded by a very different one built around the ideas of second counselor in the First Presidency, J. Reuben Clark. A recent arrival in church leadership, Clark had led a long and brilliant career in law and Republican politics that included such posts as Solicitor General in the State Department during the Taft administration, Undersecretary of State for President Coolidge, and culminating with his service as ambassador to Mexico during Hoover's presidency. Church president, Heber J. Grant, had watched with approval as Clark's impressive career unfolded. When Charles W. Nibley, one of his counselors died, Grant called Clark to fill the vacancy in the First Presidency—an unusual step as such positions are generally held by apostles or someone else with long experience as a general authority in the church. As for Clark, he hesitated for some time to give up his political ambitions, but when he agreed to assume his new church position in 1933, he brought with him a reputation as a respected elder statesman who possessed a practiced administrative hand and a wealth of contacts with prominent business and political leaders. Yet, based on his years of experience in the public realm, all this was mixed with a deep distrust of government, especially the Democratic variety. Though Heber J. Grant had been a long-time Democrat, he had grown increasingly concerned over the direction the party was taking under Roosevelt. Clark's partisan leanings reinforced trends in Grant's own thinking and helped move him firmly into the Republican camp.[89] Over time the new counselor's influence would prove extensive, with profound implications for the Relief Society and its role in the charity work of the church.

Clark had spent much of his adult life outside of Utah and perhaps for this reason seemed to hold an idealized conception of the Mormon community, even bragging, as he described it, about how the church had always taken care of its own—a reputation no doubt bolstered in the 1920s by Lyman's activities in the Social Service Department. However, when he returned to Utah to join the First Presidency he was dismayed to discover that his perceptions did not mesh with reality. Finding that the church was far from self-sufficient in relief matters, he frankly admitted, "I never had a greater shock in my life."[90] Already alarmed by the close cooperation taking place between the church and local governments, the creation of the FERA in May 1933 inspired him to work out a plan whereby the church itself would assume full responsibility to care for what he termed "faithful" Saints in need.[91]

When first put forward, Clark's proposals met with stiff opposition from several church leaders directly involved in relief. A record of Lyman's reaction is not available, but her views were no doubt in accord with those of Presiding Bishop Sylvester Q. Cannon, with whom she worked closely and who had come to share her perspectives in most relief matters. Cannon was very outspoken in his criticism of Clark's plan and indicated that it was unrealistic in its estimation of how much could be accomplished through the limited resources available to the church. Figures on public relief expenditures gathered in 1934 show that Cannon had the weight of evidence on his side: In Salt Lake County alone, excluding administrative costs, nearly $1,750,000 was spent on direct relief (a substantial sum at the time), sixty to seventy-five percent of which went to LDS families. "If the Church were to undertake to take care of this amount, it would bankrupt us," Cannon noted. He observed, as well, that in the six Salt Lake stakes that had established successful self-help programs, nearly twice as many members were receiving public assistance as were being helped by the church. In light of these facts, Cannon believed—and later observations by Lyman indicate she agreed—the church would better spend its limited resources on making public relief more efficient by preventing duplication of services and by filling gaps in the new federal system. In short, it should seek to supplement rather than supplant still inadequate federal efforts.[92]

If aspects of Clark's plan at first seemed unrealistic, some critics felt it may have been because it was based on ideology rather than practical experience. Lyman herself often observed that unless one was directly involved in relief matters, he or she could not fully understand the magnitude of need that existed in the community—a principle she felt applied to public officials and high ranking church leaders alike.[93] Although he held the best of intentions, seeking to safeguard the temporal well-being of individual saints while protecting them and the church from what he saw as a dangerous dependency on government, not only was Clark personally inexperienced in such matters, but in formulating his plans he avoided consulting many who were experienced—including Lyman.[94] Yet, as it was Lyman who was directly responsible for the very system Clark was seeking to displace, his decision to avoid consulting her seems understandable.[95]

It should be noted, however, that even those who felt the ultimate goal of Clark's plan was impractical found aspects of his proposal appealing. Like most social workers, Lyman shared Clark's dislike of direct relief, or "the dole" that she felt was demoralizing and stripped the individual of initiative.[96] Though she recognized the necessity of direct aid in times of emergency (something that was broadly turned to during the early New Deal), she agreed that work relief (slower and initially, at least, less consistently utilized during the first years of Roosevelt's administration) should be the foundation of any long-term solution. What undoubtedly appealed to her most about Clark's plan was the idea of bringing welfare matters under a strong, centralized, committee that could focus exclusively on the issue and wield the full resources of the church in addressing it. She had struggled along for years with the Relief Society's modest means, largely the small monthly donations made by the rank and file, and her efforts had enjoyed only partial support from general and local priesthood leaders. She therefore recognized that the increased emphasis given to welfare matters under Clark's plan represented its most significant and far-reaching departure.[97]

Yet Lyman, with her years of experience, was no doubt considerably less pleased when she found out, as the program was finally enacted, that both she and Cannon were to be excluded from the powerful committee Clark proposed to oversee church relief matters, even as was Relief Society president, Louise Robison.[98] In this manner the creation of a central welfare committee, the linchpin in Clark's plan, was to follow national trends whereby those with long years of experience in relief matters—most often women—were shunted aside from new loci of power in dramatically expanded public agencies, while new figures—generally men informed less by practical experience than by political and ideological concerns—took their place.[99]

In the face of stiff opposition, for the time being Clark's plan was shelved. But the counselor bided his time and fleshed out his ideas while he worked patiently to gather support, especially from Heber J. Grant. In the meantime the uncertain course of early New Deal reform, typified by starts and stops and frequent missteps, gave him plenty of opportunities to point out the underlying danger of becoming dependent on federal measures. Further support for his position came in a September 1935 survey of church members that found that 17.9 percent of the church was receiving some kind of relief, with the vast majority coming from public, rather than church sources—the latter provided aid to only 1.6 percent of the membership. Facing the possibility that the church might have to again assume the huge burden of helping unemployed members and the sobering reality of how little it was currently doing, Clark received the support he had long sought for a more robust church response. In April 1936, now with the full backing of the church president, he announced in General Conference the establishment of the new "Church Security Program." Grant himself explained that, after much contemplation and prayer, he was convinced that the program was the will of the Lord for the church. After Grant's statement, while questions about details remained, resistance toward the plan subsided as leaders loyally sought to give it their full support.[100]

Clark's plan marked a turning point in church assistance in that priesthood leaders rather than the Relief Society now assumed the dominant role in managing charity activities. Announced with significant fanfare, it received a great deal of publicity in local and national publications. While it signaled a dramatic expansion of the contribution made by the church to the poor, as early critics such as Sylvester Cannon had anticipated, the Church Security Plan (or Church Welfare Plan as it came to be known in 1938) was neither then nor later able to fully live up to either Clark's hopes or inflated public assessments of its success. Indeed, Utah, where the plan was most effectively carried out, remained among the states most heavily dependent on federal relief throughout the Great Depression. During the first years of the plan, Utah ranked fifth among all the states in the amount of direct relief it received on a per capita basis and was 20 percent above enrollment averages for the Works Progress Administration (the largest of the New Deal public works programs) as well as a third higher for enrollment in the National Youth Administration, and double the average for those receiving aid through the Civilian Conservation Corps.[101] Without the significant federal assistance its residents received—both non-Mormons and faithful Mormons alike—the suffering would have been extreme even with the impressive church efforts Clark was able to orchestrate. Clark was well aware of this and sometimes quite embarrassed by claims that the goals of the Welfare Plan had already been achieved, assertions that even appeared in national publications.[102] Nevertheless, the accomplishments of the plan were impressive, albeit more, as some anticipated, in adding resources to still inadequate federal efforts rather than replacing them, and especially in encouraging self-sufficiency and preparation for unexpected contingencies among members.[103]

As the program developed, what part the Relief Society, in particular the general board, might play in the new system was initially unclear.[104] At first the board's role seems to have been limited to support activities, such as training women in home production and encouraging them to supply their energies to Church Security Plan projects.[105] However, getting the plan up and running on the local level required an enormous contribution from women of the organization. During the summer of 1936, ward Relief Societies were asked to gather information about the amount of food, clothing, fuel, and bedding needy members required to see them through the coming winter. More to the point, they were charged with helping to provide the necessary commodities. This resulted in such a flurry of sewing and canning—with still more in demand—that it created so much stress that in the October conference of 1936, Louise Robison noted that "we have had more resignations of ward presidents this fall than we have had at any other time." This is telling indeed when one considers the feverish pace carried on by Relief Society women in the 1920s.[106]

The contributions by local women were greatly appreciated by the committee steering church relief, but it was less impressed with the general board itself. As late as the fall of 1937 it complained in a letter to the First Presidency that general Relief Society leaders seemed apathetic toward the new program.[107] If that was true, perhaps their lack of enthusiasm stemmed from feelings of powerlessness over an area in which they formerly held sway. In this regard, they were surely not alone among American women in the 1930s.

While a supportive role was not new for Relief Society women, the limited focus on home production advocated by the church plan reflected a shift toward more conservative views regarding the proper role of women, not just in the church, but across the nation. In the chaotic and uncertain economic climate of the era a backlash arose against strong, independent women, one that seemed to imply that if women would only remain in the home in "traditional" roles, somehow society's ills might disappear. Even New Deal programs focused on reestablishing men in their role as family providers while such figures as Grace Abbott and Secretary of Labor Frances Perkins, themselves non-traditional, urged the creation of relief programs that encouraged women to develop domestic skills. In fact, federal programs provided sewing jobs for women as well as training for domestic service.[108] Lyman had hoped the Relief Society would avoid the limiting effects of this reactionary slide, but the changes in church charity instead seemed to reinforce them.

Given Lyman's increasing marginalization within the Relief Society, it is doubtful whether she could have successfully influenced the course of events in a manner that might have proved more advantageous to Mormon women. But whatever possibility she had was lost at the time when a new assignment took her far away from the center of church decision making. In a move that caught everyone in the family by surprise, in June 1936, Richard was called to preside over the European Mission, a responsibility that required the family's move to England.[109] This resulted in a flurry of activity: financial affairs had to be hastily put in order and arrangements made to look after their home. Amy Kathryn, now eleven, was to accompany them, as would the family housekeeper, South Africa-born Gladys Jenkin. After a large farewell tribute, the Lymans departed in September.[110]

7

MISSION INTERLUDE

> You will, of course, realize our problem in trying to meet the needs of the women of so many different Nations, each with a different background . . .
>
> —GENERAL BOARD RELIEF SOCIETY[1]

> With it all there seemed to be grave international anxiety everywhere. There was a feeling of tenseness [and] an apparent dread of impending conflicts. Nobody seems to want war [and] still everybody feels that it may break out at any time.
>
> —AMY BROWN LYMAN[2]

On September 15, 1936, as Amy Brown Lyman stepped off the ship in Plymouth, England, she left behind extended family, friends, social networks, and most business affairs to embark on a unique period in her life. Although missionary work was becoming a rite of passage shared by increasing numbers of young Mormon men at the time—and, to a lesser extent, young Mormon women—Amy was now sixty-four and Richard sixty-five, ages when most were nearing completion of their life's work and preparing for retirement. Instead, they had been asked to assume new and demanding responsibilities that would require them to make drastic adjustments in their routines and activities when such adjustments were becoming increasingly difficult.[3] In Amy's case, this step was even harder because she was leaving behind the work for which she had prepared most of her adult life: that of wielding the resources of the Relief Society to assist those in need. The timing of her absence was especially critical because it left her unable to help the organization realign its agenda to bring it into harmony with the new Church Security Plan.

While Lyman found it trying to be far away from the individuals and responsibilities that had been the focus of her attention for decades, she also discovered the experience to be, to a degree, liberating. As Amy was to recall, like other missionaries she and Richard reveled in their ability to be "free to devote ourselves wholly to missionary work."[4] For

Amy, these years represented an important interlude when she could fully utilize her expertise in a new venue as she assisted in the development of programs and practices aimed at strengthening the church and its members in Europe. But unlike her work back home, where, as counselor to Louise Robison she had been significantly constrained in developing her own initiatives to address issues of pressing import, in Europe, laboring alongside Richard, she enjoyed broad autonomy within her sphere of activity.

Along with new opportunities for church service and greater latitude in determining how to carry it out, Lyman also highly valued other aspects of her years abroad. Having never traveled outside the United States and Canada, she looked forward with eager anticipation to the chance to know Europe and its peoples firsthand, not as hurried tourists but as residents. This was especially exciting to Amy as it allowed her and Richard to retrace the steps taken by their parents in their own missionary sojourns. Richard's father, Francis M. Lyman, had served three missions that took him to Europe, the last in 1901 when he, like Richard, as an apostle was called to preside over the European Mission. Amy found great satisfaction as well in visiting the scenes of her father's mission to England three-quarters of a century before. With the love of literature and history instilled in her from her youth she also found it thrilling to travel to sites that she had known before only in the pages of books.

The Lyman's time abroad would prove especially eventful as well, as they were to oversee celebrations marking the centennial of the British Mission, and with it, the beginning of missionary work in Europe. Elaborate festivities were planned, accompanied by visits from a host of church dignitaries, including, if health allowed, seventy-nine-year-old Heber J. Grant.

Amy arrived on her mission a practiced administrator and an innovative leader in the affairs of the Relief Society and the church. In fact, Louise Robison herself declared that while regretting her counselor's absence, as far as the Relief Society itself was concerned, she was thankful Lyman had been called to preside over the organization in Europe, as Amy "was so well informed in Relief Society work."[5] Of course, Lyman was acknowledged as well as a pioneering leader in the profession of social work and a determined advocate in the cause of women. Much of this previous experience proved to be vital preparation for her activities during these mission years. But her time in Europe also led her into largely unchartered territory insofar as she was confronted with a different culture of Mormonism than that to which she was accustomed.

Over the previous decades, Mormon leaders had developed detailed programs and curricula of instruction intended to meet the needs of rising generations of Latter-day Saints as they transitioned to the modernizing world of the early twentieth century. Lyman had played a vital role in this, in particular, leading out in the development of the broad agenda of the Relief Society.[6] But while these programs and activities had proven extremely effective in serving the saints in the United States, Lyman's experiences in Europe would cause her to rethink their adequacy for members living outside the Mormon heartland. As she came to understand with great clarity, church members in Europe faced circumstances very different from those familiar to their American co-religionists. Joining the vanguard of those responding to these realities, during her mission years Lyman helped blaze a path that in decades to come would become well-trodden as Mormonism increasingly expanded its presence beyond its North American core.

It was (and is) often common practice in the functioning of LDS affairs to ask lay-leaders to assume a wide-range of church positions, shifting frequently from one to another, generally with little or no time given for a transition period. Mission presidents in the 1930s were no exception. Consequently, the time available to initiate the Lymans into their new responsibilities was very limited. Amy and Richard had only eight days to be briefed by the outgoing mission president, Richard's fellow apostle Joseph F. Merrill, and his wife, Annie Hyde Merrill, about conditions in the European Mission. After this, the Merrills departed for home and the Lymans were left with full responsibility for mission affairs. Making matters even more difficult, three experienced senior missionaries who were special assistants to the Merrills were scheduled to depart at about the same time. Recognizing his need for practiced hands to draw upon in getting up to speed in mission affairs, and alarmed by this pending drought of such resources, Richard convinced one of the young missionaries to stay an additional three months to ease the transition.[7] On top of this hurried assumption of a host of rather daunting and initially, at least, half-understood ecclesiastical responsibilities, more mundane tasks demanded the Lymans' immediate attention as well. These included everything from housing for the family, to schooling for granddaughter Amy Kathryn.

Housing turned out to be fairly simple: apartments at the headquarters of the European Mission or "mission home" at 5 Gordon Square, London, became their place of residence. They occupied the fourth and fifth floors of a building that compensated to a degree for its want of an elevator by its possession of that commodity—rare in England at the time—of central heating. In a country where, as Lyman observed, "one often has to go out of doors to get warm," she saw that the mission offices and family accommodations were heated with unheard of liberality. For Amy, long sensitive to the cold, this was a decided advantage. Among the missionaries, 5 Gordon Square gained a reputation as the warmest building in England.[8]

Finding a suitable school for Amy Kathryn, then eleven, turned out to be more of a challenge. Lyman had a few non-negotiable priorities in selecting an institution, which turned out to be a little difficult to meet given the English educational system. First of all, she wanted no boarding schools. Then, she was determined to find an institution with central heating; sixty degrees Fahrenheit was her minimum standard. Finally, and most importantly, she wanted one that did not make use of corporal punishment of any kind—Amy wanted no Dickensonian experiences for her young granddaughter. After much searching, a suitable school was located and everything seemed perfect. However, Lyman never learned about something that, had she known, would have prompted her to withdraw Amy Kathryn in an instant: the students shared a common drinking cup suspended from a chain, a gross violation of the basic rules of hygiene.[9]

In addition to such adjustments of location and family life, mission presidents and their wives assumed significant obligations in representing the church and promoting its interests. In this capacity the Lymans found themselves occasionally attending receptions and banquets, often held in the company of high society, in private homes or at such venues as the American Embassy or the American Chamber of Commerce, as well as at other clubs and professional organizations, especially when prominent church members were in town.[10] This is where the couple's previous experiences and contacts proved a special boon to the church. Richard remained a well-connected member of important engineering societies, such as the American Society of Civil Engineers and engineering fraternities, like Sigma Xi, and was experienced functioning in sophisticated social circles. As for Amy, her long history of leadership in social work activities, in the Relief Society, and in organizations like the National Council of Women gave her significant prominence of her own that opened doors for the church in this new arena of action.

In fact, Lyman's first experiences in Europe, and her introduction to the complexities that characterized conditions there, emerged from her work with the National Council. Within days of her arrival in England, Amy embarked on a journey to serve as a delegate of the National Council of Women of the United States to the triennial meeting of the International Council of Women held on the other side of the continent, in Dubrovnik, Yugoslavia. Her decades of association with the National Council had been extremely satisfying, making her a well-known figure and helped her build bridges between women in the Relief Society and those in the larger community. In so doing, it also raised the profile of the church in a positive way. She therefore saw, as did other church leaders, her ongoing activities with the council as a legitimate and valid part of her Relief Society work both at home and now in Europe.

Her journey to Dubrovnik was, in itself, a notable achievement, one that, in retrospect, she allowed was "quite brave" on her part. It also led her to observe that she had "no idea that Europe is so large and that travel connections are so poor."[11] The eight days of meetings the Lymans had spent with the Merrills had delayed Amy's departure, preventing her, as she had intended, from accompanying the British delegation to Dubrovnik. So, traveling alone for four days across unfamiliar territory, without speaking a word of any language but English, she made her way through several countries, negotiated border customs, made a number of difficult train and ferry connections, and dealt with uncomprehending government officials and ticket agents. On one occasion she was confronted with both a taxi driver and baggage handler who screamed at her with up-raised arms. She listened, perplexed, until she finally realized the problem: she was trying to pay them in English pounds rather than the local currency.[12]

Nevertheless, she managed to make her way successfully and safely to Dubrovnik—the latter just barely, as at one point while walking from car to car on a train, she opened a door expecting to find the next coach, but instead was shocked to discover herself standing at the end of the moving train watching the tracks rapidly pass by. She was so startled she nearly fell off, threatening the termination of her mission before it really started. That she arrived at her destination on time after four days of such adventures revealed her inner pluck and determination, yet all things considered, it is little wonder that upon her return to London she revealed privately to family members that at times the experience had given her "heart palpitations."[13]

Conditions at the conference in Dubrovnik dramatically revealed a whole new set of obstacles that would impact Lyman's activities. By this time international tensions were already running high in Europe, a circumstance Lyman found quite apparent.[14] Hitler had taken over all governmental power in Germany early in 1933. In March 1936 he had sent an army of thirty-five thousand to reoccupy the Rhineland in violation of the terms of the Treaty of Versailles ending the First World War. Meanwhile, as civil war raged in Spain, Italy—under the Fascist leader Benito Mussolini—was engaged in military adventures in North Africa. It seemed to many in Europe and America that another major war was close at hand.

Not surprisingly then, Lyman found evidence at the conference of significant tensions between the different European delegations and even among factions within the host country. Yugoslavia was a recent creation dating from the end of the First World War which united the various Slavic peoples of the Balkans. Tensions were rife as ethnic groups jostled for greater autonomy. Representatives of a local women's organization, for instance, one unaffiliated with either the International Council or the National Council of Yugoslavia, and noted for its radical positions on sensitive regional political issues involving the nation's ethnic groups, demanded recognition and official status at all the council's meetings. This led to the canceling of a reception hosted by Dubrovnik's mayor rather than create circumstances that might provoke a potentially explosive confrontation. The region's status as a tinderbox was implied in another reception as well. It was hosted by Queen Marie of Yugoslavia whose husband, King Alexander, had been assassinated just two years before by an ethnic nationalist during a visit to Marseilles, leaving his widow to deal with affairs of state while raising a young crown prince.[15]

A more pointed illustration of the tensions then roiling Europe as a whole occurred in one of the conference sessions as the president of the Italian Council rose to speak and several women stormed out in protest of that nation's occupation of Abyssinia. Later, in a session devoted to labor issues, Scandinavian delegates argued bitterly with the same Italian representative about the compulsory nature of unions under Mussolini.[16] Meanwhile, Dr. Alice Salomon, veteran leader in the International Council and a prominent social worker from Germany—who was also a long-time acquaintance of Lyman's—sent a letter announcing her resignation. She had been forced to give up her position when Hitler dissolved Germany's national council, and, as a Jew, was preparing to leave home to begin a lengthy lecture tour of the United States.[17]

Despite these drawbacks, Lyman maintained that the International Council was able to accomplish a great deal. Delegates approved a long list of resolutions endorsing women's rights, equal moral standards for men and women, and promotion of a host of social reforms. Seemingly most urgent was a resolution advising women everywhere to support the League of Nations in its work for world peace. New officers were installed as well, including a president, the Baroness Pol Boël of Belgium. Lyman had a long interview with this physically imposing and very personable woman who possessed extensive social work experience. During their conversation the Baroness acknowledged the American council's role in creating the International, as well as its importance during the early years of the movement. But she lamented that American women now seemed to have distanced themselves and urged Lyman to "Go home and see if you cannot stir up more interest." It would be some time before Lyman could return home and carry out this task, but in the meantime she would energetically do what she could to promote the work of the council among European Saints.[18]

At the conclusion of the conference, Lyman gained additional education about conditions in Europe. It took her six days to return to London—this time traveling in company with the English delegation, which gave her an opportunity for careful observations along the way. What she witnessed provided her with insight into the great economic and social disparities that existed in Europe. In a letter home to family she recounted that in Sarajevo and Zagreb, she saw peasant women in colorful costumes arriving at market, balancing large bundles on their heads, while in the countryside she watched women and children "working like pack horses." She had never seen, she continued, "such poverty [and] such hard work."[19] As a social worker, Lyman was well aware of the class and social differences that existed among Americans, some very pronounced (even increasingly among some Latter-day Saints), but these paled in comparison to the disparities she observed at this time.

She also noted that tense feelings seemed to be everywhere, "an apparent dread of impending conflicts." "Nobody," she concluded, "seems to want war [and] still everybody feels that it may break out at any time."[20] These experiences, coming as they did at the beginning of her time in Europe, gave her an early understanding of the obstacles to lasting peace, as well as the fears and concerns that weighed heavily upon members of the church. As to the conference itself, it reinforced her views on the special role required of women in fostering cooperation and promoting harmony, amid what Lyman described as "a condition of tenseness, a suspicion and lack of confidence between nations."[21]

Upon her return to England, Lyman soon found events of another kind vying for the public's attention. King George V had died, and his son took the throne as Edward VIII. But his reign was to be brief as rumors of his relationship with an American divorcee and their planned marriage soon reached the press. In December 1936, amid a flurry of controversy, he abdicated and his brother succeeded him as George VI. The Lymans were thus witnesses not only to gathering war clouds, but to the melodrama of a royal scandal. In the months to come they would also witness all the pomp and pageantry connected with a coronation. When the ceremony took place in May, Amy and Richard were able to use connections to view the royal procession up close from a curbside position where they "saw everything gloriously." A full foot shorter than Richard, five-foot-three Amy stood on a small step-stool to look over the crowd. Granddaughter Amy Kathryn, meanwhile, was among a select group of school children who viewed the procession from prominent bleacher seats.[22]

While this was playing out during the first year of her mission, Lyman's travels continued, as did her education about the conditions affecting European Saints. By December 1936 she had toured England and Ireland on church business and trips to other nations soon followed.[23] The European Mission counted under its direction the ten individual missions located in Great Britain and continental Europe, as well as the Palestine-Syrian Mission and the South African Mission.[24] To be responsible for this varied assortment, each with its individual circumstances and unique problems, was challenge enough, but the Lymans' task was more complex as it was the presidents of the individual missions who directly supervised the missionaries and oversaw the success of their work as well as the well-being of the church and its members in their assigned areas.

Amy and Richard's responsibilities therefore required not only an ability to perceptively analyze a wide-range of circumstances, but also that they find a way to tactfully steer and coordinate the activities of the mission presidents whose strong-will and demonstrated administrative skills no-doubt played a role in winning them their positions in the first place. In many ways, given the organizational realities of the work, the most important roles the Lymans had were, first, as cheerleaders so to speak, in helping the presidents maintain their focus and dedication to the church's larger goals for missionary work; and second, as facilitators to provide these same leaders with the training, support, and resources they needed to accomplish those goals.

As the wife of the president of the European Mission, Amy shared responsibility for mission affairs with Richard. As elsewhere in the church, this required that they divide their labor along separate but complementary lines while they worked toward common goals. Through her many years in leadership positions, she had learned that the same held true church-wide across all the organizations. Common practice at the time, for example, called for regular "union meetings" of the heads of the Sunday School, the Mutual Improvement Associations, and the Primary Associations as well as the priesthood organizations and the Relief Society, to coordinate their activities on the ward and stake basis. Similar meetings took place among the general leaders of each of these organizations. This coordination crossed not just organizational boundaries, but boundaries linked to gendered responsibilities as well. For Amy, then, her work as the wife of the mission president was much like that she had pursued for decades as a leader in the Relief Society, working with priesthood and auxiliary leaders. Similarly, presiding in tandem over mission affairs with Richard required little personal adjustment for Amy as the couple enjoyed a congenial and mutually supportive relationship. Over the forty years of their marriage (the Lymans had sailed for Europe on their fortieth anniversary) they had nurtured an easy rapport and developed the habit of discussing in-depth topics ranging from church responsibilities, to family obligations, to current events, as well as the personalities involved in each. They also regularly shared views regarding strategies to address issues that required their attention. Amy and Richard cultivated other habits as well to sharpen their keen minds and facilitate open discussion: at home they often read the same books then (along with Amy Kathryn as she grew older) discussed them together as a family, subjecting the volumes to a thorough analysis in the process. Their difference in approach to this task was revealing: Amy read through the books quickly, cutting swiftly to the heart of any argument. Richard took more time, usually a week longer to get through a book, but when he was done the margins were filled with detailed notes and observations.[25] Taken together, their styles of analysis were complementary rather than contradictory and produced a creative synergy that led to significant insights. The combined analytical approaches, a result of their very different thinking patterns, continued to suit them well as they tackled the issues involved in missionary work.

Amy's mission responsibilities included overseeing the affairs of women's organizations in each of the missions: the Relief Society, the Young Women's Mutual Improvement Association, or YWMIA (the name of the organization had changed from the Young *Ladies* Mutual Improvement Association in 1934), and the Primary Association. She was convinced that all these organizations had to be fully functioning and active if the work of the church was to be effectively carried out. Thus in her own capacity, she worked tirelessly—spending long hours visiting local branches and conferences, meeting with Relief Society and auxiliary leaders, and working on correspondence and instructional materials back in the mission offices—to ensure the successful contributions of women to the work of the mission. As she had during the busy years of the 1920s, marshaling her strength, many times she worked out of her bed, wielding a Dictaphone, for example, to compose correspondence to the wives of the individual mission presidents, the so-called mission mothers, who bore the same responsibilities as she in each of their missions. All this, of course, helped ensure that her vision of active womanhood was carried out in Europe even as her efforts back home had ensured that it was carried out in communities throughout the Mormon core.[26]

Though she had followed developments among Relief Society members in Europe in her capacity as a general leader in the organization, and indeed for many years in her long-running "Notes from the Field" column in the *Relief Society Magazine* had regularly chronicled the activities of church units there, once on the scene it did not take her long to recognize that conditions for church members were far more complex than she had imagined. Adapting church programs to the needs of European saints, given the realities of their daily lives, proved an especially daunting responsibility.

In overseeing the affairs of Relief Society women back in the United States, Lyman and other general leaders of the organizations had decided advantages over the sisters supervising the work of the mission. The general board consisting on average during Lyman's decades of service of about twenty-four women experienced in the workings of the organization, made regular visits to the wards and stakes, gaining in the process detailed information about how the programs developed at headquarters were being carried out in the field. Under the best of circumstances, however, even with local women presiding over ward and stake organizations who were themselves skilled and experienced leaders, constant supervision, correction, and counseling was required by general Relief Society leaders to ensure the work was being carried out correctly.[27] If these general leaders observed wide-spread difficulties indicating an ongoing pattern of problems extending beyond a few local units, such issues could be addressed in the general conferences of the Relief Society, followed up with articles and lessons in the *Relief Society Magazine,* and additional focused counsel in future stake and ward Relief Society conferences.

In contrast, in the European missions, wives of the mission presidents had very limited resources to help them carry out the work. Few members had extensive experience in church leadership. In addition, these so-called mission mothers had a broad and demanding range of responsibilities incumbent upon them, including overseeing the health and well-being of the missionaries, in addition to their work supervising, not just the Relief Society, but all three of the women's organizations. And while there might be mission-wide boards for each composed of local members who could assist in supervision, frequently there were not. Likewise, local leaders, while perhaps willing and dedicated, were often ill-prepared or fulfilling several church responsibilities simultaneously and thus overstretched. Consequently, when problems arose, the mission mother was often on her own in finding solutions to address them.

With her years of experience as general secretary of the Relief Society, one of the first things Lyman recognized was the need for better record-keeping to track progress and problems in each of the missions. Given the short transition between incoming and outgoing mission presidents and their wives, coupled with the regular rotation of local leaders, keeping thorough records was an imperative. But in practice, efforts in the missions to record and preserve insights gained through hard-won experience were uneven at best, and overall, inadequate. More to the point, without a standardized set of records, there was no way to accurately gauge the success of the work in each mission individually, or in relationship of one to another. Lyman thus made it an early priority to begin to address this circumstance, first, by adapting for the use of the mission Relief Societies the record books she had instituted two decades previously in the United States.[28] She also seems to have taken a lead in systematizing the minutes of meetings and conferences, even as she had done for the Relief Society General Board Minutes, in order to make the insights gained in such venues more readily accessible. In the process, she created a valuable resource for current and future mission leaders.[29]

Lyman was to draw heavily upon these records herself as she sought to develop a comprehensive view of the circumstances affecting the success of the work. While her initiation into this role might have been harried, she prepared herself to carry out her responsibilities in a characteristically thorough manner. As was common for the wives of mission presidents, she continued to make use of regular visits to local congregations to gain insight into the functioning of the work. Less typically, however, she seems to have pored over the mission records, especially those of the 1936 conference of mission presidents, held just months before the Lymans' arrival, to gather information about pressing issues demanding attention in the various areas over which Richard and she presided. These issues involved matters both transitory and perennial in Mormon missionary endeavors.[30]

Revealed in these conference records is the recognition on the part of the mission presidents that the glory days of decades past, when large numbers of converts were harvested in Europe, were over.[31] Conversion rates were low—many missionaries working to win only handfuls of converts—and amid the ongoing international depression and mounting tensions in Europe, seemed unlikely to significantly pick up anytime soon. In addition, policies of earlier decades had encouraged migration to the Mormon Zion in Utah, which had the result of siphoning off many motivated and talented members—leaving the church in Europe without a strong, established institutional presence and with few experienced leaders.[32] The issue of leadership was a common matter of concern, voiced not only in the 1936 meeting, but in annual mission presidents' conferences held in subsequent years as well. In particular, members able to administer high quality programs, the kind likely to attract and retain new converts, were few in number.[33] Consequently, the work seemed stagnant, leaving mission leaders frustrated. Likewise, the missionaries themselves sometimes became disillusioned about the effectiveness of their efforts with many feeling they were there simply to glean those few souls left behind by earlier missionary harvests.[34]

In this 1936 meeting, the mission presidents seemed perplexed, but struggled nonetheless to define problems hindering the work and share possible solutions to the situation. A number complained about the poor quality or inappropriateness of the missionary pamphlets. Seen as particularly ineffective was a series marking the centennial of missionary work in Europe that relied on reason and philosophy rather than biblical proofs. The quality of translations of scriptures, tracts, and handbooks was also seen as problematic, as was the cost of copies of the *Book of Mormon*—the equivalent of one dollar in U.S. currency, not an insignificant sum in depression-era Europe.[35]

In addition, the mission presidents voiced their concerns about the quality of those joining the church, as well as their desire to enlist a "better class" of converts who could serve as leaders in local congregations. The presence of such individuals might enhance the prestige of the church, the presidents believed, which would encourage more to investigate the Mormon message, especially those from among the middle and upper classes where leaders were often found. The president of the French Mission, O. F. Ursenbach, related how missionaries in his area had found some success in this regard through referrals from church members. The results, he related, were far more effective than "doorbell ringing" had been. T. Edgar Lyon, president of the Netherlands Mission made a number of suggestions ranging from better tracts, to the construction of distinctive, self-built chapels that would have greater appeal for those investigating the church. He even advanced the idea of developing a Mormon colony in the Netherlands as a missionary tool to show the advantages of Mormon values in a real-world setting.

Lyon advocated, as well, a crack-down on a polygamous community "thriving among Hollanders in Utah."[36] Others advised a variety of means to increase the effectiveness of proselytizing, including the utilization of the sports programs of the MIA to stimulate interest in the church.[37] The need for better training for local leaders was also widely acknowledged. Solutions advanced included suggestions for the creation of more comprehensive programs to foster the acquisition of leadership skills, beginning with the youth. This would allow the church, in the words of O. F. Ursenbach, "to grow our own saints." At the same time, several presidents advocated a simplification of church programs to place fewer demands on the time and energies of the members.

The presidents also saw the missionaries themselves as a cause for concern. Amy and Richard would later note how they had been inspired by the idealism and enthusiasm of many of these young men and women. However, as the activities of some missionaries revealed, in the field of labor, enthusiasm did not completely make up for the shortcomings of callow youth. At the 1936 conference, several presidents called for better preparation of the missionary force and better screening to ensure greater maturity. In a comment that summed up the views of most of the others, Alma L. Petersen, the president of the Danish Mission observed: "We do not have time and means to convert them to the Gospel after they arrive in the field." He further urged no missionaries under twenty or over sixty be called—the younger because of lack of maturity, the latter due to lack of energy. Going still further in his criticism, the president of the Czechoslovakian Mission, Wallace F. Toronto, himself only twenty-eight-years-old, complained "I am astonished at the lack of talent, testimony, conviction and maturity I find among the missionaries now in the field." (To illustrate the perennial challenge posed by this situation, in a later conference, Gustive O. Larson, president of the Swedish mission wondered whether it might not be better to have individuals called to be permanent missionaries.) In response to such concerns, European Mission president Joseph Merrill reminded the presidents of the realities that faced them. While the greatest problem confronting the presidents might well be their missionary force, they should be grateful for what they have and rather than focus on the inadequacies of the young men and women, instead work to transform them into more effective agents of the church.[38]

Problems like these posed long-running challenges that extended over decades as Mormonism sought to spread its message: they were certainly not about to be resolved in the immediate wake of the 1936 conference, or for that matter, during the relatively brief period the Lymans were in Europe. However, other more immediate concerns also drew the attention of the mission presidents in this Berlin meeting shortly before the Lymans' arrival. For example, anticipating quandaries of the kind many future church leaders would face as they sought to balance church values with political realities as Mormonism expanded outside the United States—including into countries with authoritarian governments—the presidents of the German-Austrian and the Swiss-German missions expressed anxiety over the need to develop better relations with the Nazi regime in Germany. "Our only hope of being allowed to remain," asserted Philemon Kelly, president of the Swiss-German Mission, "rests upon our ability to convince the Government that we desire to work with them." Going further he recommended that articles favorable to Germany should appear in church publications, and that the church-owned *Deseret News* should be prevented from publishing any anti-Nazi articles or editorials as it had done in the past.[39]

Informed by expressions of concern such as these, Amy resolved to work with the wives of the mission presidents to assist in finding solutions. Seeking to flesh out her understanding of mission affairs as they developed over the months since her arrival in Europe, immediately following the coronation of Britain's new king in May 1937, Amy joined Richard on her first tour of the continent on mission business. Their travels took them first to Berlin where they attended a four-day conference of the German-Austrian mission. Writing to her siblings, she recounted how impressed she was by the beauty and cleanliness of Berlin and by the large number of Saints in attendance at the conference—some eight hundred—and how enthusiastically she was received when she spoke during one of the sessions, especially when she highlighted her own German heritage.[40] Whatever negative observations she might have had of the Nazi regime she did not share them in her letters, which was wise, as mail was being read by government censors.[41]

After their meetings in Berlin the couple toured the Potsdam palaces of the former Kaisers before traveling on to other conferences in Belgium, France (where they were joined by the presidents of the European missions for another conference in Paris), and then on to meetings in the Netherlands, before finally returning to London.[42] In their travels, as Amy and Richard developed greater familiarity with mission leaders they gained, as well, a better understanding of the unique circumstances in each of the missions.

Through all this, Amy remained herself: outgoing and quick paced, while displaying her keen intellect to good advantage in a variety of circumstances. Among the wives she earned a reputation as someone who could be depended upon to provide well-informed advice and as one sensitive to the needs of others. Not surprisingly, many found her an especially appealing figure. Mark Garff, who was to serve as president of the Danish mission, described her in glowing terms: "Sister Lyman impresses me as being a very fine woman, she is intelligent, pleasent [sic], never overbearing and appreciative of all kindnesses shown to her."[43] In Amy, the person these leaders met was neither arrogant nor domineering, but nevertheless mature and self-assured in her manner. She had long-since grown confident and comfortable in her role as a leader. In religious affairs she remained orthodox and devout, proud of her faith and her heritage. But she was not one to wear her religion on her sleeve. While she knew the scriptures well, she felt no need to quote them constantly—nor to present herself with a solemn or pious air. While secure in her religious beliefs, which centered around a practical, active faith, she was certainly no fanatic. Indeed, privately in one of her letters home she was even a little concerned (temporarily, as it turned out, as it was just a youthful phase) that young Amy Kathryn was "getting so religious I am wondering what the outcome will be."[44] And while both Amy and Richard recognized the need for following established practices and clear codes of behavior, they did not seem obsessed with rigid adherence to prescribed rules, but instead focused more on achieving desired goals. Of course, it must be admitted, while his journal reveals his own deep devotion to his faith, Richard was a little more free in his behavior than Amy, even to the point of letting out a rare expletive or two when driven to distraction by what seemed to be a willfully foolish young missionary, or a particularly vexing circumstance.[45]

At the end of May 1937 when they arrived in Paris for their ten-day conference with the mission presidents and their wives, the Lymans already had a good grasp of the work.

But they looked to these Paris meetings as an opportunity to join with the leaders of the missions to lay out more definite pathways leading toward greater effectiveness.[46] Most striking about this conference in comparison to the June 1936 meeting presided over by the Merrills was the much larger role played by the wives of the mission presidents. This provides a useful case study of the sometimes unanticipated consequences of the regular rotation of mission leaders. Serving before the Merrills as leaders of the European Mission had been Richard's fellow apostle (and former head of the Utah State Agricultural College) John A. Widtsoe and his wife, Leah Dunford Widtsoe, daughter of Susa Young Gates. Leah Widtsoe was an accomplished worker in the field of public health and together with her husband (and like the Lymans), she held broad views regarding the role of women. Consequently the Widtsoes too had expanded the part played by the "mission mothers" during their years in Europe, even establishing the practice of holding separate sessions where the problems of the women's organizations could be discussed in detail. However, the Merrills had reversed that trend, leading to some significant consternation on the part of the wives of the mission presidents who felt their concerns about the women's work were not being sufficiently addressed and that their talents were not being fully utilized.[47]

During the period when the Lymans presided over mission affairs, the role of these women leaders again expanded, returning them to a position of valued co-workers. In taking these steps, the Lymans built on and apparently even moved beyond some of the Widtsoes' innovations. This change was obvious during the Paris meeting in 1937 and held true in the next year's conference in Copenhagen. In both, women made presentations before joint sessions on such topics as leadership training and how to engender a greater sense of unity among the Saints, following which they then led group discussions of their topics, just as did their husbands. In addition the wives participated in two full days of separate sessions, presided over by Amy, which focused exclusively on their areas of purview. These included detailed considerations of the women's work in each of the missions, making use of roundtable discussions. Lyman encouraged full participation for all as she intended that this interaction would turn these sessions into a clearinghouse of ideas for solving mission problems. In this manner she also helped the women develop greater confidence in their own leadership ability.

For the women's organizations a perennial challenge involved how to adapt the programs developed in the United States for the use of European members. In the Relief Society, for example, there were ongoing problems in regard to the educational curriculum. Much of this was related to the significant social and economic divisions that existed among European members, which had profound consequences for the applicability of the standardized lessons. Many Mormon women in Europe were from working class backgrounds and enjoyed limited educational opportunities. In consequence, they had only a few years of formal education, restricted largely to that in the primary grades.[48] Under the circumstances, Lyman quickly perceived that the curriculum developed along Utah's Wasatch Front was frequently unsuitable. It had been intended to stretch the intellect of American women who possessed far greater educational opportunities and many of whom, as well, had experience in the woman's club movement with its agenda of continual education—reflecting this, the 1928–29 literature course included study of Shaw's "The Devil's Disciple," and Ibsen's "The Doll's House." Lyman came to understand that to many—although certainly not to all—European Saints, such a curriculum was simply too advanced. During the Paris meeting, Hannah Ursenbach, wife of the president of the French Mission noted that many of the women were only just learning to read in their Relief Society meetings and thus were unprepared for advanced subjects.[49] Not merely in content, Lyman noted, but in grammar as well, the lessons were written at too high a level.

In addition to the difficulty of the topics, the kinds of issues selected for study were also problematic. European members complained that the material in the lessons was "too American," with not enough emphasis given to local issues and culture.[50] To address this Lyman assigned Virginia Larson, wife of the president of the Swedish Mission to lead a discussion during the Paris meeting on "Coloring Course of Study with Local Background." Several of the other women shared solutions they were developing in their own missions, such as substituting alternative lessons in lieu of inappropriate ones in the regular curriculum. These included studies of women who were national heroes, or pioneer women in Utah who had migrated from the various countries of Europe. In other areas young mothers were allowed to develop topics of interest to them to replace one of the standard lessons each month.[51]

In addition to problems resulting from lack of educational opportunity in some of the missions, many Relief Society women were recent converts who had limited understanding of church history and doctrine. Indeed, institutionalized knowledge of church beliefs and practices had been hindered by the continual exodus of converts to America. This brain drain of experienced members was a situation that had changed only comparatively recently when Lyman arrived.[52] Given these circumstances in which a thorough knowledge of even Mormonism's basic beliefs was lacking, the organization's theology lessons were simply too advanced. Related to this, many European sisters had no reasonable hope of ever gathering to America and, indeed, were by then being urged by church leaders to build a revised version of Zion in their home countries. Not surprisingly then, they felt that there was too much glorification of the American Zion in the standardized theology lessons.[53]

Further complicating matters, Lyman observed that unlike most of their Mormon sisters in America, the majority of European women worked and had little time to struggle with concepts that oft-times over-stretched their intellect. Writing to Relief Society leaders back home, Lyman suggested that lessons be made simpler, that they focus more on the rudiments of church doctrine and history, and that they be written in a style that a tired sister could easily comprehend with one reading after a long day of work. All this left Lyman to wonder pointedly "if we better not have different lessons, or differently written lessons for Europe." Like Leah Widtsoe before her, she began to adapt some of the materials herself.

Other aspects of the curriculum seemed to be well-received. Social work lessons, for example, Lyman judged "very satisfactory and well-liked by everybody," no doubt because of their down-to-earth subject matter (including child welfare) and simple approach.[54] This was, of course, one of her areas of special concern, and in both the 1937 and 1938 conferences she arranged for close attention to the topic in the women's sessions. Despite its popularity with local women as part of the curriculum, however, the reinvigoration of the charity work as an aspect of Relief Society activities in the mission Relief Societies presented special problems given the variety of structures and regulations involved in state sponsored welfare programs in many European countries.[55] In both the

Netherlands and Nazi Germany, for example, charity work was strictly limited, with no additional assistance to be given to those already receiving government aid.[56]

It was here that Lyman's experience in the changing circumstances of social welfare work in America came into use. A master of adaptation to new conditions, she searched for and found ways for Relief Society women to make meaningful contributions to the welfare of church members in ways that did not conflict with established systems. She organized training sessions utilizing materials adapted for the use of Relief Society charity workers in Europe that highlighted the special history and advanced development of the social work in their own countries. In addition, there was a great deal of interest among Relief Society women about matters regarding family health and nutrition. Consequently, in Britain for example, she developed a series of lessons that incorporated materials provided by the government.[57]

Other problems substantially limited the efficacy of church programs as well. For example, in local branches of the church where members were often scattered over large areas, leaders found it too difficult to carry out the full range of church activities. There were simply too many jobs to fill, and consequently, most members served in multiple positions and thus overstretched, frequently did all of their jobs poorly.[58] Attempts by local women to carry out the Relief Society's program of visiting teaching were similarly hindered, especially by the long distances between the homes of members. In an additional complication, most LDS women worked and had to make their visits at night, which raised concerns about safety. Also, most at the time did not have telephones and it was therefore difficult for them to arrange or readjust visits. In reporting these circumstances to the general board Lyman suggested that significant modifications and adjustments be made to Relief Society programs and practices.[59]

One of the ongoing challenges to the work, not just in the Relief Society, but in all the activities of the church, lay in finding ways to encourage members to step beyond their comfort zone to embrace new ideas and activities. Hannah Ursenbach of the French Mission, for example, remarked that a frequent comment heard from members asked to accept a new innovation was "We are not accustomed to doing that." Others recorded that same view in regard to what in the United States had been standard practices, such as Relief Society bazaars and church socials.[60] In eastern Germany, however, Elizabeth Welker reported on a very successful innovation: a spiritual play presented on Sunday evenings. However, several of the other wives responded that the members in their areas were very much against anything like a play on Sundays, while in Germany itself, Welker reported that members were dead-set against allowing women speakers during regular Sunday services. This of course, raises a question of how much of the program of the church was rooted in fundamental beliefs of Mormonism, and how much of it was simply a product of American culture. Then as now, the answer was not always clear-cut.

Of course, one of the biggest problems faced in each of the missions was the perennial need for better leadership training. Early in 1937, Lyman had authored a piece for the *Relief Society Magazine* in which she had been rather overly optimistic in indicating that the transition had been made from relying on missionaries to developing local leadership. In reality there was still a long way to go on this task. It remained an ongoing subject of discussion among the various presidents and their wives whether it was better to look to missionaries raised in the faith to preside over church programs in the branches because of their superior knowledge of how such programs should function, or whether it would be preferable to have these programs run less efficiently but have them presided over by local members in order to help them develop their leadership skills. Among the wives, Margaret M. Peterson of the Norwegian Mission felt compelled because of strife among local women to come down on the side of efficiency. Virginia B. Larson of the Swedish Mission also had to step into leadership roles herself for similar reasons, but then made leadership training a priority, backed up with an impressive program to carry it out. Both Amy and Richard felt that building up local leaders was the ultimate goal and to that end Amy, who was very impressed with Larson's approach, encouraged a wide variety of efforts to achieve it.[61]

In each of these areas, following her by now well established practice—born of her social work experience—of carefully diagnosing problems and then prescribing suitable treatment, together with the mission wives, Lyman was able to make significant progress. However, she was not successful with all of her endeavors. Knowing the advantages that had come to American Saints in breaking down barriers of prejudice (a major concern in Europe) through their participation in the work of such organizations as the National and International Councils of Women, Lyman had urged the wives of the mission presidents to enlist the Relief Societies, the YWMIAs, and the Primary Associations in the respective national councils in the countries over which they presided. She hoped this would reestablish bridges between Mormon women and their non-Mormon sisters in Europe and also revitalize the Relief Society as it took up the agenda of organized womanhood in their regions. Yet, despite her efforts, such work would largely languish, not to be picked up again until a more stable environment emerged after the Second World War.[62]

In regard to the other women's organizations, Lyman learned that the MIA was doing well in most of the missions, with large numbers in attendance, members and non-members alike, who were attracted to its wholesome and enjoyable program of activities. Germany represented one of the few areas where there were problems—not with the program itself, or with the support it enjoyed from the members, but because of suspicions regarding it on the part of the government. Nazi officials could not comprehend the reasons for church meetings on days other than Sunday and did not like programs that competed with the agenda of the Hitler Youth. Already in 1936, Roy Welker, president of the German-Austrian mission, was predicting that the MIA work was doomed, although it was still flourishing among German Saints in 1938.[63]

Yet even in the generally successful MIA work there were some problems to be found. In several of the missions it was carried out unevenly, hindered in part by a lack of adequate materials and especially by aspects of the program that were not well suited to conditions in Europe. Consequently the wives of the presidents were urging a simplification of the program for the benefit of young women, many of whom were giving up on it in discouragement. In particular, the Beehive work, which had drawn considerable attention from Leah Widtsoe during her years in the mission leadership, was considered too difficult as it was laid out in the handbook.[64]

Overall, however, the consensus on the MIA remained positive. The Primary work, on the other hand, was almost universally seen as the problem child of the missions. According to the reports from the wives of the mission presidents, it only attracted children of "the lower sort." By that was meant children of working mothers—most often not even church members—who left them to fend for themselves on the streets during the day. Rather a rough lot, they scared away children from what were termed "more respectable" families who might be in a better to position to build the church and its reputation.[65]

In one area the Primary work was struggling so badly that the only solution seemed to be to dissolve it and start over with children of a "better sort." Despite these depressing realities, some were eager to gloss over problems and present rosier views than conditions justified. In one case, Lyman was alerted to an account from a missionary published in a hometown newspaper in Utah describing huge successes in one Norwegian Primary. Upon consultation with Margaret Peterson, the wife of the mission president, Lyman learned the truth. Peterson later shared details of the story at the Copenhagen conference. "I know that it was reported that we had such a wonderful Primary here in the North—one primary had an attendance of 80," she related. "In investigating this, we found that it was only during a couple of months in the winter under extreme cold that the children came." The children also found attractive the "all-day suckers" offered every week by the missionaries. "Then," Peterson continued, "the Elders stopped doing this, [and] the children stopped coming."[66]

Like other issues confronting the wives of the mission presidents, the "Primary Problem" offered no easy solutions. Yet, as Lyman noted, it too illustrated the need for better materials for leadership training in the missions. She encouraged the wives of the mission presidents to explore ways to meet such requirements in their respective areas, even as she passed on specifics of the challenges they faced to the leaders of the women's organizations back in Salt Lake City.[67]

Working with the wives collectively at these conferences, or one on one through visits to the individual missions as well as through regular correspondence, Lyman's efforts at making adjustments in mission programs continued apace even as other activities claimed her attention. Amid all this work, she found time here and there for recreation as well. As any expatriate knows, visitors from home are always a welcome diversion. In letters she made frequent reference to travelers, students, and missionaries with links to home and loved ones. A special treat came in June 1937 when Alice Louise Reynolds visited for much of the summer. Alice had traveled widely during her years at BYU and had close relatives and many friends in England. Amy was thrilled as she anticipated seeing her long-time friend, in a letter home exclaiming: "I don't know who is the happiest over her visit—her cousin or me."[68] This latest trip to Europe would be Alice's last. Already suffering serious health problems, cancer would take her life a year and a half later. But these two old school mates and veterans of general board work made the most of their time together; they attended the theater, toured the countryside, and visited mutual friends. Alice also took young Amy Kathryn on a trip to such sites as Shakespeare's Stratford-upon-Avon. When in London, Alice shared Amy's room at the mission offices and the two talked late into the night as they reminisced about old times and companions who had passed on. For them, the summer's end with its final parting came much too soon.[69]

Also that summer Amy joined Richard in hosting an extended visit by church president Heber J. Grant and first counselor J. Reuben Clark and his wife, Luacine Savage Clark, there to take part in celebrations marking the centennial of missionary work in Britain. Richard and Grant traveled extensively throughout the summer touring the individual missions and meeting with the members. Grant's visit—the first time a church president had traveled so far afield—buoyed the spirits of the Saints. In the middle of their travels, at the end of July and beginning of August 1937, Richard, Grant, Clark, and other church dignitaries visiting for the occasion joined in the elaborate centennial celebrations held in Preston, England, where the first convert baptisms were made, and in Rochdale, near Manchester. The Lyman's granddaughter was part of a large program put on by the Primary Association that was part of the festivities, while the activities centering around the MIA were considered extremely impressive.[70]

In addition to these activities, a week-long tour of the British Mission made with the Clarks provided Amy with some much valued sight-seeing between visits to local congregations. An avid reader and history buff, Clark directed the party to shrines of British literature and history along the way.[71] This close association with Clark over the summer allowed Amy to become better acquainted with the influential first counselor. In turn, Clark came to know her as an individual rather than simply as an adversary in matters of welfare. These experiences, it seems, led him to a greater appreciation of her abilities. Similarly, the time Richard spend with President Grant allowed him to impart to the church leader a detailed understanding of the problems mission leaders as well as their missionaries faced in furthering the work in Europe.

After this eventful summer, ending with the departure of church leaders and Alice Louise Reynolds in September, Amy's efforts supervising the work of the women's organizations were renewed over the following fall and winter. In the spring of 1938, Amy and Richard, along with young Amy Kathryn, traveled to each of missions on the continent, bracketing their travels around the annual mission presidents' conference, held that year in Copenhagen, Denmark. In these latest journeys they again visited local congregations and attended conferences in each of the missions. Amy Kathryn, now thirteen, proved a popular figure with the missionaries who bribed her with candy to speak to them with the English accent she had mastered at school.[72]

Once again the Lymans found time to take in cultural and historic sites along the way, often guided by the presidents of the respective missions. In Germany during their 1937 tour of the missions they had visited sites associated with Martin Luther and the beginnings of the Reformation, then enjoyed a boat trip down the Rhine that culminated in a visit to Cologne Cathedral. Now, in 1938, after attending meetings at a local congregation in Dresden, they took a side trip to view the art treasures for which the city was famous, including, most notably, Raphael's *Sistine Madonna*. They also stopped at nearby Meissen, noted for its fine china, but especially dear to Amy because it was the birthplace of Karl Maeser, the influential Mormon educator who was her early mentor and in many ways like a second father to her. They visited "the sacred little slant ceilinged upstairs bedroom where he first saw light," and signed a visitor book left by Richard's fellow apostle and Lyman family friend, the late James E. Talmage.[73] On this trip they also managed to steal away for nine days of uninterrupted sight-seeing in Italy, joined for a time by Amy's grandnephew who was serving a mission there. Their visits took them to Genoa, Florence, Naples, Pompeii, Capri, Venice (where granddaughter Amy Kathryn was disappointed that the gondoliers were garbed in ordinary attire), and Rome where they spent two days touring the Vatican and St. Peter's Basilica. They departed Rome just as elaborate street decorations were being set up in preparation for a visit by Hitler.[74]

This tour also provided significant opportunities to promote the interests of the church with government officials and community leaders. In Germany, for example,

Richard spoke before a well-attended meeting of the American Chamber of Commerce about a street numbering system he had devised that had gone into wide usage. Meanwhile, Amy spoke on the development and status of social work in the United States before a packed luncheon hosted by the Carl Shurz Foundation, founded to promote German-American unity.[75] The luncheon meeting was filled with "some of the most interesting people I have ever met," she recalled, mostly social workers (as well as a representative of the American Embassy and one from the German propaganda ministry) who besieged her with questions. So much so, that "we could hardly get away," she recalled.[76]

Their travels in 1938 culminated in Scandinavia. In Denmark Amy felt homesick because the faces of the members were reminiscent of Danish neighbors during her childhood back in Pleasant Grove. In Sweden, the Lymans attended a mission-wide meeting of the MIA where, Amy noted, she "never saw a better organized auxiliary conference." The trip wrapped up with a final visit to conferences with the saints in Norway.[77] After this long and adventure-filled journey, the Lymans concluded their tour with a memorable thirty-hour voyage from Scandinavia across the North Sea back to England. As they set sail, Amy "became suspicious" when a steward came around and fastened paper cups to the sides of each of the beds. When she asked him if he expected rough seas, he answered, "Well, the wind is blowing rather hard." The first swells were encountered at dinner time, sending dishes flying from the table, Amy noted, and sending her flying back to her cabin "none too soon" where she vowed never to take another ocean voyage other than the one home.[78]

By now in the late spring of 1938, Lyman had a very good grasp of the conditions in each of the missions and, together with the wives of the mission presidents, was far along in developing needed adjustments in church programs and curriculums. Yet as the Lymans had made their way through Europe it was clear that war clouds hung even heavier than before over the continent. Hitler had annexed Austria in March and during the Lyman's visit to Vienna at the beginning of May, long swastika banners hung from all the downtown buildings. Amy noted that the "former care-free Austrian people" had become "a serious anxious group." Tensions had been especially high during their visit to Czechoslovakia where government officials indicated that the situation was "most serious," and that "almost anything might happen as the Czech's are determined to maintain their independence." In Germany, meanwhile, civil liberties continued to deteriorate. Ida Rees, the wife of the new East German Mission president reported that among the changes needed in the Relief Society curriculum were those necessitated that year by the standard theology lessons that dwelt so much on the role of the Jewish folk she was afraid the Nazi government might forbid their use.[79] All in all, it was an extremely sobering experience.

The climactic event of Lyman's mission only reinforced such impressions. In July, Amy again served as a delegate to the International Council of Women, which held its meeting in Edinburgh, Scotland. Nine hundred representatives from thirty-one countries were in attendance and the subject of war weighed heavily over the proceedings. Lyman reported in a letter home that "there was not a single session where it did not come up in one connection or another." She noted with approval that strong resolutions were passed urging women to work for peace by promoting economic justice and political education. However, indicating just how desperate the organization judged the crisis to be, one leader made an ecumenical call for prayer by the women of the world despite the fact that the International Council had long avoided any reference to religion because of its divisiveness.[80]

With war imminent, Amy and Richard became increasingly concerned about their situation. While they found great satisfaction in missionary work, like most missionaries, they were tremendously homesick, longing for the company of family and friends, and anxious about unsettled business affairs. It was thus with a certain degree of relief that they received word that, because of the worsening situation in Europe, their term of service was to be shortened by a year. In September they sailed for the United States.[81]

Though pleased to be home, Lyman had much to reflect upon regarding her experiences in Europe. One matter that remained on her mind was a deep concern for the well-being of the European Saints and the need for discretion to protect them, especially those in Germany, from provocative words uttered in an official capacity. But Lyman came home, as well, very aware of the need for greater continuity in addressing the tenacious problems confronting successive waves of mission leaders. The realities of regular rotation of mission presidents, as Lyman had come to understand, was a double edged sword. Church leaders were naturally concerned that mission presidents be free to innovate as circumstances dictated and as moved by the spirit and not feel themselves tied down to outmoded policies. But in practice this often forced the presidents to constantly reinvent the wheel as they attacked problems from scratch rather than being able to build upon the insights gained through the experience of their predecessors. The lack of institutional continuity in programs and practices frequently meant that large problems requiring long-term solutions were inadequately addressed. (Though she did not foresee it at the time, this same phenomena would eventually have profound consequences for the Relief Society itself.) Lyman's efforts to provide a thorough-going upgrade of record-keeping practices represented a first step toward dealing with this issue.

Also of concern to her was the matter of competence linked to the comparatively short periods of service of missionaries and mission leaders. As generations of Mormon missionaries could attest, the generally two-year terms they came to serve (or the year-and-a-half that came to be standard for women) allowed them to become successful as missionaries just about the time their term of service was finished. Mission presidents, who were themselves moving toward a standard three-year term of service, given their far greater responsibilities, found much the same thing. However, in light of the lay-nature of leadership in the Mormon Church where volunteers served at their own expense, these still lengthy but limited terms were about all that could be asked from those embarking on such service.

As far as getting acclimated to the demands of the life of mission leaders, the Lymans experience was fairly typical. In their first year, Amy and Richard struggled to grasp the intricacies of the work and comprehend the issues they needed to address. By the second year they were taking effective steps to systematically deal with problems in their areas of responsibility. In Amy's case, an important part of this was trying to insure that the insights she and Richard had gained would be available, through improved record-keeping, to benefit their successors in managing the work. Their third year would have brought them to a highpoint of effectiveness. But, of course, with their early departure, and then the advent of the war, that was not to be.

As Lyman returned home she was now fully committed to the quest of adjusting programs and practices to the realities confronting Latter-day Saints in areas outside the Mormon core. Vital to this was the job of creating better lessons for the missions, adapted to the interests and capacities of these women. In addition, she saw the need for greater emphasis on leadership training as well as better preparation of potential missionaries so when they entered their fields of labor they might be more effective. All these issues would claim her attention as she again took up her full responsibilities on the Relief Society General Board.

As to conditions back in Utah, Lyman found at best limited improvement in her relationship with Louise Robison. Drawing upon her mission experience, new assignments came to her linked to missionary work. First, she was to prepare a series of supplementary lessons for the missions, incorporating the insights she had gleaned about the special needs of European women. In addition, she was named head of the board's missionary committee, with the task of helping mothers better prepare their sons and daughters for missionary work. On the other hand, while not solicited by the Relief Society, the Church Security Plan (now known as the Church Welfare Plan) requested that she organize another social service institute to prepare Relief Society women to better assist in the new program of church charity. These were significant responsibilities, and Lyman certainly let her voice be heard again in meetings of the general board. But as before, she found her influence constrained and her talents underutilized.[82]

By this time, the Relief Society's role in the Church Welfare Plan had become clearer, but was still undergoing significant adjustment. The plan, as it had developed in her absence, was impressive, with the stakes organized into regions where goods were produced for distribution through regional warehouses to needy members, many of whom contributed their labor in return for assistance. This was taking place in a national economic climate that seemed to be markedly improved since its darkest days of the depression, though the recovery was still far from complete. In Utah, though unemployment had declined sharply from its depression high, it remained elevated and despite efforts made through the Church Welfare Plan, Utahns still received a disproportionate share of federal aid compared to residents of other states and ranked among those Americans most heavily dependent on government assistance.[83] Indeed, as elsewhere around the nation, full recovery in Utah would have to wait until the massive wave of government spending related to the Second World War provided enough of an economic stimulus to break the back of the depression. In so doing, the degree of government expenditures would make the outlays of the New Deal look minuscule by comparison.[84] On the other hand, the contributions of the Welfare Plan should not be forgotten as without the full resources of the church as channeled through its auspices many more would have continued to suffer.

In her travels, from the perspective of a social worker, Lyman had come to admire much about the well-established European systems of welfare that she saw as more effective in providing aid than that which resulted from the uneven and comparatively limited efforts of the New Deal. In this context, she also found much to her liking in the Welfare Plan with its emphasis on work-relief (which she believed tended to promote self-reliance), rather than the dole.[85] Given the insights gained from her mission experiences, Lyman no doubt saw opportunities for further activism in the circumstances she found upon her return from Europe. Her mission years were rewarding and significantly broadened her horizons. But they had taken her away from the Relief Society during an important period of adjustment. Of course, even before her mission, her push to the periphery had already limited her capacity to use her talents and abilities to steer the organization to effectively address the crisis of the Great Depression. Now, however, she found the Relief Society with fewer prerogatives than previously in the realm of social welfare work. Indeed, under the priesthood-led Welfare Plan, it was supporting rather than directing the kinds of charity activities it had previously pioneered.

Lyman's life course had seemed mapped out by providence to prepare her to play a key role during a crisis such as that which was just beginning to pass as the Lyman's returned home. The Great Depression seemed to have provided an opportunity through which all of her experience and talent could have been utilized to benefit church and community. Instead, neither her full resources nor those of the Relief Society had been tapped in that task. While she recognized the importance of her work in Europe, she must have found the course of events curious, to say the least and no doubt disappointing in their outcome.

Yet, typically, she wasted little time dwelling on what might have been. Not long after her return from Europe, now far better informed about the state of Mormon women than ever before, she began to develop clear ideas about how the Relief Society could maximize its contributions to the church, the community, and the cause of women given the circumstances in which it now found itself. Marshaling its energies in more effective support for the Welfare Plan seemed one key to this endeavor. Using her network of contacts among church leaders she seems to have begun to work her way from the fringes of Relief Society affairs and back toward the center of action. It was her improved relationship with Clark and their areas of shared priorities that likely gave her room for such a repositioning. Indeed, given his ongoing influence as counselor to Heber J. Grant, it seems that his greater appreciation of her abilities and ideas played an important role in bringing new opportunities to Lyman—and the Relief Society.

In December 1939, Vera White Pohlman, Lyman's friend and former personal secretary, entered the lobby of the Hotel Utah. She had been summoned to a luncheon appointment, but told to keep the meeting strictly confidential. As she walked through the door, she heard her name called in a stage whisper from the balcony of the upper lobby. Looking upward, she saw Amy beckoning. As she made her way upstairs, Pohlman, then head of the Bureau of Statistics in the Utah State Department of Public Welfare, was intrigued and a little puzzled by all this secrecy, but the reasons for it soon became clear. While there had yet been no official announcement, Lyman informed her that a change was about to take place in the Relief Society leadership. Lyman herself had been called as the new president. She then asked Pohlman if she would be willing to give up her job with the state to serve as the new general secretary-treasurer. Despite the security and promise of her current position, Pohlman agreed, knowing that under Lyman's leadership important tasks would be undertaken. She sensed as well that she was about to work harder than ever before in her life.[86]

8

A PRESIDENCY PUSHING AGAINST NEW LIMITS

> . . . the Relief Society has not clung to customs and functions for which there is no need today, but it has adapted its human services to a changing era, risen to meet new needs, expanded its program, and endeavored always to improve the methods by which it carries forward its timeless objective.
>
> —VERA WHITE POHLMAN[1]

> Only a permanently able, active and working womanhood can produce a permanently able and active manhood.
>
> —AMY BROWN LYMAN[2]

Shortly after her meeting with Vera Pohlman, the church-owned *Deseret News* carried the announcement that Amy Brown Lyman had been called as president of the Relief Society. For Latter-day Saint women this seemed a harbinger of a new era for the organization, one in which the practices of its accomplished past were expected to re-emerge.[3] Despite her shift from center stage in the 1930s, Lyman remained a powerful presence in the Mormon community; a confidant of politicians and civic leaders who ranked among the church's most admired figures. A strong link to organized women throughout the United States—even around the world—she was also a firm advocate for the equality of her sex and an eloquent spokesman for how Mormonism and the Relief Society furthered the cause of women. As the organization looked forward to its 1942 centennial, no one better symbolized its accomplished past and its hopes for the future. There was thus every reason to believe that her administration would be an eventful one. Eventful it would be, but not in the ways imagined. Instead, Lyman was to encounter a daunting array of obstacles as she sought to restore to the organization its legacy of activism, obstacles that fully tested and ultimately overwhelmed even her formidable capabilities.

When Lyman took charge, the organization had lost a significant amount of momentum as well as a clear sense of purpose. Its former activism in public health and social welfare that had motivated Relief Society women in the past now seemed less compelling as much of the work of previous years had been taken over by government programs and the Welfare Plan. The economic hardships of the previous decade had enervated the organization as well, as the middle class women who comprised the bulk of its membership had been forced to focus more of their energies on family finances and stability at the expense of collective endeavor aimed at community improvement. If the Relief Society was to recover from this diminution of its influence and regain its cohesive power, new issues—both relevant and compelling—would have to be found to recapture the interests and energies of a rising generation.

While confronted with issues left long simmering, Lyman enjoyed some significant advantages resulting from the organization's growth and the improving economic environment in Utah and the nation. At the beginning of her presidency the Society counted a membership of eighty-six thousand dues-paying members—this a legacy of a membership drive mounted under Louise Robison in anticipation of the Relief Society's 1942 centennial. In addition, despite the challenges and sometimes wrenching changes of the 1930s, the organization retained the structure and a number of the prerogatives that had led it to a highpoint of accomplishment little more than a decade before. And by 1940 the church and the Relief Society were reaping rewards from the aggressive public relations campaign waged since the turn of the century—one in which Lyman herself had participated. Now seen less as outcasts tainted by polygamy or under the thumb of an oppressive church hierarchy, instead Mormons were increasingly viewed as patriotic citizens who supported their country and looked after their own. Hard won gains, achieved through tireless effort in previous decades, they reminded Lyman of how even the most daunting challenges could be overcome with determination.[4]

In the larger community, Lyman saw still more encouraging signs. Despite lingering economic hardship, Salt Lake was now a vibrant and modern city of some one hundred and fifty thousand inhabitants, a conduit for the region's agricultural and mineral production and a transportation hub, the so-called Crossroads of the West, in a still-developing national system of rail and highway transport. Indeed, the changes since Lyman's arrival as a school teacher nearly a half-century before must have been almost unbelievable. Not only in Salt Lake City, but throughout Utah, the last vestiges of the pioneering period were fast disappearing. As to the Depression, though the effects of the economic crisis lingered, significant progress had been made. Of those still in need, most now received aid from government programs or the church Welfare Plan.[5] While the events of the previous decade had dramatically altered the role of the Relief Society in charity matters, current circumstances promised the organization greater resources while imposing more manageable demands upon it. This granted Lyman some breathing room to devise new goals.

On a personal level Lyman was ready to take charge. Although still limited by a mild heart condition, she had experienced no recurrence of her earlier kidney problems and all in all, her health was very good.[6] In fact, her attitude and physical vigor belied her sixty-eight years and her pace of work often exceeded that of board members far younger than she.[7] Home conditions also allowed Lyman to focus her attention on new responsibilities. Amy Kathryn, now in her mid-teens, had become less of a responsibility and more of a companion and helper. Richard, still active as an apostle and engineering consultant, remained solicitous of Amy's well-being, still her greatest support and biggest booster.[8] Only in the matter of her wardrobe did she have to make adjustments. She was accustomed to wearing old, made-over clothes—a top from one dress attached to the skirt from another—partly due to her thriftiness, partly to make her clients feel at ease, and perhaps because, as a social worker, she belonged to a group at the time somewhat notorious for their indifference to fashion. But as president of the Relief Society some of her associates felt Lyman needed to project a more sophisticated image. They discreetly approached Amy's daughter Margaret for aid, and Lyman soon began to appear in clothing deemed more appropriate to her position.[9]

Now totally prepared, Lyman lost no time in moving ahead to develop her plans. Like Clarissa Williams, her first step was to orchestrate a thoroughgoing reorganization of the general board, starting with the release of many of those who had served for more than ten years. This spared older women the heavy demands that were anticipated to come, cleared out those who stood in the way of more progressive goals, and allowed for the recruitment of board members representative of a younger generation. Some welcomed the release from active service: when learning of the change longtime board member, Emma A. Empey, for example, expressed the feelings of pleasure that had come from her years of service, but was now "happy to be retired."[10] Not all were totally at peace with these changes: Annie Wells Cannon, for example, lamented the loss of institutional experience represented by the shunting aside of older women such as herself in favor of "mere youth." Yet Lyman did what she could to mitigate such strained feelings—in Cannon's case by inviting her to continue her long-running "Happenings" column in the *Relief Society Magazine*, which focused on the achievements of women.[11]

As counselors Lyman chose Marcia Knowlton Howells and Donna Durrant Sorensen, already experienced general leaders with impressive organizational skills and a demonstrated record for innovative thinking. (Board member Belle S. Spafford would replace Sorensen in 1942, who requested a release from her calling at that time.)[12] As for the new blood she brought to the board, she found it in a variety of venues: some were locally prominent women whom Lyman came to know through her visits to the stakes and wards. One, Gertrude Ryberg Garff, was the wife of a former president of the Netherlands Mission who caught her attention when she and Richard were in Europe. Still others, often long-time acquaintances, were selected for their special skills or experiences. Leona Fetzer (Wintch), for example, was a talented veteran of the Social Service Department, while Achsa Eggertsen Paxman was a long-time president of the Utah Stake Relief Society, a former state legislator, and a noted and committed social worker.[13] In addition a few could count important family ties among their advantages. These included the daughters of Heber J. Grant and J. Reuben Clark—although Lyman had to promise Clark, for one, she would not use these connections to circumvent traditional lines of authority. Not all her board members were fans of Lyman, but all were the best she could find—a remarkable group of intelligent and accomplished women who were unafraid to speak their mind and who possessed abilities that proved a great benefit to the Society.[14]

Nor did all her selections meet with the immediate approval of church leaders: in particular, J. Reuben Clark balked at Lyman's choice of Vera Pohlman as her general secretary-treasurer. According to Pohlman's recollection, to Clark, with his lengthy service to the Republican party, her work helping distribute aid in the Democratically controlled state government seemed to "taint" her with the very corruption he hoped his Welfare Plan would root out. But Lyman knew Pohlman possessed precisely the organizational skills demanded for the position and, in her eyes, Pohlman's years of experience with the State Welfare Commission only enhanced her already proven worth. Willing to give in on minor points, Lyman held firm on matters of principle: this was just such a case. Pohlman joined her administration, but in Lyman's words she "had to fight" for her.[15]

At the first meeting of the new board in January 1940, Lyman stressed the need for the women as leaders to be examples of devotion to the church and its principles. They were to strive to live lives above reproach, to follow church standards of behavior exactly, to be loyal to the priesthood as it was "the medium through which order and system is achieved throughout the Church." She also asked that they support the Welfare Plan, "which is a great undertaking, and, because of its newness and scope, a difficult assignment." And she urged them especially to be loyal to one another as members of the board. She asked them not to hold back, but to give their honest opinion in open discussion, but as always in the church, when the final decision was made by a vote of the board, they were to put aside differences and loyally support the will of the majority. To reaffirm their commitments and strengthen their sense of unity, Lyman arranged for the entire board to participate together in a special session of worship in the Salt Lake Temple.[16]

As president, Lyman granted her board ample opportunity to demonstrate their abilities through her delegation of important responsibilities and her reluctance to micromanage. In return, she expected, and generally received, the best they had to offer.[17] Together they charted a course for a revitalized Society; their first task was to rekindle a sense of unity and purpose among the women of the organization. Making effective use of the tools at their disposal, they began with the March issue of the *Relief Society Magazine,* the first prepared entirely under the supervision of Lyman and her board. On its cover was an illustration of a young woman in profile, eyes lifted in an expression of resolute anticipation, below her the words "Looking Forward." To anyone perusing the publication, it was clear that a firm hand had shaped its content.

A central theme was the approaching hundredth anniversary of the Society that Lyman and her board saw as an important occasion to engender a renewed sense of mission among the membership. Board members wrote short articles that extolled past activities and called the current generation to "accomplish even greater things." To give direction to this exhortation, the *Magazine* highlighted aspects of a new agenda in education, social work, and spiritual uplift.[18] The issue also emphasized the centennial membership drive mounted under Louise Robison with a stated goal of enrolling one hundred thousand members by the March 1942 anniversary. One board member predicted that along with growing numbers a new determination would come to the women of the Society while the organization would exercise an increasing influence for good.

Sounding the keynote was an article by Lyman herself entitled "Relief Society as a Community Builder" that focused in detail on the Society's impressive accomplishments in the realm of social welfare, including the dynamic activism of the 1920s. "The achievements of Relief Society women, both in public life and in the home," Lyman observed, "stand today as a monument to the power of their faith and service and as a challenge to the coming generation."[19] Clearly, Lyman envisioned the Relief Society pursuing a renewed agenda of social activism of the kind it had in the past.

Just as the new leadership turned to the pages of the *Magazine* to signal a sea change, so the publication was used to help steer the organization toward a reinvigorated agenda. Knowing its potential as a tool for the promotion of unity and coordinated activity, Lyman and the board threw their energies behind a subscription drive aimed at keeping pace with the expanding membership. New readers soon discovered the *Magazine's* most effective feature: the monthly "Notes from the Field" column, now penned by Vera Pohlman, that once again served as a clearing house for ideas and a means of inspiring local branches to find new outlets for their collective energies. Yet, even as Lyman and the board were creating momentum along this new pathway they encountered a significant roadblock to their plans. One week before the Relief Society's April conference, Lyman, along with the heads of the other auxiliaries, was summoned to a meeting with J. Reuben Clark, now first counselor to Heber J. Grant, to discuss a "Memorandum of Suggestions," regarding the simplification of church programs.[20]

Among church leaders of the time, perhaps none was more closely attuned to trends in conservative political and social thought than Clark. And due to the declining health of church president Heber J. Grant, and a lengthy period of ill-health that afflicted Second Counselor David O. McKay, Clark wielded an unusual amount of influence over church affairs. He was thus a man whose views could not be ignored. By 1940 he was expressing concerns then current among some commentators about the economic and social pressures leading women out of the home. Statistics show that the stresses of the Great Depression had taken a tremendous toll on American families, resulting in a decrease in marriages, a decline in the birthrate, and a breakdown of family stability—trends from which Mormons were not immune.[21] Clark concluded that some of the blame for this might lie at the doorstep of the church itself. Given that women in their roles as wives and mothers were seen as the linchpin of family life, he felt the value of demanding programs that took them out of the home had to be weighed against the destructive impact these activities had on the family unit.

In the March meeting with the auxiliary leaders, Clark spelled out his concerns in this regard, as well as his overall discomfort with plans and programs that strained the church's budget and taxed the energies of its leaders. A central part of his memorandum was his suggestion that church organizations cut back on their agendas. For the Relief Society, this meant it should turn away from activities he deemed non-essential and instead concentrate on fulfilling its role, which he later expressed at the organization's October conference as being "the handmaid to the priesthood." In social welfare work he recommended it should narrowly focus its energies in support of the Welfare Plan. By implication it should not mobilize, as previously, in cooperation with government or with other groups interested in community reform.

Based on the agenda implied in the March *Magazine*—and possibly from details of the Relief Society's emerging plans he might have been hearing from his daughter Marianne who served on the board—it must have been clear to Clark that such activities were precisely what Lyman had in mind. In its curriculum, he urged the Society to limit itself to "promotion of faith and testimony," with the "merely social, cultural, and educational" left to other agencies outside of the church.[22] In other words, parts of the Society's programs that Lyman and many others in the organization felt to be vital and valued—the legacy of the club movement in self-education and social reform that had played such an important role in the organization's revitalization and contributed significantly to the cause of community improvement in the 1910s and 1920s—should be surrendered to enable Mormon women to devote themselves exclusively to the tasks of supporting the Welfare Plan, developing personal piety, and meeting the needs of their families. In the next meeting of the general board, Lyman shared Clark's concerns and the women immediately began to discuss ways to address the issues he raised. Soon representatives of the Relief Society began to meet regularly as well in committee with the leadership of other auxiliaries to discuss ways to implement the counselor's recommendations.[23]

It is important to note that Clark, who had spent most of his adult life outside of the pale of Mormon settlement, may have been unfamiliar with the full range of Relief Society activities and the benefits that had previously accrued to church and community in consequence. In any case, he seems to have valued the organization's earlier accomplishments to a lesser degree than many other church leaders. In addition, his outlook toward gender roles was no doubt shaped in part by a hectic work schedule that had kept him away from home for lengthy periods and forced him to rely almost completely on his devoted wife to preside over family affairs. For him, this limited and focused support role for women seemed natural and even divinely ordained; a way of thinking no doubt reinforced by the collective experience of his eastern peers in the world of law and politics.[24] Several years later, not long after Lyman's release as Relief Society president, Clark neatly encapsulated his views in a Relief Society conference address: "[D]o not try to be anything else but good mothers and good homemakers," he admonished the women of the organization, "for that will exhaust all the time, all the effort, and pay the greatest dividends of anything else you can do in the world."[25] Clearly, such a vision for women was at odds with the more expansive views held by Lyman.

And yet, it would be a significant mistake to view Clark as simply a misogynist or a male chauvinist. As was the case with church charity, in practice his behavior was complex and nuanced: not nearly as rigid as his rhetoric. One had to look no further than his own family to see this. He was no remote or domineering patriarch of stereotype, and while focused on career, he sought to be available to his children—including his daughters. Indeed, Lyman's choice of Clark's daughter Marianne Clark Sharp was not merely a currying of favor with the great man. Like her father, Sharp was an accomplished woman with a brilliant mind. Her father had seen that she received a first-rate education, and was supportive of her personal achievements as well.[26]

While Clark's prescriptions for women were in part generalized from the experience of his own marriage, Lyman and her husband made difference choices. While some of Lyman's life-course was the consequence of unforeseen opportunities, she nevertheless benefitted from a supportive husband who encouraged her to take full advantage of them. Amy and Richard forged a relationship that allowed both to pursue active career paths. Of course, through nurture, inclination, and experience, Lyman could best be termed a feminist—not a radical one, friends and family members were quick to point out, but someone who believed strongly in equal pay for equal work, and equal opportunity in employment. Indeed, years later granddaughter Amy Kathryn remembered Amy lecturing her while doing laundry about how women should get the same pay as men.[27] Yet at the same time, Lyman felt through nature and environment women were especially suited to excel in certain areas of society—including, of course, social work. Scholars term such views "cultural feminism." While Clark made exceptions for the choices made by women on an individual basis, in broad terms, he was *not* a feminist, cultural or otherwise. Lyman would have to find a way to cause him to see the limits of his expectations for women if she was to be able to hold on to the essentials of an agenda that had proved so meaningful and fulfilling for members of her organization.

Lyman had confronted opposing agendas among church leaders on previous occasions and had often found a path toward accommodation with them. But complicating her efforts this time was another aspect of Clark's personality: his approach to decision making. Here again his style was no doubt shaped by his professional experiences and, as was common in the world of business and politics, was strongly top-down in nature.[28] Clark had a great deal of confidence in his own judgement—and for good reason. With his brilliant mind he carefully sought to examine all sides of a problem himself before he threw his support behind a plan of action and rarely encountered an argument persuasive enough to force him to second-guess a decision. This exacerbated a tendency Clark himself commented upon, namely a family propensity for stubbornness and strongly held opinions. "We Clarks are a good deal like the Harvard man," he once observed to his brother, "you can tell a Harvard man wherever you see him—but you can't tell him much."[29] As an administrator he was often very direct and outspoken, repeating the main thrust of his views several times in both written and oral communications. When confronted with a perspective with which he did not agree, he left no room for confusion in his views, stating on one occasion: "When you tell people no, you better tell it in emphatic terms; if you say it in a nice way they think you indicate yes."[30] And Clark, who gave his absolute loyalty to President Grant, expected the same in return from those under his authority. All this proved a formidable challenge to Lyman.

Lyman, of course, was often direct and outspoken herself, but her manner as an administrator was very different; more in line with earlier practices in the church—and one that remained valorized by her sex. In sum, she utilized a paradigm that prioritized consensus.[31] When large issues came before the Relief Society leadership for discussion she did not dominate the process, but encouraged board members to speak their minds freely before a decision was made. And when that decision was reached, it generally reflected the collective input of all involved.[32] And just as Lyman followed a template for decision-making that differed from the male/business model utilized by Clark, in regard to lines of authority she also looked to a pattern that was more typical of her sex. American women, excluded from traditional seats of power, had often drawn upon personal ties to develop alternative sources of influence, with women of the Relief Society representing no exception.

Since 1920, Relief Society leaders had been assigned an apostle liaison to work through when dealing with the First Presidency, but in reality, contact with the president of the church and his counselors during this period remained a fairly frequent occurrence. Nevertheless, under the circumstances, Lyman found it both natural and prudent to develop personal relationships with church leaders as well as with their wives and daughters.[33] Through such informal links, even if she encountered resistance to her ideas from her immediate Relief Society or priesthood leaders, she had options to appeal her case, even, if warranted, to the president of the church. Aware of the power of such informal avenues, Lyman carefully cultivated and managed them.[34]

Clark, however, sought to limit such short-circuiting of formal lines of authority even as he valued efficiency over consensus in church government. Already by the mid-1930s, his style of management was beginning to predominate. Many came to applaud the firm hand with which he wielded his administrative power, although his manner raised the eyebrows of others. Some even felt his approach was lending an unduly authoritarian tone to church decision-making.[35] By the 1940s, Clark's powerful influence in church affairs coupled with Grant's declining health made Lyman's efforts to work around the formidable counselor increasingly difficult. As he sought to safeguard the health of the ailing president, Clark restricted access to him, becoming, in essence the gatekeeper of the First Presidency. By 1940 he was already responsible for much of the day to day management of church affairs—since the mid-thirties, he had even handled most of President Grant's mail. Although he tried to ensure that his decisions reflected the desires of the president, given the compelling reasoning (a product of his years in the law) with which he presented his perspective and the growing trust that Grant demonstrated in his judgment, it is not surprising that Clark's own views frequently seemed to hold sway.[36]

To be fair to Clark, this was a very difficult time when the already fragile Grant experienced a debilitating stroke just a month after Lyman assumed the Relief Society presidency. In addition, Second Counselor David O. McKay was often ill due to a chronic lung ailment and other afflictions. These circumstances would remain largely constant over the course of Lyman's presidency—although Grant was able to make a partial recovery from his stroke, his overall health continued to decline, and even when McKay felt well, he was often away traveling on church business. The circumstances of March 1940 were thus to be fairly typical: Clark was struggling with tremendous burdens that pressed heavily upon him.[37] Lyman was aware of the pressures on the first counselor and was no doubt sympathetic toward his plight; she had been in a similar position as general secretary during the Emmeline B. Wells and Clarissa Williams administrations. Under the circumstances, she would not have been surprised to find that Clark was seeking to limit the agenda of the Relief Society as part of a strategy to simplify church programs. But while sympathetic to Clark, and supportive of his leadership, Lyman strongly disagreed with some specifics of his recommendations. How to successfully achieve the goals she felt essential for the organization thus became one of the primary challenges of her presidency.[38]

From Clark's perspective, concerned as he was about the growth of demanding church programs, it must have seemed reasonable to ask the Relief Society to reduce its educational curriculum, especially as alternative opportunities were readily available through schools, colleges, and universities. And in light of the growth of public sector services, he may also have felt it appropriate to urge that the Relief Society trim its social work activities aimed at the larger community. But based on her decades of experience building up the Relief Society, Lyman saw these as intertwined with its mission and key to holding the loyalty of its members: the educational curriculum provided vital intellectual stimulation for women in a congenial social setting even as significant gaps remained in social programs carried out by the public sector. In addition, there was a perennial need for citizen oversight of existing programs by experienced and interested women like those in the Relief Society. In light of this, the strong-willed Lyman seems to have decided to initiate a series of maneuvers designed to engage the equally strong-willed Clark in a dialog concerning the Relief Society's future.

Lyman was well aware that differences of opinion were common among church leaders, characterized, as they were, by powerful personalities and absolute dedication to their callings. And these differences sometimes led to difficult and lengthy behind-the-scenes struggles over developing policies—as had been the case with the Welfare Plan.[39] Once a course of action was decided upon, however, the leadership tended to loyally fall in line behind it, masking any previous differences from the general membership. From the onset there was no doubt that Lyman would ultimately do the same—she had been taught to follow the priesthood in her youth, and associates noted that she continued to do so as president.[40] Yet, while some room for negotiation still remained, she was willing to vigorously press her case. This was potentially a risky course and she knew it. If she pushed too hard she might alienate herself from the members of the First Presidency (especially the influential first counselor), under whose authority she served, something that had to be kept in mind by all Relief Society general presidents, especially since the release of Emmeline Wells broke the tradition of lifetime tenure. In addition, President Grant's declining health and the growing restrictions on access to him meant Lyman had to deal with a diminished (and ever diminishing) ability to informally appeal her case. Yet Lyman was willing to walk this tightrope if that was what was required to fulfill her stewardship to the women of the organization.

In her favor, however, Clark, while self-confident and often opinionated, made no claims of personal infallibility—quite the contrary. And he certainly understood the give and take of decision making even at the highest levels of the church.[41] Although he expected compliance, on those rare occasions when he was confronted with a coherent, compelling, and *determined* counter-argument, he had been known to readjust his plans. In possession of a first-rate intellect of her own, Lyman was just the individual to make the attempt.[42]

In light of these circumstances, Lyman adopted a two-fold response to Clark's proposals. On the one hand, she cultivated support for her position among other church leaders, including LeGrand Richards, who succeeded Sylvester Q. Cannon as presiding bishop, and especially his second counselor, Joseph L. Wirthlin, with whom she worked closely, and as much as possible with the ailing but still involved Heber J. Grant. On the other hand, she reached out to Clark himself, perhaps most significantly as she expanded the Relief Society's support for the Welfare Plan.[43] As a first step, Lyman sought to clarify the Society's role in the program by asking speakers to address the topic during the organization's conferences, beginning with the first over which she presided in April 1940. These talks were later given extensive space in the *Magazine*, a signal to Clark of the importance her administration gave to his agenda.[44]

Lyman also increased the Society's productivity under the plan when she established regional centers where women used industrial machines to sew welfare articles. And Lyman turned the organization's monthly work and business meetings—long used to produce articles for local families in need—to the support of the Welfare Plan and directed stake and local leaders to coordinate their production schedules with the needs of regional welfare storehouses. Finally, she saw that the Mormon Handicraft Shop, a highlight of Louise Robison's administration created to allow Mormon women to earn extra money during the Great Depression, was incorporated under the Welfare Plan.[45] With only a reservation or two, Clark must have been extremely pleased by much of what Lyman did. And for good reason: with her support the plan achieved new levels of efficiency.[46]

Lyman also made meaningful concessions to Clark's concerns: she re-emphasized testimony building and spiritual matters in the Relief Society curriculum and trimmed "unnecessary meetings" that took women out of the home. Under her direction the curriculum year was shortened from nine months to eight and stake Relief Society conferences were reduced from two days to one.[47] She deferred to Clark in other ways as well, including his desires that the organization limit its interaction with other groups. Lyman, declined, for example, at his recommendation, an invitation from the General Federation of Women's Clubs to send delegates to a national meeting on the topic of defense. In short, she sought to follow the same advice she frequently offered to others: "Compromise on the lesser things, but hold firm to essentials."[48] For Lyman the essentials were encapsulated in an address she delivered at the Utah State Agricultural College in July, 1940.

In many ways, this speech simply reiterated ideas that Lyman had been expressing for years.[49] But coming as it did so soon after the Relief Society's concessions to Clark, it carries weight as a compelling example of Lyman's own vision for the proper role of women. She began by reviewing the results of women's collective endeavor over the century since the Seneca Falls Convention signaled the beginnings of the organized struggle for women's rights, then called for like efforts by the current generation. "I would like to advocate the idea of women becoming more interested in politics and government, both local and national," she declared. Noting that it had taken seventy-two years to obtain the vote, she lamented: "There are many today who are not even interested enough to make the effort to go to the polls." She saw the need for a renewed push for the cause of equality: "It is a strange thing," she observed, "that men in general have so obstinately opposed the activity and development of women, but stranger still that many women have also joined the opposition. . . ." Women should not only vote, she argued, they should play an active role in the political process, helping select candidates and should run for office themselves "in fields where they are especially qualified."

Meanwhile, "Women's organizations," and here she presumably included the Relief Society, "should be interested in city, county, state and national administration and finance; in industrial problems and economics; in personal health, both mental and physical; in public health and health education; in the schools and school programs; in recreation; in housing." In a nod to Clark, she agreed that younger women should be encouraged first and foremost to fulfill their nurturing roles as mothers and wives. However, she explained that modern conveniences and hired help had, by 1940, freed even these women for at least some activities outside the home. More to the point, she knew that there were "many middle-aged women whose children are gone and whose duties in the home have become greatly lessened." These, she asserted, should be encouraged to devote their energies to the interests of their communities. Lyman concluded by advocating a broad agenda to bring women back into the forefront of social work and reform. "Let the women of Utah work for security through employment, security through buying power, and security through Government," she urged. "Let us work against destructive forces, such as the use of alcohol, tobacco and other narcotic drugs; disease, crime, prejudice, war. Let us work for opportunity through education and opportunity through proper leisure."[50]

Lyman may have hoped that her effective support for the Welfare Plan coupled with her meaningful concessions to Clark's concerns would have allowed her to preserve vital prerogatives for Relief Society women. If so, a major test of her strategy came later that summer—its outcome seemed to confirm the course she was steering. At that time, the church board set up to consider Clark's recommendations in detail took up the idea of consolidating church magazines, in particular a plan to combine the *Relief Society Magazine* with the *Children's Friend*—the organ of the Primary Association.[51] After Lyman discussed the matter with the general board, together they responded with a lengthy defense of the status quo. Their rhetoric was revealing. They noted that the Relief Society was one of the oldest women's organizations in existence and had long been regarded as the premier woman's organization of the church, a "companion to the Priesthood." As such, it stood higher in the estimation of LDS women than any of the other church auxiliaries, while its membership, like that of the church and unlike that of the other auxiliaries, was perpetual. Once a woman joined the Relief Society, in other words, she could remain a dues-paying member the rest of her life while the Primary and YLMIA were aimed at narrow age-brackets of girls and young women.

For all these reasons, the board asserted, the organization deserved a periodical of its own. Indeed, it had been served with its own publications for nearly seventy years, first by the *Woman's Exponent*, then, after 1914, by the *Magazine*, organs tailored to the specific needs of Mormon women. They not only entertained and inspired, but provided invaluable sources of information to women in even the most isolated areas, serving to unify a large and diverse organization. Practically, the board pointed out as well that the cost savings through consolidation would be minimal to non-existent as official materials, such as lesson manuals, official notices, etc., would still have to be distributed from time to time, thus requiring the maintenance of separate mailing lists and the means to publish and disseminate such materials. Together these objections formed a strong and ultimately convincing argument that led Clark to back away, which spared the *Relief Society Magazine*, as it turned out, for another thirty years.[52] This experience no doubt indicated to Lyman that more of the Society's prerogatives might be protected if she marshaled her resources effectively.

One area that was vital to Lyman's agenda and seemed in harmony with Clark's priorities was social service work. Drawing her immediate attention, Lyman was cognizant of significant gaps in the provision of church welfare services that the women of the Relief Society could continue to profitably fill. Specifically, the assistance rendered by trained social workers in the wards and stakes was vital if the Welfare Plan was to function smoothly and successfully. Lyman therefore prepared for another series of social service institutes to initiate a new generation of workers and began to prepare a handbook with standardized procedures and forms to provide procedural continuity over time.[53] Conference addresses were used to support these moves while also emphasizing the importance of the role of Relief Society women in working with the bishops and coordinating relief efforts with community agencies. While valorizing these social work activities, such messages also contributed to a renewed sense of *esprit de corps*.[54]

To gauge the status of the Society's welfare work and evaluate progress in the revitalization of the organization in general, at the end of 1940 stake Relief Societies were asked to prepare year-end histories of their activities. These reports revealed wide-ranging endeavors including some outstanding efforts in public health and child welfare work, much of it involving the interest on the Relief Society wheat fund. Like earlier work performed under Sheppard-Towner, these efforts, some now coordinated with aspects of the Social Security Act, involved the voluntary services of physicians and dentists and cooperative endeavors with county welfare boards and public health nurses. To highlight such activities and encourage others to do likewise Lyman asked stake Relief Society presidents who presided over especially noteworthy programs to speak in the organization's general conference. Their reports were later published in the *Magazine*.[55] Here were examples that validated Lyman's contention that, while public and church programs had assumed the bulk of the relief burden, Relief Society women still had valuable contributions to make at the margins. Then, as now, America's social safety net left many gaps in its assistance to those in need. Relief Society women, therefore, did definite good in their communities as they organized well-baby clinics, bought needed items such as eyeglasses, and provided dental services for children. One stake even helped upgrade public housing for some of its members. All were tasks not generally handled by government programs at the time or the church's Welfare Plan.[56]

To finance activities like these, the Society had in part relied on the interest from the funds obtained when its wheat was sold at the end of World War I, but these monies were about to be diminished. In the spring of 1939, the Church Welfare Committee had asked the general board to contribute a portion of the principal of its wheat fund toward the purchase of grain to be stored in new elevators being constructed in Salt Lake City. Mindful of the organization's long-standing responsibility for wheat storage, Louise Robison and the members of her administration agreed, and soon after Lyman took office, one fourth of the fund was thus converted.[57] Though Lyman acquiesced to this change, she knew the larger issue of Relief Society autonomy was involved as this diversion reduced the funds available for its own charitable work.

A featured speaker at the dedication ceremony for the grain elevator in August 1940, Lyman recounted the history of grain storage, noting past occasions when the wheat had been "borrowed" by local bishops. "I am afraid the sisters were not very energetic in getting the receipts" she observed wryly, "because they were not, the Bishops were not very energetic in paying the wheat back." While the decision to convert a portion of the wheat interest had already been made, Lyman could not be accused of lack of energy in safeguarding the resources and prerogatives still in her control. Despite pressure from local bishops to utilize Relief Society charity funds for welfare projects, she directed ward and stake presidents to allow the use of such resources only for activities sponsored by the Relief Society itself.[58] More pointedly, she recommended that local charity funds be used to supplement the now diminished interest on the Wheat Fund to sponsor public health work.

Apart from her efforts to guard the Society's prerogatives, a major preoccupation of Lyman during the first years of her presidency was the impending celebration of the Relief Society centennial.[59] To promote an appreciation of past accomplishments, she encouraged wards and stakes to stage elaborate pageants, written and produced by local talent, around the March 17 anniversary. In addition, the general board itself planned to host a large central celebration lasting eleven days to be held in conjunction with the Society's regular conference in April 1942. A number of commemorative items including a centennial history and souvenir plates and pins were also in preparation.[60] To stimulate interest, each of the four conferences in 1940 and 1941 discussed the coming centennial at length, including postings on the ongoing membership drive.[61] Relief Society leaders also provided updates on what emerged as the capstone of the celebration: the dedication of a permanent monument on Temple Square. After much discussion they had decided to erect a bell tower or "campanile" in a prominent location in front of the Tabernacle to house what they believed was the bell from the Nauvoo Temple. Women of the organization made contributions toward construction of the structure and its bronze bas relief panels that depicted aspects of the Relief Society's mission. By late fall of 1941, the first contracts had been let.[62] By that time, the wards and stakes were also far along in preparation for their own centennial celebrations.

Then on December 7 came the attack on Pearl Harbor. Like countless other Americans, Lyman greeted the news with shock and dismay. Despite the threat of world conflict that had hung heavily over the first years of her presidency, Lyman had dearly hoped for peace.[63] Yet, as the nation moved toward a wartime footing in expectation of being drawn into growing conflagration in Europe, she had begun to prepare the Society for its anticipated role on the home front. Early in 1941, for example, she arranged for the organization to cooperate with the Red Cross in conducting a survey of nurses to assist with training sessions in first aid.[64] Along with such opportunities for service, the war created daunting challenges for the Relief Society. Surprising, even to Lyman, was the extent of wartime dislocations and the rapid entry of increasing numbers of women into the workforce. These demographic shifts so heightened the concerns of the First Presidency about family stability that they recommended further cutbacks in the activities of the auxiliaries. The restrictions imposed by church leaders at this time threatened to significantly limit Lyman's ability to create new avenues for activism. With war also came government imposed limitations on travel that severely hindered supervision of existing Relief Society programs. In addition, motivated by a desire to demonstrate the church's commitment to the war effort, the First Presidency also urged cancellation of all unnecessary activities.[65]

Consistent with the wishes of priesthood leaders, Lyman and the board reluctantly canceled all of the organization's general conferences, including the elaborate central celebration of the centennial. They also discouraged stake festivities and urged Relief Society women instead to throw their energies into more modest ward celebrations.[66] Also, at the direction of church leaders, dedication of the Relief Society campanile was first delayed, then canceled for the duration of the war.[67] To assuage the disappointment of the rank and file, a special radio broadcast featuring Lyman and Heber J. Grant was scheduled and phonograph records with messages from the two leaders were circulated to all the wards. The *Magazine* also contained special centennial features throughout the year, including Lyman's own serialized autobiography. Progress on the membership drive was carefully tracked, as well, with the final total in March exceeding by fifteen thousand the goal of one hundred thousand members. Despite wartime restrictions, Relief Society women from Wyoming to California and in missions around the world were thus able to utilize the centennial year as intended, coming together on a ward basis to celebrate past accomplishments while recommitting themselves to future achievement.[68]

The war also forced Lyman to modify or place on hold other activities. Soon, all meetings beyond the ward level that required motor transport were curtailed, bringing much of the work of the Society to a standstill. Plans for the new social service institutes were also scrapped due to travel restrictions after a single two-week session was held in San Francisco.[69] Similarly, general board members limited their travel to the stakes, leaving supervision of the organization's routine activities to take place through circular letters, bulletins, or announcements in the *Magazine*. This placed fewer demands on the board, though not on Secretary-Treasurer Pohlman, who was responsible for an ever increasing flood of queries from local leaders.[70] Many of these involved war-related activities. As was the case during the First World War, Relief Society women patriotically joined in common cause with their American sisters in performing Red Cross work. Given wartime shortages of medical personnel, Lyman also urged Relief Society women to take Red Cross classes in nursing and to create first-aid kits for their homes and wards.[71] Meanwhile, Relief Society women continued to sew tens of thousands of items for the Welfare Plan. Lyman knew from experience that these seemingly simple activities had both immediate, practical benefits and, over the long run, helped grant legitimacy and value to the Relief Society as an organized body. Evidence of a growing sense of common purpose was revealed in the enthusiastic manner in which the membership attacked their new assignments.[72]

Lyman called for activism in other areas as well, though clearly, given wartime limits, she knew that much of her agenda would have to wait until the conflict was over. A glimpse at her evolving roster of current and future projects—which also reveals some of the concerns of other American women at the time—is found in the pages of the *Magazine*. For example, in January 1943, Relief Society women were asked to join in a drive mounted by the National Council of Women to petition the wartime Office of Price Administration to require manufacturers to provide clothing labels with content and care instructions.[73] This followed up a series of lessons in 1941 and 1942 on the topic of "Better Buymanship," which started with a discussion of the consumers' movement.[74] At the same time, articles and conference addresses continued to raise a variety of public health issues, not least of which was the glamorization of tobacco and alcohol use in the movies.[75]

Lyman and the board also saw to it that the *Magazine* focused closely on helping members with the immediate wartime hardships they faced in common with other American women. For example, articles instructed housewives on how to plan nutritious meals with limited amounts of such rationed commodities as meat and eggs.[76] The board also used its pages to announce a pamphlet by the National Council of Women, entitled, "How to Win on the Home Front," that encouraged participation in a national drive to save fat and scrap metal.[77] Other articles provided advice on how to help children cope during the troubled period, including a letter from Katherine Lenroot, then chair of the Children's Bureau, on "The Care of Children in Wartime." Lyman herself wrote another piece on the importance of maintaining stability in the home during times of crisis.[78] On the lighter side, other articles advised mothers about finding wholesome entertainment for their families, while original short stories continued to appear, serving as diversion from wartimes stresses.[79] On the spiritual front, the women of the Society were urged to stay close to the faith even as they were reassured that church leaders were taking steps to guard the spiritual welfare of their loved ones in the military.[80] Informative pieces also warned readers how easy it was for unreasoning hatred to grow in a wartime environment while in the "Notes to the Field" column, visiting teachers were admonished to avoid fanning panic by repeating sensational rumors when making their monthly rounds.[81] And while the Relief Society followed J. Reuben Clark's recommendations discouraging its official mobilization as a body in war-related activities, Lyman and the board used the *Magazine* to encourage the membership to actively move forward in such areas as individuals. All in all, the *Magazine* dispensed information both cautionary and reassuring, practical and spiritually uplifting, of interest not only to Mormons, but reflecting the concerns of most American women during the period.

Despite Lyman's attempts to broaden the membership base of the Society, even in wartime, its program remained geared toward women able to attend its Tuesday afternoon meetings. This generally excluded from full participation those engaged in wage work—a growing minority of Mormon women during the war years. But there were already hints that realities for LDS women were changing and that the Relief Society would have to respond with adjustments of its own. A case in point occurred in Vanport, Oregon, where Mormon women joined their husbands in working at the Kaiser shipyards. Most of the men worked days, while many of the women found support positions on the swing shift. As working women of the time (and indeed, even today) generally remained responsible for household duties, these staggered shifts gave them a chance to prepare dinner for their families before going to work. However, their schedule left no time for the Relief Society's standard Tuesday afternoon at 2 p.m. meeting. Sensibly, in anticipation of such an adjustment by the whole organization a generation later, the local branch president shifted the meeting to accommodate their schedules. These women were "all doing their bit to win the war," it was reported, "but they haven't lost their desire to meet at Relief Society." Vera Pohlman, herself a working mother, made sure this helpful innovation (as well as those by other women) reached the pages of her "Notes from the Field" column.[82]

Throughout 1942 and 1943, the Relief Society settled into patterns of sustained activity that created meaningful outlets for the women of the organization while providing familiar routines that created a semblance of normalcy in an otherwise chaotic environment. Despite daunting roadblocks that confronted Lyman as she navigated through the challenges of the era, it seemed that she was triumphing in her quest to maintain the organization's vigor and prerogatives. Yet, amid wartime hardship and suffering, she was about to encounter a different kind of tragedy, one that would prove more devastating to her personally than any she had yet encountered. Somehow she found the strength to rise above it, but it destroyed her professional life and overwhelmed her legacy.

After nearly half a century of marriage, Amy and Richard Lyman seemed to have settled into a comfortable and extremely congenial relationship. They were a powerful and influential pair, movers and shakers in the most important affairs in their community. Talented and accomplished, they found great satisfaction and pride in each other's accomplishments. Amy was proud of Richard and his record of achievement. In return, Richard seemed to dote on Amy, and showered praise on her and her accomplishments whether in her company or with others. He recognized how much support she provided him as well. On her birthday in 1937, for example, while he was away from her making a tour of the missions on the continent, he telegraphed "Birthday greetings to the finest and most efficient helpmeet in the world."[83] Indeed, Richard seemed very pleased with his wife in his private thoughts as well, writing of her in his journal at the time of a college reunion in Michigan in 1935: "I am surely proud of her for her health [and] beauty, youth (compared with the other women present) and her brilliant intellect."[84] Their lives focused on their demanding church careers and family, including a growing number of grandchildren and ongoing interaction with siblings and extended relations. With their lives closely intertwined, their home environment was active, but peaceful.

There was no fighting, no harsh words exchanged. Their relationship seemed exemplary and free of any apparent tensions. They socialized often and were considered first-rate company, they enjoyed having a good time and did their share to contribute to one.

But despite their comingled, indeed unified lives in so many ways, in others they remained two very different people. Both enjoyed sharing a little gossip, but Richard spoke much more freely and often loosely, while Amy was careful and sensitive—when she had information to share her sources were impeccable and her confidants few and discreet. In manner they differed as well: Amy moved through life with a sense of urgency, always hurrying from one important engagement to another. While she remained compassionate by nature and could be counted on to be lively and amusing in social settings, in professional matters she was often intensely focused and task oriented. True to her upbringing, she saw the key to her success in self-mastery. A serious and effective leader in his own right, Richard, on the other hand, was much more relaxed in manner. Open and affable, he was ever ready with a good joke or a clever observation. Sometimes indiscreet, he was frequently a source of mild embarrassment to his wife who often exclaimed after one of his stories, "Oh Richard!" accompanied by a brush of the hand.[85] But his actions now brought more than simple embarrassment.

Details first reached the public on Saturday afternoon, November 13, 1943, when the church-owned *Deseret News* carried a small announcement on its front page stating that Apostle Richard R. Lyman had been excommunicated for "violation of the Christian law of chastity." One cannot overestimate how traumatic the announcement was for Latter-day Saints. In the eyes of the faithful, Richard was one of the Lord's anointed and seemed to be a deeply devout and dedicated church leader. Indeed, a perusal of his journal, especially during the years he presided over the European Mission, reveals the great depth and sincerity of his beliefs. Given all this, the news of his fall thus shocked the entire membership all the way from Heber J. Grant at the top, who looked upon Richard as a son, down to the most humble member, who knew him as a popular speaker and a beloved general authority. Soon picked up by the national press, the impact of the story was so great that decades later members could remember exactly where they were and what they were doing when they heard it. For church leaders, his fall represented not just a shock, but also a great embarrassment, a serious setback to efforts to create a positive and wholesome public image for the faith.[86]

Though the news took nearly everyone by surprise, with the advantage of hindsight many could recall signs that something had long been amiss with the gregarious apostle who was unusually affectionate in his manner. Rumors had been swirling about him for years. Those who knew him well generally dismissed such concerns, finding his warm, open manner a refreshing change from other, more austere, church leaders. But a few had reasons for real concern about conduct that seemed completely out of place from one in his position—conduct that led some women in positions of church leadership to dread traveling with him on church business. Meanwhile, a number of rank-and-file members felt that his talks manifested an obsessive concern over moral purity that in retrospect seemed revealing.[87]

When the news broke, church officials attempted to downplay the impact of the case by withholding details. However, a flood of rumors quickly filled the void.[88] The facts, though certainly serious enough to justify his excommunication, were less spectacular than many believed at the time or have since imagined. Seeking to get to the bottom of persistent allegations regarding Richard's conduct, J. Reuben Clark had assigned Harold B. Lee, then a junior apostle, to use every means possible to find out the truth. Lee soon discovered that Richard was regularly accompanying a woman to her Salt Lake apartment where the two spent a significant amount of time together alone. After consulting with one another, Clark and Lee felt it necessary to obtain firsthand evidence of the suspected behavior. Thus, in a move that would now send constitutional watch-dogs into apoplexy, Lee enlisted the assistance of fellow apostle Joseph Fielding Smith and of officers from the Salt Lake City police department, some of whom only knew they were going after a "big shot."[89] On Thursday evening, November 11, after carefully timing their actions, the group burst into the apartment and caught the couple in a compromising situation.[90]

Taken back to church headquarters, the seventy-three-year-old Lyman was notified that the next day he was to be tried before his fellow apostles for his membership. It was at this time that Amy herself heard the news. Completely overwhelmed, she reportedly exclaimed over and over: "I don't believe it! I just don't believe it!"[91] The following afternoon at his church trial Richard sat stunned and ashen before the body of men, many of whom had been his colleagues and friends for a quarter of a century. As he responded to their questioning a story soon emerged that was in some ways very familiar, in others, uniquely Mormon. He had met the woman some twenty years before through his responsibilities as an apostle. A Scandinavian emigrant, roughly the same age as he, she married as a plural wife in 1905 after her future husband told her that the practice was still secretly sanctioned by church leaders—although in fact, he had no such sanction himself. In the wake of the Smoot hearings, such cases were dealt with harshly and both she and her husband soon faced church action. She was excommunicated, but knowing her to be a good-hearted woman, local leaders urged her reinstatement, which led to interviews and counseling with members of the Quorum of the Twelve. In the early 1920s, the case was turned over to Lyman and eventually, at his recommendation, her membership was restored. Their counseling relationship continued, however, and as Richard admitted, gradually developed into something more.[92]

The reasons are not hard to understand. Despite his real affection for Amy, Richard found himself unable to comply with her wishes concerning cessation of physical intimacy in their marriage. He was a child of polygamy, believed it to be of God, and no doubt as a young man had anticipated entering into the practice himself. Under the circumstances, he had undoubtedly developed certain expectations. Yet he had come of age at the very time of polygamy's public renunciation through the Manifesto and, once married himself, was required to maintain the rigid self-control of the Victorian Age. Ultimately, as the physical intimacy of his own marriage ceased, this proved too difficult a transition for him to bear, especially as he knew that some among the apostles had, for a time, secretly sanctioned post-Manifesto plural unions. Though his own father, particularly during his years as president of the Quorum of the Twelve, eventually championed harsh punishment for those violating the injunctions against polygamy, Richard found his own and the church's continuing belief in plural marriage—even if it was only to be practiced in the hereafter—a beguiling way to rationalize his later actions. Using concepts that echoed those that emerged in the early days of the church, Richard would later justify his union as a "potential plural marriage," one that might be properly solemnized if the practice was again publicly sanctioned.[93]

As they heard these details, the members of the twelve knew they had no choice. To a man they voted for excommunication. All were in tears except Richard, who, seemingly in a daze, shook hands around the room and left. Suddenly stripped of his position, his life work ruined, Richard remained in a dreamlike state of shock for weeks. Available evidence indicates that he broke down to show the full extent of his emotions only once during this period, on the afternoon of his excommunication when, at Amy's urging, he revealed what had happened to his granddaughter before the news became public.[94]

Amy herself was so devastated that, according to family members, she lay prostrate in bed for days. The man whom she had completely trusted, who had been her biggest booster, her support and confidant, her partner and friend, had betrayed and humiliated her before the entire world. Lyman had felt she enjoyed a close, companionate marriage and it must have struck her particularly hard that while her own generation was largely spared the heartaches and insecurities associated with plural marriage like those endured by their mothers, her current distress was rooted in the practice. Not lost on her, as well, would be the ironic twist that the marriage that she valued so greatly, that had opened the door to career and accomplishment, now threatened to destroy it all. Adding to her grief, given the nature of Mormon beliefs regarding the eternity of family relationships, Richard's excommunication called into question the legitimacy of her temple marriage and her status in the hereafter.[95] It is little wonder that this, among all her tragedies, was the blow that came closest to overwhelming her. Friends, family members, and church leaders who came by to visit following the announcement found her extremely distraught. "Just pray that I won't go bitter and just pray that the depth of my understanding of the gospel will carry me through," she told her counselor, Belle Spafford. Another visitor found Lyman so troubled that, as she expressed it, "she feared that she might lose her mind."[96]

Beyond her personal dilemma, at stake was her credibility as a leader. She had advocated an activist stance for women, one that led them outside their homes and into the larger community. Her own life had seemed to set the example of what might be accomplished by women if they seized the opportunities before them. She had sought to balance her public life with the needs of her family, but even before—at Wendell's death, for instance—some, including Amy herself, had questioned just how successful her balancing act had been. Now many openly wondered at the cost she and her family had paid for her successes.[97] Though it was ultimately Richard's decisions that led to this disaster, she knew that some of the blame could be reasonably placed on her.

The question was what to do? With the best of intentions, some church leaders advised her to leave Richard and move away—to flee the scandal—perhaps to California where she had family. But she would not do it. Indeed, even at the darkest moments of the crisis she kept her perspective, stating that Richard had been "in every other way an ideal husband and father," and "she was not going to leave him now." As she had so often advised others during her years of social work, "You cannot run away from your problems," and she was not about to do so herself. Somehow she would find a way to face them squarely and overcome the blow.[98]

It is perhaps her greatest triumph that this is exactly what she did. When teaching others about social welfare work, Lyman had long repeated something she had learned in her first days at the Denver Public Charities—that the hardest problem to overcome was getting clients to realize there *was* a problem. Now confronted with the seriousness of the dilemma in her own life, she could have become mired in self-pity or anger, second-guessing all of Richard's previous kindnesses, or allowing herself to become steeped in self-blame. She refused to do any of this. Instead she summoned every fiber of her iron will to look ahead.[99] For her own sake, and for the sake of Richard and their family, she was determined that their marriage would be saved, a view Richard shared. Together they faced the consequences of his actions and the public humiliation that resulted.

In a first step, Amy gathered family members around her and charged them not to speak of the matter again, that to do so would only make matters worse. Instead, they were to follow her example, put it behind them, and try to forgive Richard. Family members stayed remarkably faithful to this charge, even as—in the absence of firm information—often wild rumors continued to swirl around the story.[100] As for Richard, though it would take years before he was prepared to grasp the real import of what he had done, and more than a decade before his membership in the church was restored, for his part he did not shy away from immediate consequences of his actions. He attended meetings regularly in his local ward, despite his embarrassment.[101] And at Amy's request, Richard, so open and willing to engage in conversation with almost anyone, refused to meet with fundamentalist Mormons who came to his door looking to him for additional justification to their own polygamous cause.[102]

Amy was also faced with the issue of her church position. As rumors and speculation continued to fly, Lyman knew the scandal had undermined her credibility, and apparently she offered to resign for the good of the church. With great compassion, however, she was encouraged by second counselor in the First Presidency, David O. McKay, to hold on, at least for the time being, and try to forge ahead. While she struggled to rebuild her relationship with her husband, Lyman thus forced herself to go forward with her responsibilities and even attended the regular meeting of the general board in the first week of December. Sensing her discomfort at returning to work for the first time since the excommunication, McKay picked her up at home and escorted her through each of the offices in Relief Society headquarters in an implicit demonstration of the support she enjoyed from many in the church hierarchy, as well as their confidence that she still had meaningful contributions to make. At the conclusion of the meeting, she thanked the board for "holding up her arms" during the crisis, then hurried to her office with her counselors. This step, difficult as it was, broke the tension, allowing Lyman and her co-workers to move ahead. As the board and staff returned to their duties they were grateful that Lyman was back and full of admiration for the personal strength she demonstrated.[103]

Despite the tragedy, Lyman did not lag at the helm of the organization, but continued to push ahead with the Society's ongoing contributions to war work and the Welfare Plan. As a result, the year 1944 was even more productive than 1943, with Relief Society women donating another three-quarters of a million hours of labor, during which they sewed nearly two hundred thousand articles for the Red Cross and the Welfare Plan.[104] In these darkest days of the war, when casualties continued to mount and the end was not yet in sight, Lyman also saw that the *Magazine* focused even more closely on providing spiritual comfort to the women of the organization. It also continued to supply diversions: a new series of articles by former board member Alice Merrill Horne on Utah women artists, for example, appeared in 1944 and 1945. More practically, the *Magazine* provided expert advice on ways to deal with the wartime crisis and the adjustments of returned servicemen, disabled veterans, and mothers leaving the workplace for the home. As a result of all this, *Relief Society Magazine* subscriptions rose markedly in 1944 and attendance at meetings, which had lagged somewhat with the onset of the war, began to rise as well.[105] In addition, steps were taken to show the women of the organization that Lyman was still actively at the helm. She authored an article, for instance, in the March 1944 *Magazine* entitled "Relief Society in Action Today." At the same time, tributes to her leadership penned by her associates also appeared.[106]

Meanwhile, the continued development of the Welfare Plan brought additional changes to the Relief Society. Lyman's strategy of filling gaps in the plan had allowed much of the Society's previous work to continue. Priesthood leaders, however, had learned from the Society's example and were now urging the bishops to assume greater responsibility for funding medical care, making many of the Society's activities in these areas unnecessary. While Lyman and her board viewed this surrendering of responsibility with mixed emotions, they recognized the need to make efficient use of resources by relying on the growing capacities of the Welfare Plan. This was especially clear as their own funds continued to shrink; to be specific, the wheat interest, which disappeared as the principal in the account was converted into grain for storage in church elevators. The Society's leaders had sought to make up for the resulting shortfalls through use of donated charity funds supplemented with monies from bazaars and other fund raising activities, but as time went on it became clear to many among the organization's leadership that the Welfare Plan called into question the need for Relief Society charity funds altogether.

By the spring of 1944 the handwriting was on the wall and board members were discussing—sometimes heatedly—the possibility of ceasing the collection of charity funds by visiting teachers. One such discussion led to a memorable teaching moment by Lyman. In a committee meeting considering the subject, General Secretary-Treasurer Vera White Pohlman had been involved in an intense debate with board member Vivian McConkie. Lyman, who was not in attendance, nevertheless overheard the raised voices from her office and queried board member Leona Wintch, asking pointedly "What was going on in there?" After Wintch briefed her, Lyman asked her what she had said during the dispute. Wintch replied that she had been so upset by the strong clash of opinions that she had said nothing. Lyman then admonished her never again to be afraid to speak her mind, even when close associates were involved. "Principles rather than personalities" should have the highest priority in determining one's actions, Lyman revealingly advised.[107]

That opinions on the subject were strongly held was not surprising. Giving up the last of its charity funds was no small step. Since its inception the organization had collected such monies to be used at the discretion of Relief Society leaders. The surrender of this right would result in further dependence on the priesthood for funding, and with it, closer supervision of its activities. Some board members at first found this too great a departure from the past and too dangerous a precedent for the future. Ultimately, however, all were convinced the change was inevitable. Lyman came to agree and announced in September through the *Magazine* that charity funds were no longer to be collected.[108] An emergency fund from general revenues was to be maintained for short term uses, but the Relief Society women would now look to the resources of the bishops and stake presidents for supplying all other welfare needs. From one perspective, this new policy represented another small step in the ongoing decline of the organization's autonomy as the Relief Society was subsumed within the larger church organization. Yet Lyman saw opportunity in the change as well, and emphasized that this new departure, which required closer cooperation by ward and stake Relief Society leaders with bishops and stake presidents in welfare planning, furthered the long term goal to coordinate the actions of priesthood and Relief Society leaders. The *Magazine* soon began to carry accounts of Relief Society charity work arranged in just this manner.[109]

Even as Lyman made this latest adjustment to new realities, another shadow loomed over her presidency. Given current restrictions in access to church records, especially the deliberations of the First Presidency of the church, it is impossible to say with any certainty what factors and personalities were involved. But while the full circumstances surrounding events remain unclear, it can be said with certainty that sometime late in the summer of 1944, First Counselor J. Reuben Clark asked for Lyman's resignation.[110] Perhaps the move was initiated by Heber J. Grant, but it is more likely to have been arranged by Clark himself, who, though careful to consult Grant, seems to have been steering the day-to-day affairs of the church by this time.[111]

Clark's papers for the period are silent on the subject, but if he was responsible it would have been a logical time to make such a move. His wife had died in August after an extended illness and it is possible that he now felt free to deal with some issues long left unresolved.[112] With the successful landing of allied forces in Normandy signaling that the war was nearing an end in Europe and with the Relief Society poised to terminate its period of limited activity due to travel restrictions, he might have seen a change in its leadership as one such issue needing his attention. However, if this is indeed what happened, a number of factors could have strengthened Clark (or even President Grant) in his decision. First and foremost, Lyman's presence was a constant reminder of Richard's transgressions and thus of the embarrassment he had caused the church. Moreover, despite longstanding Mormon emphasis on a single standard of morality for men and women, Richard had reportedly sought—rather ungallantly—to shift blame for his errors to Amy because of her failure to perform her so-called wifely duties.[113] Some church leaders seemed to have accepted this explanation, even as many among the rank and file speculated that Amy's frantic schedule left her with little time to be attentive to her husband.[114] Whether Clark or Grant shared such views, the consequences of such ideas on Lyman's credibility as a leader could not have been lost on them. And at a time when Clark, in particular, was calling upon women to assume a role centered more closely on family and home, he could easily have viewed Lyman's family life as an object lesson on the consequences of wrong choices.

Of lesser, though no doubt real concern, especially to Clark, might have been Lyman's continued advocacy of cooperation with government and her injunctions for Relief Society women to be active in community affairs and politics. For reasons such as these, he could not have been entirely happy with her activities as Relief Society president despite her proven willingness to accede to his council in most matters and the extremely effective support she orchestrated for his Welfare Plan. Similarly, in September he began a renewed effort to streamline and economize church administration, one that would require ongoing concessions from all the auxiliaries, including the Relief Society.[115] Concerned about maintaining as much as possible of the Society's autonomy, as Clark well knew, Lyman enjoyed a well-earned reputation as a tough adversary when such issues were decided. Perhaps a new incident of this sort related to his plan, which included provisions for a committee to screen all material appearing in church publications, led Clark to conclude that now would be the opportune time to release the determined Lyman.

All this, of course, is based on a great deal of circumstantial evidence leaving any conclusions deep within the realm of speculation. What can be said with some certainty is that whatever contributory factors might have made such a decision seem desirable, Richard's indiscretion gave Clark—or perhaps even President Grant himself—a compelling reason to release Lyman.

Amy had been aware from the start of the implications of Richard's excommunication on her ability to lead the Relief Society. Indeed, she had been regularly reminded of the fact: traveling to and from work on the streetcar she encountered stares and whispered communications from the other passengers, something she found especially difficult to endure.[116] Yet, she knew she still had much to contribute, a view that friends, co-workers, and several priesthood leaders reaffirmed when they urged her to remain in her position at the time of the scandal. That in her heart she was personally so inclined, there can be no question. From her childhood she had been taught to accept all church callings and to serve in them until honorably released. Quitting when faced with a challenge was not in her nature. Furthermore, the Relief Society had been her life for thirty-five years. She had worked tirelessly for the organization, helping to revitalize it in the 1910s and 1920s, and had done so again during the challenging years of her presidency. Despite setbacks she had been largely successful in preserving the activist legacy of the organization and forging a strong link between its accomplished past, its vital present, and its promising future. There can be no doubt that her deepest desire was to continue, to build on the foundation she had laid, to lead the organization to new heights of achievement as it moved toward the postwar period.

And, for a short time, at least, her desire was granted. Once tendered, her resignation was temporarily refused. Perhaps due to Clark's bout of poor health in September, the inability to find a suitable successor, or a last minute intervention on the part of President Grant, she was not released, as expected, at October conference. Instead, she was informed that as long as the war continued the limits placed on the Relief Society made any change of leadership unwarranted.[117] Like the circumstances surrounding her resignation, those affecting its rejection are unclear. Whatever the explanation, Amy certainly seemed grateful to the church president. In an editorial in the November *Magazine* in celebration of Grant's birthday—a signed piece, which was itself somewhat of a departure from normal practice—Lyman nearly gushed when praising him. She noted that he had "always been a true friend to the women of the Church" and had "recognized their contributions" to its welfare and development. Perhaps most tellingly, she observed that he had "honored them in their various callings." "For this generous attitude toward women," she continued, "and this whole-souled recognition of their abilities and service, we are deeply grateful."[118]

With the assurance of a temporary reprieve, Lyman returned to the ongoing tasks of managing the organization. A year previously she had asked Belle Spafford and Vera Pohlman to tour Relief Societies in the western states to determine their status. After three months and thousands of miles of travel, they reported back that many were functioning as intended, but others, left without regular supervision by the general board, seemed to be drifting, and were beset by a variety of problems.[119] Now, pondering the time when wartime travel restrictions were to be lifted, Lyman began to discuss plans with the board to bring local affairs back into order. She also continued to press forward with another item long on the organization's agenda: the creation of the handbook for stake social service aids. By the spring of 1945, the materials for it had been approved by church leaders and were ready for printing and distribution to the stakes.[120]

The *Magazine* also began to address issues of anticipated import in the postwar period. In 1944 a series of articles appeared dealing with nations such as Poland, Turkey, and Palestine that would be foci of international attention after the war.[121] Relief Society women were also urged to join this cause of building a lasting peace. Emerging avenues of activism highlighted in the *Magazine* included renewed campaigns to combat liquor and tobacco use. Receiving attention as well was the upcoming centennial of the arrival of the Mormon pioneers in the Salt Lake Valley.[122]

Yet even as she looked ahead, Lyman realized that the day of her release from the Relief Society presidency was drawing close and that this time there likely would be no reprieve. In mid-February, 1945, the First Presidency informed the General Board that Lyman's resignation had been accepted.[123] The board was then asked to recommend, by vote, her successor. Talented and ambitious Belle Spafford, long-time editor of the *Magazine* and since November 1942, Lyman's second counselor, was considered the most likely candidate. In the event, she proved to be the choice both of the board and of the First Presidency.[124]

Before her release was made public in April, Lyman wrote another editorial, one that provided her a final opportunity to speak to the society as its president. First lauding the service offered by the members of the organization during the past year, she then broadened her focus to celebrate all that women of the Relief Society had been able to achieve in the generations since its creation. The society, "which was founded by a prophet of God on a broad, liberal, and adequate foundation," had "brought unusual opportunity to the women of the Church who have partaken of its advantages—opportunity for human service and opportunity for spiritual, intellectual, and emotional development." She paid tribute to the women of the past: "We are indebted to them for their vision, self-sacrificing efforts, and untiring labors. They have left us a rich heritage of faith and devotion to the Relief Society cause and to the restored gospel." Then she turned to those with whom she had shared the struggle, "To our co-workers, we offer congratulations for their like devotion and fortitude and for their great accomplishments in these days of apprehension and anxiety." Finally, she offered a plea for the future: "to the new and vigorous young leaders and workers who are coming into the service we say, look backward as well as forward; strive to properly evaluate the past and use it as a foundation for the future; and look forward with faith and a long view."[125] With these words as her valedictory, Amy Brown Lyman departed the leadership of the organization that she loved so dearly.

9

A FADED LEGACY

> All good is far reaching, nothing good is lost.
>
> —AMY BROWN LYMAN[1]

By all accounts, Belle Spafford was a logical successor to the accomplished Lyman.[2] But with her call came new realities: while Lyman had sought to maintain a certain amount of autonomy and independence for the Relief Society in choosing its own agenda, Spafford soon found that the broad prerogatives of years past were no longer available. When J. Reuben Clark called Spafford to her new position at the beginning of April 1945, he told her that the Relief Society would now come more closely under priesthood supervision. The society, the "companion organization to the priesthood," was henceforth to be a supporter rather than an initiator of policy.[3] In essence, with this transition, the society moved closer to its denoted status as an auxiliary and farther from that of an organization for women that paralleled the priesthood quorums. This shift reflected a new reality, that in a church growing in membership and complexity of administration, it was deemed necessary to limit the auxiliaries—including the Relief Society—in their ability to develop and pursue their own agenda.[4]

With Grant near death at Spafford's call (he would pass away the following month), and with Clark soon to fulfill the same role as manager and gatekeeper in an effort to protect the health of Grant's successor, George Albert Smith—and perhaps without the powerful constituency of supporters among the other general authorities that Lyman had cultivated for decades—Spafford had little recourse but to move the organization into line with Clark's priorities.[5] And indeed, this might have been more in keeping with Spafford's own priorities as well. Speaking in Relief Society conference in 1949, she gave her assessment of the organization's guiding responsibilities. "The Relief Society," she asserted, "since its inception, has accepted as one of its major responsibilities the task of guiding, directing, and training its members in their vital role of mother and homemaker." She maintained further that "to develop within the members a firm and abiding testimony of the gospel, and to make of them good mothers and homemakers is one of the Relief Society's first concerns."[6] Whether or not she was merely following the directives of church leaders—her stated priorities for the organization are notably the same as those advocated for years by Clark—or was herself inclined toward this new path, under Spafford there would be no return to the large-scale activism of times past. Symbolizing this era of new limits, the organization's semi-annual conferences, suspended during wartime, were now limited to annual meetings held just once a year in October.

This is not to say that Spafford completely surrendered all remnants of the society's independence. Despite ongoing pressure for the consolidation of programs, she held onto the *Relief Society Magazine* for another twenty-five years and the organization's separate educational curriculum throughout her presidency. As a body, Relief Society women continued to assist in the welfare plan, and, notably, in the immediate postwar period, provided aid to war-torn Europe. Collective charity work was also pursued, albeit on a much more limited basis than previously, as members raised funds for such causes as the March of Dimes' drive against polio.[7]

Spafford herself won local and national recognition as she continued Lyman's efforts to expand and professionalize the church's social services at the general offices of the organization. However, developments at the local level marked a significant shift from Lyman's approach: Social service institutes were terminated under Spafford's administration, and though previously cleared for publication, the planned social service handbook never appeared in print. Further, the use of Lyman's trained army of social work paraprofessionals was abandoned. This left often inexperienced bishops and Relief Society presidents without the assistance of skilled aids as they administered local charity matters. Under Spafford, the emphasis in charity work for the rank and file shifted, according to one account, "to training the sisters to give more effective compassionate service as individuals rather than as part of a group."[8] In other words, away from the vision Lyman had advanced in regard to social work, and back toward that advocated decades before by Susa Young Gates. While this move away from skilled lay workers reflected national trends in the social work profession at large, Lyman and those most closely involved with her in Relief Society welfare work knew that a vital role for informed volunteers remained. The cessation of regular training coupled with the failure to follow through on the publication of the handbook for social service aides thus left a void in the proper functioning of the church's Welfare Plan that some argue still exists today.[9]

Taken together, all this reveals that the society that emerged in the postwar period was noticeably less activist than it had been in previous decades and far less so than Lyman had anticipated.[10] In addition, Clark kept Spafford and the organization she led hemmed in within fairly narrow bounds. For instance, while she was given permission to raise money for a new Relief Society headquarters building—a highly visible legacy of her presidency—he did not allow her to draw on those funds to begin construction. Only in 1951 when David O. McKay became president did she gain access to them.[11]

Yet her eventual success in this matter raises the question of why Spafford did not expand the agenda of the Society when McKay's leadership might have provided a more congenial environment for a return to the activities of the past. Perhaps by then patterns of behavior had already been set for her presidency, with forces of administrative inertia seeming too powerful to overcome. Or perhaps President McKay's views regarding the Relief Society and the role of women were substantially in line with Clark's. On the other hand, perhaps Spafford, a generation younger than Lyman, simply did not feel a compelling need for continued collective activism of the kind that had characterized an earlier era.

Larger trends affecting American society during this period must also be accounted for in any discussion of developments affecting Mormon women. In particular, after the chaotic decades of the Great Depression and Second World War, many craved the kind of stability a settled family life seemed to represent. As the postwar recovery gave way to Cold War tensions, a variety of often conflicting signals bombarded women about their proper role in society, but those that proved most influential portrayed family and home as the avenue to feminine fulfillment and even as an expression of patriotism.[12] Strong families were the building block of a strong nation, according to many experts of the day, and strong families were thought dependent on a male provider and a mother who made the home a nurturing environment for husband and children.[13] Given such national realities, perhaps the things that the society managed to retain for its agenda in the 1950s and 1960s—the *Relief Society Magazine*, its own educational curriculum, a limited program of activities such as socials, sewing for welfare projects, and occasional drives for charity funds—were those many Mormon women of the period cared about the most, or at least in the context of the times felt it appropriate that they should care about.[14] It must also be remembered that Spafford and other Relief Society leaders could point to signs implying that this approach seemed to work. Using active participation rates and vigorous growth in its numbers as a gauge for the appeal of their agenda, two decades after her call to the Relief Society presidency, Spafford's administration would boast a record of uninterrupted increase.[15] In addition to Clark's continued presence as counselor when McKay's presidency began, there are thus any number of reasons that must be considered when seeking to understand why Spafford did not return the Relief Society to the large scale collective activism of the past.

Of course, many women of the time either willingly or by necessity rejected or sought a modification of the domestic ideal others were trying to impose on them, a fact often ignored then as now. By 1950, one quarter of American women over thirty-five were working, a proportion that continued to grow as the decade progressed.[16] According to social scientists, while most left the home due to economic necessity, others were driven by their search for intellectual and emotional outlets. Far more, generally middle class women, sought fulfillment not in the workplace, but through club work, the PTA, or other forms of service.[17] It was these latter women in the Mormon community—driven not by economic need but by a desire for meaningful activity—that Lyman had in mind when she pushed for broader opportunities during the years of her presidency. Under Spafford's leadership, neither these women, nor those forced into the workplace found as many opportunities in the Relief Society's activities and agenda that were as relevant to their lives as those Lyman had anticipated to pursue.

In retrospect, the changes that took place in the prerogatives and programs of the Relief Society after the Second World War now seem somewhat inevitable. It is possible, however, that under different circumstances, the course of events might have turned another direction and the organization's activism in community affairs—as well as the broader control over its own agenda it had long enjoyed—might have survived to be adapted for the use of subsequent generations. Certainly there were ample causes that both priesthood and Relief Society leaders might have agreed upon as appropriate venues for the collective action of Mormon women, just as similar issues had in previous decades. And given the church's accelerating expansion internationally, this legacy could eventually have been turned to the benefit of members in less developed nations than the United States. If Richard Lyman had not engaged in the actions that led to his excommunication, Amy's position as a leader might have been more secure and she might have been able to marshal her capital among other church leaders to successfully pursue a more expansive agenda in the postwar era. Perhaps she could have found greater support during the administration of George Albert Smith or even, had she remained as president that long, under David O. McKay, who was a strong admirer. And had she managed to remain president, undoubtedly Lyman would have sought to continue along the path marked out during her long years of church and community service, fighting hard along the way to retain what remained of the Relief Society's autonomy and programs.

One can be sure that under her direction the society's ties to other women's organizations would have remained strong and vital and that she would have found ways to highlight the Relief Society's contribution to the cause of women's equality. To facilitate these ends, in addition to continuing association with the National Council of Women, which Spafford herself so successfully pursued, Lyman could have tapped into strands of women's activism in the larger community that remained viable in the postwar era. Of course some such pathways moved into improbable venues for Mormon women: given the church's practice at the time of excluding African Americans from full membership, civil rights work, for example, would have been unthinkable.[18] Likewise, despite the efforts of an earlier generation in behalf of world peace, with the rise of the Cold War and the vitriolic anti-communism of the McCarthy Era, such activism would have been seen by many as un-American, even playing into the hands of communist subversives. This would have been out of harmony with the church's long-running efforts to promote a positive public image and directly at odds with the strongly conservative political views of several influential church leaders. Indeed, by this time, some authorities of the faith were quite outspoken in their belief that the Relief Society as an organization had no role whatsoever in matters with political implications, broadly defined.[19]

In light of these realities, Lyman would have, by necessity, steered clear of activities smelling even remotely of politics and instead marshaled the organization to address ongoing concerns in areas such as public health, home and practical nursing, fighting tuberculosis and polio, as well as substance abuse—all causes in which she remained active after her release. Collective action in these areas would have made valuable contributions to the well-being of the community and could have been comfortably accommodated within the framework church leaders were advocating for the organization. The same could be said for the cause of improving public education. In the judgment of some of her coworkers, Lyman would have attempted to raise the visibility of the organization much higher in areas such as these.[20]

On the other hand, even if Lyman, who lived well into her eighties and remained vigorous until her death, had been able to hang on to her position, there is no guarantee that events would have turned out differently, swimming as she was against the tide in both the larger society and the church. In the event, Spafford's twenty-nine years presiding over the Relief Society, reflective as they were both of the circumstances of the day and her own priorities, left a deep imprint on the organization and helped shape the self-image of generations of Latter-day Saint women. Lacking from that image was Lyman's compelling vision of the power of organized womanhood. Without official promotion of such a course, the society's legacy of activism faded from collective memory until it was all but forgotten. Decades before as they pursued new priorities suited to the needs of their times, Lyman's generation had not paid proper heed to the warnings of Emmeline Wells and neglected to jealously guard all of the prerogatives and authority that was their legacy.[21] Now, another powerful legacy of the past was surrendered, and as in the former case, only in retrospect has the full magnitude of the loss become clear.

The Relief Society's shift in focus, evident soon after Lyman left the presidency, may have dismayed her. If so, she loyally kept such reservations to herself and typically, rather than brooding over the past, looked ahead. Though she spoke of this period as her retirement, she remained very active. Her influence over Relief Society affairs had ended with her release, but she retained interest in the organization, though from a distance, allowing Belle Spafford to set her own course without any unsolicited input or advice. Most of Amy's involvement in Relief Society was now limited to the local level. Due to her past accomplishments, members in her own ward saw her as a little intimidating, a perspective reinforced, no doubt, by the no-nonsense, quick paced manner she maintained from her years of harried Relief Society work. Even when well into her eighties it was said she could part a crowd merely by walking resolutely toward it. Despite the awe, bordering on fear, that she engendered, shortly after her release, her ward Relief Society president summoned her courage and asked Lyman to teach the monthly literature lessons. Predictably, she accepted and served in the position until her death. Her lessons became legendary for their well-informed eloquence and the weeks she taught always saw the highest attendance in the month.[22]

Lyman was also invited on occasion to contribute to larger Relief Society matters as well, because of the admiring respect shown to her by Belle Spafford. Asked by her successor to speak at the October 1945 Relief Society General Conference, the first held since 1941, Lyman also participated in several subsequent conferences as well.[23] And in 1953 and 1954 she was a guest at the ground breaking and cornerstone ceremonies for the long awaited Relief Society building.[24] Lyman was also asked to contribute a number of features to the *Relief Society Magazine*, including a series on pioneer life for the centennial of the arrival of the Mormon vanguard in the Salt Lake Valley.[25]

Socially, Lyman was very active: she not only joined what came to be known as the General Board Emeritus Club, but renewed her active status with the Authors Club while she continued to enjoy her association with the Friendship Circle.[26] In community affairs, she maintained ties with the Visiting Nurses Association, the Utah Tuberculosis Association, and the Traveler's Aid Society, as well as a favorite group, the Organization of Women Legislators (OWLS), who gathered to discuss current affairs and matters of import for women.[27] In venues such as these, she remained outspoken in her commitment to the issues that had animated her life: church and Relief Society on the one hand, social welfare work and women's rights on the other.[28]

Family also remained a focus of her attention. Her relationship with Richard, of course, required time to regain a sense of normalcy. Before the scandal, the couple had frequently socialized in a number of civic associations, but it was years before she again felt comfortable at his side in public.[29] However, their relationship was more relaxed with close friends and family members who reported that the couple seemed at ease with one another and appeared to have put the past behind them.[30] Missionaries during their time in Europe were also frequent visitors and Amy and Richard even attended a missionary reunion.[31] Her daughter Margaret and husband Alexander Schreiner now lived nearby and she had time now to enjoy their company and that of their children who were themselves growing to maturity and soon started families of their own. Grandchildren, and soon great-grandchildren livened her days as well. She kept a rocking chair in the kitchen where she would rock the younger ones while reading them stories and teaching them songs.[32] A multitude of extended family was close at hand as well, providing ample opportunities for sociability and even service. Amy continued in her role as family matriarch to the clan during these years and, as before, was often turned to in times of crisis. When a niece was paralyzed by fear on her first day as a school teacher, for instance, Amy appeared in the classroom to reassure her.[33]

Her relationship with granddaughter Amy Kathryn, who married in 1946, proved especially gratifying.[34] Like the senior Amy, she was called to teach literature lessons in her ward Relief Society and the two shared many hours preparing their lessons together. Amy Kathryn had important opportunities for church service of her own. As she took on new tasks she was both inspired and intimidated by her grandmother, often feeling a nagging sense of inadequacy because she was unable to rise to the same heights. Over the years, Lyman herself had often been praised for her accomplishments. When this occurred, she had responded simply: "I had the opportunity." As her granddaughter began married life, she faced a different environment, one in which such opportunities were growing harder to find and exploit. Particularly limiting, child care was more difficult to obtain and socially less acceptable for women who were now more than ever expected to devote their full energies to home and family. For this new generation, well-educated and talented, the avenues that led their grandmothers to prominence in community service were no longer viable.[35]

Though concerned about such circumstances, Lyman focused more on making the best use of the time still before her. Though the pace of her life certainly slowed, she remained not just busy, but interested and involved. As the years passed, her activities kept her from becoming old in body or spirit and she remained active and quick-paced to the very end, always trying to squeeze more into life than was possible for most mortals. She had been ahead of her time during her years of Relief Society work: now, she was a pioneering a role for vital senior citizenship.[36]

Lyman was well-known because of her accomplishments outside the home, but she had always maintained a domestic role throughout her married life—she had seen no contradiction in this—and her retirement years were no exception. She baked and put up endless jars of fruit. She helped out family members who needed a hand, mending clothes and even an occasional teddy bear. She remained a fanatical house cleaner, especially when time came for spring cleaning, and continued to function as a practical and frugal household manager. For example, she dry-cleaned Richard's suits on their back porch using gasoline—a practice that caused trepidation among family members lest she burn the house down. Ironically, it was her combination of frugality and energetic activity in domestic affairs that precipitated her death.

At the beginning of December 1959, the eighty-seven-year-old Lyman was in her kitchen making soap—a skill she learned rather late in life, during the Second World

War. While moving hurriedly about her task, she slipped on some grease, fell, and fractured her arm near the shoulder. It was a serious break, requiring hospitalization and then a move to her daughter Margaret's apartment to recover.[37] However, the shock to Lyman's system proved hard on her already weakened heart and she clearly was not doing well.

On the evening of December 4, she called up her old friend Vera Pohlman. The two women had kept in close contact and recently the Lymans had asked Pohlman to prepare a brief biography of Amy for submission to a Brigham Young University committee selecting names for new women's residence halls; Lyman found satisfaction in being among the prominent women considered for the honor. She began by discussing progress on the biography but soon moved to other topics and the conversation eventually became quite lengthy. Knowing that Lyman was not well, Pohlman tactfully tried several times to end the call, but Amy clearly seemed reluctant to hang up, repeatedly shifting the discussion to new areas, reminiscing about people and events from long ago. Finally, the hour having grown quite late, the two said goodnight. Early the next morning, Pohlman received another call, this time from Amy's daughter Margaret, informing her that Lyman had died during the night. Pohlman then realized that her mentor and friend of nearly forty years, sensing her time was short, had called up to say goodbye.[38]

Lyman's passing was given lengthy notice in the Utah papers while her funeral three days later was well attended by family and friends as well as church and community leaders. Speakers included Belle Spafford, who gave the eulogy extolling Lyman's long years of service and accomplishment, and David O. McKay, then president of the church, who discoursed on Mormon theology regarding eternal life. Pohlman came as well, providing a final service by taking minutes of the proceedings. Her presence also made for a lighter moment when, unable to find a ride to the cemetery, she joined the funeral director in the front seat of the hearse. Seeing her there, steno book in hand, the family laughed about faithful Vera, sitting at the ready to take any last dictation.[39]

Richard outlived Amy by four years, remaining to the end his wife's greatest booster. When BYU declined to name a dormitory after her, in part because he had blamed her for his own indiscretions, he was then negotiating to donate Amy's papers to the institution. The university's decision caused him to question the gift because, he wrote in a letter composed at the time, of the slight given to "the greatest and most prominent WOMAN LEADER that the State of Utah or the Church has produced." He relented, however, and many of Lyman's papers now reside at her beloved BYU. As for Richard, he remained at the family home on Third Avenue, assisted by a recently married granddaughter and her husband. Late in 1963, he began to show signs of jaundice, a condition that doctors soon determined was the result of liver cancer. He died a few weeks later at age ninety-three.[40]

By this time, Amy's legacy was already beginning to fade. It had been nearly two decades since her departure from the Relief Society leadership and a new generation of Mormon women had come on the scene who knew little of her and less of the activism that had typified her era. It had been for this very reason that a quarter-century previously, the centennial committee had conceived the idea of a permanent monument to draw the attention of subsequent generations of Mormon women to their heritage. To women who had served on her general board, Lyman's death was a frustrating reminder of the continued inaction with regard to the Centennial Campanile.[41]

The campanile, its components completed, paid for, and in storage ready for final assembly, was left unfinished after the war. For the most part, the monument seems simply to have fallen through the cracks as Spafford focused the organization's energies first on construction of the new Relief Society headquarters and then on other projects.[42] Lyman herself had tactfully reminded her successor of this unfinished bit of business a number of times, but to no avail. Finally, several years after Lyman's death, former board member and chair of the centennial committee Rae Barker took it upon herself, with the assistance of her husband, a member of the church building committee, to see that the project was completed.

Their first step was to track down the various components that, over the intervening years, had been scattered to the wind. Most vexing of all, the tower itself and some of its decorative grillwork had been mistakenly sold as scrap. Purchasing these pieces with their own money, Barker and her husband soon rounded up the remaining parts and then began to wend their way through a church bureaucracy that had grown quite formidable, to find a site where the structure could be erected. The original location that had been selected for it on Temple Square was now slated for a large flag pole, but another was chosen in the rose garden adjacent to the Tabernacle.[43] Finally, at the end of September 1966 between sessions of the Relief Society's annual conference, Belle Spafford (no doubt with considerable relief that the long delayed task was finally complete) dedicated the campanile, paying tribute, as she did, to the past generations of women it honored. By then, like Lyman, many who had commissioned the monument's construction and sacrificed so much to finance it, were gone.[44]

A few years after the dedication, nearly a quarter-century after Spafford assumed the presidency, change again came to the prerogatives of the Relief Society. In September 1971, a church correlation committee terminated the collection of dues by the organization.[45] In the future, all adult women in the church would be considered members of the Relief Society, a move designed to make the organization more inclusive, but the price paid for larger membership was the loss of the last vestige of its financial independence. But another more wrenching change had already preceded this—one that had hit Spafford herself especially hard—when in December 1970, again at the direction of a church correlation committee, the *Relief Society Magazine* ended its fifty-seven year run as the voice of LDS women. In place of its sixty-plus pages written for and by women, the Relief Society, along with the other women's organizations of the church, were to share a single page in a new church periodical.[46] Yet more was to come: though the process would be a slow one spanning the better part of two decades, the Relief Society was to lose most of its separate curriculum as well. Church leaders made these changes in order to ensure the best use of limited resources, as they sought ways to strengthen members spiritually while building unity during a time of phenomenal church growth. Though not aimed intentionally at institutionally disempowering LDS women, some felt the changes had that very effect.

Four years after the demise of the *Magazine*, Belle Spafford was released from the presidency of the Relief Society. At the time she was called, she was led to believe that her term of service might last for only five years. Her three decades at the helm of the organization seemed to belie the idea that Relief Society presidents were to hold office for only a limited time. In so doing, she helped reverse a trend for shorter terms of service, and with it, diminishing status for Relief Society leaders that began with the release of unwilling Emmeline Wells. However, this reversal was only temporary: Spafford's successors held office for significantly shorter periods of time, eventually tending toward five year terms, which became the new norm. And with the more frequent arrival of new presidents, often came all new boards who brought with them significant shifts in priorities and practices. As Lyman learned on her mission, freedom to innovate is a valuable asset, but lack of institutional continuity—and especially institutional memory—can hinder an organization by forcing it to constantly reinvent the wheel while leaving inadequately addressed deep-seated problems that require years of focused attention. This regular change of leaders further contributed, of course, to the decline in the special status the Relief Society and its leaders had enjoyed during earlier years. Again, a phenomenon that Emmeline B. Wells had warned of decades before, and to which, in retrospect, younger women at the time—including Lyman herself—had not paid adequate heed. Despite the changes in practices, curriculum, and leadership and all they represented, for the most part, Relief Society members faithfully accepted them, although many found the process wrenching nonetheless.[47]

Ironically, all these steps tending toward diminishing autonomy took place even as feminism's second wave was cresting in the larger society, bringing with it demands for a greater role for women in public life. This call for change came from a chorus of voices drawn from a variety of sources. One prominent branch arose from middle-class women. Well educated and discontented with the exaggerated domesticity of the 1950s, in the 1960s large numbers of them responded to Betty Friedan's *Feminine Mystique* and its call for a richer and more fulfilling life.[48] Their goals included full citizenship for women, equal opportunity in the workplace, equal pay for equal or equivalent work, and shared responsibility between the sexes in the home. Another highly visible branch grew out of the civil rights, New Left, and student antiwar movements. Far more radical, these women did not stop at renegotiated relations between the sexes and an equal place in the existing order, but called for a complete restructuring of society. Their voices become the more strident and often the more visible. In the popular mind at least, they came to be seen as the public face of a movement some thought had spun out of control.[49] It was this more extreme element that left behind women like those in the Relief Society.[50] In the latter 1960s and early 1970s, most LDS women joined a backlash against this radical challenge to the status quo, embracing conservative conceptions of womanhood even as those conceptions seemed less and less descriptive of their own lives.

This rejection of radical feminism should not come as a surprise. First generation Mormon women, like Emmeline Wells, had embraced an agenda of cultural feminism when equality and broader spheres for women were seen as advancing the goals of the faith. Lyman's generation had inherited already well-developed feminist concepts that proved compatible to their own efforts to maintain an independent but complementary program for the Relief Society in church and community affairs. Such ideas did not seriously conflict with the positions of most church leaders until the 1930s when, reflecting similar tensions in the larger society, the relation between feminism and Mormonism grew increasingly problematic, even as the tradition of LDS women's participation in community affairs came under fire. With the rise of second wave feminism in the 1960s, especially in its more radical forms, feminist discourse among the mainstream of Mormon women at the time was largely submerged or abandoned and rather than being seen as supportive of the church and its mission, was most often portrayed as subversive to it.

Given these trends, what then to make of Lyman and the legacy of her generation? What do her experiences teach us about the history of women in general and about women of her faith in particular? Patterns of Mormon feminism indicate that Relief Society women stood at the intersection of trends affecting both Mormon society and the larger culture. Sometimes these influences worked in parallel, at others in opposition to one another. An important part of the legacy left by Lyman and other Relief Society leaders before her, was their ability to play the hand dealt them in a way that both advantaged and empowered their sex. In the world of Lyman's mother, trends in American society aimed at suppressing Mormon social and political practices worked at cross purposes with church goals to establish a commonwealth in the Great Basin—circumstances women used to broaden their sphere of usefulness and opportunity. In Lyman's case, it was parallel trends in American and Mormon society moving toward improvement in public health and social services that proved most useful to women in promoting benefits for their sex.

One of the most striking consequences for LDS women of Lyman's generation that emerged from this latter agenda is that many actively worked for the expansion of governmental influence in society. Currently, when stereotypes of Latter-day Saints often portray them as marching in lockstep with the conservative wing of the Republican Party and ready to reject any governmental intervention in society, one is taken aback by accounts of LDS women lobbying for the expansion of government services. Of course, the attitudes of this earlier generation of Mormons were formed in circumstances vastly different from today, a time when government was small and designedly ineffective. The women of Lyman's generation knew from personal experience that the consequences of lax or nonexistent government oversight were far from felicitous. Lyman and her peers worked for greater government intervention, not because they naively felt the state could solve all problems, but because they knew, after long experience, that only by tapping into the more abundant resources available through the public sector could the societal problems that surrounded them be effectively addressed. For like-minded members of her generation of Mormon women—like other Progressives across the nation—government was not the enemy, but a tool to be used to carry out the collective will of an interested and well-informed citizenry. For them, any intrusive aspect of the Sheppard-Towner Act, for example, was far less fearsome than the very real dangers of infant and maternal mortality. The same could be said of local, state, and federal measures designed to protect women and children in the workplace, to provide a minimum wage, disability insurance, or old age pensions for workers.

These women were not blindly accepting of government action—Lyman, it will be remembered, lamented the New Deal's frequent dependency on direct relief rather than works projects—but through informed participation in community affairs, they became convinced that an increasingly complex society demanded a vigorous government role in order to protect the well-being of individuals against the power of unrestrained big business and the uncertainties of economic fluctuations. Like others of her generation, however, Lyman knew that government action was only the beginning of the solution. She recognized the truth in the time-honored aphorism that the price of liberty (and it might be added, effective legislation) is eternal vigilance. The women of Lyman's generation paid the price for the kind of society they wanted not only through their own diligent participation in community life, but also through unrelenting attention to the goal of making government services—many that were the result of their own efforts—more responsive and effective. This vision of societal involvement was at the heart of the legacy Lyman was trying to preserve for Relief Society women.

Like her predecessors, Lyman's greatest talent was in finding ways to maintain the legacy of activism she inherited: in every situation she found opportunities to do so that were compatible with, even essential to, the larger mission of the church. This allowed her to retain her expansive vision even during the 1930s and 1940s as many women's organizations in the larger society were losing ground in the public sphere. Lyman was a master, in other words, at working the system. Blessed with phenomenal energy, capability, and intelligence, few could match her. What resulted was essentially a middle-class activism, progressive, though not radical in tone, that bore fruit in a charity system based on modern methods of social work and a public health program that benefitted women throughout the West and beyond. In addition, largely through Lyman's efforts, the lot of the mentally handicapped was improved, and under her guidance, the Church Welfare Plan reached a peak of efficiency. During two world wars, she helped marshal the women of the organization into an effective source of support for wartime measures while providing assistance for those on the home front. In all this, Lyman saw that ties were strengthened between the Relief Society and other women's groups even as women of the society gained an increased sense of their collective power. For Mormon women of the period, the Relief Society had served as a pathway to accomplishment and their own fulfillment. Perhaps, not surprisingly, Lyman herself best summed up the feeling women had for an organization that had opened so many doors to them. "Isn't the Church wonderful?" she observed late in life. "It is surely the greatest thing in the world." "And next to it," she pointedly continued, "comes the blessed Relief Society."[51]

While recognizing the importance of this nearly forgotten legacy, those who lament its loss must be careful not to idealize the past. The Relief Society opened avenues for activism to LDS women, but it did so at a time when they had few other alternatives for meaningful activity outside the home. While the rhetoric of first and second-generation women glorified equality, few ever really achieved it. If the Relief Society's past triumphs are largely forgotten, if much of its power often lies dormant and its functions reduced, the women of the Society today benefit from a more liberal environment in the larger society and laws prohibiting discrimination in employment. Despite continuing limitations, the granddaughters and great-granddaughters of Lyman's generation enjoy opportunities and a degree of real equality that earlier Mormon women, including Lyman, could hardly have dreamed. Nor should the cost of winning the opportunities enjoyed by today's women—including costs incurred by those of the Mormon church—be forgotten, for such were dearly bought through many decades of hard work and sacrifice, as Lyman's life so poignantly illustrates.

As for the organization Lyman served so faithfully, the Relief Society today reflects not only continuity but also significant change from Lyman's day. Its leaders continue to assist bishops in distributing relief at the local level and women regularly provide valued and necessary services to those in need during times of illness or other family emergency. The rank and file participate fairly regularly in local humanitarian relief projects, occasionally—to great effect—on a church-wide basis. But by and large the Society's function is now primarily spiritual, its role largely in keeping with the vision Clark had laid out for it—to foster sisterhood and solidarity among women of the faith.

Yet, in an environment as threatening to family and personal stability as anything in Lyman's day, such functions should be recognized for the benefits—limited as they may be—that they provide.

But, the broader potential that past Relief Society leaders such as Lyman marked out for the organization is still there, always lingering, just below the surface. If called upon by church leaders today—which seems quite plausible as opportunities for service increase with the church's growing presence in the third world—and if Mormon women desire it enough, it might reveal anew a powerful manifestation of organized womanhood. If such a revitalization does occur, the example of Lyman and her generation might serve as a guide to future action.

For the present, however, much of the organization's potential lies unused, even forgotten. Perhaps nothing better symbolizes this faded Relief Society legacy than the Centennial Campanile. In the early 1980s, renovation work led church leaders to move the structure to an area along the west wall of Temple Square. It stands there today, often ignored, mentioned only by tour guides because of the Nauvoo Bell it is believed to hold. Yet, when one understands its history and meaning, it serves as an evocative relic of a remarkable generation of women, of whom Lyman was first among equals. And in its current site, somewhat off the beaten track, visitors can find a congenial setting for contemplation of the monument and all it represents.

The centerpiece of the structure is, of course, the bell, simple yet substantial in form—it was meant to represent the Relief Society's Nauvoo origins, but reflects a heritage that became much richer after the move west. To the careful observer, even more striking is the workmanship of the rest of the campanile, from the stylized bees and beehives on the border along the top of the tower, symbolizing industry and collective endeavor, to the intricate hand-wrought grillwork emblazoned with the monogram of the Relief Society. Along the base are three impressive bas-relief sculptures by nationally prominent Utah artist Avard Fairbanks. Entitled: "Pioneering," "Education," and "Benevolence," each reveals in the heroic fashion of the 1940s much about the Relief Society's perception of its accomplishments and legacy at the time of its centennial.

When the monument is approached from the front, however, it is the inscription panel that one sees first. It is there that words seek to give meaning to the memorial and the generations of women it celebrates:

> It is with gratitude that this monument is dedicated to the thousands of unsung Relief Society heroines who over a period of one hundred years have stimulated intellectual development and given compassionate service without thought of honor or reward. These valiant women have nourished the hungry, clothed the needy, nursed the sick, [and] buoyed up the discouraged and disconsolate . . . [52]

Though unmentioned, like Lyman, they often did so at great personal sacrifice, continuing their efforts even in the face of enormous hardship and personal tragedy. While to the uninformed the Relief Society represents little of import to the advancement of women, for generations of Mormon women it provided a path to satisfying and valuable service in the community, to stimulating and useful educational experiences, and to a fulfilling sense of sisterhood in a cause that they felt was leading to equality of their sex.

In her funeral eulogy for Lyman, Belle Spafford read words Amy had used to describe her own mother, finding in them an appropriate description of Amy Brown Lyman herself: "[F]orceful, dynamic, and efficient; wise, far-seeing, and of good judgement. She was a woman's woman."[53] In turn, these words seems an apt description of the generation of Mormon women of which Lyman was a part, a generation that made a difference and found rich meaning for their lives in the process.

NOTES

ABBREVIATIONS USED

ABLP	Amy Brown Lyman Papers, L. Tom Perry Special Collections, Harold B. Lee Library, Brigham Young University, Provo, Utah.
ABLPRS	Amy Brown Lyman Papers, Relief Society, CR11 45, Church History Library, Church of Jesus Christ of Latter-day Saints, Salt Lake City, Utah.
EFP	Engar Family Papers. Materials formerly in the possession of Amy Kathryn Lyman Engar, copies of which are in possession of the author.
CBRUF	Children's Bureau Records, Utah Folder, National Archives and Records Administration, College Park, Maryland.
CHL	Church History Library, Church of Jesus Christ of Latter-day Saints, Salt Lake City, Utah.
JRCP	J. Reuben Clark Papers, L. Tom Perry Special Collections, Harold B. Lee Library, Brigham Young University, Provo, Utah.
LFP	Lyman Family Papers, MS 15998, Church History Library, Church of Jesus Christ of Latter-day Saints, Salt Lake City, Utah.
RRLP	Richard R. Lyman Papers, L. Tom Perry Special Collections, Harold B. Lee Library, Brigham Young University, Provo, Utah.
RSGBM	Relief Society General Board Minutes, CR 11 10, Church History Library, Church of Jesus Christ of Latter Day Saints, Salt Lake City, Utah.

INTRODUCTION

1. Amy Brown Lyman, "Relief Society as a Community Builder," *Relief Society Magazine* 27 (March 1940): 179.
2. For feminism during Lyman's generation of American women, see Nancy F. Cott, *The Grounding of Modern Feminism* (New Haven: Yale University Press, 1987).
3. Lyman left behind a short autobiography of limited circulation and also received some additional attention in the work of several scholars of Mormon history. Amy Brown Lyman, *In Retrospect: Autobiography of Amy Brown Lyman* (Salt Lake City: General Board of Relief Society, 1945); Loretta L. Hefner, "This Decade was Different: Relief Society's Social Services Department, 1919–1929," *Dialogue: A Journal of Mormon Thought* 15 (Autumn 1982): 64–73; Loretta L. Hefner, "The National Women's Relief Society and the U.S. Sheppard-Towner Act," *Utah Historical Quarterly* 50 (Summer 1982): 255–67; and Loretta L. Hefner, "Amy Brown Lyman: Raising the Quality of Life for All," in Vicki Burgess-Olson, *Sister Saints* (Provo: Brigham Young University Press, 1978), 96–116. See also Thomas G. Alexander, "Between Revivalism and the Social Gospel: The Latter-day Saint Social Advisory Committee, 1916–1922," *Brigham Young University Studies* 23 (Winter 1983): 19–39; Thomas G. Alexander, *Mormonism in Transition: A History of the Latter-day Saints, 1890–1930* (Urbana: University of Illinois Press, 1986); and Thomas G. Alexander and James B. Allen, *Mormons and Gentiles: A History of Salt Lake City* (Salt Lake City: Pruett, 1984). For Lyman and the Relief Society, see Jill Mulvay Derr, Janath Russell Cannon and Maureen Ursenbach Beecher, *Women of Covenant: The Story of Relief Society* (Salt Lake City: Deseret Book, 1992).

4. Jill Mulvay Derr, "'Strength in our Union': The Making of Mormon Sisterhood," in Maureen Ursenbach Beecher and Lavina Fielding Anderson, eds., *Sisters in Spirit: Mormon Women in Historical and Cultural Perspective* (Urbana: University of Illinois Press, 1987), 153–207; and Derr, Cannon, and Beecher, *Women of Covenant.* See also the following articles by Carol Cornwall Madsen, "Emmeline B. Wells: 'Am I Not a Woman and a Sister?'" *Brigham Young University Studies* 22 (Spring 1982): 161–78; "'The Power of Combination': Emmeline B. Wells and the National and International Councils of Women," *Brigham Young University Studies* 33 (1993): 647–73; and "Schism in the Sisterhood: Mormon Women and Partisan Politics, 1890–1900," in Davis Bitton and Maureen Ursenbach Beecher, eds., *New Views on Mormon History: A Collection of Essays in Honor of Leonard J. Arrington* (Salt Lake City: University of Utah Press, 1987), 212–41.
5. Lawrence Foster, "Polygamy and the Frontier: Mormon Women in Early Utah," *Utah Historical Quarterly* 50 (Summer 1982), 268–89; Jessie L. Embry, *Mormon Polygamous Families: Life in the Principle* (Salt Lake City: University of Utah Press, 1987); Kathryn M. Daynes, *More Wives Than One: Transformation of the Mormon Marriage System, 1840–1910* (Urbana: University of Illinois Press, 2001); Lola Van Wagenen, *Sister-Wives and Suffragists: Polygamy and the Politics of Woman Suffrage, 1870–1896* (Provo, UT: Joseph Fielding Smith Institute for Latter-day Saint History and BYU Studies, 2003); and Sarah Barringer Gordon, *The Mormon Question* (Chapel Hill: University of North Carolina Press, 2002).
6. Eleanor Flexner, *Century of Struggle: The Woman's Rights Movement in the United States* (Cambridge: Belknap Press of The Harvard University Press, 1959); Karen J. Blair, *The Clubwoman as Feminist: True Womanhood Redefined, 1868–1914* (New York: Holmes and Miller, 1980); Theodora Penny Martin, *The Sound of Our Own Voices: Women's Study Clubs, 1860–1910* (Boston: Beacon Press, 1987); Anne Firor Scott, *Natural Allies: Women's Associations in American History* (Urbana: University of Illinois Press, 1991); Kathleen D. McCarthy, ed., *Lady Bountiful Revisited: Women, Philanthropy, and Power* (New Brunswick: Rutgers University Press, 1990); Rosalyn Terborg-Penn, *African American Women in the Struggle for the Vote, 1850–1917* (Bloomington: Indiana University Press, 1998); and Paula Baker, "The Domestication of Politics: Women and American Political Society, 1780–1920," in Linda Gordon, ed., *Women, the State and Welfare* (Madison: University of Wisconsin Press, 1990).
7. Madsen, "The Power of Combination": 647–73; Jill Mulvay Derr, "Scholarship, Service, and Sisterhood: Utah Women's Clubs and Associations, 1877–1977," manuscript copy in author's possession; Derr, "Strength in our Union," 153–207; and Sharon Snow Carver, "Club Women of the Three Intermountain Cities of Denver, Boise and Salt Lake City between 1893 and 1929," (PhD Dissertation, Brigham Young University, 2000).
8. Gordon, *Women, the State, and Welfare*; Robyn Muncy, *Creating a Female Dominion in American Reform, 1890–1935* (New York: Oxford University Press, 1991); Lela B. Costin, *Two Sisters for Social Justice: A Biography of Grace and Edith Abbott* (Urbana: University of Illinois Press, 1983); Ellen Fitzpatrick, *Endless Crusade: Women Social Scientists and Progressive Reform* (New York: Oxford University Press, 1990); Joanne L. Goodwin, *Gender and the Politics of Welfare Reform: Mothers' Pensions in Chicago, 1911–1920* (Chicago: University of Chicago Press, 1997); Seth Koven and Sonya Michel, eds., *Mothers of a New World: Maternalist Politics and the Origins of the Welfare State* (New York: Routledge, 1993); Molly Ladd-Taylor, *Mother-Work: Women, Child Welfare and the State, 1890–1930* (Urbana: University of Illinois Press, 1994); Kathryn Kish Sklar, *Florence Kelley and the Nation's Work: The Rise of Women's Political Culture, 1830–1900* (New Haven: Yale University Press, 1995); and Theda Skocpol, *Protecting Soldiers and Mothers: The Political Origins of Social Policy in the United States* (Cambridge: Harvard University Press, 1992).

9. John S. Haller Jr. and Robin M. Haller, *The Physician and Sexuality in Victorian America* (Urbana: University of Illinois Press, 1974); Judith Walzer Leavitt, *Brought to Bed: Childbearing in America, 1750–1950* (New York: Oxford University Press, 1986); and Judith Walzer Leavitt, ed., *Women and Health in America: Historical Readings* (Madison: University of Wisconsin Press, 1984).
10. Scholars of Western history have long acknowledged the strong federal role in the affairs of the region and this is reemphasized in works of "new" Western history. See, for example, Richard White, *It's Your Misfortune and None of My Own: A New History of the American West* (Norman: University of Oklahoma Press, 1991); Patricia Limerick, *The Legacy of Conquest: The Unbroken Past of the American West* (New York: Norton, 1987); and Patricia Limerick, Clyde Milner II, and Charles E. Ranken, eds., *Trails: Towards a New Western History* (Lawrence: University of Kansas, 1991).
11. Roy Lubove briefly examined this topic in his 1965 study, *The Professional Altruist: The Emergence of Social Work as a Career* (Cambridge, MA: Harvard University Press, 1965), but the issue has not been addressed since that time.
12. Goodwin, *Gender and the Politics of Welfare Reform.*
13. Muncy, *Creating a Female Dominion*; Ladd-Taylor, *Mother Work*; and Skocpol, *Protecting Soldiers and Mothers.*
14. Hefner, "The National Women's Relief Society and the U.S. Sheppard-Towner Act."
15. See Muncy, *Creating a Female Dominion*, for the best summary of this process nationally.
16. Jill Mulvay Derr, "Changing Relief Society Charity to Make Way for Welfare, 1930–1944," in Davis Bitton and Maureen Ursenbach Beecher, eds., *New Views of Mormon History: Essays in Honor of Leonard J. Arrington* (Salt Lake City: University of Utah Press, 1987); and Garth L. Mangum and Bruce D. Blumel, *The Mormon's War on Poverty: A History of LDS Welfare, 1830–1990* (Salt Lake City: University of Utah Press, 1993).
17. Elaine Tyler May, *Homeward Bound: American Families in the Cold War Era* (New York: Basic Books, 1988); Susan Ware, *Still Missing: Amelia Earhart and the Search for Modern Feminism* (New York: Norton, 1993); Leila J. Rupp and Verta Taylor, *Survival in the Doldrums: The American Women's Rights Movement, 1945 to the 1960s* (New York: Oxford University Press, 1987); Joanne Meyerowitz, ed., *Not June Cleaver: Women and Gender in Postwar America, 1945–1960* (Philadelphia: Temple University Press, 1994); and Amy Swerdlow, *Women Strike for Peace: Traditional Motherhood and Radical Politics in the 1960s* (Chicago: University of Chicago Press, 1993).

CHAPTER 1

1. Emmeline B. Wells, "To the Women of Utah, in Mass Meeting Assembled, March 6th, 1886," *Woman's Exponent* 14 (April 1, 1886): 164.
2. Amy Brown Lyman, "Achievements of Women, 1926," 15, Amy Brown Lyman Papers, L. Tom Perry Special Collections, Harold B. Lee Library, Brigham Young University, (hereafter cited as ABLP).
3. Maureen Ursenbach Beecher, "The Leading Sisters: A Female Hierarchy in Nineteenth-Century Mormon Society." *Journal of Mormon History* 9 (1982): 25–39.
4. Amy Brown Lyman, *In Retrospect: Autobiography of Amy Brown Lyman* (Salt Lake City: General Board of Relief Society, 1945), 38.
5. See Jonathan A. Stapley and Kristine Wright, "Female Ritual Healing in Mormonism," *Journal of Mormon History*, 37 (Winter 2011): 1–85.
6. See Anne Firor Scott, *Natural Allies: Women's Associations in American History* (Urbana: University of Illinois Press, 1991).

7. A prime factor in this was the *Woman's Exponent*, which was a strong advocate for women and women's causes. See Carol Cornwall Madsen, *An Advocate for Women: The Public Life of Emmeline B. Wells, 1870–1920* (Provo: Brigham Young University Press, 2006).
8. John Zimmerman Brown, ed., *Autobiography of Pioneer John Brown, 1820–1896* (Salt Lake City: Press of Stevens and Wallis, 1941), 31–32. For Joseph Smith and the early church, see Richard Lyman Bushman, *Rough Stone Rolling: A Cultural Biography of Mormonism's Founder* (New York: Knopf, 2005).
9. Brown, *Autobiography*, 49–50.
10. Brown, *Autobiography*, 66–80.
11. Lyman, *In Retrospect*, 5.
12. Amy Lyman Engar interviews, 1990–94; Susan Elizabeth Swenson Driggs interviews, 1991, 1994.
13. Lyman, *In Retrospect*, 6; Brown, *Autobiography*, 146–47.
14. B. Carmon Hardy, *Solemn Covenant: The Mormon Polygamous Passage* (Urbana: University of Illinois Press, 1992), 1–38; Richard S. Van Wagoner, *Mormon Polygamy: A History*, (Salt Lake City: Signature Books, 1986), 84.
15. For recent estimates on the numbers involved in the practice, ranging between 20 to 40 percent of the total Mormon population, see Kathryn M. Daynes, *More Wives Than One: Transformation of the Mormon Marriage System, 1840–1910*, (Urbana: University of Illinois Press, 2002), 98–101. Daynes indicates that in 1860—a high point for such relationships—men, women and children living in polygamous families made up 43.1 percent of the population in Manti, Utah, a figure that she feels is not atypical of other areas. By 1870, that number fell to 36.0 percent, and by 1880, 25.1 percent. By 1900, only 7.1 percent in Manti were in such families. See also Van Wagoner, *Mormon Polygamy*, 91; and Hardy, *Solemn Covenant*, 16–17. For variations within the Mormon community regarding the practice, see Jessie L. Embry, *Mormon Polygamous Families: Life in the Principle* (Salt Lake City: University of Utah Press, 1987), 29–40. For the Reformation's impact on Mormon society, see Thomas G. Alexander, "Wilford Woodruff and the Mormon Reformation of 1855–1857," *Dialogue: A Journal of Mormon Thought* 25 (Summer 1992): 25–39; and Gene Sessions, *Mormon Thunder: A Documentary History of Jedidiah Morgan Grant* (Urbana: University of Illinois Press, 1982).
16. Brown, *Autobiography*, 138.
17. Rose Brown Hayes and Mrs. Clark interview, February 1, 1936, 3, John Brown file, Kimball Young Collection, L. Tom Perry Special Collections and Manuscripts, Brigham Young University; Sarah Barringer Gordon, *The Mormon Question: Polygamy and Constitutional Conflict in Nineteenth-Century America* (Chapel Hill: University of North Carolina Press, 2002), 100–101.
18. For the variety of circumstances within polygamy, see Embry, *Mormon Polygamous Families*, 161–66.
19. Annie Clark Tanner, *A Mormon Mother: An Autobiography of Annie Clark Tanner*, (Salt Lake City: University of Utah Tanner Trust Fund, 1983), 270.
20. Tanner, *A Mormon Mother*, 64–69, 272; Gordon, *The Mormon Question*, 100–101; Daynes, *More Wives Than One*, 173. For expectations regarding romance in American society during this period, see Michael Goldberg, "Breaking New Ground, 1800–1849," in Nancy F. Cott, ed., *No Small Courage: A History of Women in the United States*, (New York: Oxford University Press, 2000), 180–81.
21. Tanner asserted that few plural marriages survived until old age. Tanner, *A Mormon Mother*, 273. For estimates of divorce statistics, see Daynes, *More Wives Than One*, 142–64.
22. Hayes and Clark interview, 4; Engar interviews; Driggs interviews.

23. Hayes and Clark interview, 3; "Mary Ann Brown Clark," in Kate B. Carter, *Our Pioneer Heritage* (Salt Lake City: Daughters of the Utah Pioneers, 1965), 7:452; Driggs interviews.
24. Hayes and Clark interview, 4.
25. Nevertheless, there was not a complete rejection of the system. Margaret's eldest daughter Rose supported her own husband when he took a second wife. Engar interviews; Driggs interviews.
26. Mark Knight Allen, a psychologist who prepared a number of articles for the *Relief Society Magazine* during the 1930s and 1940s, recalled being advised to avoid the topic in his writings because it created controversy among Relief Society women. Mark K. Allen interviews, 1991, 1994.
27. For the experiences of one such plural wife, see Maria S. Ellsworth, *Mormon Odyssey: The Story of Ida Hunt Udall, Plural Wife* (Urbana: University of Illinois Press, 1992). The 1882 Edmunds Act had stripped polygamous wives of the traditional protection from being forced to testify against a spouse. For an extended discussion of this period, see Gustive O. Larson, *The "Americanization" of Utah for Statehood* (San Marino, CA: Huntington Library, 1971).
28. Leonard Arringon, *Great Basin Kingdom: An Economic History of the Latter-day Saints, 1830–1990* (Cambridge, MA: Harvard University Press, 1958), 353–79.
29. Amy, for one, had a lifelong fear of being alone, particularly at night, which perhaps is rooted in the experiences of this period. Lyman, *In Retrospect*, 74; Engar interviews.
30. Hayes and Clark interview, 7; Brown, *Autobiography*, 347–49.
31. Driggs interviews; Engar interviews.
32. Hayes and Clark interview; Vervene Hayes Pingree interview, with Barbara Carlson, 1984, copy in author's files.
33. Embry, *Mormon Polygamous Families*, 89–104.
34. For examples treating the circumstances of western women, see Sandra L. Myres, *Westering Women and the Frontier Experience: 1800–1915* (Albuquerque: University of New Mexico Press, 1982); Glenda Riley, *Women and Indians on the Frontier, 1825–1915* (Albuquerque: University of New Mexico Press, 1984).
35. Servant, was, of course, a euphemism for slave. The individual in question was Betsy Crosby Brown. Brown, *Autobiography of Pioneer John Brown*, 145; Engar interviews.
36. Step-daughters recalled that it was said "give Sister Brown a knife and she can earn a better living than any man in town." Hayes and Clark interview, 8.
37. Hayes and Clark interview, 3.
38. Lawrence Foster, "From Frontier Activism to Neo-Victorian Domesticity: Mormon Women in the Nineteenth and Twentieth Centuries," *Journal of Mormon History* 6 (1979): 3–21; Maureen Ursenbach Beecher, "Under the Sunbonnet: Mormon Women with Faces," *Brigham Young University Studies* 16 (Summer 1976): 471–84. In a later article, Beecher revised these views. See Maureen Ursenbach Beecher, "Women's Work on the Mormon Frontier," *Utah Historical Quarterly* 49 (Summer 1981): 276–90.
39. Lyman, *In Retrospect*, 14; Hayes and Clark interview, 5; Brown, *Autobiography of Pioneer John Brown*, 49–50, 138–39, 146–48.
40. Lyman, *In Retrospect*, 14; Hayes and Clark interview.
41. Tanner, *A Mormon Mother*, 24, 33, 269–70; Embry, *Mormon Polygamous Families*, 94–98; Madsen, *An Advocate for Women*, 49. In an interview, noted lawyer and women's rights activist Belva Lockwood opined that Mormon women "are fully up to the standard of intelligence and progressiveness; that each is the head of her own house, governs her own children, and is far more independent of men than the Gentile women." "Belva A. Lockwood, and 'Mormon' Mothers," *Woman's Exponent* 14 (March 1, 1886): 150.

42. I am indebted to Jessie Embry for clarifying this for me.
43. Like others of her generation, Tanner had been taught that a woman "should never oppose her husband as he was supposed to have superior wisdom." Tanner, *A Mormon Mother,* 116–17, 271.
44. Hayes and Clark interview, 5; Brown, *Autobiography*, 452.
45. Lyman, *In Retrospect*, 5, 21; Brown, *Autobiography*. 18–20. For this mixture of church and state positions in Utah, see Eugene E. Campbell, *Establishing Zion: The Mormon Church in the American West, 1847–1869* (Salt Lake City: Signature Books, 1988), 147–61; Dale Morgan, "The State of Deseret," *Utah Historical Quarterly* (April, July, October, 1940): 65–239; Gordon, *The Mormon Question*, 93.
46. The United Order required the deeding of all goods and property to local orders operated by communal labor and administered by local leaders. Over two hundred were organized, most in the spring and summer of 1874. The Pleasant Grove order operated a number of enterprises including honey production and dairy products, which were the most successful. A lumber mill purchased in 1876 was able to pay wages to workers and liquidate the cost of its purchase, but other ventures, such as a coal mine, proved failures. By 1880, the Pleasant Grove order ended, leaving Brown with his own farm equipment returned, now badly worn out, and little other than the satisfaction of having made the attempt in good faith. Leonard J. Arrington, *Great Basin Kingdom: An Economic History of the Latter-day Saints* (Cambridge, MA: Harvard University Press: 1956), 323–52; Leonard J. Arrington, Ferramorz Y. Fox, and Dean L. May, *Building the City of God: Community and Cooperation Among the Mormons* (Urbana: University of Illinois Press, 1976): 206–9; "United Order," February 19, 1936, Hayes and Clark interview; Brown, *Autobiography of Pioneer John Brown*, 340–46.
47. Lyman, *In Retrospect*, 21.
48. Brown, *Autobiography*, 419; Lyman, *In Retrospect*, 5–6.
49. Lyman, *In Retrospect*, 9.
50. Hayes and Clark interview, 5; Lyman, *In Retrospect*, 7; "Mothers of Our Executive Officers: Margaret Zimmerman Brown," *Relief Society Magazine* 7 (July 1930): 354.
51. Lyman, *In Retrospect*, 4–7; Brown, *Autobiography*, 19–20; "Mothers of Our Executive Officers," 353; Howard R. Driggs, *Timpanogos Town: Story of Old Battle Creek and Pleasant Grove, Utah* (Manchester, NH: Clarke Press, 1948), illustrations, 11; Thomas G. Alexander, *Utah: The Right Place* (Salt Lake City: Gibbs Smith, 1996), 104–5. Historian Frederick S. Buchanon noted the low quality of many schools in Utah, which opened the door to Protestant missionary schools that were well attended by the children of many Mormons who sought a better education. Frederick S. Buchanon, *Culture Clash and Accommodation: Public Schooling in Salt Lake City, 1890–1996* (San Francisco: Smith Research Associates, 1996), 1–23.
52. Brown, *Autobiography*, 20, 449–68; Hayes and Clark interview, 1, 3; Pingree interview; Engar interview.
53. Engar interview; Driggs interview.
54. Brown, *Autobiography*, 390; Jan Shipps, *Mormonism: The Story of a New Religious Tradition* (Urbana: University of Illinois Press, 1985), esp. 109–129. See also, Arrington, May, and Fox, *Building the City of God.*
55. See Thomas G. Alexander, "Between Revivalism and the Social Gospel: The Latter-day Saint Social Advisory Committee, 1916–1922," *Brigham Young University Studies* 23 (Winter 1983): 19–39.
56. See Lowery Nelson, *The Mormon Village: A Pattern and Technique of Land Settlement*, (Salt Lake City, University of Utah Press, 1952); Driggs, *Timpanogos Town.*

57. Rose Brown Hayes interview, February 1, 1936, 5, John Brown file, Kimball Young Papers, L. Tom Perry Special Collections and Manuscripts, Harold B. Lee Library, Brigham Young University.
58. Lyman, *In Retrospect*, 10–11.
59. Thomas G. Alexander, *Utah: The Right Place*, 149–55; and Thomas G. Alexander and James B. Allen, *Mormons and Gentiles: A History of Salt Lake City* (Boulder, CO: Pruett Publishing, 1984), 55–107.
60. Lyman, *In Retrospect*, 1; Driggs, *Timpanogos Town*, 115.
61. Lyman, *In Retrospect*, 2, 3; Annie Eggertsen "Autobiography," Eggertsen papers, L. Tom Perry Special Collections and Manuscripts, Harold B. Lee Library, Brigham Young University. Eggertsen, mother of labor activist and presidential advisor Esther Peterson, came to Utah from Denmark as a young woman. She recalled that it took years for Scandinavians to rise to leadership in Mormonism's lay ministry.
62. Lyman, *In Retrospect*, 1.
63. Visiting lectures included Philo Dibble, who reportedly had known the prophet Joseph Smith, and Scandinavian convert C.C.A. Christiansen who came with his large scroll of paintings depicting scenes of the church's founding and the exodus to the West. Lyman, *In Retrospect*, 14.
64. Lyman, *In Ret*rospect, 12–13; Brown, *Autobiography of Pioneer John Brown*, 335.
65. Lyman also alludes to the lingering effects of scarlet fever among those in Pleasant Grove. Lyman, *In Retrospect*, 13; for rheumatic fever, see Amy Brown Lyman to Margaret Brown, March 12, 1897, original in possession of Barbara Carlson, copy in author's possession; Engar interviews; Vera White Pohlman interviews, 1990–1994.
66. Lyman, *In Retrospect*, 12–13. Asafetida gives off a garlic-like smell. The book Margaret Brown turned to was likely John C. Gunn, *Gunn's Domestic Medicine, Or, Poor Man's Friend, in the Hours of Affliction, Pain and Sickness* (Madisonville, TN: Johnston and Edwards Publishers, multiple editions). For family medicine in the era, see James Harvey Young, "Patent Medicines and the Self-Help Syndrome," in Judith Walzer Leavitt, ed., *Sickness and Health in America: Readings in the History of Medicine and Public Health* (Madison: University of Wisconsin Press, 1985), 71–80.
67. Engar interviews.
68. Lyman, *In Retrospect*, 13; Brown, *Autobiography*, 449; Eggertsen, "Autobiography."
69. Lyman, *In Retrospect*, 13; "General Presidents of Relief Society: Amy Brown Lyman," *Relief Society Magazine* 30 (February 1943): 146–47.
70. In words rich with meaning for Mormon women, Smith said: "I now turn the key to you in the name of God and this Society shall rejoice and knowledge and intelligence shall flow down from this time." Jill Mulvay Derr, Janath Russell Cannon and Maureen Ursenbach Beecher, *Women of Covenant: The Story of Relief Society* (Salt Lake City: Deseret Book, 1992), 1.
71. For the activities of the Nauvoo period, see Derr, Cannon, and Beecher, *Women of Covenant*, 23–58.
72. Arrington, *Great Basin Kingdom*, 293–305; *Women of Covenant*, 86.
73. Jill Mulvay Derr, "Brigham Young and the Awakening of Mormon Women in the 1870s," in Susan Easton Black and Larry Porter, eds., *Lion of the Lord: Essays on the Life and Service of Brigham Young*, (Salt Lake City: Deseret Book, 1996), 322–27.
74. This, of course, was not always the case. Mormon women were often stung by remarks rebuking their pride, or calling them to repentance for not supporting their husbands. Tanner, *A Mormon Mother*, 116–17; Derr, "Woman's Place in Brigham Young's World," *Brigham Young University Studies* 18 (Spring 1978): 377–95.

75. Derr, Cannon, and Beecher, *Women of Covenant*, 85–86.
76. Susa Young Gates, *History of the Young Ladies Mutual Improvement Association from November 1869–June 1910* (Salt Lake City: General Board of the Y.L.M.I.A., 1911), 5.
77. Her companions, included, among others, Emmeline B. Wells, Zina D. H. Young, Bathsheba Smith, and Sarah Kimball. Most were veterans of the Nauvoo experience and all were destined to be notable both in Relief Society affairs and in the struggle for women's suffrage in Utah. Gates, *History of the Young Ladies Mutual Improvement Association*, 1–5; Maureen Ursenbach Beecher, "The Leading Sisters: A Female Hierarchy in Nineteenth-Century Mormon Society," *Journal of Mormon History* 9 (1982): 25–39; Jill Mulvay Derr and Carol Cornwall Madsen, "Preserving the Record and Memory of the Female Relief Society of Nauvoo, 1842–92," *Journal of Mormon History* 35 (Summer 2009): 88–117.
78. Derr, Cannon, and Beecher, *Women of Covenant* 92–93.
79. Linda King Newell, "Gifts of the Spirit: Women's Share," in Maureen Ursenbach Beecher and Lavina Fielding Anderson, eds., *Sisters in Spirit: Mormon Women in Historical and Cultural Perspective* (Urbana: University of Illinois Press, 1987), 111–43; Stapley and Wright, "Female Ritual Healing in Mormonism," 1–85; Susanna Morrill, "Relief Society Birth and Death Rituals: Women at the Gates of Mortality," *Journal of Mormon History* 36 (Spring 2010): 128–59.
80. Derr, Cannon, and Beecher, *Women of Covenant*, 105; "Pleasant Grove," *Woman's Exponent*, 5 (March 1, 1877): 150.
81. Previously, Pleasant Grove women had contributed to a variety of causes including rendering "assistance to many public improvements" and raising funds to sponsor the immigration of European converts to Utah, the latter a frequent focus of Relief Society charitable activities. "Pleasant Grove," *Woman's Exponent*, 5 (March 1, 1877): 150; "F. R. Society Reports," *Woman's Exponent* 1 (April 1, 1873): 162.
82. Jill Mulvay Derr, "Woman's Place in Brigham Young's World," *Brigham Young University Studies* 18 (Spring 1978): 392; Miriam B. Murphy, "Women in the Utah Work Force from Statehood to World War II," *Utah Historical Quarterly* 50 (Spring 1982): 149.
83. For Wells, see Carol Cornwall Madsen, "A Mormon Woman in Victorian America," (PhD Dissertation, University of Utah, 1984) and Madsen, *An Advocate for Women*.
84. For the definitive treatment of grain storage, see Jessie L. Embry, "The Relief Society Grain Storage Program," (Master's Thesis, Brigham Young University, 1977).
85. General Board of Relief Society, *A Centenary of Relief Society* (Salt Lake City: General Board of Relief Society, 1942), 67.
86. Lyman, *In Retrospect*, 37.
87. See, for example, "Pleasant Grove, Apr. 24th., 1878," *Woman's Exponent* 6 (May 15, 1878): 186; and Pleasant Grove Ward Relief Society Minutes for the period, Church History Library, Church of Jesus Christ of Latter-day Saints, Salt Lake City, Utah (cited hereafter as CHL).
88. Amy Brown Lyman, "Grain Elevator Dedication, August, 1940," 7, ABLP; "Pleasant Grove," *Woman's Exponent* 6 (May 15, 1878): 186.
89. Gates, *History of the Young Ladies Mutual Improvement Association*, 5; Arrington, *Brigham Young*, 370.
90. Of her sisters, Rose was old enough to focus her activities in the Relief Society, but Lydia and Margaret played leading roles in the MIA. For the activities of the Pleasant Grove YLMIA, see Carter, *Our Pioneer Heritage*, (1971), 13:156; Minutes of the Pleasant Grove Young Ladies Mutual Improvement Association, CHL.
91. For examples, see the entries for this period in the Pleasant Grove Young Ladies Mutual Improvement Association Minutes, and Spring City Mutual Improvement Association Minutes, CHL; "R.S. Reports," *Woman's Exponent*, 5 (March 1, 1877): 150.

92. While exact data is not available for the Relief Society and YLMIA, based on available figures it can be assumed that by 1890 somewhere between one quarter and one half of all Mormon women and girls YLMIA age or older were involved in one or both of the organizations. Using church membership data for 1895, with approximately 65,000 female members of the church (which accounts for the vast majority of Utah's female population eight years of age and up), the combined reported membership of the Relief Society and the YLMIA was 32,884. The YLMIA used more accurate reporting methods by that year so its membership of 14,884 seems relatively reliable. The Relief Society's reported 18,000 members, while a less reliable figure is by no means unreasonable. See population and membership figures in Richard D. Poll, ed., *Utah's History* (Provo: Brigham Young University Press, 1978), 688, 692; *Deseret News 1993–1994 Church Almanac* (Salt Lake City: Deseret News Press, 1992), 397; *Report of the Population of the United States, Eleventh Census: 1890* (Washington D.C., Government Printing Office, 1895), 874.
93. The Primary was supplemented with the Sunday School, a national movement for religious education that Mormons adopted in the 1860s. Lyman attended both. B. H. Roberts, *A Comprehensive History of the Church of Jesus Christ of Latter-day Saint, Century* I, 6 vols. (Salt Lake City: Deseret News Press, 1930), 5:478–80. For the Primary, see Carol Cornwall Madsen and Susan Staker Oman, *Sisters and Little Saints: One Hundred Years of Primary* (Salt Lake City: Deseret Book, 1979). In the early years of the Primary, girls significantly outnumbered boys.
94. Amy Brown Lyman, "For the Deseret News, January, 1930," ABLP.
95. Amy Brown Lyman, "Augusta Winters Grant on her 84th Birthday," and "Augusta Winters Grant for Friendship Circle," ABLP. For Mary Winters on women's rights, see "W.S.A. Pleasant Grove," *Woman's Exponent* 18 (April 15, 1890): 175.
96. This close connection led one male leader in the 1890s to exclaim that they were "all so closely connected that I could not tell where one begins and the other ends." Madsen and Oman, *Sisters and Little Saints*, xv.
97. See Lola Van Wagenen, *Sister-Wives and Suffragists: Polygamy and the Politics of Woman Suffrage, 1870–1896* (Provo, UT: Joseph Fielding Smith Institute for Latter-day Saint History and BYU Studies, 2003), 6–7; and Lola Van Wagenen "In Their Own Behalf: The Politicization of Mormon Woman and the 1870 Franchise," *Dialogue: A Journal of Mormon Thought* (Winter 1991): 31–43.
98. Wyoming women would not vote in their first election until the following fall. For Utah suffrage, see Van Wagenen, "In Their Own Behalf"; and Carol Cornwall Madsen, ed., *Battle for the Ballot: Essays on Woman Suffrage in Utah, 1870–1896* (Logan: Utah State University Press, 1997); Derr, Cannon, and Beecher, *Women of Covenant*, 111–112.
99. Madsen, *An Advocate for Women*, 56.
100. See Van Wagenen, *Sister-Wives and Suffragists.*
101. "Mass Meeting, Pleasant Grove," *Woman's Exponent* 7 (January 1, 1879): 117; "F[emale]. R[elief]. Society Reports: Pleasant Grove," *Woman's Exponent* 1 (April 1, 1873): 162.
102. Louise L. Greene, "A Blow Aimed at Woman Suffrage," *Woman's Exponent* 1 (March 15, 1873): 156; Madsen, *An Advocate for Women*, 201.
103. "Letter to the Sisters at Home," *Woman's Exponent* 14 (April 1, 1886): 164. For Wells's outspoken championship of this position, see Madsen, *An Advocate for Women.*
104. Alice Louise Reynolds, "Woman's Intellectual Renaissance," *Young Woman's Journal* 1 (January 1889): 5, 6; Lelia, "Working Women of the Bible," *Young Woman's Journal* 5 (July, 1894): 475.
105. Mary Howe, "Professional and Business Opportunities for Women," *Young Woman's Journal* 3 (October 1891): 24–25. See also subsequent articles under the same title that appeared in the *Young Woman's Journal* throughout 1892.

106. "From Missionary Fields," in "Our Girls," Column, *Young Woman's Journal* 10 (January 1899): 47–49. The Author was Jennie Brimhall (Knight) who, along with her friend and eventual sister-in-law, Inez Knight (Allen), would later serve for many years in the general leadership of the Relief Society. Both would become close associates with Lyman. See also Lettie Dewey Campbell, "A Missionary Letter," in "Our Girls" column, *Young Woman's Journal* 10 (July 1899): 331–33. Emmeline B. Wells was among those following the progress of the pair. See "Ladies Semi-Monthly Meeting," *Woman's Exponent* 26 (July 1, 1897): 168.
107. See, for example, May Bell Thurman Davis, "A Mormon Girl's Experience in a College Town," *Young Woman's Journal* 10 (July 1899):, 312–17; "Cactus," "Leaves from the Journal of a Medical Student," *Young Woman's Journal* 1 (June 1890): 265–68; Susa Young Gates, "A Biographical Sketch of R. B. Pratt," *Young Woman's Journal* 2 (September 1891): 531–36.
108. A Member, "Miscellaneous," *Young Woman's Journal* 4 (June 1893): 427–29; "The Recent Triennial in Washington," *Young Woman's Journal* 10 (April 1899): 196–215; Susa Young Gates, "International Council of Women," *Young Woman's Journal* 10 (October 1899): 435–50.
109. "W[oman's]. S[uffrage]. A[ssociation]. Pleasant Grove," and "U[tah]. W[oman's]. S[uffrage]. A[ssociation]. Convention," *Woman's Exponent* 18 (April 15, 1890): 175. The latter also mentions the involvement of one of Amy's half-sisters-in-law in the suffrage organization in nearby Lehi.
110. Lyman, "Achievements of the American Woman," 15.

CHAPTER 2

1. Emmeline B. Wells, "Women in the Legislature," *Woman's Exponent* 27 (January 15, 1899): 92.
2. Amy Brown to Will Hayes, Feb. 24, 1895, 2, original in possession of Barbara Carlson, copy in author's possession.
3. Amy Brown Lyman, *In Retrospect: Autobiography of Amy Brown Lyman* (Salt Lake City: General Board of Relief Society, 1945), 17; Gary James Bergera and Ronald Priddis, *Brigham Young University: A House of Faith* (Salt Lake City: Signature Books, 1985), 2; Kenneth L. Cannon II, *Provo & Orem: An Illustrated History* (Windsor Publications: 1987), 18–23; Allen Kent Powell, ed., *Utah History Encyclopedia* (Salt Lake City: University of Utah Press, 1994), 437.
4. Harriet Sigerman, "Laborers for Liberty, 1865–1890," in Nancy F. Cott, ed., *No Small Courage: A History of Women in the United States* (New York: Oxford University Press, 2000), 313–14.
5. These would be the 1882 Edmunds Act and the Edmunds-Tucker Act, passed in 1887. See Gustive O. Larson, *The Americanization of Utah for Statehood* (San Marino, CA: Huntington Library, 1971), 95, 208–12; Edward Leo Lyman, *Political Deliverance: The Mormon Quest for Utah Statehood* (Urbana: University of Illinois Press, 1986), 22–24, 42–46; Thomas G. Alexander, *Utah: The Right Place* (Salt Lake City: Gibbs Smith, 1996), 191–202. For a recent work examining the larger anti-polygamy campaign, see Sarah Barringer Gordon, *The Mormon Question: Polygamy and Constitutional Conflict in Nineteenth-Century America* (Chapel Hill: University of North Carolina Press, 2002).
6. For the tensions and adjustments in the Mormon community during this period, see Thomas G. Alexander, *Mormonism in Transition: A History of the Latter-day Saints, 1890–1930* (Urbana: University of Illinois Press, 1986); and Ethan R. Yorgason,

Transformation of the Mormon Cultural Region (Urbana: University of Illinois Press, 2003). Any discussion of the cessation of polygamy must be a qualified one as the practice for which so much was sacrificed, was not easily surrendered. Mormons settled colonies in Mexico and Canada in order to continue the practice and even in the United States a small number of plural marriages continued to be solemnized secretly by church leaders until after the turn of the century. For post-manifesto polygamy, see Carmon B. Hardy, *Solemn Covenant: The Mormon Polygamous Passage* (Urbana: University of Illinois Press, 1992); D. Michael Quinn, "L.D.S. Church Authority and New Plural Marriages, 1890–1904," *Dialogue: A Journal of Mormon Thought* 18 (Spring 1985): 90–105.

7. Polygamous wife Annie Clark Tanner maintained that after the Manifesto, people began "to live for this world," refocusing their efforts on obtaining worldly wealth and prestige rather than focusing on treasures in the hereafter. Annie Clark Tanner, *A Mormon Mother: An Autobiography of Annie Clark Tanner* (Salt Lake City: Tanner Trust, University of Utah, 1983), 222.
8. Originally known as the Timpanogos Academy, it was founded by the Dusenberry brothers, educators and Mormon converts. For sectarian educational efforts in Utah, see Robert Joseph Dwyer, *The Gentile Comes to Utah: A Study in Religious and Social Conflict, 1862—1890* (Western Epics: Salt Lake City, 1971). For the history of the Academy, see Bergera and Priddis, *Brigham Young University: A House of Faith.*
9. Lyman, *In Retrospect*, 17; Bergera and Priddis, *Brigham Young University*, 7; Amy Kathryn Lyman Engar interviews, 1990–94.
10. Engar interviews; Bergera and Pridis, *Brigham Young University*, 5.
11. Bergera and Priddis, *Brigham Young University*, 6.
12. Amy Brown Lyman, "Tribute to Karl G. Maeser," Amy Brown Lyman Papers, L. Tom Perry Special Collections and Manuscripts, Harold B. Lee Library, Brigham Young University (cited hereafter as ABLP).
13. Alice Louise Reynolds, "By Alice Louise Reynolds for the Ensign Club," ABLP.
14. Amy Brown Lyman, *A Lighter of Lamps: The Life Story of Alice Louise Reynolds* (Provo, UT: Deseret News Press, 1947), 4–11; Reba L. Keele, "Alice L. Reynolds," in Vicki Burgess-Olson, ed., *Sister Saints* (Provo: Brigham Young University Press, 1978), 280–82.
15. Engar interviews.
16. For Amasa Lyman, see Edward Leo Lyman, *Amasa Mason Lyman: Mormon Apostle and Apostate, A Study in Dedication* (Salt Lake City: University of Utah Press, 2009).
17. "Richard R. Lyman," in Andrew Jenson, *Latter-Day Saint Biographical Encyclopedia: A Compilation of Biographical Sketches of Prominent Men and Women in the Church of Jesus Christ of Latter-day Saints*, 4 vols. (Salt Lake City: Andrew Jenson History Company, 1901–1936), 3:756 (cited hereafter as Jenson, *LDS Biographical Encyclopedia).* While correct usage today in referring to the church is "Latter-day Saint," the common bibliographic citation for Jenson's encyclopedia follows that found on the title page of the volumes, "Latter-Day Saint."
18. Parry Sorensen interview, 1992.
19. John Brown to Richard R. Lyman, September 16, 1889, original in Amy Kathryn Lyman Engar Family Papers (cited hereafter as EFP).
20. Francis M. Lyman to Richard R. Lyman, December 27, 1893, EFP; Engar interviews. Francis M. Lyman's letter indicates his belief that, contrary to prevailing Victorian ideas, Amy would not be harmed, indeed, would even benefit from continuing to work after her marriage. Francis was evidently responding to a previous letter from Richard, in which the latter had apparently indicated a number of other reasons why the marriage might better be postponed, including the recent death of Amy's married sister Margaret. Francis considered and dismissed them all.

21. Lyman, *In Retrospect*, 21.
22. For Cluff, see Ernest L. Wilkinson, ed., *Brigham Young University: The First One Hundred Years*, 4 vols. (Provo: Brigham Young University Press, 1976), 1:211–21; Bergera and Priddis, *A House of Faith*, 8–13.
23. Cluff told students that he would require no more study from them than he required of himself "which is about twelve hours daily." Wilkinson, *Brigham Young University*, 1:214; Bergera and Priddis, 9, 10.
24. Priddis and Bergera, 9; Wilkinson, 1:259–60.
25. "Richard R. Lyman," in Jenson, *LDS Biographical Encyclopedia* 3:756.
26. Lyman, *A Lighter of Lamps,* 22, 23. Michigan had been coeducational for over two decades at this point. Karl Maeser had felt women unsuited to teach at the high school level and above, except in such areas as household skills. Cluff, however, did not share this view and made significant departures in staffing the academy as a result. Lyman, *A Lighter of Lamps*, 27–28
27. John Brown to Amy Brown, April 22, 1894, EFP.
28. John Brown to Amy Brown, April 26, 1893, EFP.
29. Amy Brown, "Busy Work," *The Normal* (May 19, 1893): 167–69; "Manners in School," *The Normal,* (January 15, 1894): 78; Lyman, *In Retrospect*, 21.
30. Lyman, *In Retrospect*, 23; "Amy Brown Lyman," in Jenson, *LDS Biographical Encyclopedia*, 2:664; Alice Louise Reynolds, "Amy Brown Lyman," ABLP; Engar interviews; Amy Brown Lyman, "Brigham Young University Alumni Association, June 1941," 6, EFP.
31. Mormons considered themselves part of the restored House of Israel, therefore, non-Mormons, including Jews, were often termed "gentiles." For Salt Lake City during this period, see Thomas G. Alexander and James B. Allen, *Mormons and Gentiles*, (Salt Lake City: Pruett Publishing, 1984), 87–161.; Alexander, *Utah: The Right Place*, 186–217.
32. Lyman recalled that only three LDS women served as teachers in the district when she began. Lyman, "Brigham Young University Alumni Association," 6. Despite assumptions of anti-Mormon bias, historian Frederick Buchanon notes that the reasons behind this seeming discrimination were more complicated. Superintendent Millspaugh, though a non-Mormon, was more concerned about raising the quality of education in the city than pursuing a religious agenda. Even the church owned *Deseret News* acknowledged this, observing that much of the change to "outsider" teachers was due to the lack of qualified educators within the territory. This was one of the factors that had driven Cluff to begin upgrading the academy's normal school. Under such circumstances, Amy's presence in the district indicates Millspaugh's high esteem for her abilities. See Frederick S. Buchanon, *Culture Clash and Accommodation: Public Schooling in Salt Lake City, 1890–1996* (San Francisco: Smith Research Associates, 1996), 17.
33. Brown to Hayes, Feb. 24, 1895, 4a; Lyman, *In Retrospect*, 20, 23. Tithing script could be taken to the bishop's storehouse and redeemed for goods paid in kind as tithing to the church.
34. Brown to Hayes, Feb. 24, 1895, 3, 3a.
35. Richard R. Lyman to Amy Brown, February 7, 1894, 3, EFP.
36. Brown to Hayes, Feb. 24, 1895, 2.
37. For a discussion of a similar phenomenon in a different culture of the time, see Sarah Deutsch, *No Separate Refuge: Culture, Class, and Gender on the Anglo-Hispanic Frontier in the American Southwest* (New York: Oxford University Press, 1987).
38. The results of this thinking were noted by LDS physician Margaret Roberts, who lamented there was no upcoming generation of female medical doctors to replace her own aging cadre who had followed the advice of Brigham Young. "Short Talk to

the Nurses Graduating Class, by Dr. Margaret Roberts," *Woman's Exponent* 36 (June 1907): 1–2.

39. For a discussion of Victorian views regarding limits of women's activities, see John S. Haller, Jr., and Robin M. Haller, *The Physician and Sexuality in Victorian America* (Urbana: University of Illinois Press, 1984), 47–87. Such views extended to higher education as well, with Dr. Edward Clarke, in a well-read 1871 volume, *Sex in Education* maintaining that women should save their "limited energy" to bear children, and not use it up studying and so possibly damage their "female apparatus." Quoted in Sigerman, "Laborers for Liberty, 1865–1890," 314.
40. Francis M. Lyman to Richard R. Lyman, March 3, 1891, EFP; Margaret Brown to Amy Brown, May 11, 1892, and Margaret Brown to Amy Brown, April, 1893, EFP. In the latter letters, Margaret Brown strongly urges Amy to take at least a year off from teaching or other work so she does not ruin her health.
41. Brown to Hayes, February 24, 1895.
42. Lyman, *In Retrospect*, 24, 25; Engar interviews; Brown to Hayes, February 24, 1895.
43. Brown to Hayes, February 24, 1895; Engar interviews. Interestingly, Lyman's granddaughter, Amy Kathryn Lyman Engar, though raised by the Lymans, knew nothing of the original plan to travel with Hayes, and Lyman makes no mention of it in her autobiography. Perhaps as an adult (and as a mother and grandmother), she sensed how far her scheme had strained the appearance of propriety.
44. Lyman, *In Retrospect*, 25. Lyman later quoted from a shopping list given to her by her dressmaker during this period. Considering how elaborate it was, the dress was probably created for her time in Ann Arbor. It called for "15 yards of material, 2 yards of waist lining, 5 yards of skirt linings, 1½ yards of canvas for facing the skirt, 2–5 dozen buttons as desired, whalebone for the waist, 20 yards of trimming braid, a card of hooks and eyes, and 1 yard of belting for the waist of the skirt." Amy Brown Lyman "Inaugural Address-Authors Club, Including Historical Data, 1945," EFP.
45. Zion's Cooperative Mercantile Institution (ZCMI) grew out of the cooperative movement aimed at establishing Mormon economic independence. It evolved into a department store and was a mainstay of the community until sold by the LDS Church in 2001. See Martha Sontag Bradley, *ZCMI: America's First Department Store* (Salt Lake City: ZCMI, 1991).
46. Lyman, *In Retrospect*, 24–26; John Brown to Amy Brown, July 14, 1895, EFP.
47. Richard was actually a second cousin once removed to Joseph F. Smith.
48. Lyman, *In Retrospect*, 27; "Richard R. Lyman," in Jenson, *LDS Biographical Encyclopedia*, 3:758–59. The Salt Lake Temple was completed in 1893. Amy had attended the dedication ceremonies with the Lyman family. Lyman, *In Retrospect*, 23.
49. Lyman, *In Retrospect*, 27.
50. John Zimmerman Brown, ed., *Autobiography of Pioneer John Brown, 1820–1896*, (Salt Lake City: Press of Steven and Wallis, 1941), 408–12; Vervene Hayes Pingree interview with Barbara Carlson, copy in author's possession; Engar interviews.
51. John Brown to Amy Brown, Jan 1896, EFP. A favorite apocryphal story of this period tells of a general authority visiting local congregations, dividing them down the middle and assigning one half to be Democrats and the other to be Republicans. In reality, Mormons had previously shown greater affinity for the Democratic Party that had more often sided with them in their struggle for religious rights. Church leaders did encourage members to more equally divide themselves, but natural affinity for one party over the other played a greater role. For the statehood period, see Edward Leo Lyman, *Political Deliverance: The Mormon Quest for Utah Statehood* (Urbana: University of Illinois Press, 1986).

52. Carol Cornwall Madsen, "Schism in the Sisterhood: Mormon Women and Partisan Politics, 1890–1900," in Davis Bitton and Maureen Ursenbach Beecher, eds. *New Views of Mormon History: A Collection of Essays in Honor of Leonard J. Arrington* (Salt Lake City: University of Utah Press, 1987), 221–30; Carol Cornwall Madsen, *An Advocate for Women: The Public Life of Emmeline B. Wells, 1870–1920* (Provo: Brigham Young University Press, 2006), 321–47.
53. Alexander and Allen, *Mormons and Gentiles,* 127.
54. Alexander and Allen, *Mormons and Gentiles,* 127; Alexander, *Utah: The Right Place,* 210–13.
55. "Janette Acord Hyde," in Jenson, *LDS Biographical Encyclopedia,* 2: 644–46.
56. Alexander and Allen, *Mormons and Gentiles,* 108, 109, 151–52.
57. Alexander, *Utah: The Right Place,* 211; Alexander and Allen, *Mormons and Gentiles,* 135.
58. For general works on the Progressive Era, see Richard Hofstadter, *The Age of Reform: From Bryan to F.D.R.* (New York: Alfred A. Knopf, 1956); Robert H. Wiebe, *The Search for Order, 1877–1920* (New York: Hill and Wang, 1967); Robert M. Crunden, *Ministers of Reform: The Progressive Achievement in American Civilization, 1889–1920* (New York: Basic Books, 1982); Allen F. Davis, *Spearheads for Reform: The Social Settlements and the Progressive Movement, 1890–1914* (New York: Oxford University Press, 1967); and Ellen Fitzpatrick, *Endless Crusade: Women, Social Scientists, and Progressive Reform* (New York: Oxford University Press, 1990). Another strain of reform arising during the period was the social gospel, inspired by the sermons and writings of Protestant clerics who urged Christians to come together to create more social services for the poor and to work for a more just society. See Robert T. Handy, ed., *The Social Gospel in American Thought, 1970–1920* (New York: Oxford University Press, 1966); and Ronald C. White, Jr. and C. Howard Hopkins, *The Social Gospel: Religion and Reform in Changing America* (Philadelphia: Temple University Press, 1976).
59. For discussions of the influence of the social gospel and progressivism on Mormons, see Thomas G. Alexander, "Between Revivalism and the Social Gospel: The Latter-day Saint Social Advisory Committee, 1916–1922," *Brigham Young University Studies* 23 (Winter 1983): 19–39.
60. Amy Brown to Will Hayes, January 4, 1894, and Amy Brown to Will Hayes, May 29, 1895, originals in possession of Barbara Carlson, copies in author's possession.
61. Amy Brown Lyman to Margaret Brown, November 1897, ABLP; Susan Elizabeth Swenson Driggs interviews, 1991, 1994; Engar interviews; Keith Hayes interview, 1991. Hayes, a grand-nephew of Amy, indicated life at the Lyman home was always straight-forward and orderly, and thus congenial: "You always knew where you stood with Aunt Amy."
62. Driggs interview; Hayes interview.
63. Driggs interviews, Hayes interview; Pingree interview. For responsibilities of Victorian housewives, see Susan Strasser, *Never Done: A History of American Housework* (New York: Pantheon, 1982).
64. Driggs interview; Hayes interview; Engar interviews; Pingree interview; Emmeline Wirthlin interview, 1992. Hayes recalled an occasion when his great-aunt Amy was summoned to counsel with him over a luncheon meal about an "unsuitable" young woman he was dating during the 1930s.
65. For a discussion of the threat of death represented by childbirth, see Judith Walzer Leavitt, *Brought to Bed: Childbearing in America, 1750–1950* (New York: Oxford University Press, 1986).
66. "Conference of W.H.P. Society," *Woman's Exponent* 25 (May 1, 1897), 139; Engar interviews; Amy Brown Lyman to Margaret Brown, November 15, 189[7], EFP. The women who anointed her were Sister Freeze (likely Lillie Freeze, president of the Salt Lake

Stake YLMIA, in which Amy was an active leader) and Sister Dougall (likely Maria Young Dougall, counselor to YLMIA general president Elmina Taylor). Such sources of spiritual comfort may be an indication of Lyman's status in the elite realm of Mormon society that came through her marriage. For washing and anointing before childbirth, see Linda King Newell, "Gifts of the Spirit: Women's Share," in Maureen Ursenbach Beecher and Lavina Fielding Anderson, eds., *Sisters in Spirit: Mormon Women in Historical and Cultural Perspective* (Urbana: University of Illinois Press, 1987), 111–50; and Jonathan A. Stapley and Kristine Wright, "Female Ritual Healing in Mormonism," *Journal of Mormon History*, 37 (Winter 2011): 1–85.

67. This information is obtained from fly-leaf notes in Lyman's hand from her own copy of her autobiography, *In Retrospect*. EFP.

68. For a discussion of women's clubs and associations, see Karen J. Blair, *The Clubwoman as Feminist: True Womanhood Redefined, 1868–1914* (New York: Holmes and Meier, 1980); and Anne Firor Scott, *Natural Allies: Women's Associations in American History* (Urbana: University of Illinois Press, 1991).

69. For Utah women's clubs, see Jill Mulvay Derr, "Scholarship, Service, and Sisterhood: Utah Women's Clubs and Associations, 1877–1977," in Patricia Lynn Scott and Linda Thatcher, eds., *Women in Utah History: Paradigm or Paradox?* (Logan: Utah State University Press, 2005), 249–94; Sharon Snow Carver, "Club Women of the Three Intermountain Cities of Denver, Boise and Salt Lake City between 1893 and 1929," (PhD dissertation, Brigham Young University, 2000). Amy Brown Lyman, "Authors Club Address," EFP. Historian Carol Cornwall Madsen has pointed out to me in an email that Joseph F. Smith, church president after 1901, frequently and strongly spoke out against women's clubs which he believed diverted Mormon women's energies away from church service. Carol Cornwall Madsen to Dave Hall, April 21, 2015.

70. Jill Mulvay Derr, Janath Russell Cannon, and Maureen Ursenbach Beecher, *Women of Covenant: The Story of Relief Society* (Salt Lake City: Deseret Book, 1992), 156–57; Carol Cornwall Madsen, "A Mormon Woman in Victorian America," (PhD dissertation, University of Utah, 1985), 360. An overview of the content of Relief Society meetings for the era can be seen in the *Woman's Exponent* for these years. In them, Emmeline B. Wells repeatedly laments the generational divide emerging in the latter 1890s and early twentieth century. For examples, see "Juab Stake," *Woman's Exponent* 26 (December 1, 1897): 233; "Conferences and Meetings," *Woman's Exponent* 22 (April 15, 1899): 184.

71. For early club work in Utah, see Mrs. J. C. Croly, *The History of the Woman's Club Movement in America* (New York: Henry G. Allen, 1898), 1108–117; Derr, "Scholarship, Service, and Sisterhood"; and Carver, "Club Women of the Three Intermountain Cities." For Wells and women's clubs, see Linda Thatcher and John R. Sillito, "'Sisterhood and Sociability': The Utah Women's Press Club, 1891–1928," *Utah Historical Quarterly* 53 (Spring 1985): 144–56.

72. See a discussion of this problem in Derr, Cannon, and Beecher, *Women of Covenant*, 155.

73. "The Mothers' Congress," *Woman's Exponent* 29 (June 1, 1900): 7.

74. Emmeline B. Wells, "Women in the Legislature," *Woman's Exponent* 27 (January 15, 1899): 92. Wells continued:

> Mothers teach virtue, honesty, integrity and uprightness in the home; the boy or youth goes out into society and into the wide, wide world and what happens? Many broken-hearted mothers know. It is not perhaps possible to have an ideal civilization with all the adverse influences of the age to combat with, but it is possible that better laws and their enforcement might be beneficial.

75. Madsen, "A Mormon Woman in Victorian America," 354–55; Jeanne Madeline Weimann, *The Fair Women: The Story of the Women's Building at the World's Columbian*

Exhibition, Chicago 1893 (Chicago: Chicago Review Press, 1981). For a recent treatment demonstrating how Mormon's utilized the fair to promote better relations with other Americans, with special attention given to Mormon women, see Reid Neilson, *Exhibiting Mormonism: The Latter-day Saints and the 1893 Chicago World's Fair* (New York: Oxford University Press, 2011), 75–105.

76. Amy Brown Lyman, "Inaugural Address—Authors Club, 1945–46," EFP.
77. "Rebecca Ellen Mantle Little," in Jenson, LDS *Biographical Encyclopedia*, 2:487–88. For the National Congress of Mothers, see Molly Ladd-Taylor, *Mother-Work: Women, Child Welfare and the State, 1890–1930* (Urbana: University of Illinois Press, 1994), 43–50; Theda Skocpol, *Protecting Soldiers and Mothers: The Political Origins of Social Policy in the United States* (Cambridge, MA: Harvard University Press, 1992), 333–40; and David J. and Sheila M. Rothman, eds., *National Congress of Mothers, the First Conventions, 1897–1899* (New York: Garland, 1987).
78. "Rebecca Ellen Mantel Little," in Jenson, *LDS Biographical Encyclopedia*, 2:487; Emmeline B. Wells, "The History of Woman Suffrage in Utah, 1870–1900," in Carol Cornwall Madsen, ed., *Battle for the Ballot: Essays on Woman Suffrage in Utah, 1870–1896* (Logan: Utah State University Press, 1997), 41.
79. "May Booth Talmage," in Jenson, *LDS Biographical Encyclopedia* 4:266–67.
80. Wells, "History of Woman Suffrage," 41.
81. For Cannon, see Jean Bickmore White, "Martha H. Cannon," in Vicky Burgess-Olson, ed., *Sister Saints* (Provo: Brigham Young University, Press, 1976), 385–95.
82. Harriet Horne Arrington, "Alice Merrill Horne, Art Promoter and Early Utah Legislator," *Utah Historical Quarterly*, 58 (Summer, 1990): 265–73.
83. "Harriett Bennion Harker," Jenson, *LDS Biographical Encyclopedia*, 4:186: "Elizabeth J. S. Wilcox," in Jenson, *LDS Biographical Encyclopedia*, 2:737; Annie Wells Cannon, "Dr. Margaret C. Roberts," *Relief Society Magazine* 13 (July 1926): 361–63.
84. For the Authors Club, see Authors Club minutes, Special Collections, Marriott Library, University of Utah; for club women in Utah, see Sharon Snow Carver, "Female Influence in Salt Lake City Government Policies: The Salt Lake City Federation of Women's Clubs, 1912–1930," paper presented at the annual meeting of the Mormon History Association, May 1995, copy in author's possession; and Derr, "Scholarship, Service and Sisterhood."
85. On one occasion, for example, the critic's notes record that "The word 'draftsman' should be used for one who draws, not 'drawer,'" and observed also the mispronunciation of the words satirical, duty, and facade. Lyman, "Inaugural Address"; Engar interviews.
86. It is not recorded what they decided when a general discussion was held on November 6, 1901, on "Should the color line be drawn in our Federation?" However, like most other women's club organizations across the nation during the period, the Utah Federation decided that it should. Authors Club minutes for November 7, 1900; November 6, 1901; November 27, 1901; March 12, 1902; November 18, 1902; February 13, 1913.
87. They helped entertain national club leaders traveling through Salt Lake on their way to a convention in Los Angeles, and helped sponsor a lecture by noted activist Florence Kelley, head of the National Consumers' League. Authors Club minutes, see especially, October 11, 1899; November 15, 1899; November 22, 1899; February 14, 1900; October 10, 1900; December 19, 1900; October 16, 1901; October 22, 1901; November 6, 1901; November 27, 1901; December 4, 1901; March 12, 1902; April 9, 1902.
88. Authors Club minutes, November 7, 1900; May 29, 1901; Amy Brown Lyman, "For the Author's Club," ABLP.
89. Amy Brown Lyman, "Obedience without Severity," *Woman's Exponent* 27 (May 1, 1899): 137–38; "Four Meetings of Mothers Held," *Deseret Evening News* (April 11, 1899).

In addition to the views on child rearing inculcated from her father's example, Lyman reportedly began a thorough study of child rearing literature after the birth of her own children. Mary Connelly Kimball, "Amy Brown Lyman, Relief Society Magazine, Jan. 1929" EFP, 8; Engar interviews.

90. Engar interviews.
91. Richard R. Lyman to Amy Brown Lyman, May 5, 1902, EFP; Lyman, *In Retrospect*, 29; Morris Bishop, *A History of Cornell* (Ithaca: Cornell University Press, 1962), 281–82.
92. Lyman, *In Retrospect*, 29–30.
93. For the development of social work, see James Leiby, *The History of Social Welfare and Social Work in the United States* (New York: Columbia University Press, 1978), 136–62; and Roy Lubove, *The Professional Altruist: The Emergence of Social Work as a Career, 1880–1930* (Cambridge, MA: Harvard University Press, 1965). Lyman, *In Retrospect*, 30; Engar interviews.
94. For Addams, see Jane Addams, *Twenty Years at Hull House* (1910); Allen F. Davis, *American Heroine: The Life and Legend of Jane Addams* (New York: Oxford University Press, 1973).
95. The literature relating to the settlement movement is rich. See, for example, Allen F. Davis, *Spearheads for Reform: The Social Settlements and the Progressive Movement, 1890–1914* (New York: Oxford University Press, 1967), and Ellen Fitzpatrick, *Endless Crusade: Women, Social Scientists and Progressive Reform* (New York: Oxford University Press, 1990).
96. For the development of Hull House programs as well as its physical plant, see Allen F. Davis and Mary Lynn McCree Bryan, eds., *100 Years at Hull-House* (Bloomington: Indiana University Press, 1990). For the Hull House influence, see Kathryn Kish Sklar, "Hull House in the 1890s: A Community of Women Reformers," *Signs* (Summer 1985): 658–77.
97. Lyman, *In Retrospect*, 30; Amy Brown Lyman, "Something of My Life," ABLP; Engar interviews.
98. Lyman, *In Retrospect*, 60, 61; Engar interviews; Amy Brown Lyman, "Interview at KSL," ABLP.
99. Lyman, *In Retrospect*, 31, 32.
100. Lyman, *In Retrospect*, 33; Bishop, *A History of Cornell*, 421–22.
101. Roberts was denied his seat in the 1898 election. On Smoot, see Milton R. Merrill, *Reed Smoot: Apostle in Politics* (Logan: Utah State University Press, 1990). For the Smoot hearing, see Alexander, *Utah: The Right Place*, 254. For its impact on Mormon society, see Kathleen Flake, *The Politics of American Religious Identity: The Seating of Senator Reed Smoot, Mormon Apostle* (Chapel Hill: University of North Carolina Press, 2004).
102. For polygamy after the manifesto, see Quinn, "New Plural Marriages," 90–105; Richard S. Van Wagoner, *Mormon Polygamy: A History* (Salt Lake City: Signature Books, 1986), 157–67; Hardy, *Solemn Covenant*, 167–243.
103. Alexander, *Utah: The Right Place*, 254.
104. Alexander, *Mormonism in Transition*, 67–68. It was not until 1909 that a committee of church leaders was designated to investigate marriages contracted after 1904. Chairing this committee was Richard's father, Francis M. Lyman, then president of the Quorum of the Twelve Apostles.
105. Lyman, *In Retrospect*, 33, 34. It is interesting that Lyman took the pains to point out the lecturer's sex in her autobiography. That she was indeed a woman, perhaps says something about the avenues for public speaking then available to women during the period. Regarding the charge that there were no public schools in Utah, this was a favorite if not entirely accurate charge by anti-polygamists against the church in the 1880s. While the

church had taken a stand against tax-supported free public schools before 1886 when the Mormon-controlled territorial legislature passed a measure supporting such institutions, most wards established and regulated locally supported schools from the time of the first settlement in the West. As historian Frederick Buchanon has pointed out, these schools represented a cultural lag, more common to the United States in the 1840s (when the Saints first moved west) and still not unusual in more isolated or recently settled regions of the nation. In contrast, by the 1880s many areas of the nation were adopting publicly supported generally secular schools (or at least generically Protestant ones) along the lines advocated by noted educational reformer, Horace Mann. Buchanon, *Culture Clash and Accommodation*, 4–5.

106. Engar interviews; Vera White Pohlman interviews, 1990–1994; Margaret Schreiner, *Margaret Schreiner Reminisces* (Privately Published, 1987), 40–41.
107. Lyman, *In Retrospect*, 35; Brown, *Autobiography*, 467.
108. The house still stands and is located at 1084 Third Avenue in Salt Lake City. Richard Lyman had helped survey the present campus of the University of Utah and it was here that he returned to work after their return from Ithaca. Engar interviews; Karl T. Haglund and Philip F. Notarianni, *The Avenues of Salt Lake City* (Salt Lake City: Utah State Historical Society), 100–102.
109. David and Sabey Pingree interview, 1994; Keith Hayes interview, 1991.
110. "Richard R. Lyman," Jenson, *LDS Biographical Encyclopedia*, 3:759–60. Richard's letters to Amy from this period reflect his deep homesickness for his family, and especially for his young bride. Clearly, he found the separations extremely difficult to bear. See Richard R. Lyman to Amy Brown Lyman, September, 9, 1899; July 11, 1901; August 31, 1901; and September 5, 1901, copies in author's possession.
111. Lyman, *In Retrospect*, 36; Amy Kathryn Lyman Engar, "Amy Brown Lyman: Transcribed from a talk given at the University of Utah Institute 'Women of the Restoration,' February 26, 1987," EFP.

CHAPTER 3

1. Report of Quarterly Relief Society Conference of Nebo Stake Relief Society held in Benjamin, Utah, April 26, 1907, as found in: "Relief Society Report," *Woman's Exponent* 36 (June 1907): 2.
2. Amy Brown Lyman, *In Retrospect: Autobiography of Amy Brown Lyman* (Salt Lake City: General Board of Relief Society, 1945), 37.
3. Emmeline B. Wells to Mrs. Amy Brown Lyman, October 6, 1909, Amy Brown Lyman Papers, L. Tom Perry Special Collections, Harold B. Lee Library, Brigham Young University (hereafter cited as ABLP); "General Relief Society Conference," *Woman's Exponent* 38 (October 1909): 29; Lyman, *In Retrospect*, 36.
4. Lyman, *In Retrospect*, 36.
5. "Richard R. Lyman," in Andrew Jenson, *Latter-Day Saint Biographical Encyclopedia: A Compilation of Biographical Sketches of Prominent Men and Women in the Church of Jesus Christ of Latter-day Saints*, 4 vols. (Salt Lake City: Andrew Jenson History Company, 1901–1936), 3:760 (cited hereafter as Jenson, *LDS Biographical Encyclopedia*).
6. Lyman, *In Retrospect*, 36.
7. For a comprehensive overview of the adjustments made by men and women of Lyman's generation see Thomas G. Alexander, *Mormonism in Transition: A History of the Latter-day Saints, 1890–1930* (Urbana: University of Illinois Press, 1986).
8. Lyman's entry in the *LDS Biographical Encyclopedia*, written in a gushing style—quite possibly by her husband Richard—describes her thus: "She is attractive with abundant

brown hair and soft liquid brown eyes, and very winsome indeed. With it all she makes hosts of friends and succeeds in keeping attached to herself most of those whom she wins." Jenson, *LDS Biographical Encyclopedia*, 2:665. For her reticence before large groups, see Susa Young Gates to Amy Brown Lyman, undated, ABLP.

9. The Relief Society as yet had no permanent offices and was then meeting in the offices of the *Woman's Exponent* in the Templeton Building, located across from Temple Square. Lyman, *In Retrospect*, 36.
10. These included Emma Smoot Woodruff, plural wife and widow of church president Wilford Woodruff. An experienced veteran of Relief Society work, she had served as ward and stake Relief Society president, and since 1892, had been a member of the Relief Society general board. Julina L. Smith, plural wife of current church president Joseph F. Smith, and mother of a future president (Joseph Fielding Smith), she too counted many years in the service of the society. Also present was Rebecca N. Nibley, first wife of Presiding Bishop Charles Nibley, likewise a veteran of long years of church service. See the respective biographical sketches in Jenson, *LDS Biographical Encyclopedia*: "Bathsheba Wilson Smith," 1:699–702; "Julina Lambson Smith," 4:65–68; "Emily Sophia Tanner Richards," 4:109; "Emma Smith Woodruff," 2:805–7; "Rebecca Neibaur Nibley," 2:675–78. For Wells, see Carol Cornwall Madsen, *An Advocate for Women: The Public Life of Emmeline B. Wells* (Provo: Brigham Young University Press, 2006).
11. Notable Authors Club members then serving on the board included Alice Merrill Horne and Elizabeth Wilcox. Rebecca Little had died the previous May. Annie Wells Cannon, "Mrs. Lyman as a Relief Society Executive," ABLP. List of Authors Club Members, 1893–1993, copy in author's possession; Lyman, *In Retrospect*, 36.
12. "Clarissa S. Williams" in Jenson, *LDS Biographical Encyclopedia* 2:738–40.
13. On family ties among the LDS hierarchy in general, see D. Michael Quinn, *The Mormon Hierarchy: Origins of Power* (Salt Lake City: Signature Books, 1994).
14. For Mormon beliefs and practices during this period, see Alexander, *Mormonism in Transition*; Linda King Newell, "Gifts of the Spirit: Women's Share," in Maureen Ursenbach Beecher and Lavina Fielding Anderson ed., *Sisters is Spirit* (Urbana: University of Illinois Press, 1992), 111–50; and Jonathan A. Stapley and Kristine Wright, "Female Ritual Healing in Mormonism," *Journal of Mormon History*, 37 (Winter 2011): 1–85. For the Social Gospel, see Robert T. Handy, ed., *The Social Gospel in American Thought, 1870–1920* (New York: Oxford University Press, 1966).
15. Alexander, *Mormonism in Transition*, 93–115; Alfred D. Chandler, *The Visible Hand: The Managerial Revolution in American Business* (Cambridge, MA: Harvard University Press, 1977); Robert H. Wiebe, *The Search for Order, 1877–1920* (New York: Hill and Wang, 1967).
16. The auxiliaries of the church were the YLMIA, the Primary Association, the Sunday School, and the Young Men's MIA. Alexander, *Mormonism in Transition*, 125–56; Newell, "Gifts of the Spirit," 133. For Wells's comments regarding the Relief Society's status, see *Woman's Exponent* 37 (June 1908): 1. Note also, Wells's reference to the general board as a "quorum (so to speak)," in her letter to Lyman cited at the beginning of this chapter. Wells to Lyman, October 6, 1909, ABLP.
17. Thomas G. Alexander and James B. Allen, *Mormons and Gentiles: A History of Salt Lake City* (Boulder, CO: Pruett Publishing, 1984), 129–33, 142–45.
18. Jull Mulvay Derr, Janath Russell Cannon, and Maureen Ursenbach Beecher, *Women of Covenant: The Story of Relief Society* (Salt Lake City: Deseret Book, 1992), 174–77.
19. Amy Lyman Engar interviews, 1990–94; Amy Brown Lyman, "The Role of Women in the Church", Engar Family Papers, (cited hereafter as EFP). The Relief Society's portion of the building would grow, however, at the expense of the other auxiliaries. Initially

given half of the second floor for office space, after several years, their broadening activities would lead the Relief Society to claim the majority of the building as their own. Vera White Pohlman interviews, 1990–1994.

20. "Old Memories," *Woman's Exponent* 31 (May 1909): 60.
21. On the remainder of the block, now occupied by the towering church office building, were apartment houses and private residences. I am grateful to Randall Dixon of the LDS Church History Library (now retired) for generously orienting me to the block at the time of Amy's entry into Relief Society work.
22. East of the Assembly Hall, on the other side of the main gate and south of the Temple, stood the bureau of information and the church museum. Again, my thanks to Randall Dixon.
23. Lyman, *In Retrospect*, 40–41.
24. E.B. Wells, "Relief Society Conference," *Woman's Exponent*, 31 (October 1&15, 1902): 10, 37; General Board of Relief Society, *A Centenary of Relief Society* (Salt Lake City: General Board of Relief Society, 1942), 45–46. For grain storage, see Jessie L. Embry, "Relief Society Grain Storage Program, 1876–1940," Master's Thesis, Brigham Young University, 1974.
25. "Peace Meetings," *Woman's Exponent* 35 (May 1907): 69; Leonard Arrington, "Modern Lysistratas: Mormon Women in the International Peace Movement, 1899–1939," *Journal of Mormon History* 15 (1989): 89–104.
26. Carol Cornwall Madsen, "A Mormon Woman in Victorian America," (PhD dissertation, University of Utah, 1985), 365.
27. For concerns about the loss of younger women to the organization, see Derr, Cannon, and Beecher, *Women of Covenant*, 155. For examples of long running concerns about younger women and the Relief Society, see President B. W. Smith comments, in "Conferences and Meetings," *Woman's Exponent* 27 (April 15, 1899): 131; Ida Smoot Dusenberry comments, "Relief Society Conference," *Woman's Exponent* 31 (Oct 1 & 15, 1902): 38; Annie T. Hyde comments, "Relief Society Conference," *Woman's Exponent* 36 (April 1908): 61; and Harriet B. Harker comments in "General Relief Society Conference," *Woman's Exponent* 39 (June 1910): 6.
28. Derr, Cannon, and Beecher, *Women of Covenant*, 157–61.
29. Madsen, "A Mormon Woman," 368; Derr, Cannon, and Beecher, *Women of Covenant*, 165. Emmeline Wells commented in 1910, for example, on questions "of how it is best for a great organization like the Relief Society to cover the ground of charity and of the field of philanthropic endeavor to do the greatest amount of good to the largest number of people." Emmeline B. Wells, Diary, June 17, 1910, Emmeline B. Wells Diaries, L. Tom Perry Special Collections and Manuscripts, Harold B. Lee Library, Brigham Young University.
30. Derr, Cannon, and Beecher, 157–60. For examples of mothers' classes, see "Relief Society Mothers' Classes," *Woman's Exponent* 31 (January 1903): 63, 64; "Lectures for Mothers," *Woman's Exponent* 31 (March 1903): 73; "Outline for Mothers' Work: Morgan Stake," *Woman's Exponent* 38 (August 1909): 15.
31. Joseph F. Smith made the final decision himself, but later noted that he had been in full accord with the will of the board members. Wells asked the president to choose her counselors and he named his wife Julina and Clarissa Williams. It was noted that the two women came in second and third in the voting. Madsen, "A Mormon Woman," 373–74.
32. Madsen, "A Mormon Woman," 367, 375, 378; Pohlman interviews. Pohlman stated that Wells's dress was as unusual for its time as it seems by modern standards.
33. Among those who were forced to leave at that time was Wells's daughter, Annie Wells Cannon. Madsen, "A Mormon Woman," 376.

34. Madsen, "A Mormon Woman," 379.
35. It is still known as the Lyman tract. Melvyn Lyman interview, 1992.
36. Lyman, *In Retrospect*, 74.
37. Lyman, *In Retrospect*, 74–75.
38. Lyman, *In Retrospect*, 74–77; Engar interviews.
39. Lyman, *In Retrospect*, 76–77.
40. Engar interviews.
41. Lyman, *In Retrospect*, 77; Engar interviews.
42. Olive Christiansen had been called to the position in 1911 with Lyman as her assistant. Christiansen resigned due to poor health in 1913. Lyman, *In Retrospect*, 42; Madsen, "A Mormon Woman," 369, 374; "Amy Brown Lyman," in Jenson, *LDS Biographical Encyclopedia*, 2:665.
43. Untitled typescript, Lyman Family Papers, Church History Library, Church of Jesus Christ of Latter-day Saints, Salt Lake City, Utah (cited hereafter as LFP).
44. Lyman, *In Retrospect*, 44, 47. Though the church maintained its own bureau on Temple Square, the long hours put in by Relief Society personnel—especially the general secretary—meant that they were often available to answer questions when others were not. Pohlman interviews.
45. Pohlman interviews; Lyman, *In Retrospect,* 43.
46. "Utah Women at Chicago," *Woman's Exponent,* 40 (November 1911): 29; Lyman, *In Retrospect*, 88.
47. Lyman, *In Retrospect*, 90, 91; Carol Cornwall Madsen, "'The Power of Combination': Emmeline B. Wells and the National and International Councils of Women." *BYU Studies* 33 (1993): 647–73; and Madsen, *An Advocate for Women*. On the formation of the National Council, see also Jane Stephens, "May Wright Sewall: An Indiana Reformer," *Indiana Magazine of History* 78 (December 1982): 281–83; Inez Hayes Irwin, *Angels and Amazons: A Hundred Years of American Women* (Garden City: Doubleday, 1933), 229–34. For the International Council, see Leila J. Rupp, *Worlds of Women: The Making of an International Women's Movement* (Princeton: Princeton University Press, 1997).
48. Madsen, *An Advocate for Women*, 433–58; Madsen, "A Mormon Woman," 361–62, 379–80; Lyman, *In Retrospect*, 91.
49. Reed Smoot comments in "General Relief Society Conference," *Woman's Exponent* 41 (November 1913): 78. Historian Carol Cornwall Madsen has pointed out to me that church president Joseph F. Smith was also very much against Mormon women associating with outside groups that might delete the identity of women of the faith. Email, Carol Cornwall Madsen to Dave Hall, November 19, 2014.
50. Titles of these addresses included "Prevention of Infant Mortality," "How to prevent infections from advanced cases of Consumption," "White Slave Trade," "Sterilization of the Unfit," "Patriotism of Peace," and "Womans Suffrage." "Nineteenth Annual Executive Session of the National Council of Women of the United States," program of meeting held in Chicago, Illinois, 14, 15, November, 1911, ABLP.
51. "Utah Women at Chicago," *Woman's Exponent* 40 (November 1911): 29; Lyman, *In Retrospect*, 88–89.
52. Lyman, *In Retrospect*, 88.
53. Lyman, *In Retrospect*, 88, 89.
54. Lyman, *In Retrospect*, 88, 89.
55. Rupp, *Worlds of Women*, 6–7.
56. Susa Young Gates to Amy Brown Lyman, undated letter, ABLP.
57. Engar interviews; Keith Hayes interview, 1991; Susan Elizabeth Swensen Driggs interviews, 1991, 1994.

58. Amy Lyman Engar, "Amy Brown Lyman: Transcribed from a talk given at the University of Utah Institute 'Women of the Restoration,' February 26, 1987," EFP, 16–18; Margaret Lyman Schreiner, *Margaret Schreiner Reminisces* (Privately Published), 38–41. Granddaughter Amy Lyman Engar also recalled that once they were on their feet financially Richard sent Amy "American Beauty roses" every week. Engar interviews.
59. Lyman had an inverted uterus. Engar interviews; Engar, "Amy Brown Lyman," 6.
60. Melvin Lyman interview, 1992; David and Sabey Pingree interview, 1993; Driggs interviews.
61. John S. Haller, Jr. and Robin M. Haller, *The Physician and Sexuality in Victorian America* (Urbana: University of Illinois Press, 1974), 89–137.
62. Karen Manners Smith, "New Paths to Power," in *No Small Courage: A History of Women in the United States* (New York: Oxford, 2000), 402–4. Anti-birth control rhetoric labeling it race suicide was found in the addresses of church leaders and even in the pages of the Relief Society Magazine. See "Birth Control," *Relief Society Magazine* 3 (August 1916): 432–35; and "Editorial: Our Conference," *Relief Society Magazine* 4 (June 1917): 350. Anecdotal evidence indicates a widespread negative attitude toward sex in the Mormon community of Lyman's day. One of Lyman's social workers in the late 1920s and 1930s, Evelyn Hodges Lewis, for example, remembered her grandmother's attitude that "good girls never enjoy sex." Similar accounts are found in Lyman's family and in the author's family. Evelyn Hodges Lewis interview, 1992; Driggs interviews; Dorothy Lauritzen Hall interview, 1992. For the larger birth control (and anti-birth control) movement, see: Ellen Chesler, *Woman of Valor: Margaret Sanger and the Birth Control Movement in America* (New York: Simon and Schuster, 1992).
63. Members of both the Brown and Lyman families recalled hearing details from independent sources regarding the decision and the approximate date. A cousin of Richard's living in Delta, Utah, heard from his father that in the 1910s when the couple came to visit, Richard said that Amy insisted on separate bedrooms, while another Lyman cousin also recalled the same details of the story. Similarly, the wife of Amy's grandnephew recalled that John Z. Brown, Amy's brother, related that Richard and Amy made the change in their relationship when Amy was forty. Melvyn Lyman interview; Mary Lyman Henrie interview, 1992; Pingree interview, 1993.
64. Lyman, *In Retrospect*, 42–43; Amy Brown Lyman, "R[elief] S[ociety] Address, Parley's Ward, March 1, 1957," ABLP.
65. Lyman, "R[elief] S[ociety] Address, Parley's Ward"; Vera White Pohlman, *In Memoriam: Amy Brown Lyman, 1872–1959, Biographical Summary and Funeral Services* (Salt Lake City: Privately Published, 1960), 10.
66. Mary Kimball, "Amy Brown Lyman, Relief Society Magazine, Jan. 1929," EFP. This is a longer manuscript version of an article that appeared on the above date in the *Relief Society Magazine*. Mary Connelly Kimball, "Counselor Amy Brown Lyman," *Relief Society Magazine* 16 (January 1929): 9–12; Lyman, *In Retrospect*, 55; Pohlman, *In Memoriam*, 10. For similar modernization activities in the larger church, see Alexander, *Mormonism in Transition*, 99–107.
67. Madsen, "Mormon Woman," 381; Alexander, *Mormonism in Transition*, 152; Derr, Cannon, and Beecher, *Women of Covenant*, 186–88; Lyman, "R.S. Parley's Ward," ABLP.
68. "Suggestions for the Relief Society," *Woman's Exponent* 40 (April 1912).
69. Lisa Olsen Tait, "The Young Woman's Journal: Gender and Generations in a Mormon Women's Magazine," *American Periodicals: A Journal of History, Criticism, and Bibliography*, 22 (November 30, 2011): 51–71; "Susa Young Gates," in Jenson, *LDS Biographical Encyclopedia* 2:626–29.
70. "Janette Acord Hyde," in Jenson, *LDS Biographical Encyclopedia* 2:644–46. Jeannette Hyde's name was spelled variously over the years in published sources (including in

Jenson) but the standard spelling seems to have been Jeannette Acord Hyde and that is what I use throughout when referring to her.

71. Other women who came on the board at this time were Authors Club member and educational reformer Elizabeth Crismon and public health advocate Emma Empey. "Elizabeth Turner Cain Crismon," in Jenson, *LDS Biographical Encyclopedia*, 4:183; "Emma Adams Empey," in Jenson, *LDS Biographical Encyclopedia*, 4:184; Madsen, "A Mormon Woman," 376–78.
72. Lyman, *In Retrospect,* 48–52. Susa Young Gates, head of the Historical Division of the Genealogical Society of Utah, saw standardized lessons as a means through which the Relief Society could popularize the study of genealogy. Genealogy was not only a topic of rising interest across the nation but was of special import to Mormons who were charged with seeking out information about their ancestors so that vicarious temple ordinances could be performed for them. Having inherited a full measure of her father's strength of will, Gates was not a woman easily denied. See James B. Allen and Jessie L. Embry, "'Provoking the Brethren to Good Works': Susa Young Gates, the Relief Society, and Genealogy," *Brigham Young University Studies*, 31 (Spring 1991): 115–38.
73. Wells held firm, however, that only one topic—genealogy—should be required, while the others were to remain recommended topics of study only. Alexander, *Mormonism in Transition*, 134; Derr, Cannon, and Beecher, *Women of Covenant*, 188; Allen and Embry, "Provoking the Brethren," 128–29; Madsen, "A Mormon Woman," 381, 383.
74. Madsen, "A Mormon Woman," 381, 382; Derr, Cannon, and Beecher, *Women of Covenant,* 188. Some autonomy had been surrendered with the Relief Society's move into the Bishops building that placed board members in closer proximity with the Presiding Bishopric and led to more supervision of their activities. Not to be forgotten was the ongoing shift in the organization's status to that of an auxiliary. Yet, the slow but growing constraints on the Relief Society's autonomy, of which the move towards a standardized curriculum was only one step among many, were but the continuation of a long-term trend. Relief Society minutes from Nauvoo state that Joseph Smith told the sisters that he "turned the key" to them. From a Mormon theological perspective, this implied that Smith placed the spiritual authority to lead the organization into the hands of the women themselves. After Smith's death and the Mormon exodus to Utah, church leaders including Brigham Young and his successor John Taylor realized this created problems because it implied the women had authority apart from that delegated by current church leaders. Especially problematic was that among the women to whom Smith was said to have "turned the key," was his wife Emma, who remained in Illinois and was estranged from the Utah church. Taylor, who was present at the Relief Society's organizational meeting, indicated that the term Smith must have used was that he had turned the key in their behalf, meaning that he (Smith), and thus other priesthood leaders who followed him, reserved authority for the organization in their own hands. The sisters who had been at the meeting disagreed, but acquiesced to Taylor's version of events, thereafter generally—although not exclusively—referring to the incident in the sanctioned terms. Derr, Cannon, and Beecher, *Women of Covenant*, 74, 75. For an example of the continued use of the earlier terminology, see, Anna Boss Hart, "The Cultural Strength of Relief Society," *Relief Society Magazine* 27 (March 1940): 175.
75. Allen and Embry, "Provoking the Brethren," 127.
76. Madsen, "A Mormon Woman," 383–84.
77. Relief Society General Board Minutes, 10 December, 1913, as quoted in Madsen, "A Mormon Woman," 383–84.
78. See Whitney R. Cross, *The Burned Over District: The Social and Intellectual History of Enthusiastic Religion in Western New York, 1800–1850* (Ithaca: Cornell University Press,

1950), and Susan Juster and Lisa MacFarlane, eds., *A Mighty Baptism: Race, Gender, and the Creation of American Protestantism* (Ithaca: Cornell University Press, 1996).

79. See, for example, Emmeline B. Wells, "Charity and Faith," *Relief Society Bulletin* 1 (April 1914): 2. On declining use of spiritual gifts among Mormon women, see Newell, "Gifts of the Spirit: Women's Share," 124–39.
80. Throughout her presidency, Wells would give Lyman a blessing from time to time when she had important tasks to perform. See Emmeline B. Wells Diary, June 2, 1917. Lyman co-worker Leona Fetzer Wintch recalled that her mother, as Relief Society president in their ward on Salt Lake's west side during the 1920s, had assumed the responsibility to bless women before childbirth. Leona Fetzer Wintch, phone conversation with the author, May 6, 2006. See Stapley and Wright, "Female Ritual Healing in Mormonism," 1–85.
81. See Jill Mulvay Derr, "Strength in Our Union: The Making of Mormon Sisterhood," in Maureen Ursenbach Beecher and Lavina Fielding Anderson, eds., *Sisters in Spirit: Mormon Women in Historical and Cultural Perspective* (Urbana: University of Illinois Press, 1992), 192–93.
82. This was pointed out to me by Vera White Pohlman, who began to work for Lyman as her personal secretary in 1920. She noted that between 1930 and 1940 another shift occurred and women were again addressing one another as "sister." Pohlman interviews.
83. See "Instructions," *Relief Society Bulletin* 1 (January 1914): 15, 16.
84. Lyman, *In Retrospect*, 50–52.
85. Writers were not paid. Lyman, *In Retrospect*, 53.
86. Lyman, *In Retrospect,* 53; Engar interviews; Engar, "Amy Brown Lyman."
87. Many ward Relief Societies that heretofore assembled monthly or semi-monthly, began to meet weekly. If local societies wished to study other topics, from this time on, they would have to find time outside of regular meetings to do so. In addition, in a move towards standardized practice beyond that of curriculum matters, a weekly meeting time was recommended (Tuesday afternoons at 2:00 p.m.) and guidelines were given for annual ward and semi-annual stake conferences. Furthermore, the duties and responsibilities of Relief Society leaders and members were spelled out in detail. "Circular of Instructions," *Relief Society Magazine* 2 (March 1915): 111–41. The scheduling of Relief Society meetings on Tuesday afternoons reveals some fundamental assumptions about the membership of the organization. First, that they were not working women. While a minority of Latter-day Saint women worked outside the home, most were expected to be primarily housewives and mothers. Those working outside the home—as were several on the general board—were considered an exception. It is interesting to note that afternoon meetings remained the norm for the Relief Society until the 1970s.
88. See Mary Ellen Zuckerman, *A History of Popular Women's Magazines in the United States, 1792–1995* (Westport, CT: Greenwood Press, 1998).
89. Lyman, *In Retrospect*, 56. Lyman's column began in 1916 and was carried continuously until 1928, when she moved from her position as general secretary to first counselor for President Louise Robison. The column was a compilation of items of interest culled primarily from the reports sent to the general offices by stake Relief Societies. At the time the *Relief Society Magazine* ceased publication in 1970, it counted nearly three hundred thousand subscribers, many of whom had read the publication for decades. Its demise was a deeply mourned loss by the women of the church. Derr, Cannon, and Beecher, *Women of Covenant*, 342–43. See also *A Legacy Remembered: The Relief Society Magazine, 1914–1970* (Salt Lake City: Deseret Book, 1982). As far as the *Woman's Exponent* was concerned, with the appearance of the *Bulletin* and its subsequent expansion into the *Magazine,* it was becoming clear that the *Exponent* was doomed. As her energies flagged, Emmeline

Wells was unable to meet a regular publication schedule, and rather than semi-monthly the *Exponent* sometimes appeared monthly, or even bi-monthly. By 1913, the paper that had done so much to inspire two generations of Mormon women was near collapse. As the board took steps to create the *Magazine*, Wells sought to save the paper by giving it to the Relief Society. When the board failed to act on her offer, she faced the inevitable and ceased publication in February 1914. Madsen, "A Mormon Woman," 385–86.

CHAPTER 4

1. "Greetings and Sentiments," *Relief Society Magazine* 2 (January 1915): 10.
2. Amy Brown Lyman, "General Conference of the Relief Society," *Relief Society Magazine* 2 (December 1915): 527.
3. Thomas G. Alexander, *Utah: The Right Place*, (Salt Lake City: Gibbs Smith, 1996), 23–25, 233–34, 257, 262; "General Relief Society Conference," *Woman's Exponent* 41 (May 1913): 53.
4. For maternalism, see Paula Baker, "The Domestication of Politics: Women and American Political Society, 1780–1920," *American Historical Review* 89 (June 1984): 620–47; Linda Gordon, ed., *Women, the State, and Welfare* (Madison: University of Wisconsin Press, 1990); and Theda Skocpol, *Protecting Soldiers and Mothers: The Political Origins of Social Policy in the United States* (Cambridge: Harvard University Press, 1992), 314–72.
5. "General Relief Society Conference," *Woman's Exponent* 39 (June 1910): 6; "Ogden Stake," *Woman's Exponent*, 40 (August 1911): 15; Olive D. Christensen, "Annual Relief Society Conference," *Woman's Exponent* 40 (October 1911): 23; "General Relief Society Conference," *Woman's Exponent* 41 (May 1913): 52–54, especially Annie Wells Cannon address, 52–53; Jill Mulvay Derr, Janath Russell Cannon, and Maureen Ursenbach Beecher, *Women of Covenant: The Story of Relief Society* (Salt Lake City: Deseret Book, 1992), 183.
6. Treatments of the Children's Bureau (including discussions of the living wage) can be found in Molly Ladd-Taylor, *Mother-Work: Women, Child Welfare and the State, 1890–1930* (Urbana: University of Illinois Press, 1994); Robyn Muncy, *Creating a Female Dominion in American Reform, 1890–1935* (New York: Oxford University Press, 1991); Skocpol, *Protecting Soldiers and Mothers*; and Lela B. Costin, *Two Sisters for Social Justice: A Biography of Grace and Edith Abbott* (Urbana: University of Illinois Press, 1983). For an example of the Relief Society's interest in the Bureau, see *Woman's Exponent* 40 (April 1912): 59.
7. Leah D. Widtsoe, "The Story of a Gifted Lady," *Relief Society Magazine* 32 (March 1945): 154
8. Richard A. Meckel, *Save the Babies: American Public Health Reform and the Prevention of Infant Mortality, 1850–1929* (Baltimore: Johns Hopkins University Press, 1990), 78–79; S. Josephine Baker, *Fighting for Life* (New York: The MacMillan Company, 1939), 126–32.
9. "General Relief Society Conference," *Woman's Exponent* 41 (November 1913): 77.
10. In 1914 and 1915 when city officials asked the Relief Society for further assistance, the board declined their request, although in the latter instance, ward and stake societies were allowed to decide themselves whether or not to participate. Carol Cornwall Madsen, "A Mormon Woman in Victorian American," (PhD dissertation, University of Utah, 1985), 389; Derr, Cannon, and Beecher, *Women of Covenant*, 184; Amy Brown Lyman, "Notes from the Field: Milk Stations," *Relief Society Magazine*, 3 (August 1916): 462.
11. Derr, Cannon, and Beecher, *Women of Covenant*, 184, 469n19; Amy Brown Lyman, *In Retrospect: Autobiography of Amy Brown Lyman* (Salt Lake City: General Board

of Relief Society), 68–69; "Alice Merrill Horne," *Relief Society Magazine* 4 (January 1917): 10.

12. "Circular of Instructions," *Relief Society Magazine* 2 (March 1915): 139.
13. The pamphlet, by Dr. L. W. Snow, was entitled "Safe Guarding of the Child's Sight"; "Notice," *Relief Society Bulletin* 1 (July 1914): 13; "Circular of Instructions," 139.
14. U.S. Department of Agriculture, *Report on Agricultural Experiment Stations and Cooperative Agricultural Extension Work in the United States for the Year Ended June 30, 1915* (Washington, D.C.: U.S. Government Printing Office, 1916), 145–46.
15. For an overview of this work, see U.S. Department of Agriculture, *Cooperative Extension Work in Agriculture and Home Economics, 1917: Part II of Report on Experiment Stations and Extension Work in the United States* (Washington, D.C.: Government Printing Office, 1919).
16. Madsen, "A Mormon Woman," 393; Janette A. Hyde, "Home Economics Department," *Relief Society Magazine* 3 (February 1916): 85–90. I must again thank Wells's biographer, Carol Cornwall Madsen, for clarifying to me that much of Wells's concern over loss of organizational autonomy through association with other organizations was the result of Joseph F. Smith's very strongly stated views on the matter. Email, Carol Cornwall Madsen to Dave Hall, December 2, 2014.
17. Lyman, *In Retrospect*, 56. "Guide Lessons, Home Economics: The Home Economics Movement and its Meaning," *Relief Society Magazine* 3 (November 1916): 658–60; Janette A. Hyde, "Home Scientists in Convention," *Relief Society Magazine* 3 (October 1916): 559–68.
18. Amy Brown Lyman, "Notes from the Field," *Relief Society Magazine* 3 (July 1916): 406. For examples, see "Guide Lessons, Home Economics: Mother's Condition and Diet," *Relief Society Magazine* 3 (December 1916): 728–30; "Guide Lessons, Home Economics: Correct Nursing Habits," *Relief Society Magazine* 4 (January 1917): 56–59; and Amy Brown Lyman, "Notes from the Field: Wasatch Stake," *Relief Society Magazine* 9 (April 1922): 214.
19. For this aspect of Smith-Lever, see *Fifth Annual Report of the Chief, Children's Bureau to the Secretary of Labor* (Washington, D.C.: U.S. Government Printing Office, 1917), 48–49; Skocpol, *Protecting Soldiers and Mothers*, 495; Costin, *Two Sisters for Social Justice*, 133.
20. The Relief Society, however, made it a Baby Day rather than a Baby Week. Relief Society Minutes, January 20, February 3, 1916, as cited in Madsen, "A Mormon Woman," 395; Relief Society Circular Letter, February 18, 1916, Relief Society Circular Letter File, Church History Library, Church of Jesus Christ of Latter-day Saints, Salt Lake City, Utah (cited hereafter as CHL). For Baby Week, see U.S. Department of Labor, Children's Bureau, *Baby Week Campaigns: Suggestions for Communities of Various Sizes*, Bureau Publication No. 15 (Washington, D.C.: Government Printing Office, 1915).
21. William J. Deeney to Mrs. Richard R. Lyman, April 27, 1916, Amy Brown Lyman Papers, L. Tom Perry Special Collections, Harold B. Lee Library, Brigham Young University, Provo, Utah (cited hereafter as ABLP).
22. For the Charity Organization movement, see Roy Lubove, *The Professional Altruist: The Emergence of Social Work as a Career* (Cambridge, MA: Harvard University Press, 1965), 1–21; James Leiby, *A History of Social Welfare and Social Work in the United States* (New York: Columbia University Press, 1978), 111–27.
23. Vera White Pohlman began a life-long association with Lyman when she started as her personal secretary in 1920. Later a welfare worker herself she provided valuable insight into the benefits that came through Lyman's association with other charitable agencies. Vera White Pohlman interviews, 1990–1994.

24. For the Social Advisory Committee, see Thomas G. Alexander, "Between Revivalism and the Social Gospel: The Latter-day Saint Social Advisory Committee, 1916–1922," *Brigham Young University Studies* 23 (Winter 1983): 19–39. For an example of the Relief Society's ongoing interest in what came to be called "preventative social work" in regard to the youth of the church, see Amy Brown Lyman, "Amusements," *Woman's Exponent* 39 (October 1910): 27.
25. Christopher Coble, "The Role of Young People's Societies in the Training of Christian Womanhood (and Manhood), 1880–1920," in Margaret Lamberts Bendroth and Virginia Lieson Brereton, eds., *Women and Twentieth-Century Protestantism* (Urbana: University of Illinois Press, 2002), 74–92; Wendy J. Deichmann Edwards and Carolyn De Swarte Gifford, eds., *Gender and the Social Gospel* (Urbana: University of Illinois Press, 2003).
26. Alexander, "Between Revivalism and the Social Gospel," 26–36.
27. Richard Poll, ed., *Utah's History* (Provo: Brigham Young University Press, 1978), 700–1.
28. David M. Kennedy, *Over Here: The First World War and American Society* (New York: Oxford University Press, 1980), 30–44.
29. The American suffrage movement, for example, was split with the mainstream National American Woman's Suffrage Association, which eventually threw its full weight behind the war (with the understanding that women would be rewarded by greater government support for suffrage once the conflict was resolved), and the smaller and more militant National Women's Party, which followed a confrontational path of demonstrations, civil disobedience, and hunger strikes to point out the hypocrisy of a war to make the world safe for democracy when much of the nation still denied the vote to half its citizens. J. Stanley Lemons, *The Woman Citizen: Social Feminism in the 1920s* (Urbana: University of Illinois Press, 1973), 3–11; Ellen Carol Dubois, *Harriet Stanton Blatch and the Winning of Woman Suffrage* (New Haven: Yale University Press, 1999), 204–20; Karen Manners Smith, "New Paths to Power, 1890–1920," in Nancy F. Cott, ed., *No Small Courage: A History of Women in the United States* (New York: Oxford University Press, 2000), 405–11; Leonard J. Arrington, "Modern Lysistratas: Mormon Women in the International Peace Movement, 1899–1939," *Journal of Mormon History* 15 (1989): 89–104.
30. Lola Van Wagenen, *Sister-Wives and Suffragists: Polygamy and the Politics of Woman Suffrage, 1870–1896* (Provo, UT: Joseph Fielding Smith Institute for Latter-day Saint History and BYU Studies, 2003), 154; Lemons, *The Woman Citizen*, 15–16.
31. Derr, Cannon, and Beecher, *Women of Covenant*, 208–9; "Red Cross Work in the Relief Society," *Relief Society Magazine* 4 (August 1917): 436.
32. Derr, Cannon and Beecher, *Women of Covenant*, 206–9. See for example Clarissa S. Williams, "Patriotic Department," *Relief Society Magazine* 5 (January, 1918): 35, 36; and Williams, "Patriotic Department," *Relief Society Magazine* 5 (June, 1918): 346–50.
33. Lemons, *The Woman Citizen*, 154. For a clever linkage of child health with the patriotic duty of Americans to preserve their nation, see statement of Children's Bureau head Julia Lathrop at 1918 meeting of the National Conference of Social Work held at Kansas City, as quoted in Amy Brown Lyman, "National Conference of Social Work," in "Notes from the Field," *Relief Society Magazine* 5 (August 1918): 460.
34. For a discussion of this process, see Muncy, *Creating a Female Dominion in American Reform*, 96–97; Lemons, *The Woman Citizen*, 16.
35. "General Conference of Relief Society," *Relief Society Magazine* 4 (June 1917): 329–30.
36. See Clarissa Smith Williams, "Patriotic Department" *Relief Society Magazine* 5 (April 1918): 218; and (June 1918): 347.
37. "Weigh Your Child for the Government," in Clarissa Smith Williams, "Patriotic Department," *Relief Society Magazine* 5 (June 1918): 348–49.

38. "The Red Cross Civilian Relief Plan: Organization of the Chapters and a Great Campaign for Money," and "The Task of Civilian War Relief," *The Survey* 38 (May 19, 1917): 162–65.
39. Amy Brown Lyman, "The Red Cross Conference in Denver," *Relief Society Magazine* 4 (December 1917): 687–90; Leiby, *A History of Social Welfare and Social Work in the United States*, 160–61; Phyllis Atwood Watts, "Casework above the Poverty Line: The Influence of Home Service Work in World War I on Social Work," *Social Service Review* 38 (September 1964): 314; State of Utah, *First Biennial Report of the State Department of Public Welfare, July 1, 1936–June 30, 1938, with Supplementary Date January 1935 through December, 1938 and a Review of Public Aid in Utah Prior to Establishment of the State Department of Public Welfare in May, 1935* (Salt Lake City: State of Utah, 1939): 1.
40. In addition to Lyman, Utah's delegation included Rebecca Nibley from the Relief Society, and W. J. Deeney, of Salt Lake's Charity Organization Society, charity workers Evelyn Moyle and Julia Mansfield, and E. S. Hinckley of the state industrial school. Nibley had the added advantage of being the wife of the church's presiding bishop, who was the priesthood leader in charge of charity efforts. "Mrs. Lyman, Delegate, Reports Proceedings Pittsburg [sic] Convention," *Deseret News* June 19, 1917; Amy Brown Lyman, "Social Service Work in the Relief Society, 1917–1928, Including a Brief History of the Relief Society Social Service Department and Brief Mention of Other Relief Society and Community Social Service Activities," ABLP, 3. For the Pittsburgh discussion of the Home Service work, see Eugene T. Lies, "Red Cross Work Among Families of Soldiers and Sailors," *Proceedings of the National Conference of Social Work at the Forty-Fourth Annual Session held in Pittsburgh, Pennsylvania, June 6–13, 1917* (Chicago: National Conference of Social Work), 140–43.
41. For Richmond, see Elizabeth N. Agnew, *From Charity to Social Work: Mary E. Richmond and the Creation of an American Profession* (Urbana: University of Illinois Press, 2004); Mary Richmond, *Social Diagnosis* (Philadelphia: Russell Sage Foundation, 1917); Mary Richmond, *The Long View: Papers and Addresses* (New York: Russell Sage Foundation, 1930), 418; Leiby, *A History of Social Welfare and Social Work in the United States,* 121–23; Lubove, *The Professional Altruist*, 45–49; Lyman, *In Retrospect*, 114.
42. For an overview of early Mormon charitable efforts, see Garth L. Mangum and Bruce D. Blumell, *The Mormon's War on Poverty* (Salt Lake City: University of Utah Press, 1993), 77–83. On the inadequacy of public relief agencies, see Lubove, *The Professional Altruist*, 52–54.
43. Acting on her own recommendation, the following year Lyman saw to it that representatives from the church joined an even larger Utah delegation to the next meeting of the National Conference in Kansas City. "Mrs. Lyman, Delegate, Reports" *Deseret News*, June 19, 1917; Alexander, "Between Revivalism and the Social Gospel," 27; Amy Brown Lyman, "Notes from the Field: National Conference of Social Work," *Relief Society Magazine* 5 (July 1918): 458–59.
44. Amy Brown Lyman to Emmeline B. Wells, [June] 1917, ABLP; Lyman, *In Retrospect*, 105–6; Charlotte Perkins Gilman, "Poverty and Woman," *Proceedings of the National Conference of Social Work, 1917*, 10–15.
45. As was the case with child welfare work, Williams's familiarization with Home Service work at this early stage contributed to her subsequent support of Lyman's ongoing efforts to bring modern social welfare methods into Relief Society charity practices. For the development of this aspect of the work, see Lyman, "Social Service Work," 3; and Lyman, "The Red Cross Conference in Denver," *Relief Society Magazine* 4 (December 1917): 687–90. Lyman's costs for attending the conference were paid by the Red Cross, and Williams's by the Relief Society.

46. Three of the five were from the Relief Society. They were Cora Kasius from Ogden, Mary L. Hendrickson from Logan, and Annie D. Palmer from Provo. Each was expected to assume responsibility for the war work in their communities upon their return, and each ultimately played prominent roles in the development of social work in the Relief Society and the state. Kasius eventually moved east and achieved some distinction in national social work circles while Palmer came to be a close associate of Lyman's. Lyman, "Social Service Work," 3, 4; "Relief Workers Return to Salt Lake," scrapbook clipping, Nov. 1917, ABLP; Pohlman interviews.
47. "Gertrude Vaile," in Walter I. Trattner, ed., *Biographical Dictionary of Social Welfare in America* (Westport, CT: Greenwood Press, 1986), 723–25; "Gertrude Vaile, 1878–1954," *Social Service Review* (March, 1955): 84–85; Gertrude Vaile, "Public Administration of Charity in Denver," *Proceedings of the National Conference of Charities and Correction at the Forty-Third Annual Session Held in Indianapolis, Indiana, May 10–17, 1916* (Chicago: National Conference of Charities and Corrections, 1916), 415–18.
48. See examples of correspondence between the two women and Lyman from 1917 to 1932, as contained in ABLP.
49. Smith had actually "set apart" Lyman as a delegate, in Mormon terms, something akin to ordaining her to what was clearly considered a sacred obligation. Emmeline B. Wells Diary, October 23, 1917.
50. Lyman, "Social Service Work," 4.
51. Smith and Lyman were joined by Jeannette Hyde at this meeting. Lyman, "Social Service Work," 4, 5.
52. Mangum and Blumell, *The Mormons' War on Poverty*, 52–74.
53. Poll, *Utah's History*, 434–42, 687.
54. Amy Brown Lyman, "General Relief Society Conference," *Woman's Exponent* 40 (April 1912): 59.
55. "Jottings," *The Survey* 38 (16 June 1917): 252. *The Survey* was at the time the preeminent journal of social work and reform. For the role of the publication in social work circles, see Clarke A. Chambers, *Paul U. Kellogg and the Survey: Voices for Social Welfare and Social Justice* (Minneapolis: University of Minnesota Press, 1971).
56. Lyman, "Social Service Work," 5.
57. Lyman, "Social Service Work," 5; Watts, "Casework above the Poverty Line, 305–6.
58. Pohlman interviews; Evelyn Hodges Lewis interview, 1992. Though professional social workers were trying to raise standards during this period, Lyman's brief training period was still fairly typical of many in the profession. By the early 1930s, government studies indicated that only a small percentage had lengthy training in a formal setting. See *Recent Social Trends in the United States: Report of the President's Research Committee on Social Trends,* (New York: McGraw-Hill, 1933), 1190–91.
59. Richard would work as a consultant on a number of important projects, including the Metropolitan Water District in southern California, the Chicago Sewer System, and Hoover Dam. Andrew Jenson, *Latter-Day Saint Biographical Encyclopedia: A Compilation of Biographical Sketches and Prominent Men and Women in the Church of Jesus Christ of Latter-day Saints* (Salt Lake City: Andrew Jenson History Company, 1901–1936), 3:756–760: "Richard R. Lyman, Hon. Lambda, Associated with Three of Seven "Modern Wonders," reprinted from *The Gear of Theta Tau* 48 (Spring 1959), EFP; Richard R. Lyman Journals, Richard R. Lyman Collection, L. Tom Perry Special Collections, Harold B. Lee Library, Brigham Young University (collection cited hereafter as RRLP).
60. In coming years, SAC members would prove important allies to Lyman in the cause of modernizing church charity work. Alexander, "Between Revivalism and the Social

Gospel," 27; Lyman, "Social Service Work," 5; Amy Brown Lyman, "National Conference of Social Work," in "Notes from the Field," *Relief Society Magazine* 5 (August 1918): 458–62; *Proceedings of the National Conference of Social Work at the Forty-Fifth Annual Session Held in Kansas City, Missouri, May 15–22, 1918* (Chicago: Rogers and Hall, 1918).

61. Lyman, "Social Service Work," 6.
62. On the influenza epidemic, see Alfred W. Crosby, *America's Forgotten Pandemic: The Influenza of 1918* (Cambridge, U.K.: Cambridge University Press, 1990); John M. Barry, *The Great Influenza: The Epic Story of the Deadliest Plague in History* (New York: Viking, 2004). On its impact on Utah, see Leonard J. Arrington, "The Influenza Epidemic of 1918–19 in Utah," *Utah Historical Quarterly* 58 (Spring 1990): 165–82.
63. This exposed Lyman to a wider range of social problems than she had previously encountered. Lyman, "Social Service Work," 6.
64. This assessment of Lyman's abilities was shared by those who worked under her as social workers, and by such figures as Gertrude Vaile and Katherine Lenroot of the Children's Bureau. Leona Fetzer Wintch interviews, 1991–94; Lewis interview; Pohlman interviews.
65. Lyman, "Social Service Work," 6; Pohlman interviews. For Grant's efforts to shore up the church's finances, see: Alexander, *Mormonism in Transition*, 116–25.
66. Thomas G. Alexander, "From War to Depression," in *Utah's History*, 463–72.
67. The department rendered little direct aid in the form of cash or commodities, however, and that which it did provide was generally limited to bare essentials, and then only in cases involving transients or in emergencies when bishops or local Relief Society presidents—who continued to be responsible for the bulk of LDS relief needs—could not be reached. Only in rare and difficult cases referred by local church leaders would department personnel organize long-term relief in cooperation with relatives, the county, and ward bishops. Lyman, "Social Service Work," 7, 8; Pohlman interviews; Wintch interviews; Lewis interview.
68. Anna Laura Stohl Cannon Oral History interview by Loretta L. Hefner, 1979, typescript, James H. Moyle Oral History Program, CHL; Lewis interview; Wintch interviews; Amy Brown Lyman to Florence Hutsinpillar, August 10, 1920, ABLP.
69. Lydia Alder Bean Oral History, interview by Loretta L. Hefner, 1979, typescript, James H. Moyle Oral History Program, CHL; Cannon Oral History; Pohlman interviews; Wintch interviews; Lewis interview.
70. Lyman to Florence Hutsinpillar, February 8, 1922, ABLP; Cannon Oral History; Pohlman interviews.
71. Pohlman interviews; Wintch interviews; Lewis interview.
72. Lyman worked very closely during these years with Dr. Arthur L. Beeley who was active in the establishment of the school of social work at the University of Utah. Pohlman interviews.
73. In 1919 Lyman arranged for a member of the Presiding Bishopric to visit Denver's City and County charities. A similar visit was arranged for Salt Lake County's new charity commissioner in 1923. Florence Hutsinpillar to Amy Brown Lyman, September 9, 1919 and Amy Brown Lyman to Florence W. Hutsinpillar, April 30, 1923, ABLP; Lyman, "Social Service Work," 8.
74. Vera White Pohlman reported seeing Gates call Lyman in this fashion on numerous occasions in the early 1920s. She also indicated that from her perspective as a young woman unfamiliar with the internal struggles going on behind the scenes, she saw no outward indication of tension between Lyman and Gates. Pohlman interviews.
75. Janath Russell Cannon and Jill Mulvay Derr, "Resolving Differences/Achieving Unity: Lessons from the History of Relief Society," in Mary E. Stovall and Carol Cornwall

Madsen, eds., *As Women of Faith: Talks Selected from the BYU Women's Conferences* (Salt Lake City: Deseret Book Co. 1989), 128–31. Gates's argument against using modern methods is summarized in a letter she wrote to the general board of the Relief Society. Susa Young Gates to the President and Board of the Relief Society, 4 Nov. 1919, Susa Young Gates Collection, CHL.

76. See Lubove, *The Professional Altuist,* 22–54.
77. Lyman, "Social Service Work," 6; Amy Brown Lyman, "Mrs. Annie D. Palmer," *Relief Society Magazine* 19 (September 1932): 523; Cannon and Derr, "Resolving Differences," 128–29. For the activities of the Utah Stake, see Utah Stake Relief Society Minutes, February through December, 1919, CHL; Mark K. Allen interviews, 1991, 1992. The Utah Stake Relief Society continued to serve the community for several years until its activities were finally assumed by the county government.
78. Cannon and Derr, "Resolving Differences," 130; "Program, Colorado Conference of Social Work, Denver, November 19–21, 1919, ABLP.
79. Cannon and Derr, "Resolving Differences," 130–31. Copies of Gates's letters to figures nationally prominent in charity work and some of their replies to her, are contained in the Susa Young Gates collection, CHL.
80. Cannon and Derr, "Resolving Differences," 131.
81. Since the statehood struggle and the Smoot hearings, LDS leaders had been sensitive about violating the church-state divide. In addition, considering the difficultly of adequately funding the central social service offices in Salt Lake, a church-wide effort on the pattern of Utah Stake would have been unfeasible for financial reasons. See Alexander, *Mormonism in Transition,* 16–37, 116–24.
82. Lyman, "Social Service Work," 1, 2; Wintch interviews; Lewis interview; Amy Brown Lyman, "General Relief Society Conference," *Relief Society Magazine* 7 (December 1920), 712.
83. The restrictions on Gates may have been due to an editorial celebrating Emmeline Wells's birthday in which she praised the older women for refusing to change the fundamentals of the organization—a barb clearly aimed at Lyman and Williams. "Editorial: Birthday of President Emmeline B. Wells," *Relief Society Magazine* 8 (February 1921): 113; Rebecca Foster Cornwall, "Susa Young Gates: The Thirteenth Apostle," in Vicki Burgess-Olson, ed., *Sister Saints* (Provo: Brigham Young University Press, 1978), 79. Despite Gates's release from the board, Richard R. Lyman suspected that her efforts to undermine the new directions in church charity work continued. See Richard R. Lyman Journals, July 26, 1922, RRLP.
84. Lyman, "Social Service Work," 9.
85. Dr. Arthur L. Beeley was also a member of the Social Advisory Committee and worked closely with Lyman in that capacity. Amy Brown Lyman, "Class in Charities and Relief Work: Brigham Young University Summer School," *Relief Society Magazine* 7 (August 1920): 437–40; Lyman, "Social Service Work," 9.
86. To prepare the Relief Society for Devine's lectures, Lyman arranged to have these same principles discussed at length during the Relief Society's conference the preceding April. Lyman, "Class in Charities and Relief Work," 438; Edward T. Devine, *The Normal Life* (New York: The MacMillan Company, 1917); Amy Brown Lyman, "General Relief Society Conference," *Relief Society Magazine* 7 (June 1920): 335–46. On Devine's prominence during this period, see John F. McClymer, *War and Welfare: Social Engineering in America, 1890–1925* (Westport, CT: Greenwood Press, 1980), 165. Lyman, *In Retrospect,* 116–17.
87. Lyman, "Social Service Work," 2, 28–31.
88. Cora L. Bennion, "Social Service," *Relief Society Magazine* 11 (June 1924): 288–89.

89. Paul L. Benjamin to Mrs. Amy Lyman, July 15, 1921, ABLP. I have found no evidence that Lyman wrote the report Benjamin requested. For estimates of Relief Society membership growth, see General Board of Relief Society, *A Centenary of Relief Society, 1842–1942* (Salt Lake City: General Board of Relief Society, 1942), 86, 87. Membership numbers for these early years of the twentieth century are considered estimates at best, though the perception among members at the time was of a noticeable amount of increased interest and participation in the organization.
90. Clarissa S. Williams, "General Officers Meeting," *Relief Society Magazine* 8 (December 1921): 679.
91. Lyman's leadership would extend nearly a decade from 1925 until 1934. Vera White Pohlman, *Amy Brown Lyman, 1872–1959, Biographical Summary and Funeral Services* (Privately Printed: 1960), 17; Clarissa Smith Williams and Amy Brown Lyman, "The Official Round Table," *Relief Society Magazine* 7 (April 1920): 225–26; Lyman, *In Retrospect*, 110–11.
92. Madsen, "A Mormon Woman," 402–5.
93. Annie Wells Cannon Journal, July 1, 1925, Annie Wells Cannon Collection, Harold B. Lee Library, Brigham Young University, Provo, Utah.
94. Madsen, "A Mormon Woman," 405–6.
95. Annie Wells Cannon Journal, April 1, 1921. Cannon disapproved of the term.
96. "General Conference of Relief Society," *Relief Society Magazine* 8 (June 1921): 353; Cannon Journal, April 14, 1921.

CHAPTER 5

1. Jeannette A. Hyde, "Responsibility of Woman as a Citizen," *Relief Society Magazine* 10 (June 1923): 308–10.
2. Amy Brown Lyman, "The Federal Children's Bureau and the Sheppard-Towner Work," *Relief Society Magazine* 12 (December 1926): 627.
3. Amy Brown Lyman, "Notes from the Field: National Conference of Social Work," *Relief Society Magazine* 5 (July 1918): 461–62; R. N. Baldwin, "An Industrial Program for After the War," *Proceedings of the National Conference of Social Work at the Forty-Fifth Annual Session Held in Kansas City, Missouri, May 15–22, 1918* (Chicago: Rogers and Hall, Co., 1918), 426–29; James H. Tufts, "Why Social Workers Should Study the Need of Health Insurance," in *Proceedings of the National Conference of Social Work at the Forty-Fifth Annual Session*, 407–16. For the postwar backlash and the Red Scare, see David M. Kennedy, *Over Here: The First World War and American Society* (New York: Oxford, 1980), 231–95; and J. Stanley Lemons, *The Woman Citizen: Social Feminism in the 1920s* (Urbana: University of Illinois Press, 1973), 209–27. For the experience of women after passage of the Nineteenth Amendment, see Kristi Andersen, *After Suffrage: Women in Partisan and Electoral Politics before the New Deal* (Chicago: University of Chicago Press, 1996).
4. State of Utah, *First Biennial Report of the State Department of Public Welfare, July 1, 1936–June 30, 1938, with Supplementary Data January, 1935 through December, 1938 and a Review of Public Aid in Utah Prior to Establishment of the State Department of Public Welfare in May, 1935* (Salt Lake City: State of Utah, Bureau of Research and Statistics, 1939), 1, 2. Milton Bennion of the University of Utah, who was affiliated with the Salt Lake Social Welfare League as well as the LDS Sunday School General Board, was selected as chairman. State of Utah, *Report of the State Welfare Commission of the State of Utah, 1921–1922* (Salt Lake City: State of Utah, 1923), 10–14.
5. Other recommendations of the state welfare commission included the creation of "a separate colony for the feeble minded," closer supervision of prisoners, classification and

segregation of residents in the State Industrial School according to ability, creation of a commission to supervise the State Hospital, creation of a program to treat and control narcotic addicts, alteration of state laws allowing districts to require smallpox vaccinations for entering students, proper supervision of widows' pensions, and creation of a state tuberculosis sanatorium. State of Utah, *Report of the State Welfare Commission*, 10–14; State of Utah, *First Biennial Report*, 1.

6. The measure was named after its sponsors, Senator Morris Sheppard of Texas and Congressman Horace Towner of Iowa. For efforts by politicians reaching out to women after the passage of the Nineteenth Amendment, see Kristi Andersen, *After Suffrage: Women in Partisan and Electoral Politics before the New Deal* (Chicago: University of Chicago Press, 1996), 6–7, 154; Robyn Muncy, *Creating a Female Dominion in American Reform, 1890–1935* (New York: Oxford University Press, 1991), 103; Lemons, *The Woman Citizen*, 153–54.
7. "Honors for General Board Members," *Relief Society Magazine* 7 (August 1920): 485–87.
8. "Honors for General Board Members," 486–87.
9. Richard R. Lyman Journals, September 18, 19, 1922, Richard R. Lyman Papers, L. Tom Perry Special Collections, Harold B. Lee Library, Brigham Young University (collection cited hereafter as RRLP); Amy Brown Lyman, *In Retrospect: Autobiography of Amy Brown Lyman* (Salt Lake City: General Board of Relief Society, 1945), 82–84; Vera White Pohlman interviews, 1990–1994. Pohlman remembered the sponsorship of Sheppard-Towner as one of the main reasons Lyman sought election to the Legislature.
10. Amy Kathryn Lyman Engar interviews, 1990–1994; Parry Sorensen interview, 1992.
11. Lyman, *In Retrospect*, 83. H.B. No. 123, 1923 Legislature, "An Act Appropriating Two Thousand Dollars for the Study, Investigation, and Treatment of Goiter by the School of Medicine of the University of Utah," and H.B. No. 68, 1923 Legislature, "An Act to Amend Section 570X15, Complied Laws of Utah, 1917, Relating to Construction of Waterworks by Cities and the Jurisdiction of Cities over Watershed, Streams, Reservoirs, Canals and Lands," both in Amy Brown Lyman Papers, L. Tom Perry Special Collections, Harold B. Lee Library, Brigham Young University, (cited hereafter as ABLP). Though Sheppard-Towner was passed in Congress in 1921, because many state legislatures at the time only met briefly every other year, Utah was not alone in passing its enabling legislation a year and a half later.
12. "Delegates Report Biennial of National Council of Women," *Relief Society Magazine* 11 (January 1924), 19, 20.
13. For Sheppard-Towner and details of its administration, see Lemons, *The Woman Citizen*, 16, 153–80; Theda Skocpol, *Protecting Soldiers and Mothers: The Political Origins of Social Policy in the United States* (Cambridge: Belknap Press of Harvard University Press, 1992), 480–524; and Muncy, *Creating a Female Dominion in American Reform*, 93–123. For useful and detailed descriptions of the activities of Lyman and the Relief Society during this period, see Loretta L. Hefner, "This Decade was Different: Relief Society's Social Services Department, 1919–1929," *Dialogue: A Journal of Mormon Thought* 15 (Autumn 1982): 64–73; and Loretta L. Hefner, "The National Women's Relief Society and the U.S. Sheppard-Towner Act," *Utah Historical Quarterly* 50 (Summer 1982): 255–67.
14. Relief Society General Board Minutes, July 28, 1921, and January 10, 1922, Church History Library, Church of Jesus Christ of Latter-day Saints, Salt Lake City, Utah (cited hereafter as CHL); Hefner, "The National Women's Relief Society," 257.
15. Amy Brown Lyman, "General Conference of Relief Society," *Relief Society Magazine* 8 (December 1921): 693–94.
16. Amy Brown Lyman, "General Conference of Relief Society," *Relief Society Magazine* 9 (June 1922): 303–7.

17. The sale of the Society's wheat was initially met with great unhappiness by Emmeline Wells and members of the board, as priesthood leaders made the decision without consulting them. For wheat storage, see Jessie L. Embry, "Relief Society Grain Storage Program, 1876–1940," (Master's thesis, Brigham Young University, 1974); and Jessie L. Embry, "Grain Storage: The Balance of Power between Priesthood Authority and Relief Society Autonomy," *Dialogue: A Journal of Mormon Thought* 15 (Winter 1982): 59–66.
18. Muncy, *Female Dominion,* 108, 120.
19. "Relief Society Conference," *Relief Society Magazine* 10 (June 1923): 287.
20. See, for example, Amy Brown Lyman, "Notes from the Field: Health Work," *Relief Society Magazine* 11 (Jan. 1924): 44–45; Amy Brown Lyman, "Notes from the Field: Malad Stake," *Relief Society Magazine* 11 (March 1924): 147–48; and Amy Brown Lyman, "Relief Society Conference Minutes," *Relief Society Magazine* 11 (June 1924): 273–79.
21. Stakes in Murray, Ogden, and Provo sought to follow Cottonwood's example, as did a stake in Arizona. "Relief Society Conference, Address by Amanda N. Bagley, President, Cottonwood Stake Relief Society, October 3, 1925," *Relief Society Magazine* 12 (December 1925): 635–37; Mrs. Mary P. Lindsay, "Cottonwood Stake Report," *Relief Society Magazine* 13 (December 1926): 627–28.
22. "General Conference of Relief Society," *Relief Society Magazine* 9 (December 1922): 626.
23. Lela B. Costin, *Two Sisters for Social Justice: A Biography of Grace and Edith Abbott*, (Urbana: University of Illinois Press, 1983), 136; Muncy, *Creating a Female Dominion*, 98.
24. "General Conference of Relief Society," *Relief Society Magazine* 9 (December 1922): 626.
25. H. Y. Richards, M.D., Director, Bureau of Child Hygiene, State Board of Health, Utah, "The Cooperation of Lay Organizations in Maternity and Infancy Work," in Department of Labor, Children's Bureau, *Proceedings of the Third Annual Conference of State Directors in Charge of the Local Administration of the Maternity and Infancy Act,* Publication No. 157 (Washington D.C., 1926), 184–86.
26. "Recommendations of General Board Respecting Maternity and Health," *Relief Society Magazine* 11 (January 1924): 27–30; Richards, "The Cooperation of Lay Organizations," 185.
27. Amy Brown Lyman, "Notes from the Field," *Relief Society Magazine* 12 (May, 1925): 275.
28. New York and Pennsylvania, the states with the largest possible federal appropriations under Sheppard-Towner's matching grant provisions, were eligible for a maximum of $80,041.78 and $68,810.99 respectively. Not a large sum by any means, even in 1920s dollars. But when coupled with an already existent public health system and larger tax base, a distinct advantage, nevertheless. See U.S. Department of Labor, Children's Bureau, *The Promotion of the Welfare and Hygiene of Maternity and Infancy: The Administration of the Act of Congress of November 23, 1921, Fiscal Year Ended June 30, 1926*, Publication No. 178 (Washington, D.C.: Government Printing Office, 1927), 2.
29. Scholars have noted that the Act itself proscribed the funding of permanent clinics or means for women to receive long term maternity care. But it should not be forgotten, that while Shepherd-Towner was prohibited from funding these resources, it encouraged creation of them through local initiative. In 1925, for instance, Utah officials were able to report the establishment of fifty permanent health centers in Utah, all due to local funding with the encouragement and supervision of state officials working under Shepherd-Towner. The Act then facilitated and stimulated local initiative rather than attempting the much more costly (and politically unlikely) task of fully funding maternity and infancy work. But the goals pursued were the same. Gwendolyn Mink, *The Wages of Motherhood: Inequality in the Welfare State, 1917–1942* (Ithaca: Cornell University Press, 1995), 68; *The Promotion of the Welfare and Hygiene of Maternity and Infancy*, U.S. Department of Labor, Children's Bureau Publication No. 156 (Washington D.C., 1925), 58.

30. H. Y. Richards, M.D., Director, Bureau of Child Hygiene of Utah State Board of Health, "Semi-Annual Report of Maternity and Infancy Work, July 1–December 31, 1925," Utah State Board of Health, Sheppard-Towner Papers, Children's Bureau Records, Utah Folder, National Archives and Records Administration, College Park, Maryland (cited hereafter as CBRUF), 1, 2, table 23; Richards, "The Cooperation of Lay Organizations," 185.
31. H. Y. Richards, M.D., Director, Bureau of Child Hygiene of Utah State Board of Health, "Semi-Annual Report of Maternity and Infancy Work, July 1–December 31, 1926," CBRUF.
32. Mrs. Mary P. Lindsay, "Cottonwood Stake Report," *Relief Society Magazine* 13 (December 1926): 627–28.
33. Mrs. Electa S. Dixon, "Relief Society Conference: Utah Stake Report," *Relief Society Magazine* 13 (December 1926): 628–30.
34. Amy Brown Lyman, "Notes from the Field," *Relief Society Magazine* 11 (July 1924): 362–66.
35. Amy Brown Lyman, "Notes from the Field," *Relief Society Magazine* 12 (May 1925): 277.
36. For the numbers of children examined in Utah, relative to other states, see U.S. Department of Labor, Children's Bureau, *The Promotion of the Welfare and Hygiene of Maternity and Infancy*, Publication No. 137 (Washington D. C.: 1924); Bureau Publication No. 146 (1925); Bureau Publication No. 156 (1926); and Bureau Publication No. 178 (1927).
37. Amy Brown Lyman to Miss Grace Abbott, December 13, 1926, Shepherd-Towner box, Utah file, CBRUF.
38. For the numbers of children examined in Utah during the last years of the act, see *The Promotion of the Welfare and Hygiene of Maternity and Infancy*, publications Nos. 186 (1928), 110–12; 194 (1928), 139–40; 203 (1931), 103–04.
39. "Reports of Stakes on Maternity and Health Work," in "Relief Society Conference Report," *Relief Society Magazine* 12 (June 1925): 296.
40. Mrs. Electa S. Dixon, "Utah Stake Report," *Relief Society Magazine* (December 1926): 630.
41. U.S. Department of Labor, Children's Bureau, *The Promotion of the Welfare and Hygiene of Maternity and Infancy: Administration of the Act of Congress of November 21, 1921, for Fiscal Year Ended June 30, 1929*, Publication No. 203 (Washington D.C., 1931), 132–38; "Relief Society Conference Report," *Relief Society Magazine* 12 (June 1925): 312. Accurate infant mortality figures are not available for Utah before 1917, when the state began full cooperation in the Children's Bureau sponsored birth and death registry system. Baseline figures for 1917 were 69 per 1,000, and in 1918, 64 per 1,000. The 1919, 1920 and 1921 figures climbed to 71, 71, and 73 respectively, which can likely be attributed to the effects of the influenza epidemic. In 1922, they returned to the pre-war level of 69. Similar figures for maternal mortality were 59 in 1917, jumping to 86 and 84 in 1918 and 1919 during the epidemic, before declining to 73 in 1921, and down to 55 in 1922. 1924 marked the lowest figure for maternal mortality in Utah, with a rate of 45 per 10,000 live births, while 1927 was the low point for infant mortality with 54 deaths per 1,000 births.
42. "Child Welfare Plea is Made," *Salt Lake Tribune* (August 28, 1926).
43. H.Y. Richards, "Cooperation of Lay Organizations in Maternity and Infancy Work," in U.S. Department of Labor, Children's Bureau, *Proceedings of the Third Annual Conference of State Directors in Charge of the Local Administration of the Maternity and Infancy Act, Held in Washington, D.C., January 11–13, 1926* Publication No. 157 (Washington D.C.: Government Printing Office, 1926), 183–86.
44. Leona Fetzer Wintch interviews, 1990–1994; Evelyn Hodges Lewis interview 1992; Pohlman interviews.
45. U.S. Department of Labor, Children's Bureau, *The Promotion of the Welfare and Hygiene of Maternity and Infancy, Fiscal Year Ended June 30, 1929*, 104, 132–38; Blanche M.

Haines, M.D., Director, Division of Maternity and Infant Hygiene, to Dr. T. B. Beatty, [Utah] State Health Commissioner, May 14, 1927, CBRUF.

46. Haines to Beatty, May 14, 1927, CBRUF.
47. Relief Society Conference Report, *Relief Society Magazine* 12 (June 1925): 312.
48. The poem, a bit of light-hearted doggerel apparently written by Authors Club member May Booth Talmage, actually parodied several of the couples in the organization. The full text of the verse on Richard and Amy reads as follows:

    Now Richard loves Amy in some sort of way
    If she'd only "stay put" where he'd like her to stay.
    So retiring and modest, it most breaks his heart
    To have *her* voice heard in the great public mart.
    Head drooping, pride crushed, he remembers the hour
    When she promised his word should be law. Gone his power.
    Now in silent rebellion he grieves night and day
    To have her making laws which he's forced to obey.

    "'These Wives' by May Booth Talmage, Made at Social Gathering in the Home of Br. & Sist M. J. Ballard, March 28, 1923," Minutes of the Wives of the General Authorities Club, CHL.
49. John Sillito, "Richard R. Lyman, Enigmatic Apostle," audiotape of address presented at the Annual Sunstone Symposium, 1990, Salt Lake City Utah.
50. See Richard R. Lyman Journals, 1922–1925, RRLP, for entries regarding the Lyman's and their children; *Margaret Lyman Schreiner Remembers*, (Privately Published, 1982), 4.
51. John Zimmerman Brown, ed., *Autobiography of Pioneer John Brown, 1820–1896* (Salt Lake City: Stevens and Wallis, 1941), 467; Evelyn Ballif Woodruff interview, 1992; Susan Elizabeth Swensen Driggs interviews, 1991, 1994; Engar interviews and Pohlman interviews.
52. Richard R. Lyman Journal, December 31, 1925 and January 1, 1926, RRLP.
53. The extent of the shock this caused Amy Lyman is revealed in what happened next. She asked her secretary, Vera White (Pohlman) to come over right away to take a letter notifying daughter Margaret of the terrible news. Indicative of the depth of the Lyman's grief was their anxiety when they had not received Margaret's reply after a few weeks. They had taken great pains to instruct White to send the letter airmail and were eventually chagrined when someone finally realized that at that time airmail service did not extend past the East coast. Pohlman interviews.
54. Pohlman interview; Engar interviews.
55. Driggs interviews.
56. Impressively, while laboring under all her other demands, Lyman prepared a thorough account of the minutes of the National Council of Women for publication, and included a directory of member organizations and a summary of their activities. Lyman, *In Retrospect*, 71, 88–93; "National Council of Women Quinquennial Campaign," *Relief Society Magazine* 12 (May 1925): 225–29; Pohlman interviews; *The Year Book and Directory of the National Council of Women of the United States, Inc., Including the Proceedings of the Fourteenth Convention* (New York, 1928); Vera White Pohlman, *In Memorium, Amy Brown Lyman, 1872–1959: Biographical Summary and Funeral Services* (Privately Published, 1960), 14.
57. Lyman, *In Retrospect*, 104.
58. Pohlman, *In Memorium*, 14. For child placing and summer programs, see Lyman, *In Retrospect*, 66–68; Mary Jane Woodger, "Amy Brown Lyman: Mother of the Church of Jesus Christ of Latter-day Saints' Child Placement Agency," in Carol Cornwall Madsen and Cherry B. Silver, eds., *New Scholarship on Latter-day Saint Woman in the Twentieth*

Century (Provo, UT: Joseph Fielding Smith Institute for Latter-day Saint History, 2005), 68–80; Lewis interview.

59. Richards, "Cooperation of Lay Organizations," 186; Amy Brown Lyman, "The Federal Children's Bureau and the Shepherd-Towner Work," *Relief Society Magazine* 13 (December 1926): 626.
60. For opposition to the Federal Maternity and Infancy Act, see Lemons, *The Woman Citizen*, 160–75.
61. Positive reports also came in from Idaho, where Blaine Stake reported the "the physicians feel that through this health work the lives of many mothers and children have been saved." "Reports of Stakes on Maternity and Health Work," *Relief Society Magazine* 12 (June 1925): 292–94.
62. Dixon, "Utah Stake Report," *Relief Society Magazine* 13 (December 1926): 629.
63. Amy Brown Lyman, "Notes from the Field: Bingham Stake," *Relief Society Magazine* 11 (July 1924): 364.
64. "Conference Report of the Annual Conference of the Relief Society," *Relief Society Magazine* 12 (June 1925): 286–87. For linkage of economics to the national opposition of physicians to the bill, see Muncy, *Creating a Female Dominion*, 138.
65. Muncy, *Creating a Female Dominion*, 135–142.
66. Ellis D. Coombs to Grace Abbott, September 14, 1926, Utah folder, CBRUF; Lyman, "The Federal Children's Bureau and the Sheppard-Towner Work, *Relief Society Magazine* 13 (Dec. 1926): 627.
67. For opposition to Sheppard-Towner from within the Mormon community, see, for example, Susa Young Gates to William H. King, April 13, 1929, Susa Young Gates Papers, CHL.
68. The Women Patriots was an anti-suffrage organization that had turned into a right-wing women's group with rigid views of gender roles. Lemons, *The Woman Citizen*, 11–12, 172–73; Muncy, *Creating a Female Dominion*, 139–43; Kim E. Nielsen, *Un-American Womanhood: Antiradicalism, Antifeminism, and the First Red Scare*, (Columbus: Ohio State University Press, 2001), 104–7.
69. Lela B. Costin, *Two Sisters for Social Justice*, 141–42.
70. Hefner, "The National Women's Relief Society," 265.
71. Grace Abbott to Amy Brown Lyman, January 19, 1927; Amy Brown Lyman to Grace Abbott, January 28, 1927, ABLP. King had been married to Richard's sister at the time the Lymans married, but she died in 1906 and King had since remarried.
72. Hefner, "The National Women's Relief Society," 265–66.
73. *Salt Lake Tribune*, November 2, 1928; Hefner, "The National Women's Relief Society," 266n16.
74. Grace Abbott to Amy Brown Lyman, March 29, 1931, ABLP.
75. For a nuanced discussion of women's voting behavior during the 1920s, see Kristi Andersen, *After Suffrage*, 49–75.
76. Hefner, "The National Women's Relief Society and the Sheppard-Towner Act," 267.
77. Dr. Arthur L. Beeley, "Preview of the Work in Child Study for 1928," *Relief Society Magazine* 14 (December 1927): 613.
78. Jeannette A. Hyde, "Responsibility of Woman as a Citizen," *Relief Society Magazine* 10 (June 1923), 309–10.

CHAPTER 6

1. Marcia Howells, "Trends in National Legislation," in "Relief Society Conference," *Relief Society Magazine* 22 (May 1935): 281.

2. Amy Brown Lyman, "Official Instructions," *Relief Society Magazine* 22 (November 1935): 706.
3. Robyn Muncy, *Creating a Female Dominion in American Reform, 1890–1935* (New York: Oxford University Press, 1991), 146–150; Lela Costin, *Two Sisters for Social Justice: A Biography of Grace and Edith Abbott* (Urbana: University of Illinois Press, 1983), 168–79.
4. Gertrude Vaile, "Some Significant Trends Since Cleveland, 1912," Presidential Address, *Proceedings of the National Conference of Social Work at the Thirty-Third Annual Session Held in Cleveland, Ohio, May 26–June 2, 1926* (Chicago: University of Chicago Press, 1926), 7–10; Roy Lubove, *The Professional Altruist: The Emergence of Social Work as a Career, 1880–1930* (Cambridge, MA: Harvard University Press, 1965), 158.
5. "Jeanette A. Hyde," in Andrew Jenson, *Latter-Day Saint Biographical Encyclopedia: A Compilation of Biographical Sketches of Prominent Men and Women in the Church of Jesus Christ of Latter-day Saints* 4 vols. (Salt Lake City: 1901–1936) 4:188.
6. Judging by official publications, neither the YLMIA nor the Primary Association had been actively mentoring young women for a role in the larger community for some time. In addition, in 1929, the YLMIA, lost its independent voice when the *Young Women's Journal* was subsumed by the publication of the Young Men's MIA. While the changing priorities for the organizations undoubtedly were linked to shifts in social circumstances and resulting generational outlooks, more research needs to be done to better illuminate the dynamics of this process.
7. Annie Wells Cannon Journal, Feb. 4, 1921; Jan. 14, 28: 1925; L. Tom Perry Special Collections and Manuscripts, Harold B. Lee Library, Brigham Young University, Provo, Utah.
8. Cannon Journal, March 21, 1928; "Letter to President Clarissa S. Williams, January 31, 1928," *Relief Society Magazine* 15 (March 1928): 119.
9. Conference Address by President Clarissa S. Williams, in Amy Brown Lyman, "Relief Society Conference," *Relief Society Magazine* 15 (December 1928): 667–69; Cannon Journal, October 5, 1928.
10. Cannon Journal, August 11, 1928. For an earlier conversation on the same topic between Cannon and Grant, see Thomas G. Alexander, "Between Revivalism and the Social Gospel: The Latter-day Saint Social Advisory Committee, 1916–1922," *Brigham Young University Studies* 23 (Winter 1983): 37.
11. Cannon Journal, October 7, 1928.
12. Reportedly, Robison herself had been so surprised by her entry into the highest reaches of the Relief Society leadership that in 1921 when her name was announced in conference as Clarissa Williams's first counselor, she turned to a friend next to her and said "I didn't know there was another woman by that name in the Church." Jennie Brimhall Knight, "Louise Yates Robison," *Relief Society Magazine* 16 (January 1929): 3–6.
13. Robison's style of leadership seems to have been much more reactive than proactive. Vera White Pohlman interviews, 1990–1994; Evelyn Hodges Lewis Interview, 1992; Leona Fetzer Wintch interviews, 1990–1994.
14. Vera Pohlman noted this change when she came back to the Relief Society as general secretary-treasurer in 1940. Pohlman interviews.
15. Within weeks of her selection as president, Cannon noted that Robison, while not as dignified as Clarissa Williams, "will hold her own I think and look after the work better." In the context of other entries, it is clear that this means rather than simply turning it over to Lyman. Cannon Journal, October 24, 1928.
16. Cannon Journal, November, 28, 1928.
17. "Another Word of Congratulation," *Relief Society Magazine* 17 (August 1930): 422.
18. For evidence of strained relations between Lyman and Robison, see Parry Sorensen interview, 1992; Mark Knight Allen interviews, 1991, 1994; Pohlman interviews. For Cannon's

role in the deterioration of that relationship, see Cannon Journal, December 13, 1928, January 28, 1929.

19. Amy Brown Lyman, "Tributes to Clarissa Smith Williams," *Relief Society Magazine* 17 (May 1930): 223; Amy Brown Lyman, *In Retrospect: Autobiography of Amy Brown Lyman* (Salt Lake City: General Board of Relief Society, 1945), 48, 49.
20. Vera Pohlman, for one, felt quite strongly that Robison was steering an unsteady course. Pohlman interviews 1990–1994. See also Lewis interview; and Wintch interviews.
21. Alice Louise Reynolds, Conference Address, October 1, 1930, in Julia A. F. Lund, "Relief Society Conference," *Relief Society Magazine* 17 (December 1930): 676. Reynolds had requested to be released from her position due to increased work related to her responsibilities at BYU. Relief Society General Board Minutes, May 14, 1930, Church History Library, Church of Jesus Christ of Latter-day Saints, Salt Lake City, Utah (cited hereafter as CHL).
22. At the time Williams assumed the presidency, Lyman chose to remain general secretary because it was more involved with the day to day operations of the society, and thus was a position where Lyman felt she could "do the most good." Had she become counselor, she later speculated, she might have assumed the presidency herself when Williams stepped down. Sorensen interview; Pohlman interviews.
23. Pohlman interviews.
24. Amy Brown Lyman to Margaret Lyman Schreiner, December 23, 1927, and W. F. Braasch, M.D., to Mrs. Richard R. Lyman, January 8, 1929, Amy Brown Lyman papers, L. Tom Perry Special Collections, Harold B. Lee Library, Brigham Young University (cited hereafter as ABLP); Margaret Lyman Schreiner to "Dearest Mother" (Amy Brown Lyman), December 24, 1927, Engar Family Papers (cited hereafter as EFP); Richard R. Lyman Journal, January 1, 1929, Richard R. Lyman Papers, L. Tom Perry Special Collections and Manuscripts, Harold B. Lee Library, Brigham Young University (cited hereafter as RRLP); Pohlman interviews.
25. At this time Amy's daughter Margaret and her husband were living in Los Angeles, where Alexander performed and taught music at the University of California. They were starting their family and Amy enjoyed visiting with her new grandchildren, even as her presence proved a welcome help to her daughter. Amy Kathryn Lyman Engar interviews, 1990–1994.
26. Engar interviews; Amy Lyman Engar, "Amy Brown Lyman: Transcribed from a talk given at the University of Utah Institute 'Women of the Restoration,' February 26, 1987," EFP, 14.
27. Wintch interviews. For conditions affecting the mentally disabled and mentally ill in Utah before adequate state facilities were developed, see Hazel Peterson, "Administration of Public Welfare in Utah," (Master's Thesis, University of Chicago, 1928).
28. For a critical history of this process, see James W. Trent, Jr., *Inventing the Feeble Mind: A History of Mental Retardation in the United States* (Berkeley: University of California Press, 1994). Also, Mark Allen interviews, 1991, 1994.
29. "Relief Society Conference," *Relief Society Magazine* 15 (June 1928): 295–98; "Editorial: Care of the Feeble-Minded," *Relief Society Magazine* 16 (February 1929): 79–80.
30. Relief Society Circular Letter, from Louise Y. Robison and Julia A. F. Lund to the Utah Stakes, December 31, 1928, Relief Society Circular Letter Files, 1892–1985, CHL. Lyman did not sign the letter.
31. Aware of the Society's efforts, George Dern, the new governor-elect, had also mentioned the measure at his inaugural address in January, 1929. Louise Y. Robison, "Officers' Meeting, Morning Session," in Julia A. F. Lund, "Relief Society Conference," *Relief Society Magazine* 16 (June 1929): 290–91.

32. Amy Brown Lyman, "Training School for the Feeble-Minded," *Relief Society Magazine* 17 (January 1930): 22–24; Allen interviews.
33. See the account of the episode written by Lyman in: *A Handbook of Relief Society* (Salt Lake City: General Board of Relief Society, 1932), 60; Allen interviews; Pohlman interviews.
34. Sylvester Q. Cannon address, "Conference of the Relief Society," *Relief Society Magazine* 16 (December 1929): 661.
35. T. H. Watkins, *The Hungry Years: A Narrative History of the Great Depression in America* (New York: Henry Holt, 1999), 43, 44; William E. Leuchtenburg, *Franklin D. Roosevelt and the New Deal, 1932–1940* (New York: Harper and Row, 1963), 18–40; David M. Kennedy, *Freedom from Fear: The American People in Depression and War, 1929–1945* (New York: Oxford University Press, 1999), 86–87; Thomas G. Alexander and James B. Allen, *Mormons and Gentiles: A History of Salt Lake City* (Boulder: Pruett Publishing, 1984), 199; Thomas G. Alexander, *Utah: The Right Place* (Salt Lake City: Gibbs Smith, 1996), 311.
36. Robert S. McElvaine, *The Great Depression: America 1929–1941* (New York: Times Books, 1984), 66; Watkins, *The Hungry Years*, 80–103; Pohlman interviews; Wintch interviews; Lewis interview.
37. Watkins, *The Hungry Years*, 56–57; McElvaine, *The Great Depression*, 80; Kennedy, *Freedom from Fear*, 86; Alexander, *Utah: The Right Place*, 311.
38. Annie D. Palmer, "The Social Worker in the Unemployment Emergency," *Relief Society Magazine* 19 (January 1932): 17–19.
39. Alexander and Allen, *Mormons and Gentiles*, 199–202; Alexander, *Utah: The Right Place*, 311–12.
40. Jill Mulvay Derr, "Changing Relief Society Charity to Make Way for Welfare," in Davis Bitton and Maureen Ursenbach Beecher, eds., *New Views of Mormon History: A Collection of Essays in Honor of Leonard J. Arrington* (Salt Lake City: University of Utah Press, 1987), 249.
41. State of Utah, *First Biennial Report of the State Department of Public Welfare, July 1, 1936–June 30, 1938, with Supplementary Data January, 1935 through December 1938 and a Review of Public Aid in Utah Prior to Establishment of the State Department of Public Welfare in May, 1935,* (Salt Lake City: State of Utah, Bureau of Research and Statistics, 1939), 4; Pohlman interviews.
42. Louise Y. Robinson, "Officers' Meeting," in "Relief Society Conference," *Relief Society Magazine* 18 (June 1931): 311; Derr, "Changing Relief Society Charity," 246, 248; Laura A. Watkins, "What the Social Service Institute Means to Us," *Relief Society Magazine* 18 (January, 1931): 34–36; "Notes to the Field," *Relief Society Magazine* 18, (April, 1931): 225.
43. Sarah Jane Deutsch, "From Ballots to Breadlines," in Nancy F. Cott, ed., *No Small Courage: A History of Women in the United States* (New York: Oxford, 2000), 452–53; Kennedy, *Freedom from Fear*, 164; Pohlman interviews.
44. Garth L. Mangum and Bruce D. Blumell, *The Mormon's War on Poverty: A History of LDS Welfare, 1830–1990* (Salt Lake City: University of Utah Press, 1993), 202; Derr, "Changing Relief Society Charity," 250–51.
45. Mangum and Blumell, *The Mormons' War on Poverty*, 107–09.
46. Watkins, *The Hungry Years*, 100–1.
47. Alexander, *Utah: The Right Place*, 312. Six decades after witnessing the scene, Evelyn Hodges Lewis, a social worker in the department, was moved to tears by still vivid memories of the march. Lewis interview.
48. Alexander, *Utah: The Right Place*, 312–14.

49. James T. Patterson, *The New Deal and the States: Federalism in Transition* (Princeton, New Jersey: Princeton University Press, 1969), 28–32; Watkins, *The Hungry Years*, 87.
50. Relief Society General Board Minutes, 19 May, 1932, as quoted in Derr, "Changing Relief Society to Make Way for Welfare," 251.
51. Kennedy, *Freedom from Fear*, 84.
52. In February, 1932, Hoover also asked the Red Cross to distribute surplus flour to needy families across the nation. In Utah, the Relief Society assisted the Red Cross in this effort. Mangum and Blumell, *The Mormons' War on Poverty*, 109–110.
53. Kennedy, *Freedom from Fear*, 84–85; Watkins, *The Hungry Years*, 102; State of Utah, *First Biennial Report*, 4; Lewis interview; Derr, "Changing Relief Society Charity," 251.
54. "Utah Launches Probe to Learn Need of Idle," *Salt Lake Tribune*, April 15, 1931; Lewis interview; Derr, "Changing Relief Society Charity," 251.
55. "Governor Appoints Welfare Committee," *Salt Lake Tribune*, August 7, 1932.
56. Bruce D. Blumell, "'Remember the Poor': A History of Welfare in the Church of Jesus Christ of Latter-day Saints, 1830–1980," typescript, CHL, 101; Derr, "Changing Relief Society Charity," 252; Mangum and Blumell, 112.
57. Derr, "Changing Relief Society Charity," 252; Mangum and Blumell, 111–12.
58. Wintch Oral History; Amy Brown Lyman, "Transients and Transportation," *Relief Society Magazine* 19 (November, 1932): 648–49.
59. Mangum and Blumell, 110; Derr, "Changing Relief Society Charity," 251–52; Lewis interview; State of Utah, *First Biennial Report*, 4, 6; Pohlman interviews; Wintch interviews.
60. Michael Katsanevas, Jr., "The Emerging Social Worker and the Distribution of the Castle Gate Relief Fund," *Utah Historical Quarterly* 50 (Summer 1982): 239–49; Amy Brown Lyman, "Mrs. Annie D. Palmer," *Relief Society Magazine* 19 (September 1932): 523–27. The similarities between Lyman's description of Palmer and others' descriptions of Lyman are striking, a view confirmed in a telephone conversation with one of Lyman's co-workers. Leona Fetzer Wintch telephone conversation, November 9, 2002.
61. Pohlman interviews.
62. Some picked up the work easily, but others, often local leaders who were older, adjusted poorly to the demands of clearing a case and using modern business machines in their work. Wintch interviews; Pohlman interviews.
63. Kennedy, *Freedom from Fear*, 104–30.
64. This was longtime Utah social worker Kate Williams. Pohlman interviews.
65. Alexander, *Utah: The Right Place*, 312.
66. Derr, "Changing Relief Society Charity," 252. The board members were Rosanna Irvine, a relative of Annie Wells Cannon, and Marcia Howells, who would later serve Lyman as her first counselor in the Relief Society presidency.
67. Amy Brown Lyman, "Social Casework Department," *Relief Society Magazine* 20 (May 1933): 273; "State Body for Social Work Urged," *Salt Lake Tribune* (April 4, 1933). Mangum and Blumell, *The Mormons' War on Poverty*, 111.
68. Amy Brown Lyman, "Unemployment Insurance," *Relief Society Magazine* 20 (November 1933): 658–59.
69. See, for example, Amy Brown Lyman, "Adjustment—The Call of the Hour," *Relief Society Magazine* 20 (May 1933): 292–93.
70. An example of this closeness is found in two chatty, affectionate, and encouraging letters Richard sent to Wendell while the former was visiting the area of the latter's earlier missionary labors. Richard R. Lyman to Wendell Lyman, April 18, 1933, EFP; Richard R. Lyman to Wendell Lyman, April 25, 1933, EFP; David and Sabey Pingree interview, 1993; Susan Elizabeth Driggs interviews, 1991, 1994.

71. Richard R. Lyman Journal, April 15, 1933, RRLP. The dates of the above cited letters indicate that Richard may have been using them to reassure Wendell of his ongoing affection after their strained discussion a few days before.
72. "Funeral Set on Tuesday for Business Man," *Deseret News*, May 17, 1933, 1, 5.
73. Richard was so upset by the event that he recorded nothing in his journal for a year following. When he did write, he put forward the theory that Wendell had been looking for a leak in the radiator when the accident happened. Richard R. Lyman Journal, May 29, 1934, RRLP; Evelyn Ballif Woodruff interview, 1992; Driggs interviews; Pohlman interviews; Wintch interviews. While in control in public, Amy grieved privately for years over Wendell. Writing in his journal on Wendell's birthday in December 1937, Richard observed that Amy "seems never to cease to grieve over Wendell. I think she weeps herself to sleep every night." Richard R. Lyman Journal, December 18, 1937.
74. Watkins, *The Hungry Years*, 169–79; State of Utah, *First Biennial Report*, 5.
75. Utah would be among the largest beneficiaries of federal aid under the New Deal. Mangum and Blumell, *The Mormons' War on Poverty*, 112–13.
76. Mangum and Blumell comment on the continuing gap between resources and need and each of Lyman's coworkers whom I interviewed emphasized that there was "never enough" to help everyone who really required help. Pohlman interviews; Wintch interviews; Lewis interview. For a contemporary assessment, see Vera W. Pohlman, Director of Research and Statistics, [State Department of Public Welfare] to Mrs. Burton W. [Gertrude] Musser, June 20, 1939, ABLP.
77. Employees of the department received half their pay from the county and half from the church. State of Utah, *First Biennial Report*, 6; Derr, "Changing Relief Society Charity," 255–56; Mangum and Blumell, 114–15, 122; Wintch interviews.
78. Mangum and Blumell, *The Mormons' War on Poverty*, 116–17; Derr, "Changing Relief Society Charity," 255; Lewis interview.
79. Mangum and Blumell, *The Mormons' War on Poverty*, 116–18; Derr, "Changing Relief Society Charity," 256.
80. Wintch interviews; Lewis interview.
81. Wintch interviews.
82. Virginia Brand Smith, "Amy Brown Lyman," March 24, 1992, original in author's possession.
83. "Counselor Amy Brown Lyman," *Relief Society Magazine* 21 (May 1934): 287–89. See also Amy Brown Lyman, "Present Day Problems," draft of address presented at April Conference, 1934, ABLP.
84. Amy Brown Lyman, address in "Relief Society Conference," *Relief Society Magazine* 21 (November 1934): 683–86; "Job Insurance Advocated by Relief Society Leader," *Salt Lake Telegram*, October 5, 1934.
85. Amy Brown Lyman, "Official Instructions," *Relief Society Magazine* 22 (November 1935): 705–6. It is unclear whether her recommendations were followed.
86. Kennedy, *Freedom from Fear*, 265–73.
87. Louise Y. Robison, "Officers' Meeting," in "Relief Society Conference," *Relief Society Magazine* 22 (May 1935): 271–72.
88. Amy Brown Lyman, "Official Instructions," in "Relief Society Conference," *Relief Society Magazine* 22 (November 1935): 705.
89. Alexander, *Utah: The Right Place*, 330–31; Mangum and Blumell, *The Mormons' War on Poverty*, 124–25.
90. Mangum and Blumell, *The Mormons' War on Poverty*, 122.
91. D. Michael Quinn, *Elder Statesman: A Biography of J. Reuben Clark* (Salt Lake City: Signature Books, 2002), 384–87; Mangum and Blumell, *The Mormons' War on Poverty*, 119–26.

92. Mangum and Blumell, *The Mormons' War on Poverty*, 122, 125–26; Pohlman interviews; Wintch interviews.
93. Social scientist and later Provost of the University of California, Clark Kerr, who studied extensively self-help movements in that state, concluded even the best of them "has afforded no more than supplemental assistance for most participants . . . and a starvation living for those few families striving to subsist by its methods. . . ." Watkins, *The Hungry Years*, 99. While the LDS program had greater success among those it was able to support, Garth Mangum and Bruce Blumell in their study of LDS welfare efforts seem to share Kerr's conclusion. In their words: "It is unlikely that self-help ever will be able to support adequately any large number of unemployed persons." Mangum and Blumell, *The Mormons' War on Poverty*, 119–20. For ideology and Clark's views, see Pohlman interviews. For Lyman's views about the need to be properly informed regarding the work before passing judgement, see Wintch interviews.
94. Mangum and Blumell, *The Mormons' War on Poverty*, 143.
95. Pohlman interviews. Vera Pohlman, who was a close observer of developing welfare policy because of her job with the state welfare department and her ongoing links to Lyman, felt strongly that Clark's political views had a significant influence on the development of the Church Security Plan and on his attitude toward the Relief Society's role in welfare matters. For an extensive discussion of Clark's views regarding relief and church welfare, see Quinn, *Elder Statesman*, 377–424.
96. Mangum and Blumell, *The Mormons' War on Poverty*, 121–22; Engar interviews.
97. Engar interviews; Pohlman interviews; Wintch interviews.
98. Mangum and Blumell, *The Mormons' War on Poverty*, 133; Derr, "Changing Relief Society Charity," 258.
99. See Muncy, *Creating a Female Dominion in American Reform,* 124–157. Historian Judith Trolander saw a correlation between the lack of a feminist tradition among women and their loss of status and position in social work. If such a link did in fact exist, the lack of an ongoing activist tradition among Relief Society women under Louise Robison could have been a significant factor in the decline of their influence over charity work in the 1930s. Judith Ann Trolander, *Professionalism and Social Change: From the Settlement House Movement to Neighborhood Centers, 1886 to the Present* (New York: Columbia University Press, 1987), 52, 53.
100. Mangum and Blumell, *The Mormons' War on Poverty*, 127–31.
101. Mangum and Blumell, *The Mormons' War on Poverty*, 146; Quinn, *Elder Statesman*, 399. For a recent discussion about the relative contributions of the church plan in comparison to federal efforts, see Joseph F. Darowski, "The WPA Versus the Utah Church," in Brian Q. Cannon and Jessie L. Embry, eds., *Utah in the Twentieth Century* (Logan: Utah State University Press, 2009), 167–85.
102. Mangum and Blumell, *The Mormons' War on Poverty*, 137.
103. This was the assessment of both historians and well informed contemporaries. Mangum and Blumell, *The Mormons' War on Poverty*, 136; Leonard J. Arrington, Feramorz Y. Fox, and Dean L. May, *Building the City of God: Community and Cooperation Among the Mormons* (Salt Lake City: Deseret Book, 1976), 346; Vera W. Pohlman to Mrs. Burton W. [Gertrude] Musser, June 20, 1939, ABLP; Pohlman interviews.
104. As yet, there were no representatives from either the Relief Society or even the Presiding Bishopric's office involved. Mangum and Blumell, *The Mormons' War on Poverty*, 141–42; Derr, "Changing Relief Society Charity," 260.
105. Mangum and Blumell, *The Mormons' War on Poverty*, 144; Harold B. Lee, "Place of the Relief Society in the Church Security Plan," *Relief Society Magazine* 24 (March 1937): 140–43; "Message from the First Presidency," *Relief Society Magazine* 24 (November 1937): 737.

106. Louise Y. Robison, "The Church Security Program," *Relief Society Magazine* 23 (November 1936): 713; Mangum and Blummell, *The Mormons' War on Poverty*, 144.
107. Committee members noted that not one session of the printed program for the fall 1937 Relief Society conference was devoted to the topic. In response, during the conference Relief Society leaders read a message from the First Presidency calling upon the women of the organization to redouble their efforts to assist in the goal of obtaining self-sufficiency for members of the church. "Message from the First Presidency," *Relief Society Magazine* 24 (November 1937): 737; Mangum and Blummell, *The Mormons' War on Poverty*, 144; Derr, "Changing Relief Society Charity," 260.
108. Deutsch, "From Ballots to Breadlines," 462.
109. Apparently Richard first heard about his call through a published notice in the *Deseret News*. It is clear from Richard's reaction, however, that he had intuited something was coming: when he telephoned Amy to give her the news, he announced simply "the blow is struck." Parry Sorensen interview, 1992; Richard R. Lyman Journal, January 17, 1937, RRLP.
110. Engar interviews.

CHAPTER 7

1. Amy Brown Lyman, "Minutes of the Women's Division of the European Mission Presidents' Conference Held at Hotel des Champs-Elysees, Paris, France, May 26 to June 11 [1937]," 8 (cited hereafter as "Minutes of the Women's Division of the European Mission Presidents' Conference, Paris, 1937"), Amy Brown Lyman Papers, Relief Society, Church History Library, Church of Jesus Christ of Latter-day Saints, Salt Lake City, Utah (cited hereafter as ABLPRS), 8.
2. Amy Brown Lyman to "Dearest Lydia" [Lund], October 26, 1936, 2, Engar Family Papers (cited hereafter as EFP).
3. Of course, in later decades, the legions of young Mormon missionaries would be joined by smaller cadres of retired couples who, not burdened by the full responsibilities resting upon mission presidents like the Lymans, nevertheless willingly assumed (and assume) significant new responsibilities as a matter of course in their varied missionary labors.
4. Amy Brown Lyman, *In Retrospect: Autobiography of Amy Brown Lyman* (Salt Lake City: General Board of Relief Society, 1945), 124.
5. Relief Society General Board Minutes, August 26, 1936, Church History Library, Salt Lake City, Utah (cited hereafter as RSGBM).
6. See Thomas G. Alexander, *Mormonism in Transition: A History of the Latter-day Saints, 1890–1930* (Urbana: University of Illinois Press, 1986), 125–56.
7. Amy Brown Lyman to Dearest Rose [Hayes], Oct. 23, 1936, EFP; Richard complained in his journal about the fairness of the brief transition. Richard R. Lyman Journal, January 16, 1937, Richard R. Lyman Papers, L. Tom Perry Special Collections, Harold B. Lee Library, Brigham Young University (cited hereafter as RRLP). The missionary convinced to stay, after Richard shed "real tears" was mission secretary, an Elder Homer.
8. Lyman, *In Retrospect*, 124; Amy Kathryn Lyman Engar interviews, 1990–1994; Parry Sorensen interview, 1992; A. Z. Richards interview, 1992.
9. Engar interviews.
10. See, for example, "Mayfair Welcomes Apostle of Mormons," *Latter-day Saint Millennial Star* 98/51,(December 17, 1936): 807–13.
11. Amy Brown Lyman to "Dearest Rose [Hayes]," October 23, 1936, EFP; Amy Brown Lyman, "Report, International Council of Women Triennial Meeting, Dubrovnik, Yugoslavia, September 28, to October 9, 1936," 2, Amy Brown Lyman Papers, L. Tom Perry

Special Collections, Harold B. Lee Library, Brigham Young University, Provo, Utah (hereafter cited as ABLP).

12. Richard R. Lyman, "To the Folks at Home from the Lymans in London," December 10, 1936, 1, 2, EFP; Lyman, *In Retrospect*, 99, 100; Engar interviews.
13. Lyman, "Report: International Council of Women," 2, 3, ABLP; Richard R. Lyman, "To the Folks at Home," 1, 2, EFP; Amy Lyman Engar, "Amy Brown Lyman: Transcribed from a talk given at the University of Utah Institute 'Women of the Restoration,' February 26, 1987," 10, EFP; Engar interviews.
14. Amy Brown Lyman to Rose Brown Hayes, Oct 23, 1936, EFP.
15. Lyman, "Report: International Council of Women," 18, 27–31, ABLP.
16. Lyman, "Report: International Council of Women," 30, 31.
17. Lyman, "Report: International Council of Women," 12.
18. Lyman, "Report: International Council of Women," 17–19, 25; Gertrude Garff interview, 1992.
19. Amy Brown Lyman to Lydia Brown Lund, October 25, 1936, 2, EFP.
20. Lyman to Lund, October 25, 1936, EFP.
21. Amy Brown Lyman to Mrs. Ruth Haller Ottaway, National Council of Women, November 5, 1936, ABLP; Amy Brown Lyman, "Report: International Council of Women," 29–30, ABLP.
22. Amy Brown Lyman to "Dearest Lydia [Lund]," December 21, 1936, EFP; [Amy Brown Lyman to] "Ve," [Vervene Pingree], June 28, 1937, EFP; Lyman, *In Retrospect*, 124.
23. Lyman to Lydia [Lund], December 21, 1936, 1, 2.
24. At the beginning of Lyman's time in Europe, there were nine missions in Europe: these included the Netherlands Mission, the British Mission, the Swedish Mission, the French Mission, the Swiss-German Mission, the German-Austrian Mission, the Norwegian Mission, the Danish Mission, and the Czechoslovakian Mission. However, arrangements were already in the works to realign the German speaking missions into three, rather than two, missions. When this was completed by the second year of the Lymans' presidency, these were the Swiss-Austrian Mission, the West German Mission, and the East German Mission. Because of the distances involved, the Lymans supervised the Palestine-Syrian and the South African Missions largely via correspondence. Lyman, *In Retrospect*, 124.
25. Lyman, *In Retrospect*, 123; Engar, "Amy Brown Lyman," 18.
26. Sorensen interview; Garff interview. The term "mission mother" was and is commonly used to refer to the wife of LDS mission presidents. While certainly the women who preside over this work fulfill the role of mother even as their husbands fulfill the role as fathers to the missionaries, one longs for a better term, even, perhaps, the now archaic Mormon usage of "presidentess," as it would more accurately reflect the complementary relationship between the two.
27. A good example was found during the years of World War II when travel restrictions had prevented regular visits to the wards and stakes. When then counselor Belle S. Spafford and General Secretary-Treasurer Vera W. Pohlman toured a number of western state societies in 1944 to assess conditions as the war was beginning to move toward its conclusion they found serious breaches of standard practice. Pohlman interviews.
28. Amy Brown Lyman, "The Relief Society in the European Mission," *Relief Society Magazine* 24 (March 1937): 137–38; Annie Wells Cannon, "Amy Brown Lyman," *Relief Society Magazine* 27 (January 1940): 5.
29. See her "Minutes of the European Mission," ABLPRS.
30. "Report of Conference of the Presidents of the European Missions, Held in Berlin, Germany, June 1st to 15th (INCLUSIVE) 1936," ABLPRS, (cited hereafter as "Berlin Mission Presidents' Conference, 1936").

31. For the highpoint of Mormon missionary success in the 1800s, see William Mulder, *Homeward to Zion: The Mormon Migration from Scandinavia* (Minneapolis: University of Minnesota Press, 1957); and P. A. M. Taylor, *Expectations Westward: The Mormons and the Emigration of their British Converts in the Nineteenth Century* (Edinburgh: Oliver and Boyd, 1965).
32. Lyman, "The Relief Society in the European Mission," 137; Gregory A. Prince and Wm. Robert Wright, *David O. McKay and the Rise of Modern Mormonism* (Salt Lake City: University of Utah Press, 2005), 364.
33. Leonard J. Arrington and Davis Bitton, *The Mormon Experience: A History of the Latter-day Saints* (New York: Alfred A. Knopf, 1979), 139–40; "Berlin Mission Presidents' Conference, 1936."
34. "Berlin Mission Presidents' Conference, 1936," 9.
35. "Berlin Mission Presidents' Conference, 1936," 8.
36. "Berlin Mission Presidents' Conference, 1936," 6.
37. Sorensen interview. For sports as a missionary tool in the church, see Jessie L. Embry and John H. Brambaugh, "Preaching through Playing: Sports and Recreation in Missionary Work, 1911–64," *Journal of Mormon History* 35 (Fall 2009): 25–84.
38. "Berlin Mission Presidents' Conference, 1936," 22; Gustive O. Larson, "The Swedish Mission," in "Annual Meeting of Mission Presidents' and Their Wives of European Missions Beginning May 17, 1938, Copenhagen Denmark," 6, ABLPRS (cited hereafter as "Copenhagen Mission Presidents' Conference, 1938").
39. See especially comments by Alma L. Petersen, Roy A. Welker, Philemon M. Kelly, and Wallace F. Toronto, in "Berlin Mission Presidents' Conference, 1936," 8–17; "Copenhagen Mission Presidents' Conference, 1938," 8.
40. Richard had already visited a number of countries on the continent on mission business during a bitter-cold winter of 1937 and in the early spring, but this was Amy's first trip beyond the British Isles since her attendance at the meeting of the International Council of Women the previous year. On the hardship engendered by the weather Richard observed, "most of all the severity of the actual cold is something I have not had to endure since I herded sheep in snowy cold winter weather and lived in a sheep camp." Richard R. Lyman Journal, January 16, 1937, RRLP; Amy Brown Lyman to Rose [Hayes], Lydia [Lund], and John [Brown], May 15, 1937, EFP.
41. Aileen Hales Clyde, counselor in the Relief Society General Presidency in the 1990s, recalled that the letters home sent by her brother, who served as a missionary in the East German Mission during the years the Lymans were in Europe, were heavily censored. Aileen Hales Clyde interview, June 2014.
42. Amy Brown Lyman to Dearest Rose [Hayes], June 16, 1937; [Amy Brown Lyman] to Ve.
43. Mark B. Garff Journal, "Sat. May 28, 1938, Copenhagen," CHL.
44. Amy Brown Lyman to Dearest Rose [Hayes], July 7, 1937, EFP. Apparently this was only a phase as subsequent letters indicate no further concerns.
45. Missionary Parry Sorensen, who was especially close to the Lymans recalled that sometimes Richard's youthful experiences as a sheepherder would result in brief eruptions of slightly salty language. Sorensen remembered one occasion when Richard had almost been left alone on a train traveling an unfamiliar route by a careless young missionary, leading Lyman to exclaim "He ought to have his ass kicked," which Richard followed quickly with "I shouldn't be saying that." Sorensen also recalled that Lyman was quite broad-minded about appropriate behavior for missionaries. Once when Sorensen was captain of a very good missionary basketball team (created to attract new members and raise the profile of the church) he approached Lyman because the missionary team had won a national tournament and so earned the right to compete with the English team in another game. The problem revolved around the fact that the game was scheduled for

Sunday. Richard's reply was "I didn't ever hear you say that." In this case, his lenient views were seconded by Hugh B. Brown, president of the British mission. Sorensen interview.

46. Lyman, "Minutes of the Women's Division of the European Mission Presidents' Conference, Paris, 1937," 8.
47. I am indebted to Kathryn H. Shirts for bringing this information to my attention. Kathryn H. Shirts, "Priesthood and Womanhood: Complementary Gender Roles in the Writings of Leah Dunford Widtsoe," paper presented at the annual meeting of the Mormon History Association, San Antonio Texas, June 6, 2014, and email, Kathryn H. Shirts to Dave Hall, June 15, 2014. See also Letter of Martha Gaeth to Sister Widtsoe, 24 October 1935, 1–2, Utah State Historical Society, Widtsoe Family Collection, reference courtesy of Kathryn H. Shirts.
48. Amy Brown Lyman to General Board Relief Society, "About June or July," [1938], 11, EFP.
49. Lyman, "Minutes of the Women's Division of the European Mission Presidents' Conference, Paris, 1937," 7a.
50. "The Devil's Disciple by George Bernard Shaw," in "Guide Lessons for February: Literature," *Relief Society Magazine* 15 (December 1928): 683–86; "The Doll's House," in "Guide Lessons for June: Literature," *Relief Society Magazine* 16 (April 1929): 219–25; Lyman to General Board, 11, 12; Lyman, "Minutes of the Women's Division of the European Mission Presidents' Conference, Paris," 6a, 7a.
51. Lyman, "Minutes of the Women's Division of the European Mission Presidents' Conference, Paris, 1937," 3, 5a; "Copenhagen Mission Presidents' Conference, 1938," 21.
52. See Leah D. Widtsoe, Relief Society President European Mission, address in "Relief Society Conference," *Relief Society Magazine* 18, (June 1931): 340–43. Widtsoe stated that only recently, and in part because of the restrictive immigration laws of the 1920s, had European saints given up hope on migrating to Zion.
53. Lyman to General Board, 11, 12.
54. Lyman to General Board, 11, 12.
55. Lyman provided the women leaders in attendance at the conference with intensive training in the fundamentals of social work, using as her text Karl de Schweinitz's *The Art of Helping People Out of Trouble*, by then rather dated in social work circles, but it used a basic and common-sense approach that stressed the need to render aid without fostering dependency. Lyman to General Board, 2, 6; Lyman, "Minutes of the Women's Division of the European Mission Presidents' Conference, Paris," 9.
56. In Germany under the Nazis this made the charity funds collected by local sisters unneeded and unusable. Lyman to General Board, 2, 6.
57. "Health," ABLPRS.
58. Lyman to General Board, 12.
59. Lyman to General Board, 12.
60. "Copenhagen Mission Presidents' Conference, 1938," 9.
61. "Copenhagen Mission Presidents' Conference, 1938," 1–4.
62. Regarding the adaption of lessons, Lyman was typically ahead of her time, sensing the need in an international church to adapt to cultural and historical differences when formulating educational materials. "Social Service Institutes—European Mission," i–xiii, ABLP. Regarding the National Councils in Europe, see Garff.
63. "Berlin Mission Presidents' Conference, 1936," 9; Lyman to General Board Relief Society, About June or July [1938], 6.
64. "Minutes of the Women's Division of the European Mission Presidents' Conference, Paris, 1937," 17.
65. "Minutes of the Women's Division of the European Mission Presidents' Conference, Paris, 1937"; Annual Meeting of the Mission Presidents and Their Wives of European Mission, Paris," 20; Lyman to General Board Relief Society, June or July [1938], 9.

66. "Copenhagen Mission Presidents' Conference, 1938," 4.
67. Lyman to General Board Relief Society, "June or July" [1938], 12, 13.
68. Amy Brown Lyman to Dearest Rose [Hayes], July 7, 1937, EFP.
69. Amy Brown Lyman, *A Lighter of Lamps: The Life Story of Alice Louise Reynolds* (Provo, UT: Deseret New Press, 1947), 38, 72.
70. In addition to Grant and the Clarks, Grant's personal secretary, Joseph Anderson was a member of their party, as was General Young Women's Mutual Improvement Association president Ruth May Fox, with counselors Clarissa Beesely and Lucy Grant Cannon. In addition outgoing British Mission president Joseph J. Cannon and family, and incoming president Hugh B. Brown were in attendance, as was, among others, Sunday School General President George D. Pyper. Richard R. Lyman Journal, July 30–August 2, 1937, RRLP; Elder Parry D. Sorensen, "Centennial Memories," *Millennial Star* (August 19, 1937): 533–42; Lyman, *In Retrospect*, 128.
71. Lyman, *In Retrospect*, 126, 129.
72. Garff interview.
73. Lyman, *In Retrospect*, 130–31; Lyman to General Board, 7. Talmage had died in 1933.
74. Lyman to General Board, 10; Lyman, *In Retrospect*, 139.
75. Lyman, *In Retrospect*, 131; "Address before the Carl Schurz Foundation, April 12, 1938, 'Social Work in America,'" ABLP. Carl Shurz was a prominent German émigré to the United States who served as Civil War general, statesman, scholar, and reformer. The foundation named in his honor was devised by German scholars in 1930 for, among other purposes, promoting greater understanding between Shurz's homeland and his adopted country.
76. Lyman to General Board Relief Society, "June or July" [1938], 6, 7.
77. Lyman, *In Retrospect*, 138.
78. Lyman, *In Retrospect*, 138–39.
79. Lyman to General Board Relief Society, June or July [1938], 4, 5, 11.
80. Amy Brown Lyman, "International Council of Women," *Relief Society Magazine* 25 (September 1938): 578; Lyman, *In Retrospect*, 103.
81. Sorensen interview. Their unsettled personal affairs included a lawsuit filed against Richard as a result of a traffic accident that occurred when he was showing a woman how to drive during a church business trip. One of his passengers at the time was injured. Leona Fetzer Wintch interviews, 1990–1994.
82. Relief Society General Board Minutes, October 26, 1938, February 8, 1939, and February 13, 1939. Lyman's close associate Vera W. Pohlman believed that Lyman felt underutilized during this period. Pohlman interviews.
83. Pohlman interviews; Vera W. Pohlman to Mrs. Burton W. Musser, June 20, 1939, ABLP.
84. The $304 billion spent on World War II represented approximately twenty times the spending of the New Deal years. David M. Kennedy, *Freedom from Fear: The American People in Depression and War, 1929–1945* (New York: Oxford University Press, 1999), 625.
85. Amy Brown Lyman, "A Social Worker in Europe—Read before Salt Lake Council of Social Agencies, 1938," ABLP.
86. Pohlman interviews.

CHAPTER 8

1. Vera White Pohlman, "Annual Report—1940," *Relief Society Magazine* 28 (June 1941): 427.
2. Amy Brown Lyman, "Some Challenges to Women," Address, Utah Agricultural College, July 1940, 2, Amy Brown Lyman Papers, L. Tom Perry Special Collections, Harold B. Lee Library, Brigham Young University (cited hereafter as ABLP).

3. "New Relief Society Heads to Take Office January 1," *Deseret News*, December 14, 1939; Vera White Pohlman interviews, 1990–1994; Leona Fetzer Wintch interviews, 1990–1994.
4. Vera White Pohlman, "Annual Report—1940," *Relief Society Magazine* 28 (June 1941): 301–4; Thomas G. Alexander, *Mormonism in Transition: A History of the Latter-day Saints, 1890–1930* (Urbana: University of Illinois Press, 1986), 239–57.
5. Thomas G. Alexander and James B. Allen, *Mormons and Gentiles: A History of Salt Lake City* (Boulder: Pruett Publishing, 1984), 231–33; Thomas G. Alexander, *Utah: The Right Place* (Salt Lake City: Gibbs Smith, 1996), 340–46.
6. The only concession to her health seems to have been her decision to move her bedroom downstairs, but this was not much of a concession as her bedroom was more of a home office. Though her sleep habits had long been irregular, she used this to her advantage, keeping a hospital tray—secured from her physician brother—at her bedside along with a notebook. She told associates that she did most of her work in the middle of the night. Wintch interviews; Pohlman interviews; Amy Kathryn Lyman Engar interviews, 1990–1994.
7. As Vera Pohlman recalled, Lyman always seemed as if she had somewhere important to go and moved rapidly to get there. Pohlman interviews; Engar interviews.
8. Engar interviews.
9. Leona Wintch, herself a social worker, noted the commonly held belief at the time about the lack of fashion sense among social workers. Wintch interviews; Pohlman interviews.
10. Relief Society General Board Minutes (cited hereafter as RSGBM), December 13, 1939, Church of Jesus Christ of Latter-day Saints, Church History Library, Salt Lake City, Utah.
11. Annie Wells Cannon Diary, December 28, 1939, Annie Wells Cannon Collection, L. Tom Perry Special Collections and Manuscripts, Harold B. Lee Library, Brigham Young University.
12. Howells, like Lyman, also had a demonstrated devotion to public health and child welfare work, having been state chairman of Utah's May Day Child Health Day in 1939, and an active member of the board of the Utah Tuberculosis Association. Sorensen was also a longtime member of the board who had served a mission and been a teacher until her marriage. Amy Brown Lyman, "Marcia Knowlton Howells," *Relief Society Magazine* 32 (1945): 273–74; Anna Boss Hart, "Donna Durrant Sorensen," *Relief Society Magazine* 27 (January 1940): 11–13. Sorensen requested a release in 1942 to care for her young family. Pohlman interviews.
13. "Achsa Eggertsen Paxman," *Relief Society Magazine* 27 (March 1940): 148–49.
14. Pohlman interviews; Gertrude Ryberg Garff interview, 1990; Wintch interviews; "The New General Board," *Relief Society Magazine* 27 (March 1940): 147–58; "Relief Society Has New General Board," *Deseret News*, January 12, 1940; Marianne Clark Sharp interview, 1977, interviewed by Jessie L. Embry, Church of Jesus Christ of Latter-day Saints, Church History Library (cited hereafter as CHL).
15. Pohlman interviews.
16. RSGBM, January 17, 1940; Wintch interviews; Pohlman interviews.
17. Wintch interviews.
18. Donna D. Sorensen, "Relief Society Spiritually Strong," *Relief Society Magazine* 27 (March 1940): 173.
19. Mary Grant Judd, "My Relief Society Tapestry," *Relief Society Magazine* 27 (March 1940): 167; Amy Brown Lyman, "Relief Society as a Community Builder," *Relief Society Magazine* 27 (March 1940): 181.
20. Jill Mulvay Derr, Janath Russell Cannon, and Maureen Ursenbach Beecher, *Women of Covenant: The Story of Relief Society* (Salt Lake City: Deseret Book, 1992), 297–98.

21. Divorce rates actually went down during the Depression, due to cost, but simple desertions seemed to have increased dramatically. David M. Kennedy, *Freedom from Fear: The American People in Depression and War, 1929–1945* (New York: Oxford University Press, 1999), 165–66; Sarah Jane Deutsch, "From Ballots to Breadlines," in Nancy F. Cott, ed., *No Small Courage: A History of Women in the United States* (New York: Oxford, 2000), 452–53; Derr, Cannon, and Beecher, *Women of Covenant*, 282–83.
22. J. Reuben Clark, "Memorandum of Suggestions," as quoted in Derr, Cannon, and Beecher, *Women of Covenant*, 297–98; J. Reuben Clark, "Our Homes," *Relief Society Magazine* 27 (December 1940): 802.
23. RSGBM, April 10, 1940.
24. For the shift toward more conservative attitudes in regard to women in the 1930s and 1940s that might have influenced Clark, see Susan Ware, *Still Missing: Amelia Earhart and the Search for Modern Feminism* (New York: W. W. Norton and Company, 1993); Alice Kessler-Harris, "Gender Ideology in Historical Reconstruction: A Case Study from the 1930s," *Gender and History* 1 (Spring 1989): 31–49; and Margaret Hobbs, "Rethinking Antifeminism in the 1930s: Gender Crisis or Workplace Justice? A Response to Alice Kessler-Harris," *Gender and History* 5 (Spring 1993): 4–15.
25. D. Michael Quinn, *Elder Statesman: A Biography of J. Reuben Clark* (Salt Lake City: Signature, 2002), 11, 18; J. Reuben Clark, Jr., "Our Homes," *Relief Society Magazine* 27 (December 1940): 802, 810; J. Reuben Clark, Jr., "The Prophet's Sailing Orders to Relief Society," *Relief Society Magazine* 36 (December 1949): 797–98.
26. "Marianne Clark Sharp," *Relief Society Magazine* 27 (December 1940): 152; Pohlman interviews, Wintch interviews.
27. Amy Lyman Engar, "Amy Brown Lyman: Transcribed from a talk given at the University of Utah Institute 'Women of the Restoration' February 26, 1987," Engar Family Papers.
28. Quinn, *Elder Statesman*, 49–54.
29. Quinn, *Elder Statesman*, 50.
30. Quinn, *Elder Statesman*, 51.
31. For examples of a consensus model in church decision making, see Edwin B. Firmage, ed., *An Abundant Life: The Memoirs of Hugh B. Brown*, (Salt Lake City: Signature Books, 1988), 127; Alexander, *Mormonism in Transition*, 97.
32. Board member Leona Fetzer Wintch and Vera White Pohlman, Lyman's secretary-treasurer, both recalled Lyman's willingness to surround herself with strong leaders whom she encouraged to speak their minds. Wintch interviews; Pohlman interviews. Evelyn Hodges Lewis, who worked as a social worker for Lyman recalled that Amy was a strong administrator who ran a tight ship, but while she had decided opinions, was willing to listen to her workers and treated them with respect and concern. Evelyn Hodges Lewis, interview, 1992.
33. Lyman and President Grant's wife, Augusta Winters Grant, belonged to some of the same women's clubs as well, and for years the Lymans and Grants frequently socialized. Engar interviews; Pohlman interviews; "Richard Roswell Lyman," in Andrew Jensen, *Latter-Day Saint Biographical Encyclopedia: A Compilation of Biographical Sketches of Prominent Men and Women in the Church of Jesus Christ of Latter-day Saints*, 4. vols.,(Salt Lake City: Andrew Jenson History Company, 1901–1936), 3:756.
34. Engar interviews.
35. By 1936, according to a letter from Clark's wife, Albert Bowen reported that some Utah Mormons disagreed with Clark's political associations and further expressed the view that Clark "was nothing but a Dictator." Lute [Luacine Savage Clark] to JRC [J. Reuben Clark], August 20, 1936, J. Reuben Clark Papers, as quoted in Quinn, *Elder Statesman*, 80. Typically given to hyperbole, Lyman's husband Richard captured these concerns

when sometime in the late thirties or early forties he expressed the view, "We're living under a dictatorship here." Parry Sorensen, interview, 1992, 8.

36. Quinn, *Elder Statesman*, 51, 93–96.
37. Quinn, *Elder Statesman*, 92.
38. Wintch interviews; Pohlman interviews. For the relationship between Lyman and Clark and its consequences for the women of the Relief Society, see Dave Hall, "A Crossroads for Mormon Women: Amy Brown Lyman, J. Reuben Clark, and the Decline of Organized Women's Activism in the Relief Society," *Journal of Mormon History* 36 (Spring 2010), 205–49.
39. For Lyman's willingness, decades earlier, during the 1910s to press an issue when she thought it in the best interest of the Relief Society, see Janath Russell Cannon and Jill Mulvay Derr, "Resolving Differences/Achieving Unity: Lessons from the History of Relief Society," in Mary E. Stovall and Carol Cornwall Madsen, eds., *As Women of Faith: Talks Selected from the BYU Women's Conferences* (Salt Lake City: Deseret Book Co., 1989), 128–31.
40. Amy Brown Lyman, *In Retrospect: Autobiography of Amy Brown Lyman* (Salt Lake City: General Board of Relief Society), 5; Wintch interviews.
41. Quinn does an excellent job capturing the complexity and nuances of Clark's thinking and behavior in this regard. See, for example, Quinn, *Elder Statesman*, 50–54.
42. His willingness to make adjustments in the timing of the Welfare Plan is one example. Mangum and Blumell, *The Mormons' War on Poverty*, 121–24.
43. Engar interviews; Wintch interviews. See also J. Reuben Clark, Jr., "Wist Ye Not That I Must Be about My Father's Business," a series on the Bible that appeared serially in the *Relief Society Magazine* in 1943 and 1944.
44. LeGrand Richards, "The Place of the Relief Society in the Welfare Program," *Relief Society Magazine* 27 (May 1940): 309–12; Pohlman interviews; Vera White Pohlman, "Public Welfare Provisions," *Relief Society Magazine* 27 (November 1940: 767–75; and Vera White Pohlman, "Child-Welfare Provisions of the Social Security Act," *Relief Society Magazine* 28 (March 1941): 183–95. The need for public relief programs was something that even Clark himself was admitting by this point, for services to the larger community if not the church itself. Stringham A. Stevens, "Church Welfare," *Relief Society Magazine* 28 (June 1941): 411–15; Bishop Joseph L. Wirthlin, "Relief Society—An Aid to the Bishops," *Relief Society Magazine* 28 (June 1941): 415–20.
45. Vera White Pohlman, "Summary of President's Report," *Relief Society Magazine* 27 (May 1940): 291–301; Amy Brown Lyman, "President's Report and Official Instructions," *Relief Society Magazine* 27 (November 1940): 754–60.
46. At the time of Lyman's release, a letter was sent to her and her board expressing appreciation for their efforts and singling out in particular their work on behalf of the Welfare Plan. The letter said in part: "You have been of greatest support to the Priesthood in helping them to carry on their work. Particularly you have whole-heartedly cooperated with the Priesthood in the General Welfare Plan and with a desire to carry out that plan effectively. The successful operation of that Plan is, in a large part, the result of your cooperation." The First Presidency to President Amy Brown Lyman and Officers and Members of the National Women's Relief Society General Board, April 4, 1945. Copy in author's possession.
47. Lyman, *In Retrospect*, 148–149; Vera White Pohlman, "Summary of President's Report and Official Instructions," *Relief Society Magazine* 27 (May 1940): 294–95.
48. Derr, Cannon, and Beecher, *Women of Covenant*, 282; Clark Office Diary, June 10, 1941, J. Reuben Clark Papers, L. Tom Perry Special Collections, Harold B. Lee Library, Brigham Young University (cited hereafter as JRCP); Wintch interviews.

49. See, for example, Amy Brown Lyman, "Present Day Problems," draft of address for April 1934 Relief Society Conference, ABLP; "Counselor Amy Brown Lyman," in Julia A. F. Lund, "The Relief Society Conference," *Relief Society Magazine* 21 (May 1934): 286–89.
50. Amy Brown Lyman, "Some Challenges to Women," address delivered at Utah State Agricultural College, July, 1940, ABLP.
51. While church correlation (the effort to combine and simplify church programs and activities) is generally associated with the period of the 1960s and especially with Harold B. Lee, Clark was the father of the effort and his proposals for church magazines in 1940 represent an example of his ongoing desire to simplify and economize in church programs. Derr, Cannon, and Beecher, *Women of Covenant*, 297–99, 330–36.
52. Patricia Ann Mann, "A History of the Relief Society Magazine, 1914–1970," (Master's thesis, Brigham Young University, 1971), 116, 127–31.
53. Given the lay nature of church leadership and the greater mobility of members, responsibilities were reshuffled fairly regularly in ward and stake organizations. Within a year first drafts of the handbook were being circulated by board members to the wards and stakes. Wintch interviews; Pohlman interviews.
54. Vera W. Pohlman, "Public Welfare Provisions," *Relief Society Magazine* 27 (November 1940): 767–75; LeGrand Richards, "The Place of the Relief Society in the Welfare Program," *Relief Society Magazine* 27 (May 1940): 309–12; Stringham A. Stevens, "Church Welfare," *Relief Society Magazine* 28 (June 1941): 411–15; Bishop Joseph L. Wirthlin, "Relief Society—An Aid to the Bishops," *Relief Society Magazine* 28 (June 1941): 415–20.
55. Vera White Pohlman, "Annual Report—1940," *Relief Society Magazine* 28 (June 1941): 426–31; Lottie Fullmer, "A Relief Society Project in Pioneer Stake," *Relief Society Magazine* 27 (May 1940): 313–14; Alverda Partridge, "A Relief Society Health Project," *Relief Society Magazine* 28 (June 1941): 422–23; Eva G. Gillespie, "Cooperation with Community Agencies in Health Work," *Relief Society Magazine* 28 (June 1941): 423–25.
56. Amy Brown Lyman, "President's Report and Official Instructions," *Relief Society Magazine* 28 (May 1941): 294.
57. Jessie L. Embry, "Grain Storage: The Balance of Power between Priesthood Authority and Relief Society Autonomy," *Dialogue: A Journal of Mormon Thought* 15 (Winter 1982): 59–66.
58. Lyman, *In Retrospect*, 149–154; Amy Brown Lyman, "Grain Elevator Dedication," ABLP; Donna D. Sorensen, "Church Grain Elevator Dedication," *Relief Society Magazine* 27 (October 1940): 653–57; Amy Brown Lyman, "President's Report and Official Instructions," *Relief Society Magazine* 27 (November 1940): 755–56.
59. One of the first things Lyman did after assuming the presidency was to appoint a committee consisting of board members Mary Grant Judd, Anna B. Hart, Edith Smith Elliot, and Rae B. Barker, assisted by General Secretary Vera Pohlman, to plan a variety of celebratory activities. Eventually, all board members received assignments in relation to the centennial. Belle Spafford, "Relief Society Centennial Bell Tower," *Relief Society Magazine* 54 (January 1967): 14; Pohlman interviews; *A Centenary of Relief Society* (Salt Lake City: General Board of Relief Society, 1942), 88.
60. Vera White Pohlman, "General Conference of Relief Society," *Relief Society Magazine* 28 (November 1941): 752–54; Pohlman interviews.
61. The difference between Lyman's approach to achieving membership growth and Robison's is illustrative of other differences between the two leaders. Robison had advocated a blanket growth in members of one third to raise the membership of the organization from seventy thousand to one hundred thousand. Lyman and Pohlman realized this was impractical—in some areas, nearly all of the LDS women were already enrolled in

the organization, while in others, as few as one in four were members. Statistics for each stake were thus broken down and more realistic goals were thus prescribed based on this more accurate assessment of the challenge. Pohlman then created colorful pictographs that were mounted on the stage of the Tabernacle during conference to impress upon the minds of the women how far they had to go. Pohlman interviews.

62. Mary G. Judd, "Our Permanent Centennial Memorial," *Relief Society Magazine* 28 (November 1941): 769; Pohlman interviews; Telephone conversation with Leona Fetzer Wintch, August 19, 1999; Telephone conversation with Gertrude Garff, August 19, 1999.
63. The evils of warfare are a thread that appeared frequently in Lyman's public addresses throughout the interwar period. See, for example, "Counselor Amy Brown Lyman," summary of conference address in *Relief Society Magazine* 21 (May 1934): 288. This was the address that Lyman had entitled "Present Day Problems," ABLP.
64. Lyman, "President's Report and Official Instructions," *Relief Society Magazine* 28 (May 1941): 298; "Survey of Registered and Practical Nurses," in "Notes to the Field," *Relief Society Magazine* 29 (February 1942): 113–14.
65. Derr, Cannon, and Beecher, *Women of Covenant*, 281–82; Pohlman interviews. See account of conference address by David O. McKay, second counselor in the First Presidency, at the April 1943 General Conference of the church, in which he stresses the importance of family stability. Bryant S. Hinckley, "113th Annual Conference," *Relief Society Magazine* 30 (May 1943): 304. For indications that such concerns were shared in the Relief Society, see also Amy Brown Lyman, "Women and the Home Today," *Relief Society Magazine* 30 (April 1943): 236–39, 297; Ramona W. Cannon, "Woman's Sphere," *Relief Society Magazine* 30 (May 1943): 323. Cannon asserts (inaccurately) that before Pearl Harbor, one in one hundred wage earners in the United States were women, and that after, one in ten were. The statement is important in reflecting popular perception in the Mormon community about the disruptive effects of the war on family life.
66. Derr, Cannon, and Beecher, *Women of Covenant*, 283–88; Pohlman interviews; Wintch interviews; "Notes to the Field," *Relief Society Magazine* 29 (February 1942): 111–14. Tree plantings went on as scheduled on March 17, and ward celebrations took place throughout the year. The pageant, with its program of interpretive dance, the special choir of Singing Mothers from throughout the church, as well as all the other planned activities were called off. An elaborate cyclorama curtain purchased for the Tabernacle was placed in storage, while dozens of yards of blue and gold fabric purchased for decorative banners was divided up and sold to board members for quilts. Pohlman interviews; Engar interviews.
67. Individual components, when completed, were placed in storage on church property to await the cessation of hostilities. Pohlman interviews.
68. Vera White Pohman, "Relief Society Celebrates Its Centennial," *Relief Society Magazine* 29 (April 1942): 225–44; and a number of her "Notes from the Field," columns for 1942 and 1943, for example, *Relief Society Magazine* 29 (June 1942): 420–27; *Relief Society Magazine* 29 (October 1942): 715–23; *Relief Society Magazine* 30 (January 1943): 48–56.
69. Wintch interviews.
70. Pohlman interviews; Wintch interviews.
71. "Notes to the Field," *Relief Society Magazine* 30 (January 1943): 36–38; Vera White Pohlman, "Annual Report—1942," *Relief Society Magazine* 30 (June–July 1943): 413–28.
72. Vera White Pohlman, "Annual Report—1943," *Relief Society Magazine* 31 (July 1944): 369–72.
73. "Notes to the Field: Petitions on Informative Labeling," *Relief Society Magazine* 30 (January 1943): 38.
74. "Lesson Department: Work and Business, Better Buymanship, Lesson 1: The Consumer Movement," *Relief Society Magazine* 28 (July 1941): 493–95.

75. "Personal Letters Protest Picturization of Smoking and Drinking," *Relief Society Magazine* 30 (June–July 1943): 398; H. L. Marshall, M.D., "Periodic Medical Examinations of Apparently Healthy Persons," *Relief Society Magazine* 30 (October 1943): 594–95, 614.
76. Edna K. Ward, "Adequate Daily Diet and Wartime Menus," *Relief Society Magazine* 30 (April 1943): 286–91, 297.
77. The program was intended by national leaders not only to aid the war effort, but as important, to generate a sense of patriotism and common cause among American women. "Notes to the Field: Pamphlet Available, How to Win on the Home Front," *Relief Society Magazine* 30 (May 1943): 329; "Notes to the Field: Salvage Program," *Relief Society Magazine* 30 (May 1943): 328; "Fat Salvage Program," *Relief Society Magazine* 30 (June–July 1943): 395.
78. "Care of Children in Wartime," *Relief Society Magazine* 30 (May 1943): 332–33; Amy Brown Lyman, "Women and the Home Today," *Relief Society Magazine* 30 (April 1943): 236–39, 297. The latter was a reprint of a speech delivered over the radio on March 14, 1943.
79. Nellie O. Parker, "Home Entertainment," *Relief Society Magazine* 30 (April 1943): 277–80.
80. Elder Milton Bennion, "The Latter-day Saint Family: Its Ideals and Responsibilities," *Relief Society Magazine* 30 (August 1943): 461–62; Dr. Edgar B. Brossar, "Keep Close to the Church," *Relief Society Magazine* 30 (April 1943): 240–44; Elder Hugh B. Brown, Coordinator of L.D.S. Service Men, "To the Parents of Service Men," *Relief Society Magazine* 30 (September 1943): 525–28.
81. Mark K. Allen, "The Abuse of Hate in Wartime," *Relief Society Magazine* 30 (March 1943): 191–194; "Notes to the Field: Visiting Teaching," *Relief Society Magazine* 30 (May 1943): 327–28.
82. Vera White Pohlman, "Notes from the Field," *Relief Society Magazine* 32 (February 1945): 106–7. In Northern California, women whose families were involved in the construction of Shasta Dam held their meetings on Sundays, immediately after Sunday School. Vera White Pohlman, "Notes from the Field," *Relief Society Magazine,* 32 (March 1945): 185–86.
83. Melvin Lyman interview, 1992; Keith Hayes interview, 1991; Richard R. Lyman Journal, February 7, 1937, Richard R. Lyman Papers, L. Tom Perry Special Collections, Harold B. Lee Library, Brigham Young University (cited hereafter as RRLP).
84. Richard R. Lyman Journal, June 16, 1935, RRLP.
85. Pohlman interviews; Mark Knight Allen interviews, 1991, 1994.
86. Hayes interview; Mary Lyman Henrie interview, 1992; Sorensen interview; A. Z. Richards interview, 1992. For a comprehensive treatment of the event, see Gary James Bergera, "Transgression in the Latter-day Saint Community: The Cases of Albert Carrington, Richard R. Lyman, and Joseph F. Smith. Part 2: Richard R. Lyman," *Journal of Mormon History* 37 (Fall 2011): 173–207.
87. Pohlman interviews; Wintch interviews; Allen inteviews; Susan Elizabeth Swensen Driggs interviews, 1990, 1994; Henrie interview.
88. A wide variety of rumors arose, most involving variants of the speculation that Richard had been engaged in a liaison with a much younger women. Historian Dale Morgan, for example, recorded that it resulted in a variety of ribald jokes based on the premise that Richard's liaison was with a woman much younger than himself. Dale Morgan to Dean Brimhall, Morgan Papers, Special Collections, Marriott Library, University of Utah. I am indebted to Vivian Talbott for bringing this to my attention.
89. Harold B. Lee was a prominent protégé of Clark who had played an important part in the development of the Welfare Plan. Joseph Fielding Smith was the son of church president Joseph F. Smith who led the church a quarter-century before when Lyman began

her activities relating to social work. For details of Richard's case, I am indebted to John Sillito, Gary Bergera, and Ken Godfrey, who generously shared their research with me. Richard R. Lyman to Melvin A. Lyman, February 16, 1963, copy in author's possession obtained from Melvin Lyman; Melvin Lyman interview.

90. Bergera, "Transgression in the Latter-day Saint Community," 185.
91. Pohlman interviews.
92. Richard R. Lyman Diaries, February 10, 12, 16, 17, 1922, RRLP; Richard R. Lyman to Melvyn A. Lyman, February 16, 1963.
93. Bergera, "Transgression in the Latter-day Saint Community," 196–97; Richard R. Lyman to Melvyn A. Lyman. For the concept of potential plural marriages, see B. Carmon Hardy, *Solemn Covenant: The Mormon Polygamous Passage* (Urbana: University of Illinois Press, 1992), 326.
94. Engar interviews.
95. Richard's excommunication terminated the couple's temple union that, according to Mormon belief, left her without a companion in the eternities, though repentance might lead to a restoration of his blessings—including their marriage. For an insightful discussion about how Lyman's circumstances reveal changing Mormon views about remaining in a marriage relationship after it has been violated by adultery, see Bergera, "Transgression in the Latter-day Saint Community," 194.
96. Belle S. Spafford Oral History, quoted in Bergera, "Transgression in the Latter-day Saint Community," 194; Emmeline Wirthlin Oral History, 1992; David O. McKay Diary, January 18, 1944, quoted in Bergera, "Transgression in the Latter-day Saint Community," 194.
97. Pohlman intervews; Driggs interviews; Wintch interviews. Historian and researcher Loretta L. Hefner recalled a conversation she had with Hermana Lyon, wife of T. Edgar Lyon, who had presided over the Netherlands mission during the time of Lyman's mission, in which Lyon recalled a rare incident in which Lyman questioned her own earlier decisions. It came at the time that Lyon had been called to the Relief Society general board. Lyman commented, "You have small children. If I had it to do over again, I wouldn't." Hefner's statement made during oral history interview with Leona Fetzer Wintch, April 23, 1979. Interview transcript, 12, CHL.
98. Wirthlin interview; Engar interviews. Leona Fetzer Wintch invited Lyman to spend some time at her home in Manti during this period, but Lyman declined, believing it best to stay in Salt Lake and begin facing the consequences of the situation. Wintch interviews.
99. Friends and family members shared this assessment of Lyman's reaction to Richard's infidelity. Pohlman interviews; Wintch interviews; Engar interviews; Driggs intervews; Wirthlin interview.
100. Engar interviews. Engar, for her part, was very careful not to violate the trust that she felt her grandmother had required of her.
101. Jim and Harriett Bean interview, 1992. As an excommunicant, Richard could attend such meetings as Sunday School and Sacrament meeting where the general public was welcome, though he was forbidden to participate in discussion or offer prayers, and he was barred from attending other gatherings such as local priesthood meetings. He was rebaptized October 27, 1954. His full temple blessings were not restored until 1970, some seven years after his death, when Joseph Fielding Smith became church president. Smith sent word to the family of the move. Engar interviews.
102. Engar interviews.
103. Pohlman interviews; Wintch interviews.
104. Vera White Pohlman, "Annual Report—1944," *Relief Society Magazine* 32 (August 1945): 479.

105. Winnifred M. Tibbs, "Do Not Despair," *Relief Society Magazine* 31 (January 1944): 45; "The Soldier and His Health Overseas," *Relief Society Magazine* 31 (March 1944): 188–92; Alice Merrill Horne, "Mormon Pioneer Culture," *Relief Society Magazine* 31 (August 1944): 419–22; Alice Merrill Horne, "A Few of Our Gifted Utah Women Artists," *Relief Society Magazine* 31 (December 1944): 678–83. Claire P. Dorius, "Income Management in Wartime," *Relief Society Magazine* 31 (August 1944): 464–65; Editorial, M.C.S. [Marianne Clark Sharp], "Home After the War," *Relief Society Magazine* 31 (October 1944): 570–71; "Rehabilitation of Disabled Soldiers and Sailors," *Relief Society Magazine* 32 (March 1945): 176–79; Vera White Pohlman, "The Magazine Honor Role for 1945," *Relief Society Magazine* 32 (May 1945): 292; Pohlman, "Annual Report—1944," 487.
106. Amy Brown Lyman, "Relief Society in Action Today," *Relief Society Magazine* 31 (March 1944): 137–39; Marguerite Burnhope Harris, "Our Relief Society President," *Relief Society Magazine* 31 (March 1944): 139; M.C.S. [Marianne Clark Sharp], Editorial, "Gratitude to Our Leaders," *Relief Society Magazine* 31 (March 1944): 168–69.
107. Pohlman interviews; Wintch interviews.
108. "Notes to the Field: Modification in Visiting Teachers' Program," *Relief Society Magazine* 31 (September 1944): 511–12; Derr, Cannon, and Beecher, *Women of Covenant*, 288.
109. Pohlman interviews; Vera White Pohlman, "Annual Report—1944," *Relief Society Magazine* 32 (August 1945): 478–79.
110. Pohlman interviews; Wintch interviews.
111. Richard Lyman mentioned to associates that Clark had assumed a usually strong hand over church affairs, and other church members apparently agreed. Sorenson interview; Allen interviews; Quinn, *Elder Statesman*, 98–105.
112. Amy Brown Lyman, "Luacine Savage Clark," *Relief Society Magazine* 31 (September 1944): 487, 510; Quinn, *Elder Statesman*, 101.
113. Melvin Lyman interview; Wintch interviews. On other occasions, however, Richard had defended Amy from a common charge that she was "frigid." William E. Hartman, "An Intimate Portrait of a Great Man," 5, copy in author's possession; Ken Godfrey, "The Richard R. Lyman Story," 12, copy in author's possession obtained from Ken Godfrey.
114. Pohlman interviews; Wintch interviews; Driggs interviews.
115. Derr, Cannon, and Beecher, *Women of Covenant*, 298; Allen interviews; Pohlman interviews.
116. Vera Pohlman recalled that Lyman, with ingrained habits of frugality developed early in her marriage, took the streetcar to work rather than a taxicab to save money. After mentioning to Pohlman on one occasion the discomfort she often felt during her ride to and from home, Pohlman secured books of taxi coupons for her. Pohlman interviews.
117. Clark Office Journal, September, October, 1944, JRCP; Wintch interviews; Engar interviews; Pohlman interviews; Richard R. Lyman to Heber J. Grant, "September 1944," typescript of draft with penciled date, obtained from Lyman family member, copy in author's possession. In the letter Richard advised Grant that Amy had submitted her resignation only because she was asked to do so, as it was neither in her nature nor her upbringing to resign a church responsibility. It is unclear whether the letter was, in fact, sent, or if so, whether Grant read it. Its timing and content, however, given the circumstances of Lyman's temporary reprieve and her obvious subsequent expressions of gratitude to Grant indicate it may have indeed been sent and so influenced the church president to intervene in events—or at least that Amy believed this to have been the case.
118. President Amy Brown Lyman, "Editorial: Birthday Greetings to President Heber J. Grant," *Relief Society Magazine* 31 (November 1944): 630. While it was not unprecedented for Lyman or other editorial writers to sign their pieces in the *Magazine*, it was

certainly not the standard practice. If authorship was ascribed, it was generally done with initials.

119. RSGBM, December 8, 1943.
120. Pohlman interviews.
121. See, for example, Leland Hargrave Creer, "The Polish Question," *Relief Society Magazine* 31 (May 1944): 243–49; "The New Turkey," *Relief Society Magazine* 31 (October 1944): 557–64; and "Palestine," *Relief Society Magazine* 31 (December 1944): 684–88.
122. "Notes to the Field: Notice of Special War Relief Society Meeting to be Held January 30, 1945," *Relief Society Magazine* 31 (November 1944): 632–33; M.C.S. [Marianne Clark Sharp], Editorial, "A Stone in Place of Bread," *Relief Society Magazine* 32 (January 1945): 30–31; Utah Centennial Commission, "Your Part in Utah's Centennial," *Relief Society Magazine* 32 (February 1945): 70, 71, 128.
123. RSGBM, February 14, 1945; First Presidency to President Amy Brown Lyman and Officers and Members of the National Women's Relief Society General Board, April 4, 1945. If Clark was behind this decision, it would certainly have been an opportune time to make the move. Heber J. Grant's health was rapidly declining—he would die early in May—and Clark might have felt it best to release Lyman before the new president took office.
124. "Belle Smith Spafford Called to be Ninth General President of Relief Society, April 1945," *Relief Society Magazine* 32 (May 1945): 259–61. Pohlman interviews.
125. A.B.L., "An Appreciation," editorial, *Relief Society Magazine*, 32 (April 1945): 218–19.

CHAPTER 9

1. Amy Brown Lyman, "The Church in a Changing World," *Relief Society Magazine* 22 (May 1935): 297.
2. Marianne C. Sharp, "Belle Smith Spafford Called to be Ninth General President of Relief Society, April 1945," *Relief Society Magazine* 32 (May 1945): 259–261; Vera White Pohlman interviews, 1990–1994.
3. Jull Mulvay Derr, Janath Russell Cannon, and Maureen Ursenbach Beecher, *Women of Covenant: The Story of Relief Society* (Salt Lake City: Deseret Book, 1992), 304.
4. Women continued to insist on the unique status of the Relief Society well into mid-century, even as they became somewhat grudgingly reconciled to the organization's status as an auxiliary. The early idea that the organization was formed "after a pattern of the priesthood," was cited frequently. See, for example, B[elle] S. S[pafford], "Editorial: Appropriate Relief Society Programs," *Relief Society Magazine* 31 (July 1944): 386.
5. In a condition that extended back several decades, George Albert Smith had suffered several bouts of nervous exhaustion. D. Michael Quinn, *Elder Statesman: A Biography of J. Reuben Clark* (Salt Lake City: Signature Books, 2002), 93–96, 107–11.
6. Belle S. Spafford, "Woman's Role as Homemaker," *Relief Society Magazine* 36 (November 1949): 727. Clark has words of praise for this talk, understandably so, as the sentiments it expresses seem drawn directly from his own views as contained in his "Memorandum" of March, 1940. These views stand in sharp contrast, however, with the broader vision asserted by Lyman and her board as cited previously in the March 1940, *Relief Society Magazine*. For Clark's praise of Spafford, see J. Reuben Clark, Jr., "The Prophet's Sailing Orders to Relief Society," *Relief Society Magazine* 36 (December 1949): 796–98.
7. Derr, Cannon, and Beecher, *Women of Covenant*, 322; Basil O'Connor, "Infantile Paralysis and the March of Dimes," *Relief Society Magazine* 42 (January 1955): 33.
8. Derr, Cannon, and Beecher, *Women of Covenant*, 319, 335.
9. Pohlman interviews; Leona Fetzer Wintch interviews, 1990–1994.

10. This can be seen in comparison of the *Relief Society Magazine* for the period with issues produced under Lyman. This change is most obvious in the "Notes from the Field," column. Under Spafford's leadership, instead of highlighting outstanding accomplishments among LDS women in order to stimulate like action—in particular in community involvement or social activism—it came to focus more on social events, as it had in the 1930s during Louise Robison's administration.
11. Gregory Prince and Wm. Robert Wright, *David O. McKay and the Rise of Modern Mormonism* (Salt Lake City: University of Utah Press, 2005), 203. It is unclear what Clark's reasons were for withholding the funds, but his reluctance may have been related to his ongoing concerns over church finances.
12. Perhaps the best known example of this view is found in Elaine Tyler May, *Homeward Bound: American Families in the Cold War Era* (New York: Basic Books, 1988). See also, Elaine Taylor May, "Pushing the Limits, 1940–1961," in Nancy Cott, ed., *No Small Courage: A History of Women in the United States* (New York: Oxford, 2000), 473–528.
13. On the domestic conditions in the postwar period, see James T. Patterson, *Grand Expectations: The United States, 1945–1974* (New York: Oxford University Press, 1996), 10–81. On women during the period, see William H. Chafe, *The Paradox of Change: American Women in the 20th Century* (New York: Oxford University Press, 1991), 175–93; On the mixed messages aimed at American women, see Joanne Meyerwitz, "Beyond the Feminine Mystique: A Reassessment of Postwar Mass Culture, 1946–1958," *The Journal of American History* 75 (March 1993): 1455–82.
14. Derr, Cannon, and Beecher, *Women of Covenant*, 322–24.
15. "1966 Annual Report," *Relief Society Magazine* 54 (June 1965): 451–54.
16. By 1960, that figure would reach thirty-nine percent. Though few women with younger children worked, by 1960, some thirty percent of all adult women were in the workforce. William H. Chafe, "The Road to Equality, 1960–Present," in Nancy Cott, ed., *No Small Courage*, 534.
17. May, "Pushing the Limits," 523.
18. In regard to the National Council, Spafford had originally wanted to separate the Relief Society from the organization, but was convinced by George Albert Smith to change her mind. She eventually went on to become its president. Derr, Cannon, and Beecher, *Women of Covenant,* 336–38. For African Americans and the church, see Newell G. Bringhurst, *Saints, Slaves, and Blacks: The Changing Place of Black People within Mormonism* (Westport, CT: Greenwood Press, 1981); Armond L. Mauss, *All Abraham's Children: Changing Mormon Concepts of Race and Lineage* (Urbana: University of Illinois Press, 2003).
19. A series of lessons and articles appearing in the magazine in the late 1940s and early 1950s revealed a strong backlash against government intervention in society of the kind that typified the New Deal. While Relief Society women were encouraged to be politically active, these same articles made it explicitly clear that the organization as a body was to have no political role whatsoever. Derr, Cannon, and Beecher, *Women of Covenant*, 313, 324–35; Albert E. Bowen, "The Constitution and the United Nations Charter," *Relief Society Magazine* 38 (October 1951): 654–57; Elder G. Homer Durham, "Social Science: Latter-day Saint Political Thought," Lesson Department, *Relief Society Magazine* 36 (January 1949): 62–65; G. Homer Durham, "The Tasks of Modern Citizenship," *Relief Society Magazine* 36 (August 1949): 507–11. On women's activism in the larger society, see May, "Pushing the Limits," 520–28.
20. Pohlman interviews; Wintch interviews; Amy Kathryn Lyman Engar interviews, 1990–1994.
21. I am thinking specifically of the "gifts of the spirit" that faded from common practice around the turn of the century and were viewed by many women of Lyman's generation

as "old fashioned." Pohlman interviews; Wintch interviews; Emmeline B. Wells, "Charity and Faith," *Relief Society Bulletin* 1 (April 1914): 2. On declining use of spiritual gifts among Mormon women, see Linda King Newell, "Gifts of the Spirit: Women's Share," in Maureen Ursenbach Beecher and Lavina Fielding Anderson, eds., *Sisters in Spirit: Mormon Women in Historical and Cultural Perspective* (Urbana: University of Illinois Press, 1987), 124–39; Jonathan A. Stapley and Kristine Wright, "Female Ritual Healing in Mormonism," *Journal of Mormon History*, 37 (Winter 2011): 1–85. Similarly, in their pursuit of their immediate priorities, previous generations—with Lyman among them—may have helped established precedents that significantly undermined their autonomy in the long run. Lyman was possibly among those pressing for the replacement of the aged and enfeebled Emmeline B. Wells in 1921 so the Society could more effectively pursue its agenda of social welfare work. This established the precedent of releasing Relief Society presidents, who, since the time of Eliza R. Snow and like other general authorities, had previously served for life. The resignation of Clarissa Williams in 1928 due to declining health moved this innovation further along the path toward routine practice. In consequence, it was comparatively easy to release Louise Y. Robison (although she was reportedly not pleased by the move) and even more so to release Lyman, rather than allowing her to continue under the cloud that hung over her presidency.

22. Emily Pollei interview, 1992.
23. Amy used her time at the pulpit to reiterate her admonition that members of the organization "be familiar with the history, background, activities, and accomplishments of the Relief Society and of the women who have directed the work" even as they prepared themselves for future roles. Amy Brown Lyman, "Relief Society Leadership," *Relief Society Magazine* 32 (December 1945): 739–40; Amy Brown Lyman, "Highlights from the Past," *Relief Society Magazine* 38 (March 1951): 148–52; and Amy Brown Lyman, "The Spirit of Relief Society," *Relief Society Magazine* 39 (March 1952): 152; Vera White Pohlman, *Amy Brown Lyman, 1872–1959: Biographical Summary and Funeral Services* (Privately Published, 1960), 19; Pohlman interviews.
24. Derr, Cannon, and Beecher, *Women of Covenant*, 328; "The Relief Society Building Ground-Breaking Ceremony," *Relief Society Magazine* 40 (December 1953): 801; "The Relief Society Building Cornerstone-Laying Ceremony," *Relief Society Magazine* 41 (December 1954): 804; "Editorial: Congratulations to President Amy Brown Lyman on Her Birthday—February 7th," *Relief Society Magazine* 36 (February 1949): 101; "Birthday Congratulations to Amy Brown Lyman, Former General President of Relief Society, February 7, 1959," *Relief Society Magazine* 46 (February 1959): 97.
25. See, for example, Amy Brown Lyman, "Pioneer Stories and Incidents," *Relief Society Magazine* 33 (July 1946): 440, 463; and subsequent monthly pieces that appeared through 1947. Topics treated included peoples and incidents encountered enroute by the pioneers, and the experience of pioneer women.
26. Pohlman interviews; Engar interviews. Minutes, General Board Emeritus Club, in author's possession.
27. Pohlman interviews; Engar interviews. Lyman also remained a member of a club for wives of the general authorities, even though Richard was no longer among their number. I am indebted to Maureen Ursenbach Beecher for bringing the information about the Wives of the General Authorities to my attention.
28. In an address in 1947, she reflected on old and new problems confronting society, including serious threats to world peace and national security. In all these, she observed, "women should share the responsibility in solving them." See untitled 1947 address by Lyman at a woman's forum in Salt Lake City, Amy Brown Lyman Papers, L. Tom Perry Special Collections, Harold B. Lee Library, Brigham Young University.

29. Pohlman interviews.
30. This conclusion was reached by a number of friends and family members of the couple. A. Z. Richards interview, 1992; Parry Sorenson interview, 1992; David and Sabey Pingree interview, 1992; Susan Elizabeth Swenson Driggs interviews, 1991, 1994; Conversation with Chad Flake, May 29, 1992.
31. Sorensen interview; Richards interview; Amy Brown Lyman to Dearest Amy [Lyman Engar], [February, 1946], Engar Family Papers (cited hereafter as EFP).
32. Amy Lyman Engar, "Amy Brown Lyman: Transcribed from a talk given at the University of Utah Institute 'Women of the Restoration,' February 26, 1987," EFP, 15–19.
33. Emmeline Wirthlin interview, 1990.
34. Amy Kathryn's husband, Keith Engar would go on to an accomplished career in the drama department at the University of Utah. He was well liked by Amy and Richard, but they were initially concerned about the match largely because of Keith's choice of acting as a career. Their fears dissipated, however, when he decided to teach drama at the university level. Engar interviews.
35. Engar served on the general board of the Primary Organization. Engar interviews.
36. Driggs interviews; Engar interviews. Revealing of her continuing mental acuity, one grandson reported that even at this late period of her life, Amy was the only person he had ever known who could carry on two simultaneous conversations, one, with a person in the room and the other on the phone, and never miss a beat. Richard Schreiner interview, 1992.
37. Amy Engar reported that her grandmother called her up before Margaret arrived to take her to the hospital and told her that if it did not hurt so bad, she could have rotated her shoulder completely around without moving the arm. This is somewhat typical of Lyman's keen and disciplined mind to make an observation of this kind at such a difficult time. Engar interviews.
38. Pohlman interviews.
39. Pohlman interviews.
40. Richard R. Lyman to Donald T. Schmidt, July 7, 1960, Richard R. Lyman Papers, L. Tom Perry Special Collections, Harold B. Lee Library, Brigham Young University; Engar interviews; Wintch interviews.
41. Occasionally, a former board member would approach Spafford and ask her for an update and she would give apologies, note distractions and then state, jokingly, that she had to get moving on the task because she knew that the first thing Lyman would ask her when she reached the other side was why the monument had not been erected. Pohlman interviews. Florence Smith Jacobsen, a close associate of Spafford during this period, also recalled Spafford's concerns over the campanile. Phone conversation with Florence Smith Jacobsen, August 28, 1999.
42. Some of these demanded immediate action, such as putting the organization back on its feet with the lifting of travel restrictions or even more critically, providing relief supplies to suffering Saints in Europe. Derr, Cannon, and Beecher, *Women of Covenant*, 310–11.
43. To be specific, it was located between the Assembly Hall and the Tabernacle on Temple Square. Though not quite as prominent, the site was deemed appropriate as both were locations where the women of the church had held their meetings over the years. Pohlman interviews.
44. Fortunately, Wilford Wood, local businessman and collector of artifacts relating to LDS history rescued the pieces from destruction. Pohlman interviews; Belle S. Spafford, "Relief Society Memorial Bell Tower," *Relief Society Magazine* 54 (January 1967): 14–18.
45. This was a step taken with all church organizations at the time, including the priesthood quorums. Derr, Cannon, and Beecher, *Women of Covenant*, 341.

46. Derr, Cannon, and Beecher, *Women of Covenant*, 341–43. Eventually the women would turn over the content of their page to the curriculum committee as well.
47. Lyman's granddaughter recalled this period as a particularly difficult one for the women of the church. Engar interviews. See also Pohlman interviews; Derr, Cannon, and Beecher, *Women of Covenant*, 347–83.
48. Betty Friedan, *The Feminine Mystique*, (New York: Dell, 1964).
49. Chafe, *The Paradox of Change*, 194–215.
50. Derr, Cannon, and Beecher, *Women of Covenant*, 372–73.
51. Amy Brown Lyman to Leona F. Wintch, February 17, 1952, copy in author's possession.
52. "Relief Society Centennial Memorial," *Relief Society Magazine*, 29 (December, 1942): 819. The Campanile was moved from its position next to the Tabernacle because Church architects feared a new basement constructed at its old site would not support its weight. Pohlman interviews.
53. Pohlman, *Amy Brown Lyman*, 31.

BIBLIOGRAPHY

Addams, Jane. *The Second Twenty Years at Hull House: September 1909 to September 1929, with a Record of Growing World Consciousness*. New York: Macmillan, 1930.

Addams, Jane, Emily G. Balch, and Alice Hamilton. *Women at The Hague: The International Congress of Women and its Results*. Urbana: University of Illinois Press, 2003.

Agnew, Elizabeth N. *From Charity to Social Work: Mary E. Richmond and the Creation of an American Profession*. Urbana: University of Illinois Press, 2004.

Alexander, Thomas G. "An Experiment in Progressive Legislation: The Granting of Woman Suffrage in Utah in 1870." *Utah Historical Quarterly* 38 (Winter 1970).

Alexander, Thomas G. "Between Revivalism and the Social Gospel: The Latter-day Saint Social Advisory Committee, 1916–1922." *Brigham Young University Studies* 23 (Winter 1983): 19–39.

Alexander, Thomas G. *Mormonism in Transition: A History of the Latter-day Saints, 1890–1930*. Urbana: University of Illinois Press, 1986.

Alexander, Thomas G. *Utah: The Right Place*. Salt Lake City: Gibbs Smith, 1996.

Alexander, Thomas G., and James B. Allen. *Mormons and Gentiles: A History of Salt Lake City*. Salt Lake City: Pruett, 1984.

Allen, James B., and Jessie L. Embry. "'Provoking the Brethren to Good Works': Susa Young Gates, the Relief Society, and Genealogy." *Brigham Young University Studies* 31 (Spring 1991): 115–38.

Andersen, Kristi. *After Suffrage: Women in Partisan and Electoral Politics before the New Deal*. Chicago: University of Chicago Press, 1996.

Andrews, Janice L. "Female Social Workers in the Second Generation." *Affilia* 5 (Summer 1990): 46–59.

Arrington, Harriet Horne. "Alice Merrill Horne, Art Promoter and Early Utah Legislator." *Utah Historical Quarterly* 58 (Summer 1990): 261–76.

Arrington, Leonard J. *Great Basin Kingdom: An Economic History of the Latter-day Saints*. Cambridge, MA: Harvard University Press, 1958.

Arrington, Leonard J. "Modern Lysistratas: Mormon Women in the International Peace Movement, 1899–1933," *Journal of Mormon History* 15 (1989): 89–104.

Arrington, Leonard J., Feramorz Y. Fox, and Dean L. May. *Building the City of God: Community and Cooperation among the Mormons*. 2nd ed. Urbana: University of Illinois Press, 1992.

Baker, Josephine S. *Fighting for Life*. New York: MacMillan, 1939.

Beecher, Maureen Ursenbach. "The Leading Sisters: A Female Hierarchy in Nineteenth-Century Mormon Society." *Journal of Mormon History* 9 (1982): 25–39.

Beecher, Maureen Ursenbach. "Women's Work on the Mormon Frontier." *Utah Historical Quarterly* 49 (Summer 1981): 276–90.

Beecher, Maureen Ursenbach, and Lavina Fielding Anderson, eds. *Sisters in Spirit: Mormon Women in Historical and Cultural Perspective*. Urbana: University of Illinois Press, 1987.

Beeley, Arthur L. *Boys and Girls of Salt Lake City: The Result of a Survey*. Salt Lake City: University of Utah, 1929.

Bennion, Sherilyn Cox. "The *Salt Lake Sanitarian*: Medical Adviser to the Saints." *Utah Historical Quarterly* 57 (Spring 1989): 125–37.

Bennion, Sherilyn Cox. "Sisters under the Skin: Utah's Mormon and Non-Mormon Women and Their Publications." *Brigham Young University Studies* 33 (1990): 111–29.

Bennion, Sherilyn Cox. "The *Woman's Exponent*: Forty-two Years of Speaking for Women." *Utah Historical Quarterly* 44 (Summer 1976): 222–39.

Benroth, Margaret Lamberts, and Virginia Lieson Brereton, eds. *Women and Twentieth-Century Protestantism*. Urbana: University of Illinois Press, 2002.

Bergera, Gary James. "Transgression in the Latter-day Saint Community: The Cases of Albert Carrington, Richard R. Lyman, and Joseph F. Smith. Part 2: Richard R. Lyman." *Journal of Mormon History* 37 (Fall 2011): 173–207.

Bitton, Davis, and Maureen Ursenbach Beecher, eds. *New Views of Mormon History: A Collection of Essays in Honor of Leonard J. Arrington*. Salt Lake City: University of Utah Press, 1987.

Blair, Karen J. *The Clubwoman as Feminist: True Womanhood Redefined, 1868–1914*. New York: Holmes and Meier, 1980.

Bradley, Martha S. "Protect the Children: Child Labor in Utah, 1880–1920." *Utah Historical Quarterly* 59 (Winter 1991): 52–71.

Breckinridge, Sophonisba B. "The Activities of Women outside the Home." In *Recent Social Trends in the United States*. Report of the President's Research Committee on Social Trends. New York, 1933.

Breckinridge, Sophonisba B. *Women in the Twentieth Century*. New York, 1933.

Bremer, William W. *Depression Winters: New York Social Workers and the New Deal*. Philadelphia: Temple University Press, 1984.

Brown, John Zimmerman, ed. *Autobiography of Pioneer John Brown, 1820–1896*. Salt Lake City: Press of Steven and Wallis, 1941.

Burgess-Olson, Vicky, ed. *Sister Saints*. Provo: Brigham Young University Press, 1978.

Campbell, Eugene E. *Establishing Zion: The Mormon Church in the American West, 1847–1869*. Salt Lake City: Signature Books, 1988.

Cannon, Annie Wells. Journals, 1877–1942. L. Tom Perry Special Collections, Harold B. Lee Library, Brigham Young University, Provo, Utah.

Cannon, Janath Russell, and Jill Mulvay Derr. "Resolving Differences/Achieving Unity: Lessons from the History of Relief Society." In Mary E. Stovall and Carol Cornwall Madsen, eds. *As Women of Faith: Talks Selected from the BYU Women's Conferences*, 128–31. Salt Lake City: Deseret Book Co., 1989.

Carver, Sharon Snow. "Club Women of the Three Intermountain Cities of Denver, Boise, and Salt Lake City between 1893 and 1929." PhD dissertation, Brigham Young University, 2000.

Carver, Sharon Snow. "Female Influence in Salt Lake City Government Policies: The Salt Lake City Federation of Women's Clubs, 1912–1930." Paper presented at the annual meeting of the Mormon History Association, May, 1995, Park City, Utah.

Chafe, William Henry. *The Paradox of Change: American Women in the 20th Century*. New York: Oxford University Press, 1991.

Chambers, Clarke A. *Seedtime of Reform: American Social Service and Social Action, 1918–1933*. Minneapolis: University of Minnesota Press, 1963.

Chambers, Clarke A. "Toward a Redefinition of Welfare History." *Journal of American History* 73 (September 1986): 407–33.

Chambers, Clarke A. "Women in the Creation of the Profession of Social Work." *Social Service Review* (March 1986): 1–33.

Chandler, Alfred D. *The Visible Hand: The Managerial Revolution in American Business*. Cambridge, MA: Harvard University Press, 1977.

Chesler, Ellen. *Woman of Valor: Margaret Sanger and the Birth Control Movement in America.* New York: Simon and Schuster, 1992.

Clemens, Elisabeth S. "Organizational Repertoires and Institutional Change: Women's Groups and the Transformation of U.S. Politics, 1890–1920." *American Journal of Sociology* 98 (January 1993): 755–98.

Cooper, Rex Eugene. *Promises Made to the Fathers: Mormon Covenant Organization.* Salt Lake City: University of Utah Press, 1990.

Costin, Lela B. *Two Sisters for Social Justice: A Biography of Grace and Edith Abbott.* Urbana: University of Illinois Press, 1983.

Cott, Nancy F., ed. *No Small Courage: A History of Women in the United States.* New York: Oxford University Press, 2000.

Crocheron, Augusta Joyce. *Representative Women of Deseret.* Salt Lake City: J.C. Graham & Co., 1884.

Crunden, Robert M. *Ministers of Reform: The Progressive Achievement in American Civilization, 1889–1920.* New York: Basic Books, 1982.

Darowski, Joseph F. "The WPA versus the Utah Church." In Brian Q. Cannon and Jessie L. Embry ed. *Utah in the Twentieth Century,* 167–85. Logan: Utah State University Press, 2009.

Daynes, Kathryn M. *More Wives than One: Transformation of the Mormon Marriage System, 1840–1910.* Urbana: University of Illinois Press, 2001.

Derr, Jill Mulvay, "Changing Relief Society Charity to Make Way for Welfare." In Davis Bitton and Maureen Ursenbach Beecher, eds. *New Views of Mormon History: A Collection of Essays in Honor of Leonard J. Arrington,* 242–72. Salt Lake City: University of Utah Press, 1987.

Derr, Jill Mulvay. "Scholarship, Service, and Sisterhood: Utah Women's Clubs and Associations, 1877–1977." In Patricia Lynn Scott and Linda Thatcher, eds. *Women in Utah History: Paradigm or Paradox,* 249–94. Logan: Utah State University Press, 2005.

Derr, Jill Mulvay. "'Strength in our Union': The Making of Mormon Sisterhood." In Maureen Ursenbach Beecher and Lavina Fielding Anderson, eds. *Sisters in Spirit: Mormon Women in Historical and Cultural Perspective,* 153–207. Urbana: University of Illinois Press, 1987.

Derr, Jill Mulvay. "Woman's Place in Brigham Young's World." *Brigham Young University Studies* 18 (Spring 1978): 377–95.

Derr, Jill Mulvay, and Carol Corwall Madsen. "Preserving the Record and Memory of the Female Relief Society of Nauvoo, 1842–92." *Journal of Mormon History* 35 (Summer 2009): 88–117.

Derr, Jill Mulvay, Janath Russell Cannon, and Maureen Ursenbach Beecher. *Women of Covenant: The Story of Relief Society.* Salt Lake City: Deseret Book, 1992.

De Schweinitz, Karl. *The Art of Helping People Out of Trouble.* New York: Houghton Mifflin, 1924.

Deutsch, Sarah. *No Separate Refuge: Culture, Class, and Gender on an Anglo-Hispanic Frontier in the American Southwest.* New York: Oxford University Press, 1989.

Deutsch, Sarah Jane. "From Ballots to Breadlines." In Nancy F. Cott, ed. *No Small Courage: A History of Women in the United States,* 413–72. New York: Oxford, 2000.

Devine, Edward T. *The Normal Life.* New York: MacMillan, 1915.

Dye, Nancy Schrom, and Daniel Blake Smith. "Mother Love and Infant Death, 1750–1920." *Journal of American History* (1986): 328–53.

Edwards, Wendy J. Deichmann, and Carolyn De Swarte Gifford, eds. *Gender and the Social Gospel.* Urbana: University of Illinois Press, 2003.

Ehrenreich, John H. *The Altruistic Imagination: A History of Social Work and Social Policy in the United States.* Ithaca: Cornell University Press, 1985.

Ely, Richard T. *Social Aspects of Christianity and Other Essays*. New York: Thomas Y. Crowell, 1889.

Embry, Jessie L. "Grain Storage: The Balance of Power between Priesthood Authority and Relief Society Autonomy." *Dialogue: A Journal of Mormon Thought* 15 (Winter 1982): 59–66.

Embry, Jessie L. *Mormon Polygamous Families: Life in the Principle*. Salt Lake City: University of Utah Press, 1987.

Embry, Jessie L. "Relief Society Grain Storage Program, 1876–1940." Master's thesis, Brigham Young University, 1974.

Embry, Jessie L., and James B. Allen, "'Provoking the Brethren to Good Works': Susa Young Gates, the Relief Society and Genealogy." *Brigham Young University Studies* 31 (Spring 1991): 115–38.

Embry, Jessie L., and Howard A. Christy, eds. *Community Development in the American West: Past and Present Nineteenth and Twentieth Century Frontiers*. Provo: Charles Redd Center for Western Studies, 1985.

Evans, Vella Neil. "Empowerment and Mormon Women's Publications." In *Women and Authority: Re-emerging Mormon Feminism*, edited by Maxine Hanks. Salt Lake City: Signature Books, 1992.

Evans, Vella Neil. "Mormon Women and the Right to Wage Work." *Dialogue: A Journal of Mormon Thought* 23 (Winter 1990): 45–61.

Fitzpatrick, Ellen. *Endless Crusade: Women Social Scientists and Progressive Reform*. New York: Oxford University Press, 1990.

Foster, Lawrence. "From Frontier Activism to Neo-Victorian Domesticity: Mormon Women in the Nineteenth and Twentieth Centuries." *Journal of Mormon History* 6 (1979): 3–21.

Foster, Lawrence. "Polygamy and the Frontier: Mormon Women in Early Utah." *Utah Historical Quarterly* 50 (Summer 1982): 268–89.

Freedman, Estelle B. "Separatism Revisited: Women's Institutions, Social Reform, and the Career of Miriam Van Waters." In Linda K. Kerber, Alice Kessler-Harris, and Kathryn Kish Sklar, eds. *U.S. History as Women's History: New Feminist Essays*, 170–88. Chapel Hill: University of North Carolina Press, 1995.

Gates, Susa Young. *History of the Young Ladies Mutual Improvement Association*. Salt Lake City: General Board of the Y.L.M.I.A., 1911.

General Board of Relief Society. *A Centenary of Relief Society, 1842–1942*. Salt Lake City: General Board of Relief Society, 1942.

General Board of Relief Society. *The General Relief Society: Officers, Objects and Status*. Salt Lake City: General Officers, 1902.

General Board of Relief Society. *Handbook of the Relief Society of the Church of Jesus Christ of Latter-day Saints*. Salt Lake City: General Board of Relief Society, 1931.

Ginzberg, Lori D. *Women and the Work of Benevolence: Morality, Politics, and Class in the Nineteenth-Century United States*. New Haven: Yale University Press, 1990.

Gladden, Washington. *Applied Christianity: Moral Aspects of Social Questions.* Boston: Houghton Mifflin, 1897

Goodwin, Joanne L. *Gender and the Politics of Welfare Reform: Mothers' Pensions in Chicago, 1911–1920*. Chicago: University of Chicago Press, 1997.

Gordon, Linda. *Pitied but Not Entitled: Single Mothers and the History of Welfare*. Cambridge, MA: Harvard University Press, 1994.

Gordon, Linda, ed. *Women, the State, and Welfare*. Madison: University of Wisconsin Press, 1990.

Gordon, Sarah Barringer. *The Mormon Question: Polygamy and Constitutional Conflict in Nineteenth-Century America*. Chapel Hill: University of North Carolina Press, 2002.

Greenwald, Maurine Weiner. *Women, War, and Work: The Impact of World War I on Women Workers in the United States*. Westporot, CT: Greenwood Press, 1980.

Hall, Dave. "A Crossroads for Mormon Women: Amy Brown Lyman, J. Reuben Clark and the Decline of Organized Women's Activism in the Relief Society." *Journal of Mormon History* 36 (Spring 2010): 205–49.

Hall, Dave. "From Home Service to Social Service: Amy Brown Lyman and the Development of Social Work in the LDS Church. *Mormon Historical Studies* 9 (Fall 2008): 67–88.

Haller, John S. Jr., and Robin M. Haller. *The Physician and Sexuality in Victorian America*. Urbana: University of Illinois Press, 1974.

Handy, Robert T., ed. *The Social Gospel in American Thought, 1870–1920*. New York: Oxford University Press, 1966.

Hardy, B. Carmon. *Solemn Covenant: The Mormon Polygamous Passage*. Urbana: University of Illinois Press, 1992.

Hefner, Loretta L. "This Decade was Different: Relief Society's Social Services Department, 1919–1929." *Dialogue: A Journal of Mormon Thought* 15 (Autumn 1982): 64–73.

Hefner, Loretta L. "The National Women's Relief Society and the U.S. Sheppard-Towner Act." *Utah Historical Quarterly* 50 (Summer 1982): 255–67.

Iversen, Joan. "The Mormon-Suffrage Relationship: Personal and Political Quandaries." *Frontiers* 11 (1990): 8–16.

Jenson, Andrew. *Latter-Day Saint Biographical Encyclopedia: A Compilation of Biographical Sketches of Prominent Men and Women in the Church of Jesus Christ of Latter-day Saints*. 4 vols. Salt Lake City: Andrew Jenson History Company, 1901–1936.

Johnson, Dorothy. "Organized Women Lobbyists in the 1920s." *Capitol Studies* 1 (1972): 43.

Jones, Dan E. "Utah Politics, 1926–1932." PhD dissertation, University of Utah, 1968.

Katsanevas, Michael Jr. "The Emerging Social Worker and the Distribution of the Castle Gate Relief Fund." *Utah Historical Quarterly* 50 (Summer 1982): 239–49

Katz, Michael B. *In The Shadow of the Poorhouse: A Social History of Welfare in America*. New York: Basic Books, 1986.

Kennedy, David M. *Over Here: The First World War and American Society*. New York: Oxford University Press, 1980.

Koven, Seth, and Sonya Michel, eds. *Mothers of a New World: Maternalist Politics and the Origins of Welfare States*. New York: Routledge, 1993.

Ladd-Taylor, Molly. *Mother-Work: Women, Child Welfare and the State, 1890–1930*. Urbana: University of Illinois Press, 1994.

Ladd-Taylor, Molly. *Raising Children the Government Way: Mothers' Letters to the Children's Bureau, 1915–1932*. New Brunswick and London: Rutgers University Press, 1986.

Larson, Gustive O. *The "Americanization" of Utah for Statehood*. San Marino, CA: Huntington Library, 1971.

Leavitt, Judith Walzer. *Brought to Bed: Childbearing in America, 1750–1950*. New York: Oxford University Press, 1986.

Leavitt, Judith Walzer. "Under the Shadow of Maternity: American Women's Responses to Death and Debility Fears in Nineteenth-Century Childbirth." *Feminist Studies* 12 (1986): 129–54.

Leavitt, Judith Walzer, ed. *Women and Health in America: Historical Readings*. Madison: University of Wisconsin Press, 1984.

Lebsock, Suzanne. "Women and American Politics, 1880–1920." In Louise A. Tilly and Patricia Gurin eds. *Women, Politics and Change*. New York: Russell Sage Foundation, 1990.

Leiby, James. *A History of Social Welfare and Social Work in the United States, 1815–1972*. New York: Columbia University Press, 1978.

Lemons, J. Stanley. "The Sheppard-Towner Act: Progressivism in the 1920s." *The Journal of American History* 55 (March 1969): 776–86.

Lemons, J. Stanley. *The Woman Citizen: Social Feminism in the 1920s*. Urbana: University of Illinois Press, 1973.

Leonard, Glen M. *Nauvoo: A Place of Peace, a People of Promise*. Salt Lake City: Deseret Book, 2002.

Logue, Larry M. *A Sermon in the Desert: Belief and Behavior in Early St. George, Utah*. Urbana: University of Illinois Press, 1988.

Lubove, Roy. *The Professional Altruist: The Emergence of Social Work as a Career, 1880–1930*. Cambridge, MA: Harvard University Press, 1965.

Lyman, Amy Brown. *In Retrospect: Autobiography of Amy Brown Lyman*. Salt Lake City: General Board of Relief Society, 1945.

Lyman, Amy Brown. *A Lighter of Lamps: The Life Story of Alice Louise Reynolds*. Provo: Alice Louise Reynolds Club, 1947.

Lyman, Edward Leo. *Political Deliverance: The Mormon Quest for Utah Statehood*. Urbana: University of Illinois Press, 1986.

Madsen, Carol Cornwall. *An Advocate for Women: The Public Life of Emmeline B. Wells, 1870–1920*. Provo: Brigham Young University Press, 2006.

Madsen, Carol Cornwall, ed. *Battle for the Ballot: Essays on Woman Suffrage in Utah, 1870–1896*. Salt Lake City: University of Utah Press, 1998.

Madsen, Carol Cornwall. "Emmeline B. Wells: 'Am I Not a Woman and a Sister?'" *Brigham Young University Studies* 22 (Spring 1982): 161–78.

Madsen, Carol Cornwall. "A Mormon Woman in Victorian America." PhD dissertation, University of Utah, 1985.

Madsen, Carol Cornwall. "'The Power of Combination': Emmeline B. Wells and the National and International Councils of Women." *Brigham Young University Studies* 33 (1993): 647–73.

Madsen, Carol Cornwall. "Schism in the Sisterhood: Mormon Women and Partisan Politics, 1890–1900." In Davis Bitton and Maureen Ursenbach Beecher, eds. *New Views of Mormon History: A Collection of Essays in Honor of Leonard J. Arrington*, 212–41. Salt Lake City: University of Utah, 1987.

Madsen, Carol Cornwall, and Susan Staker Oman. *Sisters and Little Saints: One Hundred Years of Primary*. Salt Lake City: Deseret Book, 1979.

Mangum, Garth L., and Bruce D. Blumel. *The Mormons' War on Poverty: A History of LDS Welfare, 1830–1990*. Salt Lake City: University of Utah Press, 1993.

Mann, Patricia Ann. "A History of the Relief Society Magazine, 1914–1970." Master's thesis, Brigham Young University, 1971.

Martin, Theodora Penny. *The Sound of Our Own Voices: Women's Study Clubs, 1860–1910*. Boston: Beacon Press, 1987.

Matthews, Glenna. *The Rise of Public Woman: Woman's Power and Woman's Place in the United States, 1630–1970*. New York: Oxford University Press, 1992.

May, Elaine Tyler. *Homeward Bound: American Families in the Cold War Era*. New York: Basic Books, 1988.

McCarthy, Kathleen D., ed. *Lady Bountiful Revisited: Women, Philanthropy, and Power*. New Brunswick: Rutgers University Press, 1990.

McClymer, John F. *War and Welfare: Social Engineering in America, 1890–1925*. Westport, CT: Greenwood Press, 1980.

McElvaine, Robert S. *The Great Depression: America, 1929–1941*. New York: Times Books, 1984.

Meckel, Richard A. *Save the Babies: American Public Health Reform and the Prevention of Infant Mortality, 1850–1929*. Baltimore: Johns Hopkins University Press, 1990.

Meyerwits, Joanne, ed. *Not June Cleaver: Women and Gender in Postwar America, 1945–1960*. Philadelphia: Temple University Press, 1994.

Mink, Gwendolyn. *The Wages of Motherhood: Inequality in the Welfare State, 1917–1942*. Ithaca: Cornell University Press, 1995.

Morantz-Sanchez, Regina Markell. *Sympathy & Science: Women Physicians in American Medicine*. New York: Oxford University Press, 1985.

Morrill, Susanna. "Relief Society Birth and Death Rituals: Women at the Gates of Mortality," *Journal of Mormon History* 36 (Spring 2010): 128–59.

Morrill, Susanna. *White Roses on the Floor of Heaven: Mormon Women's Popular Theology, 1880–1920*. New York: Routledge, 2006.

Mulder, William. *Homeward to Zion: The Mormon Migration from Scandinavia*. Minneapolis: University of Minnesota Press, 1957.

Muncy, Robyn. *Creating a Female Dominion in American Reform, 1890–1935*. New York: Oxford University Press, 1991.

Murphy, Miriam B. "Women in the Utah Work Force from Statehood to World War II." *Utah Historical Quarterly* 50 (Spring 1982): 139–59.

Murphy, Miriam B. "The Working Women of Salt Lake City: A Review of the Utah Gazetteer, 1892–93." *Utah Historical Quarterly* 46 (Spring 1978): 121–35.

National Conference of Social Work. *Proceedings of the National Conference of Social Work at the Forty-Fourth Annual Session Held in Pittsburgh, Pennsylvania, June 6–13, 1917*. Chicago: National Conference of Social Work, 1917.

National Conference of Social Work. *Proceedings of the National Conference of Social Work at the Forty-Fifth Annual Session Held in Kansas City, Missouri, May 15–22, 1918*. Chicago: Rogers and Hall, Co., 1918.

National Council of Women of the United States. *The Year Book and Directory of the National Council of Women of the United States, Inc., including the Proceedings of the Fourteenth Convention*. New York: National Council of Women, 1928.

Neilson, Reid. *Exhibiting Mormonism: The Latter-day Saints and the 1893 Chicago World's Fair*. New York: Oxford University Press, 2011.

Nelson, Lowry. *The Mormon Village: A Pattern and Technique of Land Settlement*. Salt Lake City: University of Utah Press, 1952.

Nielsen, Kim E. *Un-American Womanhood: Antiradicalism, Antifeminism, and the First Red Scare*. Columbus, OH: Ohio State University Press, 2001.

Orloff, Ann Shola. "Gender and the Social Rights of Citizenship: The Comparative Analysis of Gender Relations and Welfare States." *American Sociological Review* 58 (June 1993): 303–28.

Pascoe, Peggy. *Relations of Rescue: The Search for Female Moral Authority in the American West, 1874–1939*. New York: Oxford University Press, 1990.

Peterson, Hazel Meriam. "Administration of Public Welfare in Utah." Master's thesis, University of Chicago, 1928.

Prince, Gregory, and Wm. Robert Wright. *David O. McKay and the Rise of Modern Mormonism*. Salt Lake City: University of Utah Press, 2005.

Quinn, D. Michael. *Elder Statesman: A Biography of J. Reuben Clark*. Salt Lake City: Signature Books, 2002.

Radke-Moss, Andrea G. "Polygamy and Women's Rights: Nineteenth-Century Mormon Female Activism." In Newell G. Bringhurst and Craig L. Foster, eds. *The Persistence of Polygamy: From Joseph Smith's Martyrdom to the First Manifesto, 1844–1890*. Independence, Missouri: John Whitmer Books, 2013.

Rauschenbusch, Walter. *Christianity and the Social Crisis*. New York: MacMillan, 1907.

Richards, Franklin D., ed. *Journal of Discourses*. Liverpool and London: Franklin D. Richards, 1854–1888.

Richards, H. Y. "The Cooperation of Lay Organizations in Maternity and Infancy Work." *Proceedings of the Third Annual Conference of State Directors in Charge of the Local Administration of the Maternity and Infancy Act*. Department of Labor, Children's Bureau Publication No. 157 (Washington D.C., 1926), 184–86.

Richards, H. Y., M.D. "Semi-Annual Report of Maternity and Infancy Work, July 1–December 31, 1925." Utah State Board of Health, Children's Bureau Files, Utah Folder, National Archives.

Richards, H. Y. "Semi-Annual Report of Maternity and Infancy Work, July 1–December 31, 1926." Sheppard-Towner Papers, Children's Bureau Records, Utah File, National Archives.

Richmond, Mary. *The Long View: Papers and Addresses*. New York: Russell Sage Foundation, 1930.

Richmond, Mary. *Social Diagnosis*. New York: Russell Sage Foundation, 1917.

Riley, Glenda. *The Female Frontier: A Comparative View of Women on the Prairie and the Plains*. Lawrence, KS: University of Kansas Press, 1988.

Riley, Glenda. *Frontierswomen: The Iowa Experience*. Ames, IA: Iowa State University Press, 1981.

Robertson, David Brian. "The Bias of American Federalism: The Limits of Welfare-State Development in the Progressive Era." *Journal of Policy History* 1 (1989): 261–91.

Rothman, David J. and Sheila M., eds. *National Congress of Mothers, the First Conventions, 1897–1899*. New York: Garland, 1987.

Rupp, Leila J. *Worlds of Women: The Making of an International Women's Movement*. Princeton: Princeton University Press, 1997.

Rupp, Leila J., and Verta Taylor. *Survival in the Doldrums: The American Women's Rights Movement, 1945 to the 1960s*. New York: Oxford University Press, 1987.

Scott, Anne Firor, "Mormon Women, Other Women: Paradoxes and Challenges," *Journal of Mormon History* 13 (1986–87): 2–19.

Scott, Anne Firor. *Natural Allies: Women's Associations in American History*. Urbana: University of Illinois Press, 1991.

Shipps, Jan. *Mormonism: The Story of a New Religious Tradition*. Urbana: University of Illinois Press, 1985.

Sklar, Kathryn Kish. *Florence Kelley and the Nation's Work: The Rise of Women's Political Culture, 1830–1900*. New Haven: Yale University Press, 1995.

Sklar, Kathryn Kish. "Hull House in the 1890s: A Community of Women Reformers." *Signs* (Summer 1985): 658–77.

Skocpol, Theda. *Protecting Soldiers and Mothers: The Political Origins of Social Policy in the United States*. Cambridge, MA: Harvard University Press, 1992.

Stapley, Jonathan A. and Kristine Wright, "Female Ritual Healing in Mormonism," *Journal of Mormon History* 37 (Winter 2011): 1–85.

State of Utah, Department of Public Welfare. *First Biennial Report of the State Department of Public Welfare, July 1, 1936–June 30, 1938, with Supplementary Date January, 1935 through December, 1938 and a Review of Public Aid in Utah Prior to Establishment for the State Department of Public Welfare in May, 1935*. Salt Lake City: State of Utah, 1939.

State of Utah. *Report of the State Welfare Commission*. Salt Lake City: State of Utah, 1923.

Stephens, Jane. "May Wright Sewall: An Indiana Reformer." *Indiana Magazine of History* 78 (December 1982): 273–95.

Swerdlow, Amy. "Ladies' Day at the Capital: Women Strike for Peace versus HUAC." *Feminist Studies* 8 (1982): 493–520.

Tait, Lisa Olsen. "The Young Woman's Journal: Gender and Generations in a Mormon Women's Magazine." *American Periodicals: A Journal of History, Criticism, and Bibliography* 22 (November 30, 2011): 51–71.

Tanner, Annie Clark. *A Mormon Mother: An Autobiography of Annie Clark Tanner*. Salt Lake City: Tanner Trust, University of Utah, 1983.

Taylor, P. A. M. *Expectations Westward: The Mormons and the Emigration of their British Converts in the Nineteenth Century*. Edinburgh: Oliver and Boyd, 1965.

Thatcher, Linda, and John R. Sillito. "'Sisterhood and Sociability': The Utah Women's Press Club, 1891–1928." *Utah Historical Quarterly* 53 (Spring 1985): 144–56.

Trolander, Judith Ann. *Professionalism and Social Change: From the Settlement House Movement to Neighborhood Centers*. New York: Columbia University Press, 1987.

Tullidge, Edward W. *The Women of Mormondom*. New York: Tullidge and Crandall, 1877.

U.S. Department of Agriculture. *Cooperative Extension Work in Agriculture and Home Economics, 1917*. Washington D.C.: Government Printing Office, 1919.

U.S. Department of Agriculture. *Report on Agricultural Experiment Stations and Cooperative Agricultural Extension Work in the United States for the Year Ended June 30, 1915*. Washington, D.C.: Government Printing Office, 1916.

U.S. Department of Labor, Children's Bureau. *April and May Weighing and Measuring Test: Part 1, Suggestions to Local Communities*. Children's Year Leaflet no. 2, part 1. Publication no. 38. Washington, D.C.: Government Printing Office, 1918.

U.S. Department of Labor, Children's Bureau. *Baby Saving Campaigns: A Preliminary Report on What American Cities are Doing to Prevent Infant Mortality*. Publication no. 3. Washington, D.C.: Government Printing Office, 1914.

U.S. Department of Labor, Children's Bureau. *Birth Registration: An Aid in Protecting the Lives and Rights of Children*. Monograph no. 1. Washington, D.C.: Government Printing Office, 1914.

U.S. Department of Labor, Children's Bureau. *Child Care and Child Welfare: Outlines for Study*. Publication no. 90. Washington, D.C.: Government Printing Office, 1921.

U.S. Department of Labor, Children's Bureau. *Children's Year: A Brief Summary of Work Done and Suggestions for Follow-up Work*. Publication no. 67. Washington, D.C.: Government Printing Office, 1920.

U.S. Department of Labor, Children's Bureau. *Fifth Annual Report of the Chief, Children's Bureau to the Secretary of Labor*. Washington, D.C.: Government Printing Office, 1917.

U.S. Department of Labor, Children's Bureau. Mrs. Max West. *Infant Care*. Publication no. 8. Washington, D.C.: Government Printing Office, 1914.

U.S. Department of Labor, Children's Bureau. Mrs. Max West. *Prenatal Care*. Publication no. 4. Washington, D.C.: Government Printing Office, 1915.

U.S. Department of Labor, Children's Bureau. *Proceedings of the Third Annual Conference of State Directors in Charge of the Local Administration of the Maternity and Infancy Act, Washington, D.C., January 11–13, 1926*. Publication no. 157. Washington, D.C.: Government Printing Office, 1926.

U.S. Department of Labor, Children's Bureau. *Proceedings of the Fourth Annual Conference of State Directors in Charge of the Local Administration of the Maternity and Infancy Act, Washington, D.C., January 11–13, 1927*. Publication no. 181. Washington, D.C.: Government Printing Office, 1927.

U.S. Department of Labor, Children's Bureau. *The Promotion of the Welfare and Hygiene of Maternity and Infancy: The Administration of the Act of Congress of November 21, 1921, for the Period March 20, 1922, to June 30, 1923*. Publication no. 137. Washington, D.C.: Government Printing Office, 1924.

U.S. Department of Labor, Children's Bureau. *The Promotion of the Welfare and Hygiene of Maternity and Infancy: The Administration of the Act of Congress of November 21, 1921, Fiscal Year Ended June 30, 1924*. Publication no. 146. Washington, D.C.: Government Printing Office, 1925.

U.S. Department of Labor, Children's Bureau. *The Promotion of the Welfare and Hygiene of Maternity and Infancy: The Administration of the Act of Congress of November 21, 1921, Fiscal Year Ended June 30, 1925*. Publication no. 156. Washington, D.C.: Government Printing Office, 1926.

U.S. Department of Labor, Children's Bureau. *The Promotion of the Welfare and Hygiene of Maternity and Infancy: The Administration of the Act of Congress of November 21, 1921, Fiscal Year Ended June 30, 1926*. Publication no. 178. Washington, D.C.: Government Printing Office, 1927.

U.S. Department of Labor, Children's Bureau. *The Promotion of the Welfare and Hygiene of Maternity and Infancy: The Administration of the Act of Congress of November 21, 1921, Fiscal Year Ended June 30, 1927*. Publication No. 186. Washington, D.C.: Government Printing Office, 1928.

U.S. Department of Labor, Children's Bureau. *The Promotion of the Welfare and Hygiene of Maternity and Infancy: The Administration of the Act of Congress of November 21, 1921, Fiscal Year Ended June 30, 1928*. Publication No. 194. Washington, D.C.: Government Printing Office, 1929.

U.S. Department of Labor, Children's Bureau. *The Promotion of the Welfare and Hygiene of Maternity and Infancy: The Administration of the Act of Congress of November 21, 1921, Fiscal Year Ended Jun 30, 1929*. Publication No. 203. Washington, D.C.: Government Printing Office, 1931.

U.S. Department of Labor, Children's Bureau. *Promotion of the Welfare and Hygiene of Maternity and Infancy: Text of Act of November 21, 1921*. Publication no. 95. Washington, D.C.: Government Printing Office, 1921.

U.S. Department of Labor, Children's Bureau. *Save the Youngest: Seven Charts on Maternal and Infant Mortality with Explanatory Comment*. Publication no. 61. Washington, D.C.: Government Printing Office, 1919.

U.S. Department of Labor, Children's Bureau. *Standards of Child Welfare: A Report of the Children's Bureau Conferences, May and June, 1919*. Publication no. 60. Washington, D.C.: Government Printing Office, 1919.

U.S. Department of Labor, Children's Bureau. Lydia Roberts. *What is Malnutrition*? Publication no. 59. Washington, D.C.: Government Printing Office, n.d.

Van Wagenen, Lola. *Sister-Wives and Suffragists: Polygamy and the Politics of Woman Suffrage, 1870–1896*. Provo, UT: Joseph Fielding Smith Institute for Latter-day Saint History and BYU Studies, 2003.

Van Wagoner, Richard S. *Mormon Polygamy: A History*. Salt Lake City: Signature Books, 1986.

Vinson, Michael. "From Housework to Office Clerk: Utah's Working Women, 1870–1900." *Utah Historical Quarterly* 53 (Fall 1985): 326–35.

Ware, Susan. *Beyond Suffrage: Women in the New Deal*. Cambridge, MA: Harvard University Press, 1981.

Ware, Susan. *Still Missing: Amelia Earhart and the Search for Modern Feminism*. New York: Norton, 1993.

Watkins, T. H. *The Hungry Years: A Narrative History of the Great Depression in America*. New York: Henry Holt, 1999.

Watts, Phyllis Atwood. "Casework above the Poverty Line: The Influence of Home Service in World War I on Social Work." *Social Service Review* 38 (September 1964): 303–15.

Weimann, Jeanne Madeline. *The Fair Women: The Story of the Women's Building at the World's Columbian Exhibition, Chicago, 1893*. Chicago: Chicago Review Press, 1981.

Weiss, Nancy Pottisham. "Save the Children: A History of the Children's Bureau, 1903–1918." PhD dissertation, UCLA, 1974.

Wells, Emmeline B. Diaries, 1844–1920. L. Tom Perry Special Collections, Harold B. Lee Library, Brigham Young University, Provo, Utah.

White, Jean Bickmore. "Dr. Martha Hughes Cannon: Doctor, Wife, Legislator, Exile," in Vicky Burgess-Olson, ed. *Sister Saints*. Provo: Brigham Young University Press, 1978.

White, Ronald C., and C. Howard Hopkins. *The Social Gospel: Religion and Reform in Changing America*. Philadelphia: Temple University Press, 1976.

Whitney, Orson F. *History of Utah*. 4 vols. Salt Lake City: George Q. Cannon & Sons, 1892–1904.

Witt, Linda, Karen M. Paget and Glenna Matthews. *Running as a Woman: Gender and Power in American Politics*. New York: Free Press, 1994.

Woodger, Mary Jane, "Amy Brown Lyman: Mother of The Church of Jesus Christ of Latter-day Saints' Child Placement Agency." In Carol Cornwall Madsen and Cherry B. Silver, eds. *New Scholarship on Latter-day Saint Women in the Twentieth Century: Selections from the Women's History Initiative Seminars 2003–2004, 68–80*. Provo, UT: Joseph Fielding Smith Institute for Latter-day Saint History, 2005.

Yorgason, Ethan R. *Transformation of the Mormon Culture Region*. Urbana: University of Illinois Press, 2003.

Zuckerman, Mary Ellen. *A History of Popular Women's Magazines in the United States, 1792–1995*. Westport, CT: Greenwood Press, 1998.

INTERVIEWS

Allen, Mark Knight. Interviews by David Hall, 1991, 1994.

Bean, Jim and Harriett. Interview by David Hall, 1992.

Bean, Lydia Alder. Interview by Loretta L. Hefner, 1978. Typescript. James Moyle Oral History Program. Church History Library, Church of Jesus Christ of Latter-day Saints, Salt Lake City, Utah.

Cannon, Anna Laura Stohl. Interview by Loretta L. Hefner, 1978. Typescript. James Moyle Oral History Program. Church History Library, Church of Jesus Christ of Latter-day Saints, Salt Lake City, Utah.

Driggs, Susan Elizabeth Swensen. Interviews by David Hall, 1991, 1994.

Engar, Amy Kathryn Lyman. Interviews by David Hall, 1991–1994.

Garff, Gertrude R. Interview by David Hall, 1992.

Harvey, Hilda Muller. Interview by Loretta L. Hefner, 1978. James Moyle Oral History Program, Church History Library, Church of Jesus Christ of Latter-day Saints, Salt Lake City, Utah.

Hayes, Keith. Interview by David Hall, September 10, 1991.

Hefner, Loretta L. "Amy Brown Lyman: Raising the Quality of Life for All." In Vicki Burgess-Olson, ed. *Sister Saints, 96–116*. Provo: Brigham Young University Press, 1978.

Henrie, Mary Lyman. Interview by David Hall, 1992.

Lewis, Evelyn Hodges. Interview by David Hall, 1992.

Lohlmoelder, Ruth. Interview by Loretta L. Heffner, 1978. Typescript. James Moyle Oral History Program. Church History Library, Church of Jesus Christ of Latter-day Saints, Salt Lake City, Utah.

Lyman, Melvyn A. Interview by David Hall, June 13, 1992.

Nielsen, Mary Schindler. Interview by David Hall, 1992.

Pingree, David R. and Sabey Driggs Pingree. Interview by David Hall, July 2, 1993.

Pingree, Vervene. Interview by Loretta L. Hefner, 1978. Typescript. James Moyle Oral History Program, Church History Library, Church of Jesus Christ of Latter-day Saints, Salt Lake City, Utah.

Pohlman, Vera White. *Amy Brown Lyman, 1872–1959: Biographical Summary and Funeral Services*. Privately Published, 1960.

Pohlman, Vera White. Interviews by David Hall, 1990–1994.

Pollei, Emily. Interview by David Hall, 1992.

Richards, A. Z. Interview by David Hall, 1992.

Ross, Helen Midgely. Interview by Loretta L. Hefner, 1978. Typescript. James Moyle Oral History Program, Church History Library, Church of Jesus Christ of Latter-day Saints, Salt Lake City, Utah.

Sharp, Mary Ann Clark. Interview by Jessie Embry, 1977. Church History Library, Church of Jesus Christ of Latter-day Saints, Salt Lake City, Utah.

Sorenson, Parry. Interview by David Hall, 1992.

Spafford, Belle S. Interviews by Jill Mulvay Derr, 1975–1976. Typescript. James Moyle Oral History Program, Church History Library, Church of Jesus Christ of Latter-day Saints, Salt Lake City, Utah.

Wintch, Leona Fetzer. Interviews by David Hall, 1991–1994.

Wirthlin, Emmeline. Interview by David Hall, April 4, 1992.

Woodruff, Evelyn Ballif. Interviewed by David Hall, 1992.

INDEX